THE EVERYDAY ALMANAC.

THE EVERYDAY ALMANAC ®

a copious compendium of facts, figures and fun

Edited by Bob Perlongo

SECOND EDITION

CAPRA PRESS
SANTA BARBARA

For my mother Caroline and daughter Ingrid with love and thanks.

℟

LIBRARY OF CONGRESS CATALOGING-IN-PUBLICATION DATA

Perlongo, Bob.
The everyday almanac : a copious compendium of facts, figures, and fun /
edited by Bob Perlongo. — 2nd ed.
p. cm.
Includes index.
ISBN 0-88496-398-5 (paper)
1. Almanacs, American. 2. Handbooks. vade-mecums. etc.
I. Title.
AY64.P58 1995
031.02—dc20
95-24509
CIP

Note: The first edition of *The Everyday Almanac* was published
in 1979 by Grosset & Dunlap/Ace Books

CAPRA PRESS
Post Office Box 2068
Santa Barbara, CA 93120

I remembered that half-burnt old almanac we had and I thought it might be the right weather for teaching the boy to read. I could put a point on a stick and show the letters by scratching them in the floor. So we began to do that, working at it a little each day. I would have him study a letter as it was printed and then say its name and then watch me write it with the stick.

—E. L. DOCTOROW
(*Welcome to Hard Times*)

A calendar, a calendar! look in the almanack: find out moonshine . . .

—WILLIAM SHAKESPEARE
(*A Midsummer Night's Dream*)

CONTENTS

Britain's First Cat Beats Murder Rap; Dog Tales; Matching Dog to Child; Yes, Virginia, There *Are* Other Pets; Leapin' Lizards!; Visiting the Vet; "Tracer" Implants Gaining Favor; Shipping or Schlepping a Pet

ART—FOR LIFE'S SAKE . . . *myriad Muse-ings old and new*. . . 311

Art: Who, What, Why and Wow; World's Oldest Statue Discovered; Light Shed on Buried Army; Art Imitates Death; Weird Art News; Johann, Wolfgang or Ludwig—Who's Number One?; Haydn Sonatas Are Finally Found; The Everyday Music Quiz; Rejecters' Slips; Opera on the Couch; Dizzy Atmosphere; The Joy of Sax; A Brief Concordance; Four Seasons, Umpteen Names; Notes and Lines; Czech It Out!; The Gold Singers; The Super Singles; Behave Thyself! (10 Commandments for Audience Members); Tape Recording and the Law; Photography—A Snap for Buff or Pro; Reel Riffs; 11 All-Time Highest-Grossing Films; Flicks for the Ages; *Citizen Kane* Revisited; Of Life and Art; No Kidding; One-Minute Confessions; TV Toll; Selling the Kids; Yet Another Reason to Limit Tube Time (Or, The Fatting of Junior); The Birth of the Book; Writing—as Writ; Book Notes; The Writer and His Asterisk; Albee Darned; Critic Critique; Leave Your Canon at the Door; Masters of War; Peace

FANCIFUL HUMORS   . . . *beaux jests and bits of wit* . . . 339

Rx for Melancholy; You Know It's Going to Be a Bad Day When—; Dueling Wisdoms; Laws of Life; Webster's Funabridged: A Glossary of Differenitions; A Plethora of Jokes, Quips, Cartoons and Puns

PASTIMES AND DIVERSIONS
      . . . *fun and games to go or stay* . . . 351

The All-Time Greatest Puzzle; Ask Marilyn; Unmazing; Wordy Gurdy; Ups and Downs; Word Game; Who Speaks?; Animals for Sale; Famous American Name-Finder Puzzle; How Old Is Annie?; Some Creative Calculations; A Trio of Teasers; 1,089 Number Play; 15,873 Number Play; Who's Laughing Now?; Incredible Nine; Palindromes, Anyone?; A Very Tasty Poem—Almost; The Magic Squares; Rank of Hands in Straight Poker (Nothing Wild); Poker: Averages in the Deal; Poker: Averages in the Draw; Trumping Father Time—with Bridge; Let's Play Chess; Chess for You; What's His Angle?; Puzzle Answers

PREFACE

Herewith, an almanac of fact, fancy, truth and trivia, crampacked with useful and/or useless information, ranging from the pointedly relevant to the patently ridiculous—with generous helpings of exotica, un-exotica and flat-out Americana.

Some of the goodies herein you can take straight to the bank (see, for example, "Money, Money, Money"), some you can photocopy and slap up on the wall ("Art—for Life's Sake" and/or "Now Is the Time"), and some you might just want to have some plain old brain-refreshing fun with ("Fanciful Humors," "Pastimes and Diversions"). You'll find no ponderous assemblages of statisti-speak here—there are almanacs enough for that already. Instead, you'll find the facts and stats you really need and can immediately use—in addition to a wealth of visual delights old and new.

But see for yourself. Check it out. Open it up anywhere, wherever—or, if you happen to have a special, *particular* bug up, check out the Contents or the Index. Be as logical or haphazard as you like— this is a book designed to be used in whatever way suits you best.

For the record, about a third of the material that follows is from a wide range of gifted writers and artists and is accredited as such. The assorted mini-articles and miscellany making up the rest of the book can be blamed on the editor, and in the interests of unclutteredness have in almost every case not been signed.

THE UNIVERSE
... heavenly bodies—and beyond ...

Those who study the stars have God for a teacher.
—TYCHO BRAHE

*Outer space is like Dolly Parton. You don't quite
believe it, but there it is.*
—LORNE GREEN

THE GREAT SPACE EXPLOSION

Don't look now, but the universe is exploding. And we're not just talking Big Bang. We're talking Golden Age of Astronomy, marked by discovery after discovery, "first" after "first," in unprecedented profusion. Recent years/months/weeks (that's how fast it's happening) have seen a veritable star-stream of spectacular developments, leading many astronomers to believe we may soon reach a level of technical competence sufficiently high to answer some of the most perplexing questions asked by scientists:

• **Is the universe forever?** In theory, the universe was born some 15 billion years ago, when the so-called "Big Bang" banged into existence all matter and energy, in great clouds of hydrogen and helium.

Because the consistency of the clouds varied, gravitational forces were able to collapse them into clumps of matter from which stars, galaxies and clusters of galaxies and clusters of galaxies gradually took shape. The question now is: Will the universe continue to expand? Or will it someday contract and collapse on itself? The answers could come from measuring instruments now being put into outer space.

• **What was there before the Big Bang?** If nothing, how so? If something, what? Or can one *ever* expect to unravel the eerie enigma of origin? At the heart of such mysteries is the equally mysterious question of quantum mechanics, predicated on the notion that the behavior of elementary particles is uncertain and that, contrary to Einstein, maybe God *does*, after all, play dice with the universe. That is, if there *is* a God. (If all this seems daunting, don't feel bad. Quantum mechanics is so complicated that it is said that no one person in the world fully understands all its ramifications.)

• **Are we alone in the universe?** Many scientists think this most intriguing of celestial mysteries won't be solved except by accident (i.e., by stumbling across extraterrestrial radio transmissions). Hoping to give chance a helping hand, NASA continues to use radio telescopes to scan the stars for intelligent-sounding signals. The so-called SETI (Search for Extraterrestrial Intelligence) program, boldly begun but soon staggered by deep funding cuts, has been recently rejuvenated—and fittingly rechristened Project Phoenix— by contributions from private groups and individuals. Meanwhile, major breakthroughs in our knowledge of the most distant reaches of the heavens are expected with the help of such new technological aids as the recently repaired and refurbished Hubble Space Telescope, and the Keck Telescope atop the Mauna Kea volcano in Hawaii, the largest and most powerful optical telescope in the world. (An even larger telescope than the 400-inch Keck is now being built in West Texas; due to be completed in 1997, the so-called Hobby-Eberly telescope will borrow and improve on features pioneered by the Keck, to enable scientists to probe quasars and test current theories of cold, dark matter.)

All in all, astronomy—the world's oldest science—is more than ever one of the most dynamic and exciting of scientific disciplines, thanks in recent years to an ongoing cascade of headline-making discoveries and accomplishments. Among the celestial superlatives:

• **Largest, oldest, most-distant objects.** The largest, oldest, most distant objects in the universe—gigantic, wispy ripples of matter some 15 billion light-years away—were recently observed as microwave radiation by NASA's $400-million Cosmic Background Explorer (COBE) satellite, which since 1989 has been orbiting Earth

559 miles up. (A light-year is the distance light travels in one year, about 5.87 trillion miles.)

"If you're religious, it's like looking at God," said astrophysicist George Smoot, one of the creators of the COBE project, as he announced the discovery in 1992 of the clouds of primordial matter that span two-thirds of the known universe.

Up to that time, the largest known structure in the universe had been thought to be the enormous arc of galaxies called the Great Wall; that galactic conglomerate, some 200 million light-years long, was discovered in 1989 by astronomers working at the Harvard-Smithsonian Center for Astrophysics in Cambridge, Massachusetts.

• **Largest galaxy.** The largest galaxy ever, more than 60 times the size of the Milky Way, has been discovered by astronomers at the Kitt Peak National Observatory in Arizona. The galaxy measures at least 6 million light-years across and contains more than 100 trillion stars. It is at the center of a rich cluster of galaxies known as Abell 2029.

• **Fastest-spinning object.** The fastest-spinning celestial object, a neutron star turning 645 times per second, has been detected by a team of astronomers from Berkeley and from Puerto Rico's Arecibo Observatory. One of the discoverers said scientists now have "a chance to look at what is probably a very young, extremely energetic pulsar, one that's probably in an early stage of evolution." There was particular excitement over the possibility that the newfound object is emitting gravity waves detectable on Earth, which would open an important new "window" through which to study the universe.

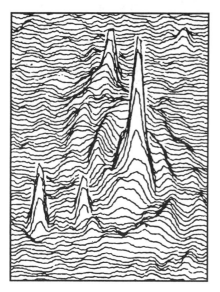

Alpine peaks pinpoint radio intensities in this computer plot of the Whirlpool galaxy, 15 million light-years away. Such seemingly three-dimensional views permit instant identification of the location and relative strength of invisible energy sources.

—Leiden Observatory, The Netherlands

17

THE HOLE IN THE MILKY WAY

A massive black hole that "dines" on stars at the rate of one every 5,000 to 10,000 years has been discovered in the center of the Milky Way by U.S. and Australian astronomers. (A black hole is thought to occur when a huge star collapses, creating an increasingly intense gravitational field. As the star shrinks, gravity overwhelms all other forces, and nothing—not even light—can escape.) Images made with the giant radio telescope near Socorro, New Mexico, indicate that the black hole is emitting an enormous amount of energy that appears to be blowing on nearby stars and on the undigested debris remaining from other stars that have already been torn apart and partially consumed.

While the Milky Way's suspected black hole is thought to have a mass of some 1.3 million suns, it is tiny compared to the extraordinarily powerful black hole in the center of the giant elliptical galaxy M87, some 50 million light-years away in the constellation Virgo. This attractive force of collapsed matter would weigh as much as three billion suns, concentrated in a space no larger than the solar system.

"PERMIT US TO INTRODUCE OURSELVES . . ."

Bearing a gold-plated plaque containing a message from Earth, Pioneer 10, traveling at 10,558 miles an hour and still beeping back strong signals after more than a dozen years in space, became in 1983 the first man-made object to escape the solar system. Earlier it had been the first spacecraft to probe the planet Jupiter. (It was followed in 1989 by Voyager 2, which, after a tour of the four giant outer planets, headed toward the farthest and darkest parts of the solar system, where it will continue to measure cosmic rays, the solar wind, and other celestial entities. The craft is expected to keep sending back useful data for another 20 to 25 years until its nuclear batteries run down.)

During its long, lonely journey through interstellar space, Pioneer 10 will come close enough to be picked up by another star system once every million years. The plaque it bears contains a brief message for any intelligent life-forms that may intercept it: drawings of a man and a woman to show them what we look—or looked—like, a diagram of the earth and the solar system, along with prominent pulsars (celestial lighthouses) to illustrate our location, and some basic science concepts to give them an index to our intelligence. If no ETs pick up Pioneer, it will wander through space, probably forever. At any rate, the spacecraft should outlive the earth, which astronomers say will be incinerated by the sun in five billion years when it swells into a red giant during its death throes.

Another remarkable spacecraft, IRAS (Infrared Astronomical Satellite), rewrote astronomy books with its discovery of five new comets, three giant rings of dust in the solar system, and interstellar clouds. Before the satellite quit functioning, its infrared telescope discovered a vast cloud of particles circling the star Vega, the third brightest star in the sky. Astronomers said it was the first direct evidence that ours is not the only solar system in the universe, and that in fact there may be as many as 50 such systems. Later, NASA astronomers released the first photo of what may be a young solar system 293 trillion miles from our own. The picture shows a swarm of particles around the star Beta Pictoris that could have been ejected into space as planets formed around the star.

U.S. RETOOLS SPACE PLANS
Despite serious questions raised by the January 1986 Challenger explosion, manned—or should we say "personned"?—spaceflight still remains perhaps the most significant area of interest for astronomer and space buff alike, with a "pre-Challenger" flurry of historic "firsts," including the first U.S. woman in space (Sally K. Ride), the first walks in space by astronauts untethered to their mother ships and the first two-shift, round-the-clock orbital operations by crew members. There is clearly more space history on the horizon since the rousing resumption of the U.S. manned-flight program with the successful fall 1988 launching of the shuttle Discovery, and the record-setting flight of the shuttle Columbia in fall 1993 (14 days).

Still, with today's tax dollars under increasing pressure from a host of social problems, funding for space exploration is proving to be harder than ever to come by, as planned projects are continually reevaluated, some being scrapped outright, others trimmed and reworked.

The most dramatic evidence of this cosmic belt-tightening have been plans for U.S. space station Freedom, envisioned in 1984 as an orbiting space laboratory/factory/service station that would house eight astronauts and cost $31 billion to build.

One decade and half a dozen revamps later, the proposed station is currently seen as an international venture involving the U.S., Russia, Japan, Europe and Canada. The newly conceived station, now referred to as International Space Station Alpha, would house not eight but six persons (including U.S. astronauts and Russian cosmonauts), and would cost the U.S. less than what had been planned under the Freedom program; it would be run from Mission Control Center in Houston with the Russian command site in Kalingrad as backup.

Provided funding is approved by Congress, construction of the station is expected to begin in 1997, after U.S. shuttles dock several times with Russia's aging Mir space station in order to lay the ground-

19

work for joint construction. Target date for completion is 2001.

Meanwhile, despite its relative infancy, shuttle research has already made great strides in developing space-oriented agricultural and manufacturing techniques, bringing us a bit closer to the still far-off goal of economically self-sufficient space activity.

Of course, the real challenge of space remains the political one: Will it be allowed to continue on its present course toward being a heavenly realm of peaceful multinational enterprise, or will it become a massively dangerous new battlefield devoted to real-life "Star Wars"?

That remains the key question, which none can answer with certainty. We can but hope that the stars are on our side.

SUPERNOVA—IT'S A BLAST!

The first "nearby" supernova—or exploding star—seen in 383 years was detected on February 24, 1987, in the Large Magellanic Cloud, actually a small satellite galaxy at the arc of the Milky Way, some 160,000 light-years from Earth.

The star—now known as Supernova Shelton 1987—blazed into view over the Southern Hemisphere and has since become the subject of intense scrutiny from astronomers chiefly interested in the quantity and composition of the light it is emitting. Changes in brightness enable observers to follow the progress of the explosion, and the composition of the light reveals the chemical elements in the explosion and the speed at which the outer layers of gas are expanding.

TWINKLE, TWINKLE, STARRY SKY

Twinkle, twinkle—my-oh-my! Just how many stars are there up above so high?

You may not be glad you asked.

We can see about 2,000 stars with the naked eye, about a million with a small telescope and about a billion with our most powerful telescopes. Altogether, there are some 100 billion stars in our galaxy, the Milky Way—and it's believed that there are as many galaxies in the universe as there are Milky Way stars. (It's estimated that a quarter of all the stars in the universe are binary, or double, stars: systems of two stars revolving about a common center of gravity.)

There are 60 known stars in our sun's "immediate" vicinity (i.e., within 17 light-years). The nearest star—not counting the sun—is Proxima Centauri, 4.2 light-years away but visible only with a telescope. In the same constellation is Alpha Centauri, at 4.3 light-years the nearest star visible with the naked eye; it can be seen in the Southern Hemisphere. The brightest of stars is Sirius (the Dog Star), the sixth nearest. It is more than three times the size of the sun and is seen best in early March, in the southern sky.

Most stars are very much farther away than that. Rigel, for instance, is 900 light-years distant. So when we look at Rigel, we're not seeing it as it is now, but as it was 900 years ago!

If we look at the stars, take a break of about an hour, then look at them again, we discover that all but the pole star (Polaris, or North Star) have changed positions. This is caused by the rotation of Earth on its axis. The stars seem to wheel across the sky from east to west, because Earth is turning from west to east.

CONSTELLATIONS AND STARS

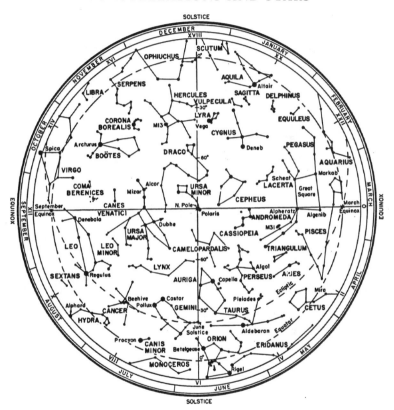

NORTHERN HEMISPHERE

Note: For best results as heavenly viewing guides, this page and the following page should be taken (preferably with the rest of the book attached) to a copy shop to have them blown up to at least twice their present size.

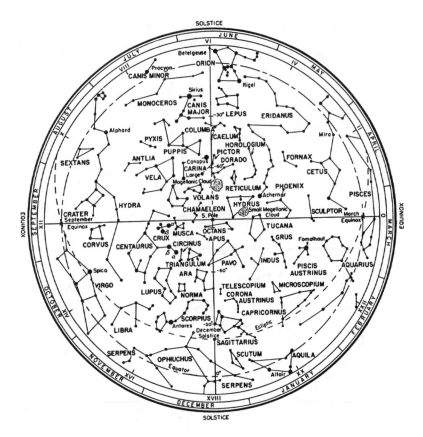

SOUTHERN HEMISPHERE

(This and the preceding illustration are from Webster's Third New International Dictionary © 1986 *by Merriam Webster Inc., publisher of the Merriam Webster ® Dictionaries. Reprinted by permission.)*

THE 20 NEAREST STARS
(OTHER THAN THE SUN)

Name	Distance in Light-Years
Proxima Centauri	4.2
Alpha Centauri	4.3
Bernard's Star	5.9
Wolf 359	7.6
Lalande 21185	8.1
Sirius	8.6

Luyten 726-8	8.9
Ross 154	9.4
Ross 248	10.3
Epsilon Eridani	10.7
Luyten 789-6	10.8
Ross 128	10.8
61 Cygni	11.2
Epsilon Indi	11.2
Procyon	11.4
E 2298	11.5
Groombridge 34	11.6
Lacaille 9352	11.7
Tau Ceti	11.9
BD + 5°1668	12.2

SUN STROKES

Our galaxy, the Milky Way—said of yore to have spilled from Juno's breast—is, in fact, a flat spiral of some 100 billion stars measuring 100,000 light-years across and 1,000 to 2,000 light-years thick. That's roughly about a dozen and a half stars for every person on Earth.

The nearest of these, our sun, is a relatively small and feeble dwarf star. Still, its 865,000-mile diameter is 109 times greater than Earth's, and its mass is about 330,000 times greater. At about 93 million miles away, it is—astronomically speaking, of course—so "near" that the next nearest star is some 270,000 times as far. It rotates on its axis once every 25 to 27 days and revolves around the galaxy one complete orbit every 225 million years. Light from the sun takes 8 minutes and 20 seconds to reach Earth.

The sun contains 99.9 percent of the solar system's entire mass and supplies Earth with 120 trillion horsepower every second—still just one five-billionth of the total energy it radiates into space.

Astronomers believe the sun was born about five billion years ago,* the spawn of a gigantic swirling nebula of gas and dust. As the particles coalesced, gravitation pulled them swiftly together and they heated up. Within a few million years—a short time in cosmic terms—the new body developed within its deep interior a temperature of millions of degrees, enough to ignite the processes of nuclear fusion. Hydrogen atoms fused to form helium atoms, giving off energy in the process, and the sun began to shine.

This stellar star of ours has changed little in its five-billion-year span, and it's likely to change little for the next five billion. But then

---

*For comparison, the age of the solar system is generally put at 4.6 billion years.

the hydrogen at its core will near exhaustion, and the outer layers will begin to expand.

Then, according to the latest theories, a strange and dire fate will confront any life on Earth. The sun will swell and redden, expanding a hundred times in diameter and eventually looming across some 25 percent of the sky—and burning a thousand times brighter than now. The process may melt the inner planets, Mercury and Venus, and reduce Earth to a desolate rock, baked at temperatures that would melt lead, its oceans completely boiled away.

And earthlings? If they have survived, they will have fled to a moon of Jupiter, or perhaps to a more hospitable part of the galaxy.

And, say the theorists, for a hundred million more years, the swollen sun—now a "red giant"—will continue to deplete its nuclear fuel. Once the enormous outer envelope has dissipated, only a tiny core will remain. Then, to quote a recent report of the National Academy of Sciences, "a frozen and presumably lifeless Earth will swing bleakly around a faint white-dwarf sun appearing no larger in the sky than the tiny planet Mars"—and with a density so great that a teaspoon of white-dwarf material would weigh a ton.

PROFILES OF THE PLANETS

MERCURY—Closest planet to the sun, Mercury is also the second smallest. Four-fifths of its mass is iron, making it second only to Earth in density. Mercury's sparse hydrogen-helium atmosphere may be made up of solar wind passingly concentrated by the planet's presence. Its 1,000-degree surface temperature range (+200° F to -800° F) is greater than that of any other planet, although its maximum is less than that of Venus. The U.S. Mariner 10 space probe relayed invaluable data and photos as it flew within 500 miles of the dark side of Mercury; they show a surface like the moon's—heavily cratered, little eroded, and with smooth areas similar to, but smaller than, their lunar counterparts. Also discovered was a faint but permanent magnetic field emanating from the planet's interior, answering the question of whether the field was, in fact, from the planet itself or was caused instead by the solar wind.

Mean distance from sun: 36 million miles
Equatorial diameter: 3,031 miles
Volume: 0.06 times that of Earth
Mass: 0.054 times that of Earth
Length of day: 58.65 Earth days
Length of year: 87.96 Earth days
Surface gravity (relative to Earth): 0.37
Number of satellites: 0

VENUS—Second planet from the sun and the brightest in Earth's sky, our nearest neighbor, Venus, is about the same size and mass as Earth. Its surface is very hot (about 900° F), waterless, corrosive and lifeless, with a pressure averaging some 90 Earth atmospheres (equal to an ocean depth of one-half mile) and gentle surface winds. Thirty to 33 miles above the surface, air streams at 200-plus mph. Only about 2 percent of incident solar radiation reaches the surface, while 75 percent is absorbed in its mostly carbon-dioxide atmosphere and its four layers of clouds—creating the "greenhouse effect" responsible for its superheated crust. U.S. and Soviet space probes of Venus detected neither a magnetic field nor radiation belts, but they did surprise scientists with revelations of spectacular scenery, including the largest known canyon in the solar system, a mountain higher than Everest, a giant plateau larger than any on Earth, periods of almost continuous lightning, and a constant strange glow near the surface. This glow allowed Russian scientists to obtain photos showing rocks on the Venusian surface. In 1990 the unmanned U.S. spacecraft Magellan pierced the thick, sulfurous clouds of Venus to reveal a surface disfigured by earthquakes and volcanic eruptions. The craft's powerful radar also showed huge meteor craters and a plain marked with amazingly regular parallel and perpendicular scars thought to have been caused by subsurface forces. Magellan completed more than 15,000 orbits around Venus before its power waned; it was then sent on its last mission—a final, fiery dive toward Venus's surface in October 1994, which scientists were hoping would tell them more about the 900°F sulfuric mist that envelops the planet.

Mean distance from sun: 67.2 million miles
Equatorial diameter: 7,521 miles
Volume: 0.88 times that of Earth
Mass: 0.815 times that of Earth
Length of day: 243.01 Earth days (retrograde rotation)
Length of year: 224.7 Earth days
Surface gravity (relative to Earth): 0.88
Number of satellites: 0

EARTH—Third planet from the sun and fifth largest. For a profile—and much more—see the following chapter, "The Earth."

MARS—Fourth planet from the sun, Mars has a year almost twice the length of Earth's, but a day only slightly longer. Photo-transmitting unmanned spacecraft have revealed to us more about Mars than any planet other than Earth itself. The main surface features include white solar caps and bright and dark regions, all showing seasonal variations; the bright areas give Mars its familiar ruddy color. Looking closer, we see a rough-hewn, forbidding planet with deep chasms and massive volcanoes, the largest of which—Olympus Mons—is taller than Mount Everest. We see, too, Martian plains pockmarked over the years by the impact of thousands of meteors. As for the Martian atmosphere, U.S. space probe Mariner 9 proved it to be much thinner than expected and to consist principally of carbon dioxide. Although soil samples scooped up by U.S. space probes Vikings 1 and 2 contained no organic material, the photographs that were taken give scientists fresh hope that primitive life once may have existed on Mars and someday may thrive there again. Many water-caused channels were seen, and there were little channels cut into big channels, a sign that the planet has gone through hot warm and cold periods. Photographs have also shown that Mars still has up to 100 times more water—in the form of permafrost, polar ice, and subsurface liquid—than was previously believed. Since temperatures increase closer to a planet's core, the ice indicates that water exists up to half a mile beneath the surface, in the pores of Martian rocks. Unfortunately, the recent loss of contact with the Mars Observer unmanned spacecraft, which was to orbit and intensively study the planet, has cast a pall on plans for future probes. As for a manned mission, the cost estimates, ranging from $50 billion to $400 billion, seem a universe away from present-day budget realities. Even so, many scientists support such a mission, perhaps as a multinational project, with funding shared by the U.S., Russia, Japan, and the European Space Agency.

Mean distance from sun: 141.6 million miles
Equatorial diameter: 4,217 miles
Volume: 0.15 times that of Earth
Mass: 0.107 times that of Earth
Length of day: 24.6 Earth hours
Length of year: 1.88 Earth years
Surface gravity (relative to Earth): 0.38
Number of satellites: 2

JUPITER—Fifth planet from the sun and the largest, Jupiter is the size of a thousand Earths, containing in fact more matter than all of the other objects in the solar system combined, except the sun. Jupiter has a dense, cloudy atmosphere consisting mainly of hydrogen and helium, along with some ammonia and methane—an atmosphere ideal for reflecting sunlight, making the planet appear far brighter than any of the stars. Parallel clouds characterize Jupiter's visible surface, divided into white-yellowish zones and reddish-brown belts, with cloud-top temperatures averaging about -220° F. Jupiter's gravitational field is two and a half times that of Earth. Its satellite system somewhat resembles the solar system itself, with a close inner system and a distant outer system. Jupiter's most prominent feature is the Great Red Spot, an immense (9,000 X 24,000 miles), hurricane-like atmospheric disturbance, discovered in 1665 and still something of a mystery. Voyagers 1 and 2 revealed that Jupiter, like neighbors Saturn and Uranus, has a ring around its equator, and that Io, one of 16 moons, has active volcanoes, the first found anywhere in the solar system outside Earth. Scientists hope that the Galileo spacecraft, launched in 1989 and due to reach Jupiter in December 1995, will verify indications received from Voyager 2 that the planet's second satellite, Europa, contains beneath its icy, rocky crust a body of water on the scale of an earthly ocean. Besides probing the planetary nature of Jupiter's four major moons, the projected 22-month survey will also reveal the intensity of electromagnetic energy produced by Jovian lightning, which is believed to be a thousand times more intense than Earth's. In July 1994, 21 fragments of a newly discovered comet, Shoemaker-Levy 9, crashed into Jupiter in spectacular fashion, to the delight of astronomers and casual gazers alike.

Mean distance from sun: 483.6 million miles
Equatorial diameter: 88,729 miles
Volume: 1,316 times that of Earth
Mass: 317.8 times that of Earth
Length of day: 9.8 Earth hours
Length of year: 11.86 Earth years
Surface gravity (relative to Earth): 2.64
Number of satellites: 16

SATURN—Sixth planet from the sun and the second largest, butterscotch-hued Saturn has been the object of considerable attention of late, thanks to the historic close-up pictures of the remote, ringed planet that Voyagers 1 and 2 sent to Earth in the early 1980s—the closest shots having been taken by Voyager 2, from a "mere" 63,000 miles. The fly-bys reaped a flood of startling new data—in fact, more information about Saturn was gathered in a few days than had been collected in all recorded history. For one thing, there was evidence of thunderstorm systems stretching 40,000 miles around the planet's equator. Also, to date nine new natural satellites have been discovered, for a total of 22, the most of any planet—and there are indications that there may be others. As for Saturn's famous rings, discovered by Galileo in 1610, the images sped back from Voyager were both wondrous and baffling. Instead of five or six discrete disks, there were hundreds of separate ringlets and structural kinks that appeared to defy the laws of orbital mechanics. And there were rings within rings, like concentric ripples in a cosmic pond, with a dusting of particles filling the gaps between the major rings. What's more, scientists—having already detected carbon dioxide in the atmosphere of Saturn's largest moon, Titan—have begun to suspect that clues to the evolution of the chemistry of life may be found in its soil. NASA plans to send a scientific probe to Titan in 2002 as part of its Cassini Mission; the probe is to be provided by the European Space Agency (ESA).

Mean distance from sun: 885.5 million miles
Equatorial diameter: 74,565 miles
Volume: 755 times that of Earth
Mass: 95.2 times that of Earth
Length of day: 10.23 Earth hours
Length of year: 29.46 Earth years
Surface gravity (relative to Earth): 1.15
Number of satellites: 22

URANUS—Seventh planet from the sun and third largest, Uranus was the first to be discovered with the aid of a telescope (in 1781, by William Herschel). So viewed, Uranus appears as a pale greenish disk, with scant detail to be seen on its gaseous surface. Adding to the mystery has been the fact that the planet's rotational axis is tilted so far over that it lies almost on the plane of its orbit, making for a climate of incredible extremes: summer in Uranus's Northern Hemisphere finds the sun almost directly over the North Pole and much of the Southern Hemisphere in total darkness, the situation reversing itself half a Uranian year later. Many old questions about Uranus were answered, and new ones raised, when in January 1986 Voyager 2 passed within 50,679 miles of the Uranian cloud tops. The fly-by confirmed previous theories that under those clouds exists an ocean of superheated water that is prevented from boiling away by the planet's thick atmosphere, but it was also found that Uranus's magnetic field is 60 degrees out of sync with its poles, and that four large methane clouds are circling Uranus the "wrong" way—that is, in the same direction as the planet's rotation. Other surprises included the discovery of 10 arc-shaped pieces of rings, and the planet's 10th full ring. There were even stranger surprises in close-ups of the five large moons, especially the bewildering variety of terrain features on Miranda, including valleys, deep fractures, long ridges, craters, glacial flows, broad terraces, and features that resemble a racetrack and a chevron. (Uranian Fly-By Trivia: Even traveling at the speed of light, the radio signals from Uranus took 2 hours and 45 minutes to reach Earth.)

Mean distance from sun: 1.78 billion miles
Equatorial diameter: 31,600 miles
Volume: 67 times that of Earth
Mass: 14.5 times that of Earth
Length of day: 16.8 Earth hours (retrograde rotation)
Length of year: 84.01 Earth years
Relative surface gravity: 1.17
Number of satellites: 15

NEPTUNE—Eighth planet from the sun and the fourth largest, Neptune has been called the twin of Uranus, although it is much farther away—too faint, in fact, to be seen with the naked eye. Orbital changes of Uranus, brought about by the gravitational pull of Neptune, led to the latter's telescopic discovery (by Johann Galle and Heinrich d'Arrest) in 1846. Variations in Pluto's eccentric orbit sometimes make Neptune the most-distant planet. Like Uranus and the other giants (Jupiter and Saturn), Neptune has a gaseous surface and, when viewed though a telescope, appears as a small, greenish-blue disk. In August 1989 the unmanned spacecraft Voyager 2 made Neptune its last port of call on its spectacular 12-year "Grand Tour" of the four giant outer planets, flying a scant 3,000 miles over the planet's frigid methane clouds and discovering four additional moons (besides Nereid and Triton, first seen from Earth) and two encircling rings, one complete and one partial. Also observed were an Earth-sized cyclone ("the Great Dark Spot") and an extraordinarily volatile atmosphere raked by 400-mile-an-hour winds—phenomena greatly at variance with Voyager 2's initial images of a beautiful and apparently serene planet. Even more startling was the discovery that Triton—about the size of Earth's moon and the only satellite to orbit counter to a planet's rotation—may still be geologically active and that its surface is pocked with massive craters and large and small "ice volcanoes." The volcanoes' activity is driven by fluid ice and compounds such as nitrogen, which can change from a solid to a liquid to a gas at temperatures of more than -300° F, making Triton one of the most bizarre and fascinating objects in the solar system. Or as Lawrence Soderblom, a member of the Voyager support team, put it: "Wow, what a way to leave the solar system!"

Mean distance from sun: 2.79 billion miles
Equatorial diameter: 31,200 miles
Volume: 57 times that of Earth
Mass: 17.2 times that of Earth
Length of day: 16.1 Earth hours
Length of year: 164.79 Earth years

Surface gravity (relative to Earth): 1.18
Number of satellites: 8

PLUTO—Ninth and farthest planet from the sun, Pluto is also the smallest. Discovered by Clyde Tombaugh in 1930 and named for the underworld god of the ancient Romans, Pluto has the solar system's most eccentric orbit, bringing it at times closer to the sun than Neptune. Since 1962 Pluto has been traveling inside Neptune's orbit, and will do so until 1999. The planet is so small and remote that the largest telescopes show it only as a yellowish speck. It takes five and a half hours for sunlight to reach its surface, which is essentially lit by starlight. In 1976 solid methane, which freezes at -373° F, was detected on Pluto's surface. In 1978 a satellite now known as Charon was discovered in orbit around the planet. The orbital distance and period of this satellite have led to the first reasonably accurate measurement of Pluto's mass and diameter. Because of the satellite's largeness, some astronomers have speculated that it and Pluto may in fact constitute a "double planet" system. In 1978 the U.S. Infrared Astronomy Satellite detected on Pluto evidence of a significant methane atmosphere.

Mean distance from sun: 3.66 billion miles
Equatorial diameter: 1,500-2,000 miles
Volume: 0.1 times that of Earth
Mass: 0.2 times that of Earth
Length of day: 6.39 Earth days
Length of year: 247.7 Earth years
Surface gravity (relative to Earth): Unknown
Number of satellites: 1

MOON LORE

The moon is nothing but a circumambulating aphrodisiac divinely subsidized to provoke the world into a rising birth rate.
—CHRISTOPHER FRY

First Quarter   Full Moon   Last Quarter   Waning Moon   New Moon   Waxing Moon

Near yet far, beguilingly beautiful yet totally barren, the moon has long had a particular fascination for earthlings. Averaging a distance of 238,857 miles from Earth, it's our nearest celestial neighbor, and so "close" it was only a matter of time before we stopped by for a neighborly cup of "sugar," as it were—*scientific* sugar, to be sure, in the form of 843 pounds of soil and rocks brought back by six astronaut teams.

The moon and its motions have undergone close and almost continual scrutiny since 2200 B.C., when the first records of lunar eclipses were made by the Mesopotamians. By about 500 B.C., the Chaldeans were predicting eclipses, and it wasn't long before distances were figured and tidal forces explained. With the advent of first the telescope and then of the age of space exploration, one shadowy lunar secret after another has yielded to the light of science.

We've learned, for instance, that there were volcanic eruptions on the moon 4.3 to 4.4 billion years ago and that these eruptions became what Galileo called the lunar marin, or "seas." We've gauged the temperatures on the moon's surface as varying 500° F from day to night (+250° to -250°) and we've calculated that it takes moonlight about a second and a quarter to reach Earth.

Some other lunar lore:

The moon has a diameter of 2,160 miles and weighs 81 billion tons, with a mass 26 million times less than the sun's. The full moon gives 1/500,000th the light of the noonday sun, but two days earlier or later, the moon is only half as bright as when it's full. The only month on record that had no full moon was February 1866.

The moon circles the Earth completely every 27 days, 7 hours and 43.2 minutes—a revolution that is irregular because of the moon's elliptical orbit. Earth's tides are caused mainly by the moon, because of its relatively extreme nearness; in fact, the ratio of the tide-raising power of the moon to that of the sun is 11 to 5.

A "blue moon" is the second full moon within the same month, a rare occurrence (hence the expression, "once in a blue moon"). Also, the presence of volcanic dust or forest-fire smoke in the air can, if viewed from the proper angle, give the moon a bluish tint. The last recorded blue-colored moon, in 1950, was visible from New England and was caused by forest-fire smoke from Canada.

If you've ever wondered why you never see the back of the man-in-the-moon's head it's because the moon does not rotate daily as the earth does, but keeps one side always facing toward us, on account of the earth's gravitational pull. Though this might lead us to expect that we can see only 50 percent of the moon, the actual figure is 59 percent—due to the moon's librations, or slow oscillations, which make it seem to rock slightly as it journeys around us.

Meanwhile, the interaction of the spheres of gravity of Earth and its moon is causing the latter to steadily pull away, at a rate of four inches a month.

31

Not all that we believe of the moon is strictly scientific or satisfactorily provable. Astrologers, for example, believe the moon to be connected with diseases of the stomach, the womb and all "left-hand parts." And many people, of course, believe there is a correlation between full moons and mental disturbances, violent crime, metabolic rate and medical emergencies—though so far there has been no irrefutable evidence establishing such a link. Statistics proving full-moon "madness" have invariably been canceled out by statistics disproving such a phenomenon. Still, the connection between the moon and bizarre behavior is strongly rooted in folklore and language (e.g., "lunacy," "lunatic," "moonstruck" and "mooncalf") and is therefore likely to persist, despite any efforts science may make to debunk it.

Traditionally, the full moon has been considered a good time for pulling down, a time to think of the end of projects and plans. It is also thought to be a good time to mow grass and make hay. The new moon, on the other hand, is thought to signal a good time for beginnings—a time, for example, to move into a new house, or begin building one. Financial astrologers say you should buy at the new moon and sell at the full. Money counted during the new moon is said to increase.

As colorful as lunar legends may be, they pale by comparison to some of the true-life moon news generated by the so-called "space race." In 1966 the USSR's Luna 9 became the first spacecraft to make a soft landing on the moon, and two years later the U.S. Surveyor 7 followed suit. Then, on July 20, 1969, Apollo 11 astronauts Neil Armstrong and Edwin "Buzz" Aldrin became the first men to set foot on the moon, taking "one small step for [a] man, one giant leap for mankind," as Armstrong [almost] put it.

When the resultant rocks were dutifully read, it was a tad disappointing to discover that the moon was dead, and always had been. Most of the lifeless rocks were in the 3.7-billion-year range, with a few as old as 4.6 billion years—that is, about the same age as the solar system itself. One moon-walking astronaut described the surface as smelling like spent gunpowder. In any case, moon matter has thus far failed to answer the central moon mystery: Where did it come from?

The lunar rocks have largely put to rest a once popular theory that Earth's gravity "caught" the moon as it drifted through space. The chemical similarities between the moon rocks and Earth samples would be an extraordinary coincidence if this theory were true. On the other hand, the shortage of rhenium and molybdenum in lunar samples, compared to their presence on Earth, has ruled out the theory that the moon split off from Earth in one piece. The moon rocks also negated the notion that the planets and moons were formed by an accumulation of rocks and boulders condensed from early nebulas or clouds of dust and gases.

Calculations supporting that theory indicated that the entire condensation process should have taken a few million years at most—yet the moon samples showed that the lunar surface had been battered by rocks or meteors for much longer than that, about 600 million years.

Another mystery is whether the moon, like Earth, has a core. There is some evidence to suggest a small metallic core may exist, but definite proof remains elusive, and it may remain so, at least for the immediate future, because, since less is known about Mars, many scientists are more interested in someday studying Mars samples than new moon rocks which may or may not prove more revealing than those studied so far.

Even so, there have arisen in the astronomy community strong voices urging a return to the moon, pointing out that it could be, for instance, a venue for arrays of optical telescopes spaced many miles apart that could make possible observations and experiments barred on earth by atmospheric effects—providing what noted astronomer Bernard F. Burke says would be "an absolutely revolutionary new view of objects in the universe."

More mundanely, a group of American space firms has a plan to restart lunar research by opening the moon to corporate sponsors, TV spectaculars and theme parks. International Space Enterprises of San Diego plans to fly Russian-made launch and landing vehicles moonward in 1997 at a cost of $100 million, a fraction of what NASA would charge had it stayed in the lunar-exploration business.

But as the world marked the silver anniversary of the historic Apollo, Buzz Aldrin—one of the astronauts making that mission—conjured up a somewhat gloomier future for would-be space wanderers:

"For one crowning moment we were creatures of the cosmic ocean, a moment that a thousand years hence may be seen as the signature of our century. Yet an eerie apathy now seems to inflict the very generation who witnessed and were inspired by these events. The past quarter-century has seen a withered capacity for wonder and a growing retreat to delusions of a risk-free society."

Could it be, then, that the *last* words spoken by a lunar-walking astronaut will have been that those of Eugene Cernan in 1972, as he got into the Apollo 17 lunar module preparatory to liftoff? If so, they are words that speak, as they say, volumes: *"Let's get this mother out of here!"*

NORTHERN LIGHTS, SOUTHERN LIGHTS

The northern lights, or *aurora borealis*, have been noted since the time of classical Greece and Rome. The spectacular, multicolored rays and curtains of light that dance and swirl above the northern horizon have South Pole counterparts called, logically enough, the southern lights, or *aurora australis*.

These celestial light shows are caused by electrons and protons hitting Earth's atmosphere with hundreds of thousands of electron volts. The attacking particles ionize atmospheric molecules, which emit visible light upon returning to their normal state. Auroral activity appears as it does—in streaks and sheets, and so on—because the incoming particles penetrate most deeply along the lines of Earth's magnetic field. Auroral displays coincide with periods of increased sunspot activity, when solar magnetic storms shoot into space unusually large numbers of electrons and protons.

The different colors of the northern and southern lights are produced as the different gases in the atmosphere change form after ionization. Oxygen atoms produce two kinds of light, greenish-white and red. Oxygen-nitrogen molecules, on the other hand, produce lavender light.

Most of the "fireworks" of the lights, both northern and southern, occur about 60 miles above Earth's surface. In 1737, Benjamin Franklin wrote a newspaper article about the northern lights appearing so bright that people believed a house was on fire.

Satellite recordings show that the lights occur during the day as well as at night—it's just that, like the planets and stars, they are far outshone by the sun.

COMET TALES

It's hard to figure how objects so beautiful got such a bad rep, but for a long time comets were considered evil omens, the heralds of war and disease. It was even thought they caused the Black Plague, which is today believed to have been spread by fleas and bats in unsanitary conditions. But we now have a more scientific appreciation of what comets are and how they behave.

Look closely at a picture of a comet and you'll see it has a starlike head and a long, shiny tail. The head, or nucleus, is a miniature planet a few thousand miles in diameter, made up of ice.

Only a few comets ever become bright enough to be easily seen (usually at dawn and only for a few days). Some "untamed" comets that orbit opposite the direction of the major planets *do* show up in the evening heavens, but most can only be seen through a telescope or binoculars. It takes a combination of a big nucleus that produces a bright tail and a fortuitous arrangement of comet orbit, Earth and sun for a comet to become bright enough to see with the unaided eye.

Comets lose an estimated 100th of their volume during each "close encounter" with the sun. From this disintegration come meteors and meteorites. The brilliant meteor showers observed at different times annually are legacies from past comets, still tracking the comet's orbit. Comets can and do strike the Earth, although very infrequently.

Some amateur astronomers use huge binoculars to search for comets. If you find a heretofore unknown comet, it is then officially named for you. Comet Ikeya-Seki, for example, was an outstanding celestial streaker spotted by two Japanese amateur astronomers. At its brightest, its tail stretched across nearly a third of the dawn sky.

In July 1994 the 21 mountain-sized fragments of the comet Shoemaker-Levy 9—named for its discoverers Eugene Shoemaker and David Levy—hit the planet Jupiter with an explosive force of about 40 million megatons of TNT, far more powerful than all the nuclear bombs ever built. The celestial bombardment provided a rare show for astronomers and lay-viewers alike, while prompting some U.S. scientists to call for a federal program to track comets and asteroids, and to prepare for such collisions.

The most famous comet, of course, is Halley's, considered a rather mystical happenstance by Mark Twain, whose life was ushered in and out by two successive appearances of the fiery phenomenon. The idea that comets portend the toppling of kings was given credence when Halley's comet appeared in 1066, the year England's King Harold got royally trounced at the Battle of Hastings. (The Bayeux Tapestry, the 231-foot wall hanging that is the historical record of the Normal Conquest, depicts Halley's in the sky while below a thoroughly flummoxed King Harold quakes on his throne.) Much later, Halley's visit in 1910 coincided with the death of Britain's King Edward VII. Other records show the comet as early as 240 B.C.

It was not until 1705 that Edmund Halley postulated that the comet that now bears his name was the same returning over and over again, every 76.1 years. Sad to report, Halley's 1986 visit was a bit of a bust, much more ballyhoo than bedazzlement. Hopefully, the 2062 trip will be more deserving of the hoopla that will inevitably precede and accompany it.

ZAPPA: A REAL ASTEROID

Many thought Frank Zappa's music was from another planet. Now a miniature planet of sorts has been picked out for him.

Besieged by letters and e-mail, a Cambridge, Massachusetts, astronomy organization has named an asteroid that orbits between Mars and Jupiter "Zappafrank" after the late musician. "I don't recall a lobby quite as extensive as this one," said Brian Marsden, director of the International Astronomical Union's Minor Planets Center.

Zappa died in late 1993 at age 52 after battling prostate cancer for two years. Outrageous and irreverent, he fused jazz, classical and rock music behind lyrics that often tested the limits of free speech. His best-sellers were usually parodies, like 1979's *Dancin' Fool*, which made fun of the disco craze, and 1982's *Valley Girl*, which spoofed the Southern California mall crowds.

Others for whom asteroids have been offically named by the IAU include Beatles John Lennon, Paul McCartney, George Harrison and Ringo Starr.

Note: The IAU reminds high-minded skygazers not to fall for ads offering to name a star after them or their loved ones for a fee. The naming of stars and other celestial bodies is not an honor one can buy.

WHY IS THE SKY BLUE?

Ever wonder why the unclouded sky is blue?

It's because of Earth's atmosphere. When a ray of sunlight enters the atmosphere, a molecule in the air bends or "refracts" it so that it is no longer going in the same direction as before. The ray is composed of all the colors in the rainbow, and each color is bent at a slightly different angle. Blue and violet light are bent the most, red and orange the least. After hitting the first molecule, the light encounters many, many more—and each time, each color is bent again. As a result, the sunlight is scattered in all directions. However, because blue light is bent the most, it is scattered farthest.

Thus, it's the blue light that appears to come from all over the sky, whereas red, orange, and yellow light rays stay close to where the sun is in the sky.

POLE STAR

"The earth lies right in the middle of the heavens," said the Greek astronomer Ptolemy, thereby hanging up people's minds for more than a millennium. And wouldn't you know, it took a starry-eyed Pole of the Renaissance named Mikolaj Kopernik (otherwise known as Nicholas Copernicus) to unseat too-proud Earth—and Man—from the center of the universe.

Copernicus (1473-1543) was a man of many interests, equally at home in law and mathematics as in physics and astronomy. After years of studying the silent, vast voyages of the planets and stars, he came up with the startling conclusion that, "as if seated upon a royal throne, the Sun rules the family of the planets as they circle around him." He also explained the alternation of day and night by the rotation of Earth upon its axis.

"The fool wants to turn the whole science of astronomy upside down," Martin Luther supposedly said—which, in fact, is exactly what Copernicus did.

GALILEO REVISITED

Galileo Galilei (1564-1642), the first astronomer to enjoy the use of the telescope, discovered the craters of the moons, the rings of Saturn, the four largest moons of Jupiter, the movement of sunspots, and the starry nature of the Milky Way. His confirmation and espousal of the Copernican theory that the sun was the center of our planetary system put him in direct conflict with the Roman Catholic church, whose teachings portrayed Earth as the system's stationary center. He was charged with heresy.

The Grand Inquisitors of the church's Holy Office threatened the ailing, 68-old sage with torture on the rack. After two days of interrogation, he could take no more, and on bended knee before the examiners in Rome on January 22, 1633, he publicly recanted the astronomical theory he had expounded for 17 years. The Inquisition sometimes ordered heretics burned at the stake but was relatively lenient with Galileo—thanks to his public renunciation. It sentenced him to unlimited imprisonment, immediately commuted to house arrest.

It took the first non-Italian pope in over 455 years—John Paul II of Poland—to offer a handsome apology to the man he referred to as "the founder of modern physics." On November 10, 1979, the pope told scientists of the august Pontifical Science Academy in the Vatican that "the greatness of Galileo, like that of Einstein, is known to all. But the former had to suffer greatly, we cannot hide it, from church institutions and men."

ENCORE FOR THE STAR OF BETHLEHEM?

According to Christian tradition, the Star of Bethlehem was the heavenly beacon that guided the Magi to the infant Jesus. Some scientists believe it could appear again in the sky at any time—for it was not a conjunction of the planets, as once thought, but a nova, the temporary flaring of a distant star. It eventually will reappear either in the constellation of Capricorn (the goat) or in that of Aquila (the eagle), according to three British scientists who based their conclusions on a study of ancient Chinese and Korean records.

The scientists suggest that the nativity nova was observed by the Chinese in 5 B.C. "Jesus was born in 4 or 5 B.C., and not 1 A.D. The monk Dionysius Exiguius, who in 533 A.D. fixed the new era, made a mistake when he overlooked four years of the reign of the Emperor Augustus," wrote the scientists in the *Quarterly Journal of the Royal Astronomical Society*. It also was the Star of Bethlehem, they say, of which St. Ignatius wrote in the second century A.D.: "Its light was unspeakable, and its newness caused astonishment."

Space has always been a subject of fascination. In this 19th-century woodcut by Camille Flammarian a medieval traveler is shown seeking that far-out world of the unknown that lies beyond the stars.

THE EARTH
. . . portrait of planet number three . . .

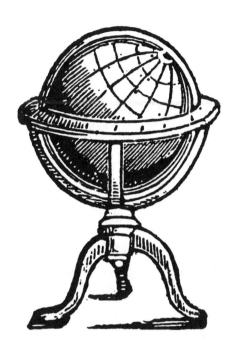

Earth does not belong to Man. Man belongs to the Earth.
—CHIEF SEATTLE (of the Suquamish and Duwamish)

If Earth was an apartment, we wouldn't get our security deposit back.
—JIM SHUBERT

EARTHLY PROFILE

Third planet from the sun, Earth is the fifth largest. Its circumference around the equator has been estimated at 24,900 miles, while its circumference around the poles is thought to be about 24,820 miles, making it nearly spherical but flattened at the poles. Various dimples and bulges give Earth a slightly pear-shaped appearance. Its sole satellite, the moon, has a diameter of 2,160 miles. Earth's total surface area is about 197,272,000 square miles, of which the land area makes up only about 57,200,000 square miles. The average land elevation is 2,700 feet; the average ocean depth is 12,500 feet. It is thought that

Earth originally had an atmospheric composition like Jupiter's—mostly hydrogen and helium, some methane and ammonia, and no oxygen—but this atmosphere was lost and the present one developed. Earth has a molten nickel-iron core with a surrounding rock mantle about 2,000 miles the beneath the surface. Friction from the sloshing of the liquid across valleys and mountains at the core-mantle boundary may explain why Earth rotates with a slight jerkiness that makes a day five-thousandths of a second longer or shorter than 24 hours every decade.

Mean distance from sun: 93 million miles
Equatorial diameter: 7,926 miles
Surface area: 197,272,000 square miles
Mass: 5.883 X 10^{21} tons
Length of day: 23 hours, 37 minutes and 4 seconds
Length of year: 365.25 days
Relative surface gravity: 1
Number of satellites: 1

THE WATER PLANET—AND HOW IT GOT THAT WAY

To ride astride a ball of blue through eternity's ageless skies—ah, what a destiny, what a strange, whirling world of wonders this is!—a matter mostly of plain old water (70 percent or so, in fact), and a whole lot of fantastically evolved mud. But first we must look to the stars, for the story of Earth begins in space, with the birth of the sun.

Science, which ought to know, says it all happened about 4.6 billion years ago, when Earth was formed from the same interstellar gas cloud that give birth to the sun and the other planets.

The cloud was mostly hydrogen, with heavier elements making up only a small fraction of its composition. As the cloud contracted under gravitational forces, the temperature and pressure at the core increased tremendously until thermonuclear reactions began, converting hydrogen into helium, releasing huge amounts of heat and light, and eventually forming the sun.

Icy stellar dust grains in the now disk-shaped cloud constantly collided and coalesced into ever-larger bodies, which in turn consolidated into planets surrounded by gaseous atmosphere.

The primeval Earth, creating and in turn being further shaped by gravity, must have been covered by craters. For as gravity increased, so did the speed at which asteroids and comets crashed into the planet. This incessant bombardment eventually melted the surface. Like its sister proto-planets, the twirling Earth grew more compact, with the heavier elements sinking ever inward and the lighter ones—such as hydrogen—escaping into space.

Such was the particular chemistry and destiny of this planetary shakeout that Earth evolved into the heaviest planet of all, with an average density about five and a half times that of water. And that's *after* a process of reduction that began with a proto-Earth five hundred times heavier and a thousand times larger than it is now.

During the first quarter of Earth's life, the new liquid-from-dust planet slowly cooled and hardened, forming a viscous crust. The earliest of earthly rocks were destroyed in the primal flux, but the oldest of those that remain are thought to be some 3.6 billion years old.

Stretched above the planet was a poisonous atmosphere of methane, ammonia and steam—life's strange primordial "soup." As Earth's surface cooled, the vapors turned liquid, and the rains came . . . and came . . . and came—literally oceans of it, as the great waiting basins filled, setting the stage for the eventual emergence of life-forms.

Meanwhile, new rock was formed by Earth's deep magma pouring forth from the ocean's ridges. In time, a simple massive earth-island was thrust up above the water—the supercontinent "Pangena," as it has since been named. About 100 million to 150 million years ago, this huge landmass began to break up, with separate continents slowly drifting to their present locations. One of the last of the units to break off—the Australia-Antarctica split—may have done so as "late" as 40 million years ago. And though the continents now seem stationary, they continue to move a few inches a year.

Evidence for so-called continental drift exists not only in how the continents can be seen to have once fit together, but also in the telling fit of rock formations and other geological structures in landmasses now separated by oceans. Studies of past positions of the magnetic poles also indicate relative movement between continents, and only continental drift can explain the scattered distribution of certain plants and animals.

Continental drift is now explained in terms of "plate tectonics." The plates in this case are the 15 rigid rock segments that make up Earth's outer shell and that extend down through the crust and floor on a semi-molten layer of the upper mantle. Seven of these plates are of major size and usually carry a continental landmass with surrounding ocean floor and island arcs. The plates are slowly moving relative to each other, driven by powerful forces within Earth's mantle.

At their boundaries, plates are either grinding past one another, or slowly separating (with new magma gushing up from below), or colliding (with one plate being ground down beneath another). These colossal machinations are the cause of equally colossal events—earthquakes, volcanic eruptions and the formation of mountains.

41

TAKING THE MEASURE OF EARTH

The history of science reveals the genius of the ancients and yields demonstrations that still amaze. In the third century B.C., the Greek astronomer Eratosthenes measured Earth's circumference within 1 percent—something anyone can do with two sticks and a distant friend.

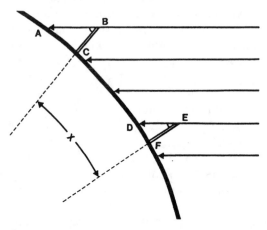

The simplest way is to stand the sticks vertically several hundred miles apart but on as near a north-south line as possible. At noon measure the angles A, B, C and D, E, F. (Divide each shadow length by its stick height to find the tangents of the angles. Then consult trig tables.) The difference between the angles equals angle X between the sticks, which, if projected, would intersect at Earth's center. The angle between the sticks is a fraction of a 360° circle. The distance between the sticks, which must be known, is the same fraction of Earth's circumference. —ROGER RAPOPORT

GAUGING A QUAKE: THE RICHTER SCALE

The Richter magnitude scale was developed in 1935 by Charles F. Richter of the California Institute of Technology as a mathematical device to compare the size of earthquakes. The magnitude of an earthquake is determined from the logarithm of the amplitude of waves recorded by seismographs. Adjustments are included in the magnitude formula to compensate for the variation in the distance between the various seismographs and the epicenter of the earthquakes. On the Richter scale, magnitude is expressed in whole numbers and decimal fractions. For example, a magnitude of 5.3 might be computed for a moderate earthquake, and a strong earthquake might be rated as magnitude 6.3.

Because of the logarithmic basis of the scale, each whole-number increase in magnitude represents a tenfold increase in measured amplitude. As an estimate of energy, each whole-number step in the magnitude scale corresponds to the release of about 31 times more energy than the amount associated with the preceding whole-number value.

Earthquakes with magnitudes of about 2.0 or less are usually called microearthquakes; they are not commonly felt by people and are generally recorded only on local seismographs. Events with magnitudes of about 4.5 or greater—of which there are several thousand annually—are strong enough to be recorded by sensitive seismographs all over the world.

Great earthquakes, such as the 1906 earthquake in San Francisco, have magnitudes of 8.0 or higher. On the average, one earthquake of such size occurs somewhere in the world each year. Although the Richter scale has no upper limit, the largest known shocks have had magnitudes in the 8.8 to 8.9 range.

The Richter scale is not used to express damage. An earthquake in a densely populated area that results in many deaths and considerable damage may have the same magnitude as a shock in a remote area that does nothing more than frighten the wildlife. Large-magnitude earthquakes that occur beneath the oceans may not even be felt by humans. —U.S. GEOLOGICAL SURVEY, DEPARTMENT OF THE INTERIOR

WE'RE LOSING ATMOSPHERE—BUT DON'T HOLD YOUR BREATH

Q—Most of the atmosphere of Mars has been lost to space because of the low gravity. Is Earth also losing atmosphere?

A—Yes, but don't hold your breath. Ninety-nine percent of the Earth's atmosphere is composed of nitrogen and oxygen, heavier elements that are held snugly by gravity. Above an altitude of 60 miles or so, remaining gases begin to separate.

The exosphere—the thinnest, outermost atmosphere that blends into interplanetary space about 500 miles up—is dominated by hydrogen, which is 16 times lighter than oxygen, and helium—both of which travel at high velocities. Because collisions of molecules are rare here, some just keep on going into space. This "leakage" is insignificant because hydrogen and helium make up such a tiny fraction of the atmosphere.

Also, in the case of helium, the gas is replaced on Earth as fast as it is lost. As for Mars, certainly some of its thin carbon-dioxide atmosphere is being lost because of low gravity, but another factor may be the planet's lack of a magnetosphere, which on Earth shields the atmosphere from solar winds.   —NEW YORK TIMES NEWS SERVICE

ELEMENTS IN EARTH'S CRUST

The seven most abundant elements in Earth's crust in parts per million:

Oxygen	466,000
Silicon	277,200
Aluminum	81,300
Iron	50,000
Calcium	36,300
Sodium	28,300
Potassium	25,900

THE CONTINENTS

Name	Area (in Sq. Miles)	% of World's Land
Asia	16,988,000	29.5
Africa	11,506,000	20.0
North America	9,390,000	16.3
South America	6,795,000	11.8
Europe	5,500,000	9.6
Australia	3,745,000	6.5
Antarctica	2,968,000	5.2

CONTINENTAL LOW POINTS

Continent	Lowest Point (in Feet)
Asia	Dead Sea, Israel-Jordan (1,312 below sea level)
Africa	Lake Assal, Djibouti (512 below sea level)
North America	Death Valley, California (282 below sea level)
South America	Salinas Grandes, Peninsula Valdes, Argentina (131 below sea level)
Europe	Caspian Sea, CIS (USSR) (92 below sea level)
Australia	Lake Eyre, South Australia (52 below sea level)
Antarctica	Unknown

HIGH MOUNTAIN PEAKS OF THE WORLD

The Himalayas, the world's loftiest mountain range, culminate in Mount Everest, the world's highest peak. The highest peaks in Europe lie in the Caucasus Mountains, a range in the CIS (former USSR) that divides Europe and Asia.

ASIA	Location	Feet
Everest	Nepal-China	29,028
K1 (Godwin-Austen)	Kashmir	28,250
Kanchenjunga	Nepal-India	28,208
Lhotse I	Nepal-China	27,923
Makalu I	Nepal-China	27,824

AFRICA	Location	Feet
Mount Kibo (a peak of Kilimanjaro)	Tanzania	19,340
Mount Mawenzi (a peak of Kilimanjaro)	Tanzania	16,896
Kenya	Kenya	17,058
Margherita Peak	Uganda-Zaire	16,795
Ras Dashan	Ethiopia	15,158
NORTH AMERICA		
McKinley	Alaska	20,320
Logan	Canada	19,850
Citlaltépetl (Orizaba)	Mexico	18,700
St. Elias	Alaska-Canada	18,008
Popocatépetl	Mexico	17,887
SOUTH AMERICA		
Aconcagua	Argentina	22,834
Ojos del Salado	Argentina-Chile	22,572
Bonete	Argentina	22,546
Tupungato	Argentina-Chile	22,310
Pissis	Argentina	22,241
EUROPE		
Caucasus Mountains (Europe-Asia)		
Elbrus	CIS (USSR)	18,510
Shkara	CIS (USSR)	17,064
Dykh Tau	CIS (USSR)	17,054
The Alps		
Mont Blanc	France	15,771
Monte Rosa	Italy	15,203
Dom	Switzerland	14,911
ANTARCTICA		
Vinson Massif	—	16,864
Tyree	—	16,290
Shinn	—	15,750
Gardner	—	15,375
Epperly	—	15,100

Note: The highest point in Australia is Mount Kosciusko, in New South Wales, 7,310 feet. The highest point in Oceania is Djaja Peak, in New Guinea, 16,503 feet.

THE LIQUID LOWDOWN

• The Southern Hemisphere has a water-to-land ratio of about 4 to 1, as compared to 3 to 2 in the Northern Hemisphere.
• Those five inland seas of the U.S. and Canada known as the Great Lakes (Superior, Michigan, Huron, Erie and Ontario) contain 65 tril-

lion gallons of water—or a fifth of the surface fresh water on Earth and 95 percent of the U.S. total. If all the water from the Great Lakes were emptied on the country's 48 contiguous states—and if somehow none was lost through absorption—people would be in water 10 feet deep.

• Kardivilliwarrakurrakurrie-apparlandoo is the name of a lake in northern Australia. Last one out has to spell it!

• The world's highest waterfall is Venezuela's Salto Angel (3,212 feet), named for its discoverer, an American flyer named Jimmy Angel, who was searching for a supposed treasure trove of gold.

• The source of the Amazon, which has about 15,000 tributaries and subtributaries, is a narrow mountain brook some 17,000 feet high in the snowcapped peaks of the Peruvian Andes.

• In every 1,000 pounds of ocean water there are about 35 pounds of salt and other materials.

• The highest tides occur in Canada's Bay of Fundy, rising up to 53 feet.

• Canada has the longest coastline in the world.

• New Zealand's coastline is longer than China's.

OCEANS AND SEAS

Ocean	Area (in Sq. Miles)	% of World's Water
Pacific	65,186,300	46.0
Atlantic	33,420,000	23.9
Indian	28,350,500	20.3
Arctic	5,105,700	3.7

Sea	Area (in Sq. Miles)	Avg. Depth (in Feet)
South China Sea	1,148,500	4,802
Caribbean Sea	971,400	8,448
Mediterranean Sea	969,100	4,926
Bering Sea	873,000	4,893
Gulf of Mexico	582,100	5,297
Sea of Okhotsk	537,500	3,192
Sea of Japan	391,100	5,468
Hudson Bay	281,900	305
East China Bay	256,600	1,539
Andaman Sea	218,100	3,667
Black Sea	196,100	3,906
Red Sea	174,900	1,764
North Sea	164,900	308
Baltic Sea	147,500	180
Yellow Sea	113,500	121

PRINCIPAL OCEAN DEPTHS

Pacific Ocean			Feet
Mariana Trench	11°22'N	142°36'E	35,840
Tonga Trench	23°16'S	174°44'W	35,433
Philippine Trench	10°38'N	126°36'E	32,995
Kermadec Trench	31°53'S	177°21'W	32,993
Bonin Trench	24°30'N	143°24'E	32,788
Atlantic Ocean			
Puerto Rico Trench	19°55'N	65°27'W	28,232
South Sandwich Trench	55°42'S	25°56'E	27,313
Romanche Gap	0°13'S	18°26'W	25,354
Cayman Trench	19°12'N	80°00'W	24,721
Brazil Basin	09°10'S	23°02'W	20,076
Indian Ocean			
Java Trench	10°19'S	109°58'E	23,376
Ob' Trench	09°45'S	67°18'E	22,553
Diamantina Trench	35°50'S	105°14'E	21,660
Vema Trench	09°08'S	67°15'E	21,004
Agulhas Basin	45°20'S	26°50'E	20,325
Arctic Ocean			
Eurasia Basin	82°23'N	19°31'E	17,881
Mediterranean Sea			
Ionian Basin	36°32'N	21°06'E	16,896

Note: Average ocean depth: about 16,400 feet.

—Defense Mapping Agency Hydrographic/Topographic Center

11 LONGEST RIVERS

River	Miles
1. Nile, Africa	4.145
2. Amazon, South America	4,000
3. Chang Jiang (Yangtze), Asia	3,964
4. Mississippi/Missouri/Red Rock, North America	3,740
5. Ob-Irtysh/Black Irtysh, Asia	3,362
6. Huang He (Yellow), Asia	2,903
7. Zaire (Congo), Africa	2,900
8. Amur/Shilka/Onon, Asia	2,744
9. Lena, Asia	2,734
10. Mackenzie/Peace/Finlay, North America	2,635
11. Mekong, Asia	2,600

15 LARGEST DESERTS

Desert	Location	Size (Approx. Sq. Miles)
1. Sahara	Northern Africa	3,500,000
2. Gobi	China and Mongolia	500,000
3. Rub al Khali	Southern Arabia	235,000
4. Kalahari	Southern Africa	225,000
5. Taklimakan	Xinjiang Province, China	180,000
6. Great Sandy	Western Australia	150,000
7. Great Victoria	Western and Southern Australia	150,000
8. Atacama	Northern Chile	140,000
9. Chihuahuan	Texas, New Mexico, Arizona and Mexico	140,000
10. Gibson	Western Australia	120,000
11. Kara-Kum	Turkmen, CIS (USSR)	120,000
12. Kyzyl-Kum	Uzbek and Kazakh, CIS (USSR)	100,000
13. Nubian	Northern Sudan	100,000
14. Syrian (El Hamad)	Northern Arabia, Iraq, Jordan and Syria	100,000
15. Thar (Great Indian)	India and Pakistan	100,000

SAVING THE EARTH

When naming "Endangered Earth" the "Planet of the Year" for 1988, *Time* magazine warned: "This wondrous globe has endured for some 4.5 billion years, but its future is clouded by Man's reckless ways."

The magazine listed these four major threats to the planet:

1. **Extinction**—Destruction of forests and other habitats is killing off a hundred species of plants and animals every day. "The losses," said *Time*, "are especially serious in the tropical forests, which cover only 7 percent of the earth's surface but are home to between 50 and 80 percent of the planet's species."

2. **Global Warming**—"If emissions of carbon dioxide and other greenhouse gases are not severely curtailed," the magazine warned, "their heat-trapping properties could raise the atmosphere's mean temperature as much as 8° F during the next 60 years." The main sources of carbon dioxide are the cars, factories and power plants of the industrial countries and the burning of tropical forests in the third world.

3. **Waste**—While nations continue to produce millions of tons of household garbage and toxic industrial waste, the world is running out of places to put them, and the danger to human health increases. The "throwaway societies" of the developed countries generate the most trash, while the developing nations have waste-related problems of their own.

4. **Overpopulation**—the world's population, presently at about 5.5 billion, is increasing by at least 8 million a year, with about 90 percent of the growth coming in the developing nations, where most people struggle to eke out an existence. The swelling ranks of humanity are sapping the environment as the urgent need to produce more food results in chopping down forests and depleting grasslands and croplands.

Faced with so awesome a roster of ruin, one may well wonder what can be done.

Some proposals were recently put forth by leaders of the country's most highly regarded environmental groups, whose agenda calls for a freeze on nuclear weapons and population growth, tougher water-pollution laws, more efficient use of natural resources, and greater protection of open lands and endangered animals.

In their report, "An Environmental Agenda for the Future," environmentalists—representing the Sierra Club, the Wilderness Society and the Environmental Defense Fund, among others—called public awareness the key to survival, and offered a plan of action on several fronts:

• **Pollution**—There should be tougher air and water laws and the Environmental Protection Agency's Superfund program to clean up toxic wastes should be bolstered. (Superfund's first decade and a half of operation has not been auspicious. Since its establishment in 1980, the program has thus far managed to clean up only 18 percent of the hazardous-waste sites on its "national priorities" list.)

• **Population Control**—To advance the goal of zero-population growth, population organizations and other public-interest groups should spread the word about the problems and possible remedies. The Agency for International Development "should incorporate family planning in all economic-assistance programs" and the World Bank and other global funding institutions "should give increased priority to population stabilization."

• **Energy**—"The best solution to the U.S. and world energy problems relies predominately on a variety of energy-efficiency improvements in all sectors of the world economy. This strategy . . . affords significant economic, social, health and environment advantages over any other approach."

• **Nuclear War**—A mutual and verifiable moratorium on production of nuclear weapons by the U.S., the republics of the former Soviet Union and other so-called nuclear nations. Those countries should also reevaluate arms-production policies for their "effect on health and the environment."

YIN AND YANG

Followers of Taoism, a Chinese mixture of philosophy and religion with mystical overtones, urge the acceptance of "all things in their natural state," believing that all life depends upon a balance of opposites, as represented by the halved circle: dark (yin) and light (yang), feminine and masculine, soft and strong, wet and dry, and so on. The yin-yang design eloquently conveys the two watchwords of Taoism, simplicity and harmony—which could also serve as an ecological motto for us all.

Note: For tips and suggestions as to what you, personally, can do to help Planet Earth survive in this, her time of angst, read on . . .

NATURE IS A MOTHER

...*flora and fauna forever*...

Hast thou named all the birds without a gun?
Loved the wood-rose and left it on its stalk?
—RALPH WALDO EMERSON

Men argue, nature acts.
—VOLTAIRE

EVERY DAY IS MOTHER'S DAY

We all know it's "not nice" to fool this mother of all mothers, but all too often we forget that it's frequently *fatal* as well—though maybe "forget" is too good a word. Maybe what we really do is put the whole complicated question out of mind on the grounds that it's simply too friggin' *big* to do anything about anyway—or maybe we're just too *busy* today, as we comfort ourselves that tomorrow, after all, is another.

But whatever the reason—whatever the easeful thought of delay—the time is still *now*, and there's much we each can do.

So let us consider this modest proposal: to waste not a zip or zap more of time with blame or regret, but rather take stock of however much of Mother Nature's good nature may be left—and act accordingly.

Part of taking stock, of course, is sharing life-preserving data and ways, and hopefully helping, meanwhile, to light proverbial fires under proverbial duffs (our own included). So let us begin . . .

WHEN MOTHER NATURE GOT BIG-BANGED

As we saw in the Universe chapter, most scientists today believe everything dates from the Big Bang—which therefore may be thought of as our good Mother Nature's most righteous birthday.

That mightiest of celestial orgasms gave rise to billions of heavenly offspring—including, eventually, Spaceship Earth, which has been sailing around the sun for some 4.5 billion years now. And from a recent study of some of the planet's oldest rocks comes evidence that life on Earth is nearly as old as Earth itself.

Scientists at the University of Maryland say they have found "molecular fossils" made of hydrocarbons in 3.8 billion-year-old, granite-like gneiss (pronounced "nice") rocks from western Greenland. The discovery pushes back the date of life's advent by some 400 million years, close to the estimated age of the Earth—4.5 billion years.

Dr. Cyril Ponnamperuma of Maryland's Laboratory of Chemical Evolution says the only question was whether the hydrocarbons were created by primitive living organisms or were formed inorganically. That question was answered, he believes, when it was determined that hydrocarbons in the rock contained elevated amounts of carbon-12 isotope produced in photosynthesis.

The first creatures on Earth may have been soft-bodied entities that left only indirect fossil evidence of their existence, in the form of fecal pellets. If so, then it means the world's animal life is at least 2 billion years old. (The accepted fossil record indicates a wide variety of animals were present 600 million years ago.) As for still-living entities, the oldest known is a 70-foot by 25-foot creosote plant discovered in the desert some 80 miles northeast of Los Angeles. Nicknamed "King Clone," it is estimated to be 11,700 years old.

NATURE NOTES

The world's tallest tree is a 368-foot redwood in Humboldt County, California—taller than a football field is long. Giant sequoias, however, closely rival the redwoods in height, with the tallest reaching as high as a 25-story office building and weighing about as much as a small oceangoing freighter.

A housefly beats its wings about 20,000 times a minute and has an average airspeed of 4 1/2 mph.

Did you know that in certain national parks, in hard-to-get-at places where dams must be built, the U.S. Department of Fish and Game drops beavers by parachute? Or that if a beaver did not chew wood every day, its teeth would grow so long that it could not eat?

The skyscraper of desert cacti is the saguaro, which can reach a height of 50 feet. Its root system is rarely more than three feet deep, but the radius is often equal to the height of the plant. After a downpour, the roots soak up the moisture and hundreds of gallons of water rise up into the expandable stem.

Sausage trees in Florida resemble outdoor delicatessens, with long sausagelike fruits hanging from the branches.

The eyes of the predator animals are usually in front so they can spot their prey. The eyes of the prey are generally placed toward the side to give a wider range of vision to watch out for the predators.

The huge Amazon electric eel (*Electrophorus electricus*) stuns its victims with a shock of up to 600 volts.

The manatee, an aquatic mammal, has a "conveyor-belt" dental system, in which the old teeth drop out in the front and new ones migrate forward, for as long as the manatee lives.

Crocodiles are quite fast on their feet, but they can't change directions very well. If you are ever chased by one, don't run in a straight line—zigzag!

Walrus bulls eat as much as 100 pounds of food a day and often weigh the same as a midsize automobile.

Lizards can be strange little beasties, indeed. The female collared lizard signals she is ready for mating when bright orange spots blossom on her shoulders, while the rather impiously named Jesus Christ lizard of Central America literally walks on water to flee its predators.

The "bug room" at the Smithsonian Institution houses 20,000 dermestid beetles, whose job it is to pick clean the skeletons of animals that are to be stored.

Just how fast—or slow—is a "snail's pace"? According to tests made in the U.S., the movement of a common garden snail (*Helix aspersa*) varies from 0.00036 mph (or 23 inches per hour) to 0.0313 mph (55 yards an hour). An English snail, Henry by name, was clocked in his progress over a two-foot stretch of glass at Truro, Cornwall. It was determined that he was traveling at *103 hours per mile!*

Grasshoppers can't hop unless the temperature is at least 62° F.

Princeton University memory researchers have reported the successful breeding of an amnesic fruit fly, which forgets odors four times as fast as a normal fruit fly.

The mayfly has no mouth or stomach. Its lifetime is but a single day.

Spiders' webs, of which no two are precisely alike, are made from a liquid which hardens when it is stretched; this liquid is produced in the spider's abdominal glands. Some male spiders strum the strands of their web to attract a mate.

How, you may ask, does a cricket chirp? It doesn't! What it does that we think of as chirping is fiddle—and only the male cricket does it, to attract female crickets. Our cricket-fiddler, so to speak, first lifts his wings and then, using one wing as a "bow," he rubs that wing against tiny ridges on top of the other wing.

Stanford University researchers recently ended a long-standing debate among owl specialists as to which sense owls rely on most to find food at night. Determining sight to be the most vital sense, they reported fitting owls with eyeglasses.

A blue-and-gold parrot was fired from its job at a British zoo recently after embarrassing parents and children alike with its foul language. Bluey, a long-tailed macaw named for his brilliant plumage and not his X-rated language, was part of a show at the Isle of Wight zoo until he suddenly started telling visitors in no uncertain terms exactly what they could do. "It was no good," said zoo manager Jack Corney. "We even got in a local elocution teacher, but Bluey told him to go on a sexual excursion too." Still, the zoo people might have expected something like this—inasmuch as Bluey's previous owner was a sailor.

Do you eat like a bird? That's fine—as long as you don't mean the pelican, which ingests a third of its weight in fish at a single meal. Or, as poet Dixon Lanier Merrit (1879-1972) once put it:

> *A wonderful bird is the pelican,*
> *His bill will hold more than his belican.*
> *He can take in his beak*
> *Food enough for a week,*
> *But I'll be damned if I see how the helican.*

Herons are the "swordsmen" of aquatic birds, often using their sharp bills to stab their prey to death.

The Rabbit

The rabbit has a charming face:
Its private life is a disgrace.
I really dare not name to you
The awful things that rabbits do;
Things that your paper never prints—
You only mention them in hints.
They have such lost, degraded souls
No wonder they inhabit holes;
When such depravity is found
It only can live underground.

—Anonymous

A squirrel's bushy tail acts as a balance factor, much as a parasol aids a tightrope walker. It is also used as a rudder when the animal leaps, as a parachute to break a fall, as an extra layer of fur on a cold day, as a shield in a fight, as an umbrella when the sun's too hot—and as a signal for emotions.

Each quill of the porcupine has about a thousand tiny barbs.

The bear can't see very well, and it hears only fairly well. But it has a well-developed snout with a wet nose, or rhinarium (the roughened skin at the tip of the snout) which sharpens the sense of smell. (*A bear*

fact: The koala—known as Australia's teddy bear—is not a bear, but a relative of the American opossum. The koala must eat eucalyptus leaves or it dies. Its digestive system does not accept any other kind of foliage.) Bears, by the way, are not the only beings that hibernate—so do whippoorwills, beetles, wolf spiders, goldfish and carp.

According to the U.S. Sheep Experiment Station in Dubois, Idaho, the chances that a ram is homosexual is 1 in 11.

The greatest reliable height recorded for a giraffe is 19 feet 3 inches, but it is thought that there are perhaps many over 20 feet tall. Giraffes, incidentally, are the only animals born with horns.

One Hump or Two?

Officials at the Sedgwick County Zoo in Wichita, Kansas, recently asked the city to remove a fire hydrant from the yard in which its camel, Tomoloc, is housed. The camel's would-be mate died not long ago, and "Tommy" has transferred his affections to the hydrant, shall we say rubbing against it vigorously at all hours. Said keeper Julie Fritz, "If it's during public hours, I just go hide somewhere. What can I say? The camel doesn't have a life."

Epalog, the official publication of the Environmental Protection Agency, recently reported a study that showed that "ten cows burp enough gas in a year to provide for all the space heating, water heating, and cooking requirements for a small house." According to the study, U.S. cows burp about 50 million tons of hydrocarbons into the atmosphere every year.

The Tambopata Wildlife Reserve, a 13,000-acre tract of unsullied rain forest in Peru, has the richest animal life of any place in the world, including 566 bird species, 145 species of dragonflies, and many other rare and endangered animals.

There have been private zoos for at least four thousand years. Today's modern zoos are havens of survival where endangered species may be saved from extinction.

A team of California researchers has concluded that, aside from humans, pigs are the only mammals capable of getting sunburned.

Reuters reports that gorillas at the Frankfurt, Germany, zoo have had a TV set installed in their cage to keep them from getting bored.

Funny Times—a truly indispensable monthly tabloid of humorous fancy and fact—recently reported the sad saga of the three dolphins who escaped from their performing pen at an exclusive resort in Key Largo, Florida, and swam away. Several days later they were discovered in a golf-course lagoon on Key Biscayne, where, on their own, they showed up at 10 A.M., 2 P.M. and 4 P.M.—the same times as the Key Largo shows—and performed tricks, obviously expecting to be fed.

The creature with the largest brain in proportion to its body is neither the human nor the dolphin, but the "lowly" ant. The ant's chief natural enemy is another ant—a situation that is true of only one other living creature: a human being.

Considering their relative sizes, a worm is a thousand times stronger than a human. The typical earthworm takes four naps between sunup and sundown.

Chimpanzees normally bear twins only once in every 87 live births— the same frequency as humans.

An average child's brain, by the time it is one year old, has attained 50 percent of its adult weight and, at six, it has reached 90 percent of its final weight of about three pounds. The adult brain, which reaches an average size of 1500 cubic centimeters, comprises only 2 percent of body weight but it consumes 25 percent of the body's oxygen.

The human body contains 206 bones, over half of which are in the feet (52) and hands (54).

Nature index: Number of heartbeats per minute—bats: 750, squirrels: 249, humans: 70.

THE ROOTS OF MAN

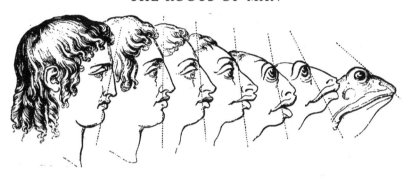

The human family is widely believed to have developed from apes from 5 million to 6 million years ago.

The common species the two families developed from—*Australopithecus*—gave rise to the modern genus *Homo*, which includes *Homo sapiens*, and a series of ape-human creatures that lived in Africa with early *Homo species* until they died out a little more than a million years ago.

In 1994 scientists in Ethiopia reported the discovery of a largely complete, 4.4-million-year-old skeleton, a representative of mankind's oldest known ancestor, *Australopithecus ramidus*. The find includes hip, foot and leg bones that may be from a time when apelike creatures first began walking.

Earlier, in 1979, anthropologist Mary Leakey, widow of noted colleague Louis Leakey, announced that in the previous summer she and her aides had found new evidence of Man's early roots in a remote area of northern Tanzania called Laetoli: a 75-foot-long trail of footprints made by hominids (humanlike beings) walking on a fresh layer of volcanic ash 3.5 million years ago.

According to Leakey, the creatures hypothesized by the prints were walking upright, with a free-striding gait not unlike that of humans. She contended that, more than anything else, walking upright is what differentiates man's forebears from other primates.

"This unique ability," she said, "freed the hands for myriad possibilities—carrying, toolmaking, intricate manipulation. From this single development, in fact, stems all modern technology. Somewhat oversimplified, the formula holds that this new freedom of forelimbs posed a challenge. The brain expanded to meet it. And mankind was formed."

However, whether Leakey's prints are indeed those of the oldest known human ancestors is a matter of some dispute in archeological circles. For example, Dr. Donald C. Johanson, director of the Institute of Human Origins, feels that his own landmark discovery of 1974—of a 3.7-million-year-old prehuman skeleton dubbed "Lucy"—proves that hominids walked on two legs long before they had a human-sized brain, and that this walking qualifies them to be classified as true ancestors, not just relatives.

Critics of the Johanson theory question whether the four-foot-tall, small-skulled Lucy really "walked" in the modern sense or was just an upward-gaited tree dweller, something halfway between a chimp and a man. Dr. Leakey and her adherents feel that Lucy is not in the mainstream of human evolution, but merely a representative of the earlier, extinct *Australopithecus* genus.

ADAM AND EVE

Arkansas bill requires
teaching of creationism
—HEADLINE, CHICAGO TRIBUNE

Adam and Eve,
sand and sieve,
were you in fact
the very first act?

Or did dirty ol' Darwin
go wee in your Garden?

—BOB PERLONGO

60

TONY THE TIGLON

Crossings of different animals have always held a freaky fascination for most of us. Do you know what we call the offspring from a union between a male lion and a female tiger? A liger, no less. And what of the fruit of a union 'between a lioness and male tiger? A tiglon, of course.

Not long ago a lioness and a male leopard did their thing and came up with a lepon, while a *really* different union of female cat and pet male rabbit resulted in an animal with a feline head and rabbity rear. (A "cabbit," perchance?) And we all know that mules derive from the breeding of male donkeys and female horses (the originators of the art of making an ass of oneself). But did you know a donkey times a zebra equals a "zedonk"?

The reason we don't see such specimens in the nation's zoos was summed up recently by an official of Chicago's Lincoln Park Zoo, who said: "We are not in the business of exhibiting freaks."

ANIMAL NAMES: MALE, FEMALE AND YOUNG

Animal	Male	Female	Young
Ass	Jack	Jenny	Foal
Bear	Bear	Sow	Cub
Cat	Tom	Queen	Kitten
Cattle	Bull	Cow	Calf
Chicken	Rooster	Hen	Chick
Deer	Buck	Doe	Fawn
Dog	Dog	Bitch	Pup
Duck	Drake	Duck	Duckling
Elephant	Bull	Cow	Calf
Fox	Dog	Vixen	Cub
Goose	Gander	Goose	Gosling
Horse	Stallion	Mare	Foal
Lion	Lion	Lioness	Cub
Pig	Pig	Sow	Piglet (Suckling)
Rabbit	Buck	Doe	Bunny
Sheep	Ram	Ewe	Lamb
Swan	Cob	Pen	Cygnet
Tiger	Tiger	Tigress	Cub
Whale	Bull	Cow	Calf
Wolf	Dog	Bitch	Pup

ANIMAL GESTATION PERIODS

Animal	Gestation Period	Animal	Gestation Period
American buffalo (bison)	270-285 days	gorilla	8 1/2 months
baboon	6 months	hamster	16-19 days
black bear	7 months	horse	11 months
camel	12-13 months	kangaroo	38-39 days
cat	63 days	lion	108 days
chimpanzee	226 days	mink	48-51 days
cow	280-290 days	otter	9 1/2-12 1/2 months
deer (whitetail)	7 months	pig	112-115 days
dog	61 days	rabbit	1 month
dolphin	9 months	raccoon	63 days
elephant	21 months	sheep	150 days
fox	49-55 days	skunk	49 days
gerbil	25-29 days	squirrel	44 days
giraffe	14-15 months	tiger	100-108 days
		wolf	60-63 days
		zebra	11-12 months

—NEW YORK ZOOLOGICAL SOCIETY

LONGEVITY OF SOME ANIMALS

The list below reflects the average maximum life-span of various animals while in captivity.

Years	Animal	Years	Animal
10	pig	25	zebra
12	robin	28	giraffe
13	rabbit	28	sea lion
14	chicken	30	dolphin
14	coyote	30	lion
15	reindeer	31	gibbon ape
15	timber wolf	31	grizzly bear
16	bullfrog	33	gorilla
16	kangaroo	35	pigeon
17	goat	37	chimpanzee
19	beaver	41	polar bear
19	leopard	45	baboon
20	cougar	46	jackass
20	cow	50	domestic horse
20	moose	51	pelican
20	rattlesnake	55	eagle
20	sheep	68	owl
20	sparrow	69	raven
22	domestic dog	70	African elephant
23	domestic cat	75	Asian elephant
25	camel	134	Eastern box turtle
25	tiger	177	giant tortoise

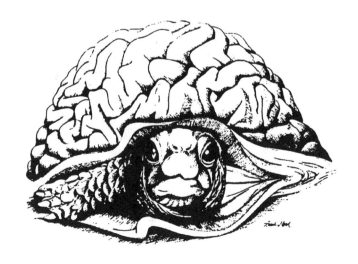

Conserving Landfill Space

For each ton of wastepaper that is recycled. 3.3 cubic yards of landfill space is conserved.

Protecting the Environment

When compared to manufacturing products made from virgin pulp materials. making products from recycled resources reduces:

Air pollution by 74%

Water pollution by 35%

Conserving Natural Resources

Right now. paper products consume 35% of the world's annual commercial wood harvest. This figure is expected to increase to 50% by the year 2000. At this rate. harvest exceeds replacement. Using a ton of recycled paper saves 17 trees.

Conserving Energy

Manufacturing from recovered resources uses 64% less energy than manufacturing from virgin pulp. By recycling a ton of paper. the equivalent of 4.100 kilowatt hours of electricity can be saved.

Saving Money $ $ $

Disposal of solid waste is the nation's third largest domestic expenditure. $6 billion is spent by the U.S. annually to collect and dispose of trash. The less garbage we generate. the less we will have to pay to get it taken away.

Providing Jobs

Harvesting wastepaper in the city creates five times as many jobs as harvesting the raw material from the forest.

Finally. recycling makes good sense. Studies show that about half of all garbage is capable of being recycled. Currently. we reuse only 10% of this.

CHART BY KATHERINE KAO

THE "FIND" ART OF RECYCLING

Mother Nature loves recyclers, and so will your budget—so keep your throwaways to a minimum by carefully checking for any items that can be used again.

If you have the room to store it, paper is a good item to save and take in to a recycling center when you have enough to make the trip worthwhile. Since the average tree yields 118 pounds of paper, recycling one ton of paper will save 17 trees from being cut down. (Machines run by electricity extract from the paper such foreign material as staples and paper clips, then de-ink it and turn it into the pulp from which new paper is made. The complete cycle takes about 90 minutes.) If you're fortunate enough to have a working fireplace, remember that old newspapers can be turned into logs by rolling them tightly and holding them together with thin tuna or cat food cans from which the tops and bottoms have been cut. (*Tip:* These paper logs will work better if you alternately soak them in water and dry them out several times before using.)

But paper is just one of many recyclable items, not all of which are readily apparent as such. According to author Carolyn Jabs, what we view as trash is very arbitrary: "It's all a matter of rethinking of things not as what you've been told it is, which might be trash, but as a raw material. For instance, once you've seen the plastic top of a coffee can as a Frisbee, you might see other things that are more applicable to your own life."

The "find" art of recycling can stimulate the inventor in all of us, claims Jabs: "There is a creative element to reusing, a resourcefulness, which is an American tradition we're losing touch with. The most beautiful reuses are those which you haven't necessarily read about in a book. Instead, you have a need and you have an object and you figure out how to bring them together. Those are really the most satisfying."

Here, then, is a handful of tidy tips, to get you started on your own recycling program:

Leftover food. Keep your trashing of edible food to an absolute minimum. After every meal, stash away anything that might conceivably make up a snack or part of another meal. Soups, salads, stews and omelets, for example, are endlessly variable as to specific ingredients, and therefore perfect as vehicles for recycling leftover meats and vegetables. No doubt you have culinary recycling secrets of your own when it comes to such less-obvious reusables as cake and bread. And—wonder of wonders!—even your "throwaways" needn't be thrown away. If you have a garden or some indoor plants, start saving your food scraps (along with fallen leaves, grass clippings, sawdust, pet manure and the like) in a box or bin for three to four weeks.

Stirred occasionally, these ripening oddments make a most excellent compost that will give your soil a real boost.

Plastic bottles and jugs. Use these for just about any type of liquid. The bottoms make excellent caddies for tools or crayons. They can also be used as catchalls for hair rollers or as leakproof saucers for plants. Or use a plastic milk jug as a bird-feeder; just cut out a square close to the bottom, large enough for birds to get in, and tie the jug to a tree by running a piece of string or wire through its handle. To fill the feeder, just take off the cap and pour in seed. And cutting a circle out of the side of a large well-rinsed bleach bottle turns it into an excellent onion or potato bin. Or fill one with water and keep it in the trunk of your car—you never know when a thirsty radiator may need a drink. Also, by cutting the bottom off a plastic bottle of just about any size, you have a crude but effective funnel; by cutting the bottom off on a long, gradual slant, you end up with a scoop that can be used for scooping up flour, sugar or rice—or even soil or pet food.

Milk cartons. Cut off and discard the tops—then use the bottoms as plant containers.

Tube-shaped potato-chip containers. These can be used again as canisters for bread crumbs, biscuits, flour or sugar—or for candles or incense sticks.

Glass containers. Sterilize and reuse them. They're great for storing leftovers, nails, screws or whatever.

Plastic bags. Don't throw them away—reuse them. If just 25 percent of all U.S. homes used 10 fewer plastic bags a month, we'd save more than 2.5 billion bags a year.

Plastic-foam meat trays. These can be used in the garden under tomatoes or cucumbers that might be touching the ground, to keep the plants from rotting on the bottom. They also can be recycled as paint palettes, or cut into strips and used as window insulation.

Plastic egg cartons. When parties and other get-togethers create an unusual demand for ice cubes, you can use these as extra ice trays.

Spice rack. An old spice rack can be given a coat of paint and hung up as a caddy for nail polish, perfume and the like.

Soap slivers. When bars of soap diminish to the point of becoming hard to handle, don't toss them—put them into an old sock or wrap them in a piece of cloth, then sew up the sock or cloth securely and you have a sudsing sack that can be used for a surprisingly long time. Or make a slit in one end of a sponge and insert the slivers. A sponge thus loaded is great for washing cups, or cleaning the sink, or for other such "quickie" cleanups.

Brushes. An old toothbrush is great for cleaning ridges and grooves on refrigerators, stoves, can openers and the like, as well as windowpane corners and cheese graters. A shaving brush can be trimmed and put into service as a shoe-polish applicator. And an old mascara brush can be used to clean typewriter keys, jewelry and such.

Self-closing shower rings. These can be recycled as king-size, "lose-proof" key rings.

Brooms and mops. Before replacing a broom or mop, you can "renew" it several times by trimming off stiff or uneven ends. Trim a broom's ragged bristles on a sharp angle and you have a most effective tool for cleaning edges and corners. Or trim the bristles evenly, cut the handle off, and use it as a whiskbroom. If the bristles are totally unsalvageable, all is still not lost: the broomstick itself can be saved and used at some future time as a replacement handle for another tool.

Rubber spatula. A rubber spatula with battered edges can be trimmed and used again. In its final stages, it can still be used to scrape out the contents of small bottles and jars.

Cotton clothing. If you're adept at sewing, turn old, absolutely-unwearable-anymore cotton garments into potholders, slipcovers or doll's clothes. And don't throw away those leftover bits and pieces of cloth—use them as rags or save them till you have enough make a patchwork apron, skirt or bedspread. Speaking of sewing, keep in mind that empty lipstick cases, carefully cleaned, make excellent needle holders, and that a plastic-topped pill bottle when empty makes a fine sewing kit for use when traveling—just put in a needle and thread (wrapped around a small piece of cardboard), snap the top back on, and you're ready to go. (These bottles can also be used as thumbtack, button or fishhook containers.) As for your empty thread spools, they can be turned into toy abacuses or used as jump-rope handles.

Carpeting. When carpeting is installed, the small leftover pieces can be saved for use as shoe polishers.

Garden hoses. An old, leaky hose may no longer be able to hold its water very well, but that doesn't mean it's altogether useless. Cut hose sections to the size of handsaws, ice skates and the like, for use as blade-edge protectors; just split the hose down the middle on one side and slide it over the blade.

Auto and truck tires. Tires too worn for further on-road use can do service as planters, or as components for a variety of playground attractions. Or the treads can be cut off and used to improve footing on stairways or ramps.

Paint thinner. After using paint thinner to clean your brushes, let it sit in a container until the sediment sinks to the bottom. Strain the thinner through a piece of cloth, and it's ready to use again.

Motor oil. Used motor oil can be re-refined and used again, or recycled as a herbicide to kill unwanted plants. It can also be used as a weatherizing liquid for the bottom of fence posts or tomato stakes; soak the posts or stakes in used oil for a week and they won't rot as readily as they would otherwise.

OTHER STEPS YOU CAN TAKE

Here are several more things you can do to help Mother Nature and yourself at the same time:

Buy larger sizes. At the supermarket and elsewhere, keep in mind that a single 16-ounce can uses 68 grams of metal. That's 40 percent less than the 95.4 grams used in two 8-ounce cans.

Buy eggs that come in cardboard rather than Styrofoam containers. Then use the containers as workshop or jewelry organizers.

Eat less meat. If all Americans reduced their meat intake by just 10 percent, the grain and soybeans saved each year could adequately feed 60 million people—the same number who starve to death worldwide each year. It takes 16 pounds of grain and soybeans and 2,500 gallons of water to produce 1 pound of beef. And cattle ranching accounts for a good deal of the rain-forest destruction in Central America.

Use your own mug and silverware at work. This is preferable to using disposable cups and utensils. It also saves money while lending your coffee and lunch breaks a personal touch.

Use cloth diapers. Biodegradable diapers don't really biodegrade and, according to *New Age Journal*, they cost up to eight times more than it costs to wash your own and three times more than most diaper services. How about a compromise? Use cloth diapers at home and disposable ones when out.

Recycle newspapers. If everyone in the U.S. recycled just one-tenth of their newspapers, we could spare about 25 million trees a year.

Plant a tree. If every U.S. family planted just one tree, more than a billion pounds of "greenhouse gases" would be removed from the atmosphere every year.

Drive a fuel-efficient car. Better yet, use public transportation or carpool. Or, whenever possible, walk or bicycle—which have the additional advantage of helping you stay fit.

EASY ON THE WATER

By making a few changes in your habits, you and your family can save many gallons of water while helping assure that there will always be enough available for such essential uses as drinking, washing, farming and business. Some examples:

In the bath. A quick shower usually draws less water than a bath, especially if you turn off the shower while soaping down. Instead of letting the water run while shaving or washing your face, stopper the wash basin. Special attachments are available to reduce water use by showers, wash basins and toilets. Put refuse, such as used facial tissues, into your trash receptacle rather than down the toilet.

Around home. Load the washing machine and dishwasher to capacity. When washing dishes by hand, use a washtub or plug the sink. Don't wash or rinse with running water. Check waterline connections and faucets for leaks. In areas with severe drought, washing the car at home is illegal, but even where it isn't, you can save water by using the hose only for a quick final rinse.

Landscaping. Watering of lawns and gardens is also illegal in some drought-stricken areas—a fact that may cause hundreds of dollars of damage to the landscaping in those places, according to the American Association of Nurserymen. Lawns and gardens in dry regions are thirsty after a dry winter, notes the association. It recommends a good soaking for your plants if they haven't had much rain for the past 10 days. The association suggests that really serious conservers can use bathtub water, soap and all, for trees and plants.

—THE DENVER WATER DEPARTMENT

ALTERNATIVE FUELS FORESEEN

Cars of the 21st century may be driven on fuel made from seaweed, algae, wood pulp or garbage. Or fuel might be made from a more conventional source, such as coal, shale or tar sands. But chances are that by the year 2000, the world's diminishing oil supply will make alternative fuel sources necessary, the experts say.

Although development of synthetic fuels isn't exactly a national priority while oil is in abundant supply and cheaper than its imitation, scientists and officials of government and industry are looking to a less abundant future. Research in the development of synthetic fuel goes on in the oil industry, at national laboratories such as Argonne National Laboratory in Illinois, and several hundred universities nationwide, which are under contract with the U.S. Department of Energy.

In a back-to-the-drawing-board approach to synthetic fuels,

researchers are seeking cheaper means than existing technology for converting coal to gas and liquid fuel. Gas produced from coal eventually may become competitive commercially with natural gas because coal gasification is a simpler process than coal liquefaction.

—ANNE LITTLE

OLE KING SOL

There's nothing new under the sun, they say—and the ongoing effort to more effectively harness the energy thereof is certainly no exception.

Thousands of years ago in the Far East, structures were being built with solar-energy factors in mind, while later, in the golden days of Greece, Socrates took time out from his more abstract expositions to explain to fellow Athenians the solar principle of orienting buildings to the south. (There was a certain urgency to his instruction, since he and his countrymen faced a fuel shortage resulting from deforestation.) So we are not the first to face fuel shortages and energy crises: throughout history, societies have had to cope with these basic challenges.

Even today's rooftop solar-energy collectors, used by over a million solar-power pioneers to heat water, were foreshadowed by similar equipment invented—in California, of course!—at the turn of the century. And thousands of the systems were mass-produced in Florida until shortly after World War II, when the solar equipment lost out to electric water heaters. Clearly, there is a lot of potential energy beaming down from Ole King Sol that simply isn't being used.

One problem is that, with present technology, the money you can save with solar power can only be realized in the long run. Solar collectors are mounted on the roof to attract and absorb the sun's radiant energy. A series of small water-filled pipes forms a grid inside the collectors. A pipe connects to a second grid of pipes in a water storage tank. The water is pumped constantly through this network of pipes. It is heated by the collectors and the heat is transferred to the stored water in the tank. A backup electric heating unit will take over on cloudy days and at night. It may take a few years before your energy-bill savings equal your initial investment, but after you cross that particular "Great Divide" the savings are continuous, since there are virtually no operating or repair costs involved. What's more, you may be eligible for federal and state tax credits equal to a certain percentage of installation costs. Then, too, solar units increase the value of your house—and some states even exclude this added value when determining your property tax assessment.

Meanwhile, as you ponder the whys and wherefores of full-scale conversion to solar power, you might want to explore some of the more popular incidental uses thereof, such as keeping your car battery charged via a panel of solar cells, and using cells to power walkway lights that cast small circles of light on the ground. These lights can be installed simply by driving a stake into the ground—a much cheaper and simpler chore than running an electric cable from the house.

One of the chancier factors in deciding if and when to go solar on more than a dabbler's scale is how quickly or how slowly research in the field may be proceeding. At the moment, breakthroughs in the development of direct and truly cost-effective converters of sunlight into electricity are still considered to be several years away. Meanwhile, research continues to center on further perfecting two types of solar cells—the photovoltaic cell, which stores the power it collects from sunlight in a large number of separate batteries, and the much-newer photoelectrochemical cell, which offers the promise of both collecting and storing energy in one efficient unit, while at the same time extracting hydrogen from water. Suffice to say, if you're thinking about installing a solar energy system, you should definitely begin by doing some research into just what state the state of the art is in.

The Better Business Bureau advises all solar shoppers to consider three basic factors that determine how much solar energy you can reasonably expect to collect and store—namely, climate, ground location and the direction a house faces. Since these factors are different for each situation, almost all present systems must be custom-designed for your home. What you must first determine is how a proposed system will compare with the heating and cooling performance of your conventional system. You may find that you still need a conventional system as a backup for the solar one.

In considering costs, besides checking out whatever tax advantages you may be eligible for, find out if you can get special-interest rates on mortgages and building loans for solar-energy systems. And be sure to get *current* local, state and federal regulations, as these tend to change fairly rapidly.

Next, and perhaps most crucially, choose the right contractor. Ask the utility company, builders, architects and solar homeowners for recommendations. Then get at least three bids—but before anyone gives you a bid, find out if there is a fee for a plan and full-cost estimate. Compare performance claims, prices, warranties and installation costs—and get thorough documentation for all claims made about a system, such as efficiency and reliability.

INVESTING IN LIFE

For reasons amplified in this and the preceding chapters, life on Earth needs all the help it can get—be it time, energy or money.

Many dedicated, effective organizations exist with whom one can easily join ecological forces, so to speak, Greenpeace being perhaps the gutsiest and most fully committed. If you would like to help the group continue its aggressive agenda of confronting polluters, "drift-net" fishers and so on, then send in the largest contribution you can. The address, along with those of other groups deserving of your support:

* **Greenpeace,** 1436 U St. NW, Washington, DC 20009.
* **Sierra Club,** 730 Polk St., San Francisco, CA 94109.
* **National Audubon Society,** 700 Broadway., New York, NY 10003.
* **World Wildlife Fund,** 1250 24th St. NW, Washington, DC 20037.
* **Worldwatch Institute,** 1776 Massachusetts Ave. NW, Washington, DC 20036.
* **Environmental Defense Fund,** 257 Park Ave. So., New York, NY 10010.

Note: For the names and addresses of other international, national and state environmental and conservation organizations, see the

Conservation Directory, published annually by the National Wildlife Federation, 1400 16th St. NW, Washington, DC 20036.

PASSING THE WORD

One company that's doing its unabashed best to raise ecology awareness is the Baltimore-based Atlantic Recycled Paper Co./N.O.P.E., which offers a variety of environmentally sensible products, including cups, envelopes, grocery bags, 100% cotton duck shower curtains, and hard-to-ignore bumper stickers, such as the above. For a free catalog, call (800) 323-2811.

WEATHER WATCH
. . . keeping abreast of the winds of change . . .

ROBERT MERZ

> *Oh, what a blamed uncertain thing*
> *This pesky weather is!*
> *It blew and snew and then it thew*
> *And now, by jing, it's friz!*
> —PHILANDER JOHNSON

> *Some are weatherwise, some are otherwise.*
> —BENJAMIN FRANKLIN

THE WIDE, WIDE WORLD OF WEATHER

Few things are as universally personal as the weather, few so intensely pervasive. Whether savoring or surviving heat or cold or storm, whether bedeviled by the itch and scratch of a sweaty summer, or sulky-gray from too much winter, we live in the realm of weather, that powerful, indifferent ruler from whom we can never quite escape. Oh

75

we may, with varying degrees of success, rise above the weather's effects by heating or cooling, or by adding moisture to or subtracting moisture from, the indoor air—but it's still out there, waiting, and few of us can manage without having to go out into it from time to time, however briefly. That the weather gets us where we live, that it takes a big part in calling our shots, we know only too well. Its. wide-ranging influence is described most vividly by *Chicago Tribune* writer William Ecenbarger:

> *It causes sniffles and suicides. It determines the outcomes of battles, horse races and love affairs. It is with us from first breath to last, predisposing our well-being, our emotions and our attitudes toward life. Each day, we must take it into account, and each day, we live by its terms.*
>
> *Weather is an American obsession, and we spend much of the time enjoying it, disliking it and avoiding it. It provides a natural topic of conversation and a source of shared experience with strangers. Weather extremes—droughts, floods, blizzards, tornadoes, hurricanes—remind us that the world is still ruled by the laws of nature.*

Yet, no matter how universal its reach and ramifications, the weather gets to us first—and most—of all in our bodies. As the saying says, "We can feel it in our bones." And just about everywhere else, one might add.

The period of low pressure and increased humidity preceding bad weather, for example, can bring aches, pains, and general physical and mental sluggishness—largely because lowered air pressure means less oxygen makes its way into your system. And less oxygen translates into less alertness. This has been borne out by research showing that we tend to think more clearly on cold, dry days. We also have better memory retention and fewer auto accidents then.

Low-pressure weather can also bring lower blood-sugar levels, while aggravating the effects of rheumatism and arthritis. (In one study of 376 arthritic patients, 72 percent reported experiencing increased levels of pain every time the barometer fell.) Other lower-pressure discomfort zones include corns, bunions, bad teeth, queasy stomachs and the sites of long-mended bone breaks. As one weather-wise bit of folklore has it:

> A coming storm your shooting corns presage,
> And aches will throb your hollow tooth with rage.

Moreover, recent scientific experiments have confirmed what French surgeon Ambroise Paré observed in the 16th century: "Gouty patients can feel and perceive changes in the weather such as rain, snow, winds and suchlike, as though they had within them built in an almanac to last their lifetime."

But being weatherwise doesn't just add insight to your own inner workings. It can also enrich your understanding of the ways weather has influenced the destiny of peoples and nations (torrid climes, for instance, discourage energetic exertion) while perhaps helping you plan your own immediate future a little better, as you become more attuned to those natural phenomena that send their little signals as to coming conditions.

HOW THE WEATHER MACHINE WORKS

The easiest way to understanding how weather gets the way it gets is, first, to think of our particular corner of the universe as a weather machine, the main cog of which is the sun. Then consider how differently the sun's rays warm different types of earthly terrain. These differences, along with the varying angles and distances involved in our rotation around the sun, produce the wide range of weather conditions we experience.

For instance, land surfaces heat up and cool down more quickly than water, making the continents hotter than the sea in summer and cooler in winter. And at the equator, the sun is either directly overhead or never far from it, and its heat is concentrated. But at the poles, the sun's rays strike obliquely, and its heat is diffuse. This imbalance in air temperatures causes the winds to blow and weather patterns to form and change, as hot air moves toward cold, and cold air is drawn to heat.

The air at the equator is heated and begins moving north; when it reaches the Arctic Circle, it is cooled and turns around for a return trip to the equator. Modifying these winds is Earth's rotation on its axis, which creates a veering off of the north-to-south course. In the Northern Hemisphere this means that most winds move from the west to the east, at least down to within 30 degrees of the equator. These fairly steady winds are known as westerlies, and they predominate over the central and northern states and across southern Canada. Any change from the prevailing west wind is apt to bring foul weather.

In the polar regions, air chilled by the ground sinks, forming a high-pressure zone from which the winds at ground level blow outward to warmer latitudes.

Seasons are caused by the 23.4° tilt of the earth's axis. The average distance of the earth from the sun is 93 million miles, with the difference between the shortest distance (perihelion) and farthest (aphelion) being about 3 million miles. When the earth passes through perihelion, the northern end of its axis is tipped away from the sun, so that the areas beyond the Tropic of Cancer receive only slanting rays from a sun that appears low in the sky.

When the sun is directly above the equator, the day is of equal length everywhere—these are the "equinoxes" that occur about March 21 and September 23. The shortest day of the year, about December 22, is the winter solstice; the longest is the summer solstice, about June 22.

YOU DON'T NEED A WEATHERMAN . . .

If kites fly high, fair weather is coming.

Have you about had it yet with all those maniacally smiling, terminally pleasant TV weatherpeople? And all their chucklesome prognostications that seem about as apt to be wrong as right? Deep down in your heart of hearts, wouldn't you just love to decorate Willard Scott's incurably happy pan with a truly humongous lemon-meringue pie?

Join the club! And while any facial pastry—however deserving—must alas remain imaginary, you *can* declare your weather independence by simply tuning out the merry meteorologists and doing your own forecasting. At the very least, when you do tune in for the weather, you can compare the Official Weather Word with the forecast you've arrived at, based on the signs around you and the messages your body has gotten.

With practice, you'll be surprised how well you can do. And why not? People have been doing it for ages: the earliest recorded weather lore dates back some six thousand years. In fact, when it comes to

78

"oldest," informed weather watching can give some other professions we could name a good run for the money.

Many giants of philosophy and literature, including Aristotle, Virgil and Shakespeare, have included weather wisdom in their works. Wrote the Bard in *Richard III*:

Small showers last long,
but sudden storms are short.

This is based on the fact that a warm front moves in slowly, usually stays a long while, and brings milder and longer rains, while a cold-front storm gives shorter warning of its approach and passes more quickly.

Of course, the main problem with "folk-casted" weather lore is separating the true from the fanciful. A good way to begin the winnowing is to disregard virtually all predictions linked to religious observances or spiritual beliefs. We can still appreciate them for their poetry and/or historical significance, but we should not take them too seriously as science.

You might also shake a few salty grains on any folk-casts that are either very detailed or very long-range. After that, it's mostly a matter of increasing your weather wisdom so that you can decide for yourself how much fact stands behind a particular bit of folklore.

For example, take the case of early farmers who expected rain if they saw their dogs eat grass, or if their roosters crowed in the evening, as reflected in this rhyme:

If the cock crows going to bed,
He will certainly rise with a watery head.

Such signs rang true because experience generally bore them out. For Farmer Jones, observed cause and effect was sufficient unto itself, and he usually understood, or at least sensed, that his observations were rooted in the hard facts of physics. For instance, a steep drop in atmospheric pressure, signaling bad weather, can sicken animals by causing gas bubbles to form in their body fluids—thus driving Fido to munch the lawn so as to vomit and thereby end his nausea. At the same time, the lowered pressure causes the rooster to voice his discomfort by crowing at the moon rather than the sun.

Or consider this famous weather-lorical gem:

Red sky at night,
sailor's delight;
red sky in the morning,
sailor take warning.

This observation has been traced at least as far back as the Bible (Matthew 16:2,3), though Jesus expressed it a bit differently:

79

> *When it is evening, ye say, It will be fair weather:*
> *for the sky is red. And in the morning, It will be foul*
> *weather today: for the sky is red and lowering.*

Either way, this folk wisdom is based on the fact that when the sun is low in the sky, its light travels a longer distance through the atmosphere, so that most of its shorter blue rays are scattered by air and dust particles and we see only the red rays. In a relatively cloudless sky, a red sunset is usually a sign of a high-pressure system to the west, which could bring several days of fair, calm weather. A red sunrise, however, generally indicates a dry mass to the east, which, as it departs, will likely be replaced by a less favorable weather system.

Closer to home, perhaps, are these everyday weather clues:

> *When windows won't open*
> *and salt clogs the shaker,*
> *the weather will favor the umbrella-maker.*
> • • •
> *When the ditch and pond affect the nose,*
> *Then look out for rain and storm blows.*

No mysteries here, as we know that air moisture expands substances like wood and salt, and that one's sense of smell is improved by a bad-weather low-pressure center, odors that had been repressed by the departing high-pressure center.

Hair, too, can signal a storm by its tendency to curl as it absorbs moisture and shortens—as Lieutenant A. P. Herbert, R.N.V., wryly observed:

> *But I know ladies by the score*
> *Whose hair, like seaweed, scents the storm;*
> *Long, long before it starts to pour*
> *Their locks assume a baneful form.*
>
> *Think of the powers of that young girl,*
> *And how much destiny must hinge*
> *On whether she can get a curl*
> *To come in her confounded fringe!*

Keeping a Weather Eye

As Yogi Berra, in another context, once said: "You can see a lot just by observing." In that spirit, we offer the following visual weather signs:

A ring around the moon means there will soon be a storm. The number of stars inside the ring was believed by many to be an indication of the number of days remaining before the storm.

• • •

If the first crescent moon in the western sky is tilted up, "so that it cannot hold water," the month will be dry.

• • •

Foul weather is said to follow the new moon and the full moon, while fair weather is said to follow the first-quarter and last-quarter moons.

• • •

With a crescent moon, when the tips—or "horns of the moon"—appear sharp, high winds are virtually certain; when dull, rain may be expected, since the dullness is a result of a humid atmosphere. As Virgil, in his *Georgics*, wrote of "Luna":

> *If with blunt horns she holds the dusky air,*
> *Seamen and swains predict abundant showers.*

• • •

"Sweating" stones or bricks are signs of rain to come, as moisture exudes from them when the humidity reaches the saturation point. The phenomenon, known as "earth sweat," also affects metal, causing rust in a short time.

Weather-watch tip: gusting winds with downdrafts, signaling rain, will cause chimney smoke to fall toward the ground.

The Heavenly Graffiti of Clouds

Clouds can tell you much about the weather to come, as they write themselves across the sky. The way they shape up, their color, their height—all these factors can be eloquent weather clues:

> *When you see a mackerel sky,*
> *Twill not be many hours dry.*
>
> —
>
> *Mackerel scales,*
> *Furl your sails.*

A so-called mackerel sky is a system of high cirrocumulus and/or altocumulus clouds resembling fish scales. These clouds are signals of an approaching warm front, which will move over cooler ground air, form thicker clouds, and produce rain, usually within a day.

• • •

The highest clouds, at 20,000 feet and above, are cirrus, which have been described variously as looking like angels' wings, mares' tails and hen scratches. They're made of ice crystals rather than the usual liquid moisture of most clouds, and they travel at great speeds. They are the first signs of the approach of a larger, slow-moving warm front and an indication of the increase in wind and possible precipitation as the front arrives several hours, or as much as a day, later. As these proverbs put it:

> *Mares' tails, mares' tails,*
> *make lofty ships carry low sails.*
> *Clouds look as if scratched by a hen,*
> *Be ready to reef your top sails in.*

• • •

A cumulus cloud is described as "a massy cloud form having a flat base and rounded outlines often piled up like a mountain." As it becomes larger and taller, there is more moisture and more vertical upthrusting. Therefore:

> *When clouds appear like rocks and towers,*
> *The Earth's refreshed with frequent showers.*

Playing It by Ear

While weather-watching, don't forget to do some weather listening as well. For you can often "hear" foul weather approaching before it arrives because the dampness in the air affects sounds in such a way that they carry farther and are heard more clearly. As this proverb advises:

> *Sound traveling far and wide,*
> *A day of rain will soon betide.*

• • •

82

Wood beams and furniture tend to creak before heavy rains.

• • •

Chirping crickets can act as living thermometers, inasmuch as they chirp faster as the temperature rises. On warm days, adding 37 to the number of chirps in a 15-second span will just about equal the Fahrenheit temperature.

• • •

Frogs croak more before a storm because they can't tolerate much evaporation of their skin's moisture. So on low-humidity days they spend most of their time in water. When conditions bespeak of a storm, however, they are more apt to emerge—croaking.

CELSIUS OR FAHRENHEIT?

25 DEGREES FAHRENHEIT   25 DEGREES CELSIUS

For most Americans, the Celsius or centigrade temperature scale is an idea whose time may have come but whose appeal is still a long way off. Yet, since most of the world uses it, it's something we really should start learning to live with. Developed in 1742 by Anders Celsius, the scale's 0° reading represents the freezing point of water, while 100° represents the boiling point, the interval between them being divided into 100 degrees.

To convert Fahrenheit (named for Gabriel Daniel Fahrenheit) to Celsius, first subtract 32, multiply the answer by 5, then divide *that* answer by 9. For instance, 66 degrees Fahrenheit minus 32 is 34, which multiplied by 5 is 170, which divided by 9 is 18.8. Or, on the lower end of the scale, say it's 17 degrees Fahrenheit. To get the Celsius equivalent, you figure thusly: 17 -32 = -15 X 5 = -75 ÷ 9 = -8.3.

To convert Celsius to Fahrenheit, multiply by 9, divide by 5, and add 32. It helps to keep in mind that a Fahrenheit degree is smaller than a Celsius degree, one Fahrenheit degree being five-ninths of a Celsius degree. (Oddly enough, there's one temperature that's the same in both systems: -40°.)

Here's a handy table offering Fahrenheit/Celsius conversions ranging from the freezing point of water (32° F, 0° C) to its boiling point (212° F, 100° C). For higher or lower temps, *go figure!*

°F	°C	°F	°C	°F	°C	°F	°C	°F	°C	°F	°C	°F	°C	°F	°C	°F	°C	°F	°C
32	0	53	11·7	72	22·2	89·6	32	103	39·4	122	50	140	60	160	71·1	180	82·2	197	91·7
33·8	1	54	12·2	73	22·8	90	32·2	104	40	123	50·6	141	60·6	161	71·7	181	82·8	198	92·2
35·6	2	55	12·8	73·4	23	91	32·8	105	40·6	124	51·1	142	61·1	161·6	72	182	83·3	199	92·8
36·5	2·5	56	13·3	74	23·3	91·4	33	105·8	41	125	51·7	143	61·7	162	72·2	183	83·9	199·4	93
37·4	3	57	13·9	75	23·9	92	33·3	106	41·1	125·6	52	144	62·2	163	72·8	183·2	84	200	93·3
38	3·3	57·2	14	75·2	24	93	33·9	107	41·7	126	52·2	145	62·8	164	73·3	184	84·4	201	93·9
39	3·9	58	14·4	77	25	94	34·4	107·6	42	127	52·8	146	63·3	165	73·9	185	85	202	94·4
39·2	4	59	15	78	25·6	95	35	108	42·2	128	53·3	147	63·9	166	74·4	186	85·6	203	95
40	4·4	60	15·6	79	26·1	96	35·6	109	42·8	129	53·9	148	64·4	167	75	186·8	86	204	95·6
41	5	61	16·1	80	26·7	96·8	36	110	43·3	130	54·4	149	65	168	75·6	187	86·1	204·8	96
42	5·6	62	16·7	80·6	27	97	36·1	112	43·9	131	55	150	65·6	168·8	76	188	86·7	205	96·1
43	6·1	63	17·2	81	27·2	97·3	36·3	112	44·4	132	55·6	151	66·1	169	76·1	188·6	87	206	96·7
44	6·7	64	17·8	82	27·8	98	36·7	113	45	133	56·1	152	66·7	170	76·7	189	87·2	207	97·2
45	7·2	65	18·3	82·4	28	98·6	37	114	45·6	134	56·7	152·6	67	171	77·2	190	87·8	208	97·8
46	7·8	66	18·9	83	28·3	99	37·2	115	46·1	134·6	57	153	67·2	172	77·8	190·4	88	208·4	98
46·4	8	66·2	19	84	28·9	99·5	37·5	116	46·7	135	57·2	154	67·8	173	78·3	191	88·3	209	98·3
47	8·3	67	19·4	84	28·9	100	37·8	117	47·2	136	57·8	155	68·3	174	78·9	192	88·9	210	98·9
48	8·9	68	20	85	29·4	100·4	38	118	47·8	136·4	58	156	68·9	175	79·4	193	89·4	210·2	99
48·2	9	69	20·6	86	30	101	38·3	118·4	48	137	58·3	156·2	69	176	80	194	90	211	99·4
50	10	69·8	21	87	30·6	101·8	38·8	119	48·3	138	58·9	157	69·4	177	80·6	195	90·6	212	100
51	10·6	70	21·1	88	31·1	102	38·9	120	48·9	138·2	59	158	70	178	81·1	195·8	91		
52	11·1	71	21·7	89	31·7	102·2	39	121	49·4	139	59·4	159	70·6	179	81·7	196	91·1		

THE HEAT INDEX

Also called the "temperature-humidity index" or "THI," the heat index below is a measure of the contribution high humidity makes with high temperatures in reducing the body's ability to cool itself by sweating. At 75° F, many are uncomfortable; at 80° or higher, just about everyone is. When the index reaches 105°, sunstroke and heat exhaustion are likely:

	Air temperature*										
	70	75	80	85	90	95	100	105	110	115	120
Relative Humidity	Apparent Temperature*										
0%	64	69	73	78	83	87	91	95	99	103	107
10%	65	70	75	80	85	90	95	100	105	111	116
20%	66	72	77	82	87	93	99	105	112	120	130
30%	67	73	78	84	90	96	104	113	123	135	148
40%	68	74	79	86	93	101	110	123	137	151	
50%	69	75	81	88	96	107	120	135	150		
60%	70	76	82	90	100	114	132	149			
70%	70	77	85	93	106	124	144				
80%	71	78	86	97	113	136					
90%	71	79	88	102	122						
100%	72	80	91	108							

*Degrees Fahrenheit

THE WIND-CHILL FACTOR

Body surfaces can lose heat not only as a result of low temperatures, but as a result of wind. A very strong wind combined with a temperature slightly below freezing can have the same chilling effect as a temperature nearly 50° F lower in a calm atmosphere. The wind-chill factor, or "wind-chill index," shows the combined effects of wind and temperature as equivalent calm-air temperatures. In effect, the index describes the cooling power of the air on exposed flesh.

To use the chart below, first find the actual (calm) temperature across the top, then determine wind speed and follow across to correct calm-air temperature. The number given is the equivalent temperature. (For example, a 10° F temperature with a 20-mph wind is the equivalent of -24°.) **Note:** A good rule-of-thumb for gauging the wind-chill is to subtract *one degree from the temperature for every one mph of wind speed.*

	Temperatures in Degrees Fahrenheit																
Calm	35	30	25	20	15	10	5	0	—5	—10	—15	—20	—25	—30	—35	—40	—45
5	33	27	21	17	12	7	1	—6	—11	—15	—21	—26	—31	—35	—41	—47	—53
10	21	16	9	3	—2	—9	—15	—22	—27	—32	—38	—45	—52	—58	—64	—70	—77
15	16	11	5	—6	—11	—18	—25	—32	—40	—45	—51	—60	—65	—70	—78	—85	—91
20	12	3	—4	—9	—17	—24	—32	—40	—46	—52	—60	—68	—75	—81	—88	—96	—103
25	8	0	—7	—15	—22	—29	—37	—45	—52	—58	—67	—75	—83	—89	—96	—104	—112
30	5	—2	—11	—18	—26	—33	—41	—49	—56	—63	—70	—78	—87	—94	—101	—109	—117
35	4	—4	—13	—20	—27	—35	—43	—52	—60	—67	—72	—83	—89	—98	—105	—113	—123
40	2	—4	—15	—22	—29	—36	—45	—54	—61	—69	—76	—85	—92	—101	—107	—115	—125
45	1	—6	—16	—22	—31	—38	—46	—55	—62	—70	—78	—87	—94	—102	—108	—118	—127
50	0	—7	—17	—24	—31	—38	—47	—56	—63	—71	—79	—88	—96	—103	—110	—120	—128

Wind speed (Miles per hour)

OUR KIND OF WINDY

Chicago's the Windy City, right?

Not really—at least not in the sense most people think. It gets windy, all right, and in the winter "The Hawk" can surely squawk—but when it comes to being the true, certified *windiest*, Chicago's not even in the top 20. The *real* windy city is Cheyenne, Wyoming, followed (in descending order of windiness) by: Great Falls, Montana; Boston, Massachusetts; Oklahoma City, Oklahoma; and Wichita, Kansas.

As for Chi-town, its "Windy" nickname actually has nothing to do with weather. It was bestowed by *New York Sun* newspaper editor Charles A. Dana, who characterized Chicago as an undeserving upstart for presuming to vie with New York and other cities for the honor of hosting the World's Columbian Exposition of 1893. Dana advised his readers to ignore "the nonsensical claims of this windy city. Its people could not hold a world's fair even if they won it."

Windy or not, Chicago managed to convince Congress that it was, in fact, *the* place for the fair—and held it successfully.

FEELING THE PRESSURE

Any understanding of the weather and its ways must include at rough idea of what air pressure is and what it does. It may seem a bit abstract at first, but it's basically not all that complicated. A good way to think of it is to picture the air as an ocean of water, with you on the bottom and the weight of a tall column or layer of air/water pressing down on you. That's air pressure. Writer Albert Lee, who draws the "ocean" parallel in his book *Weather Wisdom*, goes on to explain the kinds of things that can happen in this imaginary sea:

> The surface of the ocean is not stagnant. There are waves, constant peaks and valleys, that move across the surface above you. As a large wave goes over you, there is actually a mound of water overhead, and therefore more weight or pressure on you. This mound, or wave, because it creates more pressure, is called a high-pressure area, or just plain high. When the valley between the mounds of waves passes over you, there is less weight or pressure, and therefore we have a low-pressure area, or low. Lows are huge, normally covering hundreds of miles. Highs are much smaller.
>
> These high- and low-pressure centers create their own wind and have their own weather associated with them. Air rushes from an area of high pressure to an area of low pressure in nature's attempt to even out pressure. From a high, or mound, of pressure, the air flows away from the center, creating a wind in a clockwise direction. In a low, or depression, air flows inward, toward the bottom or center. This creates a wind that runs counterclockwise. Generally speaking, highs normally bring pleasant weather. Lows bring storms and unsettled conditions.

A number of folk sayings have been devised over the years to help us remember the significance of a barometer reading, including:

> When the glass falls low,
> Prepare for a blow:
> When it rises high
> Let all your kites fly.

A steady barometer, of course, indicates that present conditions will continue.

If you're a true weather buff, you may wish to consider getting a barometer of your own. If so, you should be prepared to take regular series of readings to determine the speed and direction of the changes in the atmosphere. Remember, too, to adjust the barometer to show equivalent sea-level pressure for the altitude at which it is to be used. For instance, a change of 100 feet in elevation will cause a decrease of 0.1 inch in the reading.

WIND/BAROMETER TABLE

WIND DIRECTION	BAROMETER ACTIVITY	WEATHER RESULTING
east to north	low and falling fast	gales with heavy rains or snowstorms
south to southeast	low and falling fast	severe storm
south to southwest	low and rising	fair weather to follow soon
southwest to northwest	high and steady	continued fair weather
southwest to northwest	falling slowly from high	rain in a day or two
southwest to northwest	extremely high and falling	temperature rising for 24 hours
west	low and rising	clearing and cooler
south to southeast	high and falling fast	high winds and rain within hours
south to southeast	high and falling slow	rain within a day
southeast to northeast	high and falling fast	high winds and rain
southeast to east	high and falling slow	rain within one day
east to northeast	high and falling fast	storms with high winds
east to northeast	high and falling slow	rain in one day
southeast to northeast	low and falling fast	storms and high winds
southeast to northeast	low and falling slow	continuing rains

CHART BY ALBERT LEE

GOVERNMENT WEATHER-WATCHING

The story of the three major governmental organizations established to map and forecast the weather begins with a flurry of highs, lows and occasional thunderstorms.

Although a national weather department of some sort would not be set up until the mid-1880s, interest in the subject dates back to the earliest days of America. People were still very close to the earth, and weather-watching was a popular pastime. Presidents Washington, Jefferson and Madison were among those who even used their own instruments to do so. At the time, predictions were still mostly a matter of folklore, the rhymed and unrhymed weather wisdom of the ages—often surprisingly accurate, but far from often enough: the margin of error was very, very wide. Jefferson, whose range of skills and interests was truly phenomenal, expressed his unhappiness with the state of meteorology, 1822-style: "Of all the departments of Science, no one seems to have been less advanced in the last hundred years."

The problem, of course, was that the "tech" was not yet high enough. Due to its global nature, the mapping and forecasting of weather entails multiple readings at points often greatly distant from one another. The advent of the telegraph in 1844 provided the first real breakthrough in making meteorology more of a science, as such, than the quasi-scientific art it had been. In 1870, President Grant established the first national weather service to keep records and warn of storms, giving the job to the Army Signal Service.

Some historians date the birth of the U.S. Weather Bureau from this time, while others consider the true birth to have occurred 20 years later, in 1890, when all meteorological functions of the Signal Service were transferred to the Department of Agriculture, pointing up the farmers' need for accurate weather data.

These early years of the U.S. Weather Bureau were not spectacularly successful and were tainted at times by scandal. Perhaps the bureau's most famous failing was the missed forecast for the inauguration, on March 4, 1909, of President Taft, when the immaculately attired ranks of dignitaries were unceremoniously dumped on by an unforeseen, and very severe, storm. The ceremonies were moved indoors and the area was left under 9.8 inches of snow.

But the outlook for the bureau would soon brighten, thanks to the coming of aviation, which gave new stature and import to the role of the weather forecaster. Funding was expanded to nearly $2 million in 1923 and $4.5 million in 1932—mammoth amounts for those times. Bureau forecasters, however, were still relying primarily on traditional methods that were rapidly becoming outmoded. In Europe, meteorology was being revolutionized by polar-front theory and air-mass analysis, with the weather map emerging as a kind of airy battlefield where are met—often with much noisome ado—airstreams and air masses of differing temperatures and humidities.

It would take a few more years, but eventually the bureau began to see which way the new weather winds were blowing. In the mid-30s, two young meteorologists from MIT were given a desk behind a screen in the bureau's forecasting room and permitted to do their thing with warm fronts, cold fronts and mathematical probabilities. The stage was thus set for the bureau to finally commit to the new methodology. But, as David Ludlum recently noted (in the *Old Farmer's Almanac*) it took World War II to move the Weather Bureau into the modern age of forecasting. And the computerized bureau of the 1990s (now known as the National Weather Service) bears scant resemblance indeed to its antiquated precursor. As Ludlum depicts it, it has been a most remarkable transformation:

> *By the end of the war 19,000 men and women were engaged in the weather work to aid the armed forces. In the 1950s the Weather Bureau began to play a major international role in weather observation and forecasting. Cooperative ventures such as the International Geophysical Year (1957), the World Weather Watch (1968) and the Global Atmospheric Research Program in the 1980s gathered tremendous amounts of information about our weather.*
>
> *Today [1990], in its 100th year, the National Weather Service employs about 4,500 people working in 300 offices throughout the 50 states. The operating budget is more than $330 million. Some 10,000 volunteer observers maintain daily temperature and precipitation records for their locations. Radar and satellite photographs have enabled us to see beyond the horizon, and computers enable us to introduce current weather conditions into a prescribed mathematical model in order to project the weather as much as two weeks in advance with a fair degree of accuracy.*

In 1992 the National Weather Service pulled onto the communications superhighway in a big way, moving into new headquarters in Silver Springs, Maryland, as part of a modernization that includes new radar and computer equipment, the consolidation of local offices, and improvements in satellites and warning systems. Despite the nearly two years it took to make the move, and the complicated systems involved, the flow of 200,000 messages a day in and out of the center was never interrupted.

The new center connects nearly 300 Weather Service offices across the country and serves as a link in the World Meteorological Organization's communications network, a circuit that links the U.S., England, France, Germany, Czechoslovakia, Russia, India and Japan.

FORECAST FOR FORECASTS

CBS weatherman and American Meteorological Society executive Todd Glickman recently ventured out on a well-weathered limb to predict that seven-day predictions about the weather will be possible within the next decade. National Weather Service records currently show forecasts to be accurate 91 percent of the time when predicting precipitation for a given 12- to 24-hour period. The temperature forecasts for a like period are accurate within 2.8° F.

IS ACCU-WEATHER ANY MORE "ACCU"?

If you're unhappy with the National Weather Service's batting average, you may do better elsewhere—for instance, at Accu-Weather of State College, Pennsylvania, most notable of the hundred or so private firms that forecast for a fee. (Clients include ski resorts, newspapers, TV stations, trucking firms and others with a vested interest in how the weather winds blow.) As for comparative accuracy, recent figures from New York City show an average error rate for the National Weather Service for one month was 4.1 percent; Accu-Weather's was 2.0.

STORMY REACTION

America's first meteorological martyr may well have been Tarley McFetters of Mobile, Alabama, who in 1911 was lynched by members of the Pascagoula Sorghum & Sporting Society for predicting fair weather for the society's annual Fourth of July crawfish festival. In fact, it snowed, hailed and there was an unscheduled eclipse of the sun.

SOME WEATHER EXTREMES

Surprise, surprise! Antarctica holds the record for the lowest temperature ever recorded: -128.6° F at the USSR's (CIS's) Vostok Station, on July 21, 1983.

• The coldest permanently inhabited place: Oymyakon, Siberia, where the temperature in 1964 reached -96° F.

• The all-time highest temperature on record is 136° F, at El Azizia, Libya, September 13, 1922.

• The greatest recorded depth of snow on the ground: 25 feet 6 inches, at Paradise, Mount Rainier, Washington, on April 17, 1972.

• The greatest rainfall in the U.S. over a one-year period is 739 inches at Kukui, Maui, Hawaii, December 1981-December 1982.

• The record for greatest snowfall in the U.S. over a 24-hour period is 76 inches at Silver Lake, Colorado, April 14-15, 1921.

• On April 18, 1858, rain began falling in the Chicago area and kept falling for 60 days. (In case you've ever wondered, the average wind speed in the Windy City is 10.4 mph.)

AN INCH OF RAIN

Ever wonder just how much water constitutes an inch of rain?

Well, this measurement, used by the National Weather Service, is based on one acre of land. Rainwater one inch deep, covering one acre of land, comes to 37,143 gallons of water—which weighs 113 tons.

So let's not take those one-inch rainfall predictions lightly!

THREE HANDY-DANDY WEATHER TIPS

- To determine what the high temperature of the day will be, a good rule of thumb is to add 18 degrees Fahrenheit to the temperature at 6 A.M.
- You need to have three consecutive days of temperatures no higher than 20° F before a pond will be safe for skating.
- Ten inches of snow reduces to one inch of water.

THE DOG DAYS

The very warmest days of summer, generally from about the Fourth of July to mid-August in temperate latitudes in the Northern Hemisphere, were called the "dog" days by the Romans, who associated weather patterns with the various stars. At that time the brightest star in the sky was Sirius, the Dog Star, and thus a (not very scientific) connection was made. Truth is, only one star—the sun—has influence upon earthly weather.

INDIAN SUMMER

Ah yes, sweet indeed is the warm surprise of Indian summer—and what more may we say of it?

It is a pleasant autumnal interlude of a certain length that takes place during a certain month or months. And that's about all you can say without courting controversy.

For most people, Indian summer means any spell of warm or

mild weather in September, October or November. *Merriam-Webster's Collegiate Dictionary* gives the time frame as "late autumn or early winter." To climatologists, it's simply a warm spell following the first frost. To the *Old Farmer's Almanac*, it is warm, windless and hazy (or smoky) weather marked by clear and chilly nights and it happens only between St. Martin's Day (November 11) and November 20.

As far as the elemental mechanics are involved, Indian summer is the result of a conversion of a moving, cool, shallow polar air mass into a deep, warm and stagnant high-pressure system that concentrates natural dust and smoke in the air near the ground and causes a large swing in temperature between day and night. It is the time of year when the temperatures of the Northern Hemisphere's land masses and oceans are nearly equal. This temperature balance between land and sea causes meteorological stability, and storms are infrequent in most regions.

Several theories have evolved concerning the origin of the term "Indian summer." The most probable, according to the *Old Farmer's Almanac*, dates back to the early settlers in New England, who welcomed each new autumn because it meant that the Indians would be slacking off their attacks with the onset of winter:

> But then came a time, almost every year . . . when it would suddenly turn warm again, and the Indians would decide to have one more go at the settlers even though it was no longer their normal raiding season. "Indian summer," the settlers called it.

LIGHTNING FLASHES

Lightning is caused by a chain of events that begins with a "charge separation" inside a thundercloud, apparently the result of updrafts in the cloud that separate the upper positive and lower negative charges.

As the types of charge separate, negative-charge accumulation may send out a "step leader" toward the ground. This faintly luminous channel is filled with free electrons and descends in jerky 150-foot "steps."

Although Earth is generally negatively charged, under a storm cell electrostatic repulsion between the planet and the negatively charged belly of the cloud induces a positive charge on the ground that tries to rise up and connect with the descending step leader. Upward-going charges leave all the sharp points on the ground, one of the charges meets a negatively charged descending leader to produce a "return stroke." It is this return stroke—the ground-to-cloud discharge—that produces the lightning bolt that is actually seen, but it all happens so fast that the brain cannot distinguish which direction the current is going.

Some lightning facts and figures:

• Lightning is one of the most deadly forms of severe weather, surpassing blizzards and tornadoes. Since 1969, only flash floods have claimed more lives in the U.S. According to the National Weather Service, in a recent year, lightning killed 68 and injured 283 Americans and caused nearly $40 million in property damage.

• When lightning strikes a person, the electrical current is traveling at 300 miles per second and may fire off a series of up to 40 different current peaks, each packing an electrical wallop of up to 50 million volts.

• A clap of thunder results when a lightning bolt heats the air, causing it to expand rapidly. The rush of expanding air creates shock waves, which change into sound waves. To figure out about how far away a storm is, count off the seconds from the time you see the flash of lightning to the time you hear the thunder, and divide by 5. (This estimation is based on the speed of sound, which is approximately 1,100 feet per second.) Thus, an interval of five seconds between lightning and thunder means the storm is just one mile away.

• Heat lightning—those diffuse flashes of light that dance on the horizon on warm summer nights—is merely a regular lightning storm occurring too far away for the accompanying thunder to be heard.

• The typical lightning bolt lasts less than half a second and has enough energy to light a 100-watt light bulb for more than three months.

• The diameter of a lightning bolt is about 6 inches.

• To learn more about the causes and inner workings of lightning, scientists launch small rockets, trailing wires, into thunderclouds to precipitate lightning strikes. The surge of electricity down a wire to the ground is recorded in photographs and measured by remote sensors and other instruments. The results are used to better predict when and where lightning will strike and to test protection systems.

• Contrary to popular belief, lightning can and sometimes does strike the same place twice—though admittedly not very often.

HUMAN HAILSTONES

In the *Reader's Digest Book of Facts* (1985) is told the tale of five glider pilots caught in the grip of a thermal updraft. These very unheavenly menaces take lethal shape in large clouds where they reach a speed of 60 mph and can be real killers.

In 1930 five glider pilots bailed out into a thundercloud over mountainous terrain in Germany—but only one survived. The others, held aloft by thermals, became entombed in giant icelike hailstones before the cloud finally released them.

WINDS THAT KILL

Stormy weather, most agree, generally sucks—figuratively for sure, and sometimes literally as well, as in the case of hurricanes and tornadoes.

But not all rains or winds or blackening clouds need be objects of dread. Spring and summer showers can often refresh, and even a sudden noisy thunderstorm can usually be endured with nary more than a grouse or a curse—or two or three.

Then there are the killers—hurricanes, tornadoes, typhoons, monsoons and cyclones. They come in various shapes and sizes and can pack winds up to 300 mph. At their worst, they kill by the thousands and cause damage in the millions of dollars.

If you live in North America, the only two kinds of lethal winds to watch—and prepare—for are hurricanes and tornadoes.

A hurricane, which forms over warm oceans, is a huge swirl of clouds rotating about a calm center (the eye). Warm air is sucked down into the eye, and warm, moist air swirls upward around the eye. Condensation creates so-called wall clouds and releases heat, increasing the upward spiral of air. Hurricanes can be up to 300 miles in diameter and strike in the North Atlantic from June to November.

The deadliest U.S. hurricane on record hit the island city of Galveston, Texas, on September 8, 1900. Hurricane-wracked gulf waters sent million-ton waves—including a massive tidal wave— shoreward, crumpling buildings like cardboard, tossing ocean steamers out of their docks and into city streets, and uprooting gravestones and coffins. When it was all over, some 6,000 people were dead and an estimated $30 million in damage had been done.

Unlike hurricanes, those violently spinning funnels of air we call tornadoes form over land, and have their own special brand of chemistry and mechanics.

Tornadoes, generally 100 to 150 feet in diameter, descend from thunderstorm cloud systems. If a funnel touches ground, it can cause considerable wind damage—both because of its killer winds and because those winds suck air from the funnel's core, drastically lowering the air pressure inside. The most frequent and destructive tornadoes occur in the prairies of North America, where abound all the necessary ingredients: broad, unobstructed plains, together with a strong jet stream above and massive doses of cold air from the north merging with moist warm air from the south.

Since 1970, the National Weather Service's tornado count has varied from 650 to 1,100 annually, ranging from single, isolated twisters to vast, multistate outbreaks. The worst outbreak in history occurred on April 3-4, 1974, when 148 tornadoes touched down within 16 hours, in an area stretching from northern Alabama to

Ontario, Canada. The twisters killed 315 people, injured 5,484 and caused millions of dollars' worth of property damage.

The worst tornado months, in order, are June, April and May.

Note: The first person to name hurricanes was 19th-century Australian weatherman Clement L. Wragge. He favored biblical names such as Sacar, Talmon and Uphaz. For many years, reflecting perhaps a gender-based bias, hurricanes were given women's names (beginning with "Louise," during World War II). However, since 1978, the World Meteorological Organization has been giving hurricanes men's names as well as women's.

SURVIVING A HURRICANE

Before the season begins:

• Each June, check supplies of boards, tools, batteries, nonperishable foods, and equipment you'll need when a storm strikes.

• Monitor radio and TV after first learning of tropical storm advisory.

• During a hurricane watch, continue normal activities, but stay tuned to National Weather Service broadcasts. A watch means possible danger within 24 hours.

Upon receiving a hurricane warning:

• Secure boat before storm arrives. Do not return to boat once wind and waves are up.

• Store drinking water.

• Check battery-powered equipment.

• Fill your car's gas tank.

• Board up windows and secure outdoor objects.

• Leave low-lying areas.

• Leave mobile homes for sturdier shelter.

• If your home is sturdy and at a safe elevation, stay there. If not, go to nearest shelter.

During the storm:

• Stay indoors. Travel is extremely dangerous when winds and tides are raging.

• Tornadoes often are spawned by hurricanes. Listen to radio and TV for storm warnings.

• Beware the eye of the storm. If the calm passes directly overhead, the lull may last only 30 minutes. However, at the other side of the eye, the storm still rages and fierce winds will strike from the opposite direction.

After the storm:

• Seek necessary medical care at disaster stations or hospitals.

• Stay out of disaster areas unless you have been qualified to help.

• Drive carefully along debris-filled streets.

- Avoid loose or dangling wires. Report them immediately to power companies or police.
- Report broken sewers or water mains.
- Prevent fires. Lowered water pressure makes fire fighting difficult.
- If power has been off, check refrigerated food for spoilage.
- Because hurricanes often cause severe flooding as they move inland, stay away from banks of rivers and streams.

TORNADO SAFETY TIPS

- Plan ahead: Family members should do advance planning and rehearse where they will go to seek safety during a tornado.
- Office buildings and factories: Stand in an interior hallway on a lower floor, preferably in the basement.
- School: Children outdoors or in portable or temporary classrooms should be taken to sturdier buildings. They should be escorted to basements or hallways without windows. Children should face interior walls and cover their heads.
- Urban areas: Seek shelter in basement or steel-framed or reinforced concrete building.
- Rural areas: Move away from tornado's path at right angles. If it is too close to escape, lie flat in a ditch or ravine and cover your head.
- While driving: Leave your vehicle and seek immediate sturdy shelter.

ROBERT MERZ

WHITHER THE WEATHER?

Much has been said about the future of the weather, especially about whether tomorrow's climate will suffer from the so-called greenhouse effect, wherein gases in the atmosphere such as carbon dioxide, methane and nitrogen oxides trap heat at the Earth's surface. If unchecked, the resultant global warming can bring an increase in droughts and famines, as well as higher ocean levels—up to a little more than two feet worldwide by 2050, according to a United Nations panel on climate change.

Other concerns about the way future climate is shaping up include the destruction of the planet's protective ozone shield and damage from acid rain—the former caused by the emission of chlorine gases (from aerosol can propellants and other products) and the latter by high concentrations of acid-forming chemicals released into the atmosphere by coal smoke, chemical manufacturing and smelting.

Adding urgency to the subject of future world climate have been studies such as those recently made by separate groups of climatologists in the United States and Britain, who reported that 1990 was the warmest year since people began measuring surface temperatures. A third group, in the U.S., reported record high temperatures from one to six miles above Earth; these were recorded by weather balloons from December 1989 through November 1990.

Some scientists said the new readings, taken together with the string of very warm years in the 1980s, strengthened the possibility that the feared greenhouse effect had already begun.

According to the climatologists, the seven warmest years in the past century have all occurred since 1980—but not all these experts are ready to blame the greenhouse effect. David Parker, of Britain's Meteorological Office, said that while a warming of this amount is consistent with the effect, "the Earth's temperature fluctuates considerably due to natural causes and no unambiguous connection can yet be made." He said it would take 20 years of temperature rises before the greenhouse effect could be detected with certainty.

Taking the least conventional position of all regarding this question have been climatologists Michael Ghil and Robert Vautard, who in a recent issue of *Nature* said that global temperatures have peaked temporarily and are headed down. Ghil said that after 1995 temperatures will "go back up to a maximum maybe in 1999, then down again until about 2002."

Meanwhile, climatologist James Hansen, head of the Goddard Institute for Space Studies, has predicted that the 1990s will be the warmest decade on record. Of the work of Ghil and Vautard, he said, "By using a mathematical approach, they are reaching a conclusion that's directly opposite to what we find [using atmosphere physics to predict climate trends]. We'll see what happens."

SOME USEFUL/USELESS INFORMATION
... depending on whether or not you need it ...

Comment is free but facts are sacred.
—C. P. SCOTT

Do not become a mere recorder of facts, but try to penetrate the
mysteries of their origin. Seek obstinately for the laws
that govern them.
—IVAN PAVLOV

SO WHO NEEDS IT?

Info, input, data, the lowdown, the skinny, the scoop, the poop—
whatever you deign to call it, whether it is useful or useless all
depends on whether or not you need it in such-and-such particular
place and at such-and-such particular time.

But remember: There's a quasi-Einsteinian warp constantly working with and against *all* facts and figures, and what may be vital right
now, *this very instant,* may by tomorrow be just more *stuff* to file, forget or recycle—and vice versa.

So the answer to who needs it is: *Maybe you.* You're the one who decides the usefulness of any of this or that. You're the human computer that knows what its operating system and files need. As for the rest, skim and pass on—but don't forget where it is. You just may need it come tomorrow, or next year, or—you never know—any moment now . . .

MEASURING UP: THEN AND NOW

Weights and measures are among the earliest known tools. Primitive societies needed rudimentary measures for many tasks: constructing dwellings of an appropriate size and shape, fashioning clothing or bartering food or raw materials.

Humans understandably turned first to parts of the body and natural surroundings for measuring instruments. Early Babylonian and Egyptian records and the Bible indicate that length was first measured with the forearm, hand or finger, and that time was measured by the periods of the sun, moon and other heavenly bodies. To compare the capacities of containers like gourds, clay pots and metal vessels, the containers were filled with plant seeds, which were then counted to measure the volumes. When means for weighing were invented, seeds and stones served as standards. For instance, the "carat," still used as a unit for gems, was derived from the carob seed.

As societies evolved, weights and measures became more complex. The invention of numbering systems and the science of mathematics made it possible to create whole systems of weights and measures suited to trade and commerce, land division, taxation and scientific research. For these more sophisticated uses it was necessary not only to weigh and measure more complex things, but to do it accurately time after time and in different places. However, with limited international exchange of goods and communication of ideas, it is not surprising that different systems for the same purpose developed and became established in different parts of the world, even in different parts of a single continent.

The English System

The measurement system commonly used in the U.S. today is nearly the same as that brought by the colonists from England. These measures had their origins in a variety of cultures—Babylonian, Egyptian, Roman, Anglo-Saxon, and Norman French. The ancient "digit," "palm," "span" and "cubit" units evolved into the "inch," "foot" and "yard" through a complicated transformation still not yet fully understood.

Roman contributions include the use of the number 12 as a base (1 foot=12 inches) and words from which we derive many of our present weights-and-measures names. For example, the 12 divisions of the Roman "pes," or foot, were called *unclae*. Our words "inch" and "ounce" are both derived from the Latin word.

The yard as a measure of length can be traced back to early Saxon times. Kings then wore sashes or girdles around their waists, which could be removed and used as convenient measuring devices. Thus the word "yard" comes from the Saxon word "gird," meaning the circumference of a person's waist.

Standardization of various units and their combinations into a loosely related system of weights and measures sometimes occurred in fascinating ways. Tradition holds that King Henry I decreed that the yard should be the distance from the tip of his nose to the end of his thumb. The length of a furlong (or "furrow-long") was established by early Tudor rulers as 220 yards. This led Queen Elizabeth I to declare, in the 16th century, that henceforth the traditional Roman mile of 5,000 feet would be replaced by one of 5,280 feet, making the mile exactly 8 furlongs and providing a convenient relationship between two previously ill-related measures.

Thus, through royal edicts, England by the 18th century had achieved a greater degree of standardization than the continental countries. The English units were well suited to commerce and trade because they had been developed and refined to meet commercial needs. Through colonization and dominance of world commerce during the 17th, 18th and 19th centuries, the English system of weights and measures was spread to and established in many parts of the world.

However, standards still differed to an extent undesirable for commerce among the 13 American colonies. The need for greater uniformity led to clauses in the Articles of Confederation and the Constitution giving power to the Congress to fix uniform standards for weights and measures. Today, standards supplied to all the states by the National Bureau of Standards assure uniformity throughout the country.

The Metric System

The need for a single worldwide coordinated measurement system has long been recognized. Gabriel Mouton, vicar of Saint Paul in Lyons, proposed in 1670 a comprehensive decimal measurement system based on the length of one minute of arc of a great circle of Earth.

In 1790 in the midst of the French Revolution, the National Assembly of France requested the French Academy of Sciences to "deduce an invariable standard for all the measures and all the weights." The commission appointed by the academy created a system that was, at once, simple and scientific. The unit of length was to be a portion of Earth's circumference. Measures for capacity (volume) and mass (weight) were to be derived from the unit of length, thus relating the basic units of the system to each other and to nature.

Furthermore, the larger and smaller versions of each unit were to be created by multiplying or dividing the basic units by 10 and its powers. This feature provided a great convenience to users of the system, by eliminating the need for such calculations as dividing by 16 (to convert ounces to pounds) or by 12 (to convert inches to feet). Similar calculations in the metric system could be performed simply by shifting the decimal point. Thus the metric system is a "base-10" or "decimal" system.

The commission assigned the word *metre*—which we spell *meter*—to the unit of length. This was derived from the Greek word *metron*, meaning "a measure." The physical standard representing the meter was to be constructed so that it would equal one ten-millionth of the distance from the North Pole to the equator along the meridian running near Dunkirk in France and Barcelona in Spain.

The metric unit of mass, called the "gram," was defined as the mass of one cubic centimeter (a cube that is 1/100 of a meter on each side) of water at its temperature of maximum density. The cubic decimeter (a cube 1/10 of a meter on each side) was chosen as the unit of fluid capacity. This measure was termed a "liter."

Although the metric system was not accepted with enthusiasm at first, adoption by other nations occurred steadily after France made its use compulsory in 1840. The standardization character and decimal features of the metric system made it well suited to scientific and engineering work. Consequently, it is not surprising that the rapid spread of the system coincided with an age of rapid technological development. In the United States, by Act of Congress in 1866, it was made "lawful throughout the United States of America to employ the weights and measures of the metric system in all contracts, dealings or court proceedings."

By the late 1860s, even better metric standards were needed to keep pace with scientific advances. In 1875, an international agreement, the "Treaty of the Meter," set up well-defined metric standards for length and mass, and established permanent machinery to recommend and adopt further refinements in the metric system. This "machinery" was an agreement known as the "Metric Convention," which was signed by 17 countries, including the U.S.

Today, with the exception of a few small countries, the entire world is using the metric system or is changing to such use.

—U.S. Department of Commerce, National Bureau of Standards

Note: In the case of the United States, it perhaps would be more accurate to say *"theoretically* changing to such use." Recent concerted efforts by government and industry have managed to raise general metric consciousness and slowly increase use, but for all its logic and symmetry, the system's still quite a few kilometers away from being "the people's cherce."

U.S. WEIGHTS AND MEASURES

Linear Measure
1 inch = 1/12 foot
1 foot = 12 inches
1 yard = 3 feet
1 rod = 5 1/2 yards = 16 1/2 feet
1 mile = 320 rods = 1,760 yards = 5,280 feet
1 U.S. nautical mile = 6,076.1033 feet
1 knot = 1 nautical mile per hour
1 furlong = 1/8 mile = 660 feet = 220 yards
1 league = 3 miles = 24 furlongs
1 fathom = 2 yards = 6 feet
1 chain = 100 links = 22 yards
1 link = 7.92 inches
1 hand = 4 inches
1 span = 9 inches

Area Measure
1 square inch = 1/144 square foot
1 square foot = 144 square inches
1 square yard = 9 square feet
1 square rod = 30 1/4 square yards = 272 1/4 square feet
1 acre = 160 square rods = 4,840 square yards = 43,560 square feet
1 square mile = 640 acres = 102,400 square rods
1 square rod = 625 square links
1 square chain = 16 square rods
1 acre = 10 square chains

Cubic Measure
1 cubic foot = 1,728 cubic inches
1 cubic yard = 27 cubic feet
1 register ton (shipping measure) = 100 cubic feet
1 U.S. shipping ton = 40 cubic feet
1 cord = 128 cubic feet
1 U.S. liquid gallon = 4 quarts = 231 cubic inches
1 imperial gallon = 1.20 U.S. gallons = 0.16 cubic feet
1 board foot = 144 cubic inches

Liquid Measure

1 gill = 1/4 pint
1 pint = 4 gills = 16 fluid ounces
1 quart = 2 pints = 1/4 gallon
1 gallon = 4 quarts
1 hogshead = 63 gallons
1 pipe or butt = 2 hogsheads
1 tun = 2 pipes

Dry Measure

1 pint = 1/2 quart
1 quart = 2 pints
1 gallon = 4 quarts
1 peck = 8 quarts
1 bushel = 4 pecks

Avoirdupois Weight

1 ounce = 16 drams
1 pound = 16 ounces
1 stone = 14 pounds
1 hundredweight = 100 pounds[*]
1 ton = 20 hundredweights = 2,000 pounds[*]

Troy Weight
(used in weighing gold, silver and jewels)

1 pennyweight = 24 grains
1 ounce = 20 pennyweight
1 pound = 12 ounces

Apothecaries' Weight

1 scruple = 20 grains
1 dram = 3 scruples
1 ounce = 8 drams
1 pound = 12 ounces

Apothecaries' Fluid Measure

1 fluid dram = 60 minims
1 fluid ounce = 8 fluid drams
1 pint = 16 fluid ounces
1 quart = 2 pints
1 gallon = 4 quarts

---

[*] When the terms "hundredweight" and "ton" are used unmodified, they are commonly understood to mean the 100-pound hundredweight and the 2,000-pound ton, respectively; these units may be designated "net" or "short" when necessary to distinguish them from the corresponding units in "gross" or "long" measure. (In long measure, 1 long hundredweight = 112 pounds; 1 long ton = 2,240 pounds.)

METRIC WEIGHTS AND MEASURES

Linear Measure
1 centimeter = 10 millimeters
1 decimeter = 100 millimeters = 10 centimeters
1 meter = 1,000 millimeters = 10 decimeters
1 dekameter = 10 meters
1 hectometer = 100 meters = 10 dekameters
1 kilometer = 1,000 meters = 10 hectometers

Area Measure
100 square millimeters = 1 square centimeter = 100 square millimeters
10,000 square centimeters = 1 square meter = 1,000,000 square mil
    limeters = 10,000 square centimeters
100 square meters = 1 are = 100 square meters
100 ares = 1 hectare = 10,000 square meters
100 hectares = 1 square kilometer = 1,000,000 square meters

Cubic Measure
1 cubic centimeter = 1,000 cubic millimeters
1 cubic decimeter = 1,000,000 cubic millimeters = 1,000 cubic cen
    timeters
1 cubic meter = 1 stere = 1,000 cubic decimeters = 1,000,000 cubic
    centimeters = 1,000,000,000 cubic millimeters

Volume Measure
1 liter = 0.001 cubic meter
1 centiliter = 10 milliliters
1 deciliter = 100 milliliters = 10 centiliters
1 liter = 1,000 milliliters = 10 deciliters
1 dekaliter = 10 liters
1 hectoliter = 100 liters = 10 dekaliters
1 kiloliter = 1,000 liters = 10 hectoliters

Weight
1 centigram = 10 milligrams
1 decigram = 100 milligrams = 10 centigrams
1 gram = 1,000 milligrams = 10 decigrams
1 dekagram = 10 grams
1 hectogram = 100 grams = 10 dekagrams
1 kilogram = 1,000 grams = 10 hectograms
1 metric ton = 1,000 kilograms

METRIC CONVERSIONS

To Convert	Into	Multiply By
inches	millimeters	25.4
inches	centimeters	2.54
feet	meters	0.3048
yards	meters	0.9144
miles	kilometers	1.6093
millimeters	inches	0.0394
centimeters	inches	0.3937
meters	feet	3.2808
meters	yards	1.0936
kilometers	miles	0.6214

EVERYDAY METRIC EQUIVALENTS

Centimeter—A little more than the width of a pencil (about 0.4 inch).
Gram—About the weight of a dollar bill.
Kilogram—A little more than 2 pounds (about 2.2 pounds).
Kilometer—Somewhat longer than 1/2 mile (about 0.6 mile).
Meter—A little longer than a yard (about 1.1 yards).
Milliliter—Five of them make a teaspoon.
Millimeter—Diameter of standard paper-clip wire (about 0.04 inch).

DECIMAL EQUIVALENTS OF COMMON FRACTIONS

1/64	.0156	19/64	.2968	37/64	.5781
1/32	.0312	5/16	.3125	19/32	.5937
3/64	.0468	21/64	.3281	39/64	.6093
1/16	.0625	11/32	.3437	5/8	.6250
5/64	.0781	23/64	.3593	41/64	.6406
3/32	.0937	3/8	.3750	21/32	.6562
7/64	.1093	25/64	.3906	43/64	.6718
1/8	.1250	13/32	.4062	11/16	.6875
9/64	.1406	27/64	.4218	45/64	.7031
5/32	.1562	7/16	.4375	23/32	.7187
11/64	.1718	29/64	.4531	47/64	.7343
3/16	.1875	15/32	.4687	3/4	.7500
13/64	.2031	31/64	.4843	49/64	.7656
7/32	.2187	1/2	.5000	25/32	.7812
15/64	.2343	33/64	.5156	51/64	.7968
1/4	.2500	17/32	.5312	13/16	.8125
17/64	.2656	35/64	.5468	53/64	.8281
9/32	.2812	9/16	.5625	27/32	.8437
55/64	.8593	59/64	.9218	63/64	.9843
7/8	.8750	15/16	.9375	1	1.0000
57/64	.8906	61/64	.9531		
29/32	.9062	31/32	.9687		

ROMAN NUMERALS

I	1	XIV	14	XC	90
II	2	XV	15	C	100
III	3	XVI	16	CC	200
IV	4	XVII	17	CCC	300
V	5	XVIII	18	CD	400
VI	6	XIX	19	D	500
VII	7	XX	20	DC	600
VIII	8	XXX	30	DCC	700
IX	9	XL	40	DCCC	800
X	10	L	50	CM	900
XI	11	LX	60	M	1,000
XII	12	LXX	70	MM	2,000
XIII	13	LXXX	80	MMM	3,000

Note: A dash line over a numeral multiplies the value by 1,000. Thus: $\overline{V}$=5,000; $\overline{X}$=10,000; $\overline{L}$=50,000; $\overline{C}$=100,000; $\overline{D}$=500,000; $\overline{M}$=1,000,000; $\overline{CLIX}$=159,000; $\overline{DLIX}$=559,000.

OTHER GENERAL RULES

1. Repeating a letter repeats its value: XX=20; CCC=300.
2. A letter placed after another of greater value adds thereto: VI=6; DC=600.
3. A letter placed before another of greater value subtracts there from: IV=4; CM=900.
4. No letter may repeat consecutively more than three times.

COSMIC CONSTANTS

Geometry

Triangle:
    Area = base x height ÷ 2
Square:
    Area = $side^2$
    Perimeter = 4 x side
Rectangle:
    Area = length x width
Circle:
    Area = π x $radius^2$
    Circumference = π x diameter
Cone:
    Surface = π x radius x length of a side
    Volume = π x $radius^2$ x height ÷ 3

Sphere:

Surface = 4 x radius^2 x π

Volume = 4 x radius^3 x π ÷ 3

Cube:

Surface = 6 x side^2

Volume = side^3

Rectangular solid:

Surface = (2 x length x width) + (2 x width x height) + (2 x height x length)

Volume = length x width x height

Cylinder

Surface = 2 x radius x π x height

Volume = radius^2 x π x height

Pyramid:

Volume = height x area of base ÷ 3

π=3.14159265358979323846264338327950288419716939937511
…(or 3.1416)

Mechanics

Speed = distance ÷ time

Force = mass x acceleration

Momentum = mass x velocity

Work = force x distance

Kinetic energy = mass x velocity^2 ÷ 2

Electricity

Ohm's law: amperage = voltage ÷ resistance

Watts = volts x amps

ELEMENTS

ELEMENT	SYMBOL	ATOMIC #	ELEMENT	SYMBOL	ATOMIC #
Actinium	Ac	89	chlorine	Cl	17
aluminum	Al	13	chromium	Cr	24
americium	Am	95	cobalt	Co	27
antimony	Sb	51	copper	Cu	29
argon	Ar	18	curium	Cm	96
arsenic	As	33	dysprosium	Dy	66
astatine	At	85	einsteinium	Es	99
barium	Ba	56	erbium	Er	68
berkelium	Bk	97	europium	Eu	63
beryllium	Be	4	fermium	Fm	100
bismuth	Bi	83	fluorine	F	9
boron	B	5	francium	Fr	87
bromine	Br	35	gadolinium	Gd	64
cadmium	Cd	48	gallium	Ga	31
calcium	Ca	20	germanium	Ge	32
californium	Cf	98	gold	Au	79
carbon	C	6	hafnium	Hf	72
cerium	Ce	58	hahnium	Ha	105
cesium	Cs	55	hassium	Hs	108

helium	He	2	promethium	Pm	61
holmium	Ho	67	protactinium	Pa	91
hydrogen	H	1	radium	Ra	88
indium	In	49	radon	Rn	86
iodine	I	53	rhenium	Re	75
iridium	Ir	77	rhodium	Rh	45
iron	Fe	26	rubidium	Rb	37
krypton	Kr	36	ruthenium	Ru	44
lanthanum	La	57	rutherfordium	Rf	104
lawrencium	Lr	103	samarium	Sm	62
lead	Pb	82	scandium	Sc	21
lithium	Li	3	seaborgium	Sg	106
lutetium	Lu	71	selenium	Se	34
magnesium	Mg	12	silicon	Si	14
manganese	Mn	25	silver	Ag	47
meitnerium	Mt	109	sodium	Na	11
mendelevium	Md	101	strontium	Sr	38
mercury	Hg	80	sulfur	S	16
molybdenum	Mo	42	tantalum	Ta	73
neodymium	Nd	60	technetium	Tc	43
neon	Ne	10	tellurium	Te	52
neptunium	Np	93	terbium	Tb	65
nickel	Ni	28	thallium	Tl	81
nielsbohrium	Ns	107	thorium	Th	90
niobium	Nb	41	thulium	Tm	69
nitrogen	N	7	tin	Sn	50
nobelium	No	102	titanium	Ti	22
osmium	Os	76	tungsten (wolfram)	W	74
oxygen	O	8	uranium	U	92
palladium	Pd	46	vanadium	V	23
phosphorus	P	15	xenon	Xe	54
platinum	Pt	78	ytterbium	Yb	70
plutonium	Pu	94	yttrium	Y	39
polonium	Po	84	zinc	Zn	30
potassium	K	19	zirconium	Zr	40
praseodymium	Pr	59			

Note: In late 1994, an international team of scientists at the Heavy Ion Research Center in Darmstadt, Germany, discovered two new, thus far unnamed, elements—110 and 111. The elements are the heaviest yet found, with atomic weights of 269 and 272 respectively.

THE RIGHT STUFF?

According to *Your Vital Statistics* by Gyles Brandeth (Citadel, 1986), adults, on average, are made of:

1. Carbon—enough to make 900 pencils.
2. Iron—enough to make a 3-inch nail.
3. Water—enough to fill a 10-gallon tank.
4. Potassium—enough to fire a toy cannon.
5. Sulfur—enough to kill all the fleas on an average dog.

Samuel Morse (1791-1872) devised the code for which he became famous in about 1838. Using the number of each letter in a printer's type tray as a guide to frequency of use, he gave the shortest signals to the commonest letters. Thus, most-popular *e* has the shortest code (one dot) and the rarely used *j*, *q* and *y* have the longest (combinations of a dot and three dashes)—not counting, however, numerals, special characters and punctuation marks.

A	·—	N	—·	á	·——·—	8	———··
B	—···	O	———	ä	·—·—	9	————·
C	—·—·	P	·——·	é	··—··	0	—————
D	—··	Q	——·—	ñ	——·——	,	——··——
E	·	R	·—·	ö	———·	.	·—·—·—
F	··—·	S	···	ü	··——	?	··——··
G	——·	T	—	1	·————	;	—·—·—·
H	····	U	··—	2	··———	:	———···
I	··	V	···—	3	···——	'	·————·
J	·———	W	·——	4	····—	-	—····—
K	—·—	X	—··—	5	·····	/	—··—·
L	·—··	Y	—·——	6	—····	(	—·——·
M	——	Z	——··	7	——···	)	—·——·—

Note: The last five marks in the last column are an aposthrope, a hyphen, a slash mark, a left parenthesis and a right parenthesis.

Next time someone stops you on the street and asks you to name the letters of the alphabet in the order of their relative frequency of use, just say: *"ETAISONHRDLUCMFWYPGVBKJQXZ!"*

For an encore, you might want to share the following facts about the wondrous world of English letters and words:

- T is the most common initial letter.
- "Strength" is the only eight-letter word with just one vowel.
- The River Wye in England was originally called the "We" because it is fed by springs named, respectively, "I." "Thou" and "He."
- The letter S was formed from the Egyptian hieroglyhpic *SE*, meaning "goose," whose shape was outlined in it.
- The 12 most commonly used words are:

1. the	5. a	9. I
2. of	6. in	10. it
3. and	7. that	11. for
4. to	8. is	12. as

- The average pencil will write about 30,000 words.
- The origin of the slang word "john" for a toilet remains tissued in mystery, but its first mention in print was in an official regulation of Harvard College in 1735, reading: "No freshman shall go into the Fellows' Cousin John," meaning the privy.
- "Clink" was the name of a prison in Southwark, England, destroyed in the so-called Gordon Riots in 1780 but persisting in language as a slang synonym for jail.
- Along about now, it might be useful to recall the immortal words of Sherlock Holmes, as portrayed by Basil Rathbone in the 1943 movie, *Sherlock Holmes in Washington:* "I shall write a monograph someday on the noxious habit of collecting useless trivia."

GOD IN, GOD OUT

[*Bill*] *Moyers:* There is a fetching story about President Eisenhower and the first computers...

[*Joseph*] *Campbell*:...Eisenhower went into a room full of computers. And he put the question to these machines, "Is there a God?" And they all start up, and the lights flash, and the wheels turn, and after a while a voice says, "*Now* there is." —*The Power of Myth* by JOSEPH CAMPBELL, with BILL MOYERS (Doubleday, 1988)

ENTER: COMP/TRIV

The first mechanical computer was the abacus, thought to have been invented by the Chinese more than 5,000 years ago. The abacus consists of a frame and crossbar, and wires that are strung with beads. The beads represent units: tens, hundreds, and so on. Calculations are made by sliding the beads up and down.

• • •

The first adding machine was invented in 1642 by French mathematician and philosopher Blaise Pascal.

• • •

It can safely be said that the first fully electronic computer was not a portable. Built in 1946 by American scientists John W. Mauchly, J. Presper Eckert, Jr., and J. G. Brainerd, the "ENIAC" (Electronic Numerical Integrator and Computer) weighed more than 60,000 pounds, cost $400,000 and was so big it filled a large room.

• • •

Lawrence Tribe, professor of constitutional law at Harvard University, has called for an amendment to the Constitution—to protect freedom of information. The proposal is aimed at extending to digital communications the First Amendment protections enjoyed by the print and broadcast media. Tribe believes it would help safeguard the rights of the increasing number of users of electronic mail and computer bulletin boards.

• • •

A Florida police aide who illegally accessed the national crime computer to check her boyfriend's arrest record now has a record of her own. The woman was recently arrested for misusing the National Information Center computer, a felony that carries a five-year prison sentence.

INTERNET OR OUT OF IT?

If you're bedazzled and amazed, but not necessarily enlightened, by the constant, trumpetous hype surrounding the shiny-new information superhighway, you may want to do some solid, old-fashioned, low-tech research before jumping aboard, or even trying to sneak across. And the first step you need to take is acceptance of this evolving electronic-brick road, quite separate and apart from the issue of whether or not you wish to travel on it.

With an estimated 30 million people worldwide now accessing the Internet, the lights on this sparkly road are green indeed, and the speed is definitely full-ahead, as cable television, telephone networks and computer services forge forward with their plans for a totally splendiferous, multimedia platform of vast power and allure. But inputter beware!— amid the bright signs and the techno-sell remain some basic questions that you alone must ask, and answer, yourself.

So let the truly significant research begin—by thoughtfully determining just how "high" your tech really needs to be to help you do the things you do. Are a computer and a printer, say, enough? Do you need a fax? Do you need a modem? Do you need to be among the estimated 20 million users of the global Internet?

Unless you have a burning urge to be "in" on leading-edge water-cooler talk about the latest Internet topics and charades, you might want to consider playing life *without* an Internet. There are still other excellent, speedy ways to get data you really need—and the charms of surfing the service for fun and knowledge can be sullied by all-too-frequent rudeness and outright hate bobbing among the fairer waves.

Even worse has been the increase in such nasty practices as eavesdropping, document copying and destruction, and various financial scams, including pyramid chain letters and artificially trumped-up penny-stock offerings of dubious worth. In fact, officials of the government-backed Computer Emergency Response Team, assessing the recent violation of a well-known computer-security expert, have warned that better security precautions must be taken before businesses tie into the Internet.

So welcome aboard the highway—but remember to look both ways!

POSTAL NOTES

Due to the steadily escalating nature of postal rates (and most other rates and prices), they have not been included here. For all rates and fees, as well as information on products and other services such as certification, registration and insurance, check with your local post office.

The Postal Service and the Federal Trade Commission both have jurisdiction over some areas of commerce by mail. The Postal Service is charged with protecting the public against fraud or misrepresentation by mail. Any information about these matters should be addressed to your local postmaster, postal inspector or chief postal inspector. The Postal Service also provides assistance with mail-service problems. Write: The Consumer Advocate, U.S. Postal Service,

Washington, DC 20260, Attention: Manager, Customer Response.

In spring 1995, some of the nation's 33,000 post offices officially began accepting charge cards. Seattle, Denver and San Diego joined Fort Worth, Orlando and Washington, where payment by credit card had been tested for 15 months prior to the official start-up. The Postal Service plans to have all branches in the program by the end of 1996. Said Michael Riley, the Service's chief financial officer: "We are moving into the electronic payment age in response to today's consumer payment habits."

The cent symbol (¢), which was banished from stamps for aesthetic reasons in the early 1980s, is being brought back to low-value stamps (9¢ or less). Such stamps have carried numerals such as 01, 03 or 05 to denote their value, which apparently has caused problems with people confusing the values and even accepting some as dollar-value stamps. So all new issues of low-value stamps will have a single digit and a cent symbol to make their value clear.

Tip: You can keep your mailing costs to a minimum by getting a good postage scale. To make sure the scale is accurate, test it every so often with pennies. Ten of them weigh an ounce.

APPROVED POSTAL-SERVICE ABBREVIATIONS

Alley	**Aly.**	Grove	**Grv.**
Arcade	**Arc.**	Heights	**Hts.**
Avenue	**Ave.**	Highway	**Hwy.**
Boulevard	**Blvd.**	Lane	**Ln.**
Branch	**Br.**	Manor	**Mnr.**
Bypass	**Byp.**	Place	**Pl.**
Causeway	**Cswy.**	Plaza	**Plz.**
Center	**Ctr.**	Point	**Pt.**
Circle	**Cir.**	Road	**Rd.**
Court	**Ct.**	Rural	**R.**
Courts	**Cts.**	Square	**Sq.**
Crescent	**Cres.**	Street	**St.**
Drive	**Dr.**	Terrace	**Ter.**
Estates	**Est.**	Trail	**Trl.**
Expressway	**Expy.**	Turnpike	**Tpke.**
Extension	**Ext.**	Viaduct	**Via.**
Freeway	**Fwy.**	Vista	**Vis.**
Gardens	**Gdns.**		

DE-JUNKING YOUR MAIL

To get your name off many national mailing lists, write to: Mail Preference Service, Direct Marketing Association, 11 W. 42nd St., New York, NY 10036. To get off pornographic-mail lists, fill out a prohibitory order form at the local post office. The mailer must remove your name within 30 days.

MOTHERS OF INVENTION

Five female inventors—or "mothers of invention":

- Elizabeth Smith Miller (bloomers, 1851; named for women's-rights activist Amelia Bloomer)
- Rose O'Neil (Kewpie doll, 1913)
- Ruth Wakefield (chocolate-chip cookies, 1933)
- Claire McCardell (stretch leotards, 1940s)
- Mary Quant (miniskirt, late 1950s)

WEDDING ANNIVERSARIES

	Traditional	**Modern**
1st	paper	clocks
2nd	cotton	china
3rd	leather	crystal, glass
4th	fruit, flowers, silk	electrical appliances
5th	wood	silverware
6th	sugar and candy, iron	wood
7th	copper or wool	desk, pen-and-pencil sets
8th	bronze or pottery	linens, laces
9th	willow or pottery	leather
10th	aluminum or tin	diamond jewelry
11th	steel	fashion jewelry
12th	silk or linen	pearls or colored gems
13th	lace	textiles, furs
14th	ivory	gold jewelry
15th	crystal	watches
20th	china	platinum
25th	silver	sterling silver
30th	pearls	diamonds

35th	coral	jade
40th	rubies	rubies
45th	sapphires	sapphires
50th	gold	gold
55th	emeralds	emeralds
60th to 70th	diamonds	diamonds

WORLD POPULATION

World population as of 1994 stood at 5.64 billion and is projected to increase to 7.92 billion by 2020. The 15 most populous countries:

Country	1994	2020
1. China	1,190,431,000	1,424,725,000
2. India	919,903,000	1,320,746,000
3. United States	260,714,000	323,113,000
4. Indonesia	200,410,000	276,474,000
5. Brazil	158,739,000	197,466,000
6. Russia	149,609,000	159,263,000
7. Pakistan	128,856,000	251,330,000
8. Bangladesh	125,149,000	210,248,000
9. Japan	125,107,000	126,062,000
10. Nigeria	98,091,000	215,893,000
11. Mexico	92,202,000	136,096,000
12. Germany	81,088.000	82,385,000
13. Vietnam	73,104,000	102,359,000
14. Philippines	69,809,000	101,530,000
15. Iran	65,612,000	143,624,000

THE GLOBAL VILLAGE

According to Development Innovations and Networks of Geneva, Switzerland, if the world were converted into a village of 1,000 people, it would have 564 Asians, 210 Europeans, 86 Africans, 80 South Americans and 60 North Americans. Religiously speaking, there would be 300 Christians, 175 Muslims, 128 Hindus, 55 Buddhists, 47 animists and 293 others of various persuasions too numerous to list here. (Figures based on data as of early 1990.)

Note: Half the human race speaks only seven languages: Mandarin Chinese, English, Hindustani, Spanish, Russian, German and Japanese.

THE UNITED NATIONS

The second worldwide attempt by nations to join in keeping the peace was the formation of the United Nations. (The first was the ill-starred League of Nations.)

On April 25,1945, representatives of 50 nations met in San Francisco to plan the UN. On October 24, 1945, the UN Charter went into effect. (In early 1995, as the UN's 50th anniversary approached, there were 184 member nations.)

The UN Charter contains four main goals:
- To preserve world peace.
- To encourage nations to deal justly with each other.
- To help nations cooperate in solving problems.
- To provide an agency for working toward these goals.

Overall, the UN has been stronger than the League of Nations in many ways, including the use of armed UN peacekeeping forces to prevent wars from breaking out or spreading. The UN has also been instrumental in bringing countries and their peoples together through its specialized agencies, which were established to deal with the issues of health, food, finances, labor, education, cultures, science, communications and weather forecasting, and their related problems.

Of course, the UN has also had its troubles and failures. Member countries involved in disputes have sometimes refused to voice their differences before the UN, or to abide by UN decisions, or to bear their share of the expense. Moreover, some conflicts and problems (such as those in Somalia or the former Yugoslav republic) have simply proved thus far to be beyond the UN's power to resolve—which doesn't mean that efforts to do so should be abandoned, or that the world would be better off without the UN.

Let's face it: the world needs all the help it can get, and the UN needs and deserves all the support *it* can get.

Note: For a complete text of the UN Charter, send $1 to the UN Sales Section, United Nations, New York, NY 10017.

TRANSLATIONAL INTERCOURSE

There are six official working languages recognized by the UN: Arabic, Chinese, English, French, Russian and Spanish. Here is the word "peace" in a dozen languages:

French	paix
Spanish	paz
Italian	pace
Chinese	ho ping
Japanese	heiwa
Russian	mir
Hebrew	shalom
Arabic	salam
German	frieden
Swedish	fred
Norwegian	fred
Polish	pokoj

U.S. POPULATION

The population of the United States—260,714,000—is larger than the estimated population of the *world* at the birth of Christ—250 million. With a current growth rate of 1.1 percent, the nation's population is expected to double by about the year 2055.

According to the 1990 U.S. census, the nation's population grew nearly two-thirds—64.4 percent, to be exact—since the first post-World War II census in 1950.

Nevada recorded the greatest percentage growth in the 40-year period (650.8 percent) as well as in the 1980-90 period (50.4). In numerical growth, California led the nation with 6,091,459 persons in the 1980-90 period, and with 19,173,798 in the 1950-90 period.

The Census Bureau projects that the number of women in the U.S. will total 166 million by 2020, or 50.9 percent of the population. That would be down a bit from the 51.2 percent they now constitute.

Other findings and projections by the bureau include:

The adult population that was married in 1991 totaled 61 percent—down from 72 percent in 1970. The report also indicated that the median age at which people marry is rising (that's the age at which half of all adults are married and half are not). It said that by 1991 the median age for women was 24.1, up from 20.8 years in 1970. For men the median age was 26.3 years in 1991, compared with 23.2 years in 1970. Although these figures represent a change over the last two decades, they're about the same as they were at the turn of the century.

In 1991 there were nearly 10 million American children living in families in which there was a stepparent or siblings who are less than full brothers and sisters. By contrast, 33.4 million children were living in "nuclear families"—that is, with both biological parents and any full brothers or sisters. Those youngsters under age 18 in nuclear families accounted for 50.8 percent of all young people.

The fastest-growing age group is expected to be the 55-to-64 component, increasing to 42.3 million people, up from 8.2 percent to 13 percent of all Americans by 2020.

The 25-to-34 group, the largest now, is expected to hold onto top place, rising to 43.5 million, although that will amount to a declining share of the total, falling from 16.6 percent to 13.4 percent.

The biggest drop, though, is expected among the early middle-age 35-to-44 group, which is expected to fall from the current 15.8 percent to 12.2 percent of Americans, even though the total increases to 39.6 million.

Whites will still make up by far the largest number of Americans, though not as big a percentage as they do now. Their numbers will increase to 254.8 million, but their share of the total will shrink from 83.3 to 78.2.

Immigration and rapid population growth are expected to make Hispanics the largest U.S. minority by 2020, totaling 51.2 million, or 15.7 percent of the population. That would be up from 9.7 percent in 1993. Blacks are projected to be the second largest minority at 45.4 million people, or 13.9 percent of the total. That would be an increase from the current 12.5 percent.

Meanwhile, Asians and Pacific Islanders are expected to see significant growth, from today's 3.4 percent to 6.9 percent, or 22.6 million. Native Americans will increase their share of the population from 0.8 percent to 0.9 percent, or 3.2 million.

POPULATION BY STATES, 1950-90

	1950 Census	1990 Census	% Change
Alabama	3,061,743	4,040,587	+ 31.9
Alaska	128,643	550,043	+327.6
Arizona	749,587	3,665,228	+388.9
Arkansas	1,909,511	2,350,725	+ 23.1
California	10,586,223	29,760,021	+181.1
Colorado	1,325,089	3,294,394	+148.6
Connecticut	2,007,280	3,287,116	+ 63.8
Delaware	318,085	666,168	+109.4
Florida	2,771,305	12,937,926	+366.8
Georgia	3,444,578	6,478,216	+ 88.1
Hawaii	499,794	1,108,229	+121.7
Idaho	588,637	1,006,749	+ 71.0
Illinois	8,712,176	11,430,602	+ 31.2
Indiana	3,934,224	5,544,159	+ 40.9
Iowa	2,621,073	2,776,755	+ 5.9
Kansas	1,905,299	2,477,574	+ 30.0
Kentucky	2,944,806	3,685,296	+ 25.1
Louisiana	2,683,516	4,219,973	+ 57.3
Maine	913,774	1,227,928	+ 34.3
Maryland	2,343,001	4,781,468	+104.1
Massachusetts	4,690,514	6,016,425	+ 28.2
Michigan	6,371,766	9,295,297	+ 45.9
Minnesota	2,982,483	4,375,099	+ 46.7
Mississippi	2,176,914	2,573,216	+ 18.1
Missouri	3,954,653	5,117,073	+ 29.4
Montana	591,024	799,065	+ 35.2
Nebraska	1,325,510	1,578,385	+ 19.1

Nevada	160,083	1,201,833	+650.8
New Hampshire	533,242	1,109,252	+108.0
New Jersey	4,835,329	7,730,188	+ 59.9
New Mexico	681,187	1,515,069	+122.4
New York	14,830,192	17,990,455	+ 21.3
North Carolina	4,061,929	6,628,637	+ 63.2
North Dakota	619,636	638,800	+ 3.1
Ohio	7,946,627	10,847,115	+ 36.5
Oklahoma	2,233,351	3,145,585	+ 40.8
Oregon	1,521,341	2,842,321	+ 86.8
Pennsylvania	10,498,012	11,881,643	+ 13.2
Rhode Island	791,896	1,003,464	+ 26.7
South Carolina	2,117,027	3,486,703	+ 64.7
South Dakota	652,740	696,004	+ 6.6
Tennessee	3,291,718	4,877,185	+ 48.2
Texas	7,711,194	16,986,510	+120.3
Utah	688,862	1,722,850	+150.1
Vermont	377,747	562,758	+ 48.9
Virginia	3,318,680	6,187,358	+ 86.4
Washington	2,378,963	4,866,692	+104.6
West Virginia	2,005,552	1,793,477	− 10.6
Wisconsin	3,434,575	4,891,769	+ 42.4
Wyoming	290,529	453,588	+ 56.1

Note: The population of the District of Columbia was 802,178 in 1950 and 606,900 in 1990, for a percentage change of -24.3.

25 MOST POPULOUS U.S. CITIES

1990	1980	City and State	1980 Pop.	1990 Pop.	% Change
1	1	New York, NY	7,071,639	7,322,564	+ 3.5
2	3	Los Angeles, CA	2,968,528	3,485,398	+17.4
3	2	Chicago, IL	3,005,072	2,783,726	− 7.4
4	5	Houston, TX	1,595,138	1,630,553	+ 2.2
5	4	Philadelphia, PA	1,688,210	1,585,577	− 6.1
6	8	San Diego, CA	875,538	1,110,549	+26.8
7	6	Detroit, MI	1,203,368	1,027,974	−14.6
8	7	Dallas, TX	904,599	1,006,877	+11.3
9	9	Phoenix, AZ	789,704	983,403	+24.5
10	11	San Antonio, TX	785,940	935,933	+19.1
11	17	San Jose, CA	629,400	782,248	+24.3
12	12	Indianapolis, IN	711,539	741,952	+ 4.3
13	10	Baltimore, MD	786,741	736,014	− 6.4
14	13	San Francisco, CA	678,974	723,959	+ 6.6

15	19	Jacksonville, FL	571,003	672,971	+17.9
16	20	Columbus, OH	565,021	632,088	+12.0
17	16	Milwaukee, WI	636,297	628,088	− 1.3
18	14	Memphis, TN	646,174	610,337	− 5.5
19	15	Washington, DC	638,432	606,900	− 4.9
20	21	Boston, MA	562,994	574,283	+ 2.0
21	23	Seattle, WA	493,846	516,259	+ 4.5
22	28	El Paso, TX	425,259	515,342	+21.2
23	25	Nashville-Davidson, TN	477,811	510,784	+ 6.9
24	18	Cleveland, OH	573,822	505,616	−11.9
25	22	New Orleans, LA	557,927	496,938	−10.9

—U.S. CENSUS BUREAU

GEOGRAPHIC CENTERS OF THE U.S.

Because there is neither a generally accepted definition of a geographic center nor a completely satisfactory method for determining it, there may be as many geographic centers of a state or country as there are definitions of the term.

No marked or monumented point has been established by any government agency as the geographic center of either the 50 states, the coterminous states, or the North American continent. However, a monument was erected in Lebanon, Kansas, by a group of citizens who had hired engineers to determine the "geographic center" of the United States

Sometimes confused with the geographic center of the U.S. is the reference point for all property lines and city, county, state, and international boundaries on the North American continent that are tied to the National Triangulation networks of the U.S., Canada, Mexico, and Central America. This point is Meades Ranch Triangulation station located at latitude 39°13'26.686", longitude 98°32'30.506", about 12 miles north of Lucas, Kansas. It is the base point or origin of geodetic positions and directions in the triangulation net of the U.S. because it is at the junction of the main east-west transcontinental triangulation arc stretching from the Atlantic to the Pacific coasts and the main north-south arc, which follows approximately the 98th meridian from the Canadian border to the Rio Grande.

In determining the centers of the states, islands adjacent to their coastlines and large bodies of water on their boundaries were excluded.

The geographic centers and positions listed below should be considered as estimates. The center of the U.S. (without Alaska and Hawaii) is approximately Lebanon, Kansas.

Center	Latitude N	Longitude W
United States (50 states)		
West of Castle Rock,		
Butte County, South Dakota	44°58'	103°46
Continental United States (49 states)		
Near Castle Rock,		
Butte County, South Dakota	44°59'	103°38'
Coterminous United States (48 states)		
Near Lebanon, Smith County, Kansas	39°50'	98°35'

—U.S. GEOLOGICAL SURVEY, DEPARTMENT OF THE INTERIOR

STATES OF THE UNION

State		Capital	Entered Union
Alabama	AL	Montgomery	Dec. 14, 1819
Alaska	AK	Juneau	Jan. 3, 1959
Arizona	AZ	Phoenix	Feb. 14, 1912
Arkansas	AR	Little Rock	June 15, 1836
California	CA	Sacramento	Sept. 9, 1850
Colorado	CO	Denver	Aug. 1, 1876
Connecticut	CT	Hartford	Jan. 9, 1788
Delaware	DE	Dover	Dec. 7, 1787
Florida	FL	Tallahassee	Mar. 3, 1845
Georgia	GA	Atlanta	Jan. 2, 1788
Hawaii	HI	Honolulu	Aug. 21, 1959
Idaho	ID	Boise	July 3, 1890
Illinois	IL	Springfield	Dec. 3, 1818
Indiana	IN	Indianapolis	Dec. 11, 1816
Iowa	IA	Des Moines	Dec. 28, 1846
Kansas	KS	Topeka	Jan. 29, 1861
Kentucky	KY	Frankfort	June 1, 1792
Louisiana	LA	Baton Rouge	Apr. 30, 1812
Maine	ME	Augusta	Mar. 15, 1820
Maryland	MD	Annapolis	Apr. 28, 1788
Massachusetts	MA	Boston	Feb. 6, 1788
Michigan	MI	Lansing	Jan. 26, 1837
Minnesota	MN	St. Paul	May 11, 1858
Mississippi	MS	Jackson	Dec. 10, 1817
Missouri	MO	Jefferson City	Aug. 10, 1821
Montana	MT	Helena	Nov. 8, 1889
Nebraska	NE	Lincoln	Mar. 1, 1867
Nevada	NV	Carson City	Oct. 31, 1864
New Hampshire	NH	Concord	June 21, 1788
New Jersey	NJ	Trenton	Dec. 18, 1787
New Mexico	NM	Santa Fe	Jan. 6, 1912
New York	NY	Albany	July 26, 1788
North Carolina	NC	Raleigh	Nov. 21, 1789
North Dakota	ND	Bismarck	Nov. 2, 1889
Ohio	OH	Columbus	Mar. 1, 1803
Oklahoma	OK	Oklahoma City	Nov. 16, 1907
Oregon	OR	Salem	Feb. 14, 1859
Pennsylvania	PA	Harrisburg	Dec. 12, 1787
Rhode Island	RI	Providence	May 29, 1790
South Carolina	SC	Columbia	May 23, 1788
South Dakota	SD	Pierre	Nov. 2, 1889

Tennessee	TN	Nashville	June 1, 1796
Texas	TX	Austin	Dec. 29, 1845
Utah	UT	Salt Lake City	Jan. 4, 1896
Vermont	VT	Montpelier	Mar. 4, 1791
Virginia	VA	Richmond	June 25, 1788
Washington	WA	Olympia	Nov. 11, 1889
West Virginia	WV	Charleston	June 20, 1863
Wisconsin	WI	Madison	May 29, 1848
Wyoming	WY	Cheyenne	July 10, 1890

THE DECLARATION OF INDEPENDENCE
In CONGRESS, July 4, 1776
A DECLARATION
By the REPRESENTATIVES of the UNITED STATES OF AMERICA,
In GENERAL CONGRESS assembled.

When in the Course of human Events, it becomes necessary for one People to dissolve the Political Bands which have connected them with another, and to assume among the Powers of the Earth, the separate and equal Station to which the Laws of Nature and of Nature's God entitle them, a decent Respect to the Opinions of Mankind requires that they should declare the causes which impel them to the Separation.

We hold these Truths to be self-evident, that all Men are created equal, that they are endowed by their Creator with certain unalienable Rights, that among these are Life, Liberty, and the Pursuit of Happiness—That to secure these Rights, Governments are instituted among Men, deriving their just Powers from the Consent of the Governed, that whenever any Form of Government becomes destructive of these Ends, it is the Right of the People to alter or to abolish it, and to institute new Government, laying its Foundation on such Principles, and organizing its Powers in such Form, as to them shall seem most likely to effect their Safety and Happiness. Prudence, indeed, will dictate that Governments long established should not be changed for light and transient Causes; and accordingly all Experience hath shewn, that Mankind are more disposed to suffer, while Evils are sufferable, than to right themselves by abolishing the Forms to which they are accustomed. But when a long Train of Abuses and Usurpations, pursuing invariably the same Object, evinces a Design to reduce them under absolute Despotism, it is their Right, it is their Duty, to throw off such Government, and to provide new Guards for their future Security. Such has been the patient Sufferance of these Colonies; and such is now the Necessity which constrains them to alter their former Systems of Government. The History of the present

King of Great-Britain is a History of repeated Injuries and Usurpations, all having in direct Object the Establishment of an absolute Tyranny over these States. To prove this, let Facts be submitted to a candid World.

He has refused his Assent to Laws, the most wholesome and necessary for the public Good.

He has forbidden his Governors to pass Laws of immediate and pressing Importance, unless suspended in their Operation till his Assent should be obtained; and when so suspended, he has utterly neglected to attend to them.

He has refused to pass other Laws for the Accommodation of large Districts of People, unless those People would relinquish the Right of Representation in the Legislature, a Right inestimable to them, and formidable to Tyrants only.

He has called together Legislative Bodies at Places unusual, uncomfortable, and distant from the Depository of their public Records, for the sole Purpose of fatiguing them into Compliance with his Measures.

He has dissolved Representative Houses repeatedly, for opposing with manly Firmness his Invasions on the Rights of the People.

He has refused for a long Time, after such Dissolutions, to cause others to be elected; whereby the Legislative Powers, incapable of Annihilation, have returned to the People at large for their exercise; the State remaining in the meantime exposed to all the Dangers of Invasion from without, and Convulsions within.

He has endeavoured to prevent the Population of these States; for that Purpose obstructing the Laws for Naturalization of Foreigners; refusing to pass others to encourage their Migrations hither, and raising the Conditions of new Appropriations of Lands.

He has obstructed the Administration of Justice, by refusing his Assent to Laws for establishing Judiciary Powers.

He has made Judges dependent on his Will alone, for the Tenure of their Offices, and the Amount and Payment of their Salaries.

He has erected a Multitude of new Offices, and sent hither Swarms of Officers to harass our People, and eat out their Substance.

He has kept among us, in Times of Peace, Standing Armies, without the consent of our Legislatures.

He has affected to render the Military independent of and superior to the Civil Power.

He has combined with others to subject us to a Jurisdiction foreign to our Constitution, and unacknowledged by our Laws; giving his Assent to their Acts of pretended Legislation:

For quartering large Bodies of Armed Troops among us:

For protecting them, by a mock Trial, from Punishment for any Murders which they should commit on the Inhabitants of these States:

For cutting off our Trade with all Parts of the World:

For imposing Taxes on us without our Consent:

For depriving us, in many Cases, of the Benefits of Trial by Jury:

For transporting us beyond Seas to be tried for pretended Offences:

For abolishing the free System of English Laws in a neighbouring Province, establishing therein an arbitrary Government, and enlarging its Boundaries, so as to render it at once an Example and fit Instrument for introducing the same absolute Rule into these Colonies:

For taking away our Charters, abolishing our most valuable Laws, and altering fundamentally the Forms of our Governments:

For suspending our own Legislatures, and declaring themselves invested with Power to legislate for us in all Cases whatsoever.

He has abdicated Government here, by declaring us out of his Protection and waging War against us.

He has plundered our Seas, ravaged our Coasts, burnt our Towns, and destroyed the Lives of our People.

He is, at this Time, transporting large Armies of foreign Mercenaries to compleat the Works of Death, Desolation, and Tyranny, already begun with circumstances of Cruelty and Perfidy, scarcely paralleled in the most barbarous Ages, and totally unworthy of Head of a civilized Nation.

He has constrained our fellow Citizens taken Captive on the high Seas to bear Arms against their Country, to become the Executioners of their Friends and Brethren, or to fall themselves by their Hands.

He has excited domestic Insurrections amongst us, and has endeavoured to bring on the Inhabitants of our Frontiers, the merciless Indian Savages, whose known Rule of Warfare, is an undistinguished Destruction of all Ages, Sexes and conditions.

In every stage of these oppressions we have Petitioned for Redress in the most humble Terms: Our repeated Petitions have been answered only by repeated Injury. A Prince, whose Character is thus marked by every act which may define a Tyrant, is unfit to be the Ruler of a free People.

Nor have we been wanting in Attentions to our British Brethren. We have warned them from Time to Time of Attempts by their Legislature to extend an unwarrantable Jurisdiction over us. We have reminded them of the Circumstances of our Emigration and Settlement here. We have appealed to their native Justice and Magnanimity, and we have conjured them by the Ties of our common Kindred to disavow these Usurpations, which, would inevitably interrupt our Connections and Correspondence. They too have been deaf to the Voice of Justice and of Consanguinity. We must, therefore, acquiesce in the Necessity, which denounces our Separation, and hold them, as we hold the rest of Mankind, Enemies in War, in Peace, Friends.

We, therefore, the Representatives of the UNITED STATES OF AMERICA, in General Congress, Assembled, appealing to the Supreme Judge of the World for the Rectitude of our Intentions, do, in the Name, and by Authority of the good People of these Colonies, solemnly Publish and Declare, That these United Colonies are, and of Right ought to be, Free and Independent States; that they are absolved from all Allegiance to the British Crown, and that all political Connection between them and the State of Great-Britain, is and ought to be totally dissolved; and that as Free and Independent States, they have full Power to levy War, conclude Peace, contract Alliances, establish Commerce, and to do all other Acts and Things which Independent States may of right do. And for the support of this Declaration, with a firm Reliance on the Protection of divine Providence, we mutually pledge to each other our Lives, our Fortunes, and our sacred Honor.

Signed by Order *and in*
Behalf *of the* Congress,
JOHN HANCOCK, President

ATTEST.
CHARLES THOMSON, Secretary.

THE BILL OF RIGHTS

The first ten amendments to the U.S. Constitution are known as the Bill of Rights. By resolution of Congress, these amendments— along with two others that ultimately were not ratified—were presented to the states for ratification on September 25, 1789. By December 15, 1791, the first 10 amendments were ratified by 11 of the 14 states, with Virginia completing the needed three-fourths majority. Georgia, Connecticut and Massachusetts did not ratify them until 1939.

AMENDMENT I

Congress shall make no law respecting an establishment of religion, or prohibiting the free exercise thereof; or abridging the freedom of speech, or of the press; or the right of the people peaceably to assemble, and to petition the Government for a redress of grievances.

AMENDMENT II

A well regulated Militia, being necessary to the security of a free State, the right of the people to keep and bear Arms, shall not be infringed.

AMENDMENT III

No Soldier shall, in time of peace be quartered in any house, without the consent of the Owner, nor in time of war, but in a manner to be prescribed by law.

AMENDMENT IV

The right of the people to be secure in their persons, houses, papers, and effects, against unreasonable searches and seizures, shall not be violated, and no Warrants shall issue, but upon probable cause, supported by Oath or Affirmation, and particularly describing the place to be searched, and the persons or things to be seized.

AMENDMENT V

No person shall be held to answer for a capital, or otherwise infamous crime, unless on a presentment or indictment of a Grand Jury, except in cases arising in the land or naval forces, or in the Militia, when in actual service in time of War or public danger; nor shall any person be subject for the same offence to be twice put in jeopardy of life or limb; nor shall be compelled in any criminal case to be a witness against himself, nor be deprived of life, liberty, or property, without due process of law; nor shall private property be taken for a public use, without just compensation.

AMENDMENT VI

In all criminal prosecutions, the accused shall enjoy the right to a speedy and public trial, by an impartial jury of the State and district wherein the crime shall have been committed, which district shall have been previously ascertained by law, and to be informed of the nature and cause of the accusation; to be confronted with the witnesses against him; to have compulsory process for obtaining witnesses in his favor, and to have the Assistance of Counsel for his defence.

AMENDMENT VII

In Suits at common law, where the value in controversy shall exceed twenty dollars, the right of trial by jury shall be preserved, and no fact tried by a Jury, shall be otherwise re-examined in any Court of the United States, than according to the rules of the common law.

AMENDMENT VIII

Excessive bail shall not be required, nor excessive fines imposed, nor cruel and unusual punishments inflicted.

AMENDMENT IX

The enumeration in the Constitution, of certain rights, shall not be construed to deny or disparage others retained by the people.

AMENDMENT X

The powers not delegated to the United States by the Constitution, nor prohibited by it to the States, are reserved to the States respectively, or to the people.

U.S. PRESIDENTS

	President	Term		President	Term
1	George Washington	1789-97	22	Grover Cleveland	1885-89
2	John Adams	1797-1801	23	Benjamin Harrison	1889-93
3	Thomas Jefferson	1801-09	24	Grover Cleveland	1893-97
4	James Madison	1809-17	25	William McKinley	1897-1901
5	James Monroe	1817-25	26	Theodore Roosevelt	1901-09
6	John Quincy Adams	1825-29	27	William H. Taft	1909-13
7	Andrew Jackson	1829-37	28	Woodrow Wilson	1913-21
8	Martin Van Buren	1837-41	29	Warren G. Harding	1921-23
9	William Henry Harrison	1841-41	30	Calvin Coolidge	1923-29
10	John Tyler	1841-45	31	Herbert Hoover	1929-33
11	James K. Polk	1845-49	32	Franklin D. Roosevelt	1933-45
12	Zachary Taylor	1849-50	33	Harry S Truman	1945-53
13	Millard Fillmore	1850-53	34	Dwight D. Eisenhower	1953-61
14	Franklin Pierce	1853-57	35	John F. Kennedy	1961-63
15	James Buchanan	1857-61	36	Lyndon B. Johnson	1963-69
16	Abraham Lincoln	1861-65	37	Richard M. Nixon	1969-74
17	Andrew Johnson	1865-69	38	Gerald R. Ford	1974-77
18	Ulysses S. Grant	1869-77	39	Jimmy Carter	1977-81
19	Rutherford B. Hayes	1877-81	40	Ronald Reagan	1981-89
20	James A. Garfield	1881-81	41	George Bush	1989-93
21	Chester A. Arthur	1881-85	42	Bill Clinton	1993-

Note: John Hanson (1715-83) is sometimes referred to as the *true* first U.S. president, inasmuch as he was the first to serve the one-year term (1781-82) under the Articles of Confederation. But his duties were merely those of a presiding officer and bore no relation to presidential duties under the Constitution.

SEQUENCE OF PRESIDENTIAL SUCCESSION

1 Vice President

2 Speaker of the House

3 President Pro Tempore of the Senate

4 Secretary of State

5 Secretary of the Treasury

6 Secretary of Defense

7 Attorney General

8 Secretary of the Interior

9 Secretary of Agriculture

10 Secretary of Commerce

11 Secretary of Labor

12 Secretary of Health and Human Services

13 Secretary of Housing and Urban Development

14 Secretary of Transportation

15 Secretary of Energy

16 Secretary of Education

THE TWO BIRTHDAYS OF GEORGE WASHINGTON

Some people have all the luck! Consider the great red-white-and-blue father, George Washington. Among the many smiles that Fortune smiled upon him was a quirk of time and fate that netted him not one birthday, but two. (And even more, if you add in the various "Presidents' Days" of recent years.)

It all started, of course, when he was born—on February 11, 1732 (in Westmoreland County, Virginia).

That would have been the date encountered in our history books except for the fact that 20 years later Great Britain belatedly got around to adopting the Gregorian calendar, which had been promulgated by Pope Gregory XIII in 1582. The American colonies, then under British rule, received the new calendar in 1752. The main reason for replacing the Julian calendar, which had been used since 45 B.C., was that it overestimated the length of the year by 11 minutes and 25 seconds, or one day in 128 years. By 1528, the Julian calendar had gained 10 days on the solar year. By the time Britain and its colonies adopted the new calendar, another day had been gained for a total of 11. Therefore, Britain's Calendar Act decreed that the day following September 2, 1752 should be September 14. So, in 1753, Washington's birthday fell on February 22, because of the 11-day difference.

As for Washington himself, he more or less simply ignored his "traditional" birthday of the 22nd and continued to celebrate on the 11th.

LINCOLN'S GETTYSBURG ADDRESS

Gettysburg, perhaps the key battle of the Civil War, was fought July 1-3, 1863. On November 19 of that year, the site was dedicated as a national cemetery by President Lincoln in a two-minute speech that has become immortal. At the time, Lincoln's simple-but-strong, biblically cadenced utterance was overshadowed by a two-hour address by Edward Everett, a leading orator of the period. The following is the text of the address as revised by Lincoln from his own notes.

Fourscore and seven years ago our fathers brought forth on this continent a new nation conceived in liberty and dedicated to the proposition that all men are created equal. Now we are engaged in a great civil war testing whether that nation, or any nation so conceived and so dedicated, can long endure. We are met on a great battlefield of that war. We have come to dedicate a portion of that field as a final resting-place for those who here gave their lives that that nation might live. It is altogether fitting and proper that we should do this. But, in a larger sense, we cannot dedicate, we cannot consecrate, we cannot hallow this ground. The brave men, living and dead, who struggled here have consecrated it far above our poor power to add or detract. The world will little note nor long remember what we say here, but it can never forget what they did here. It is for us the living rather to be dedicated here to the unfinished work which they who fought here have thus far so nobly advanced. It is rather for us to be here dedicated to the great task remaining before us—that from these honored dead we take increased devotion to that cause for which they gave the last full measure of devotion—that we here highly resolve that these dead shall not have died in vain, that this nation under God shall have a new birth of freedom, and that government of the people, by the people, for the people shall not perish from the earth.

LINCOLN/KENNEDY SPOOKY SIMILARITIES
- Lincoln and Kennedy each have 7 letters in their last names.
- Both were slain on a Friday in the presence of wives. Both presidents' wives also lost children through death while in the White House.
- Both were shot from behind and in the head.
- Both were concerned with civil rights.
- Lincoln's secretary, whose name was Kennedy, warned him not to go to the theater.
- Kennedy's secretary, named Lincoln, warned him not to go to Dallas.
- Both of their successors were named Johnson and both were Southern Democrats from the Senate: Andrew Johnson and Lyndon Johnson—each had 13 letters in their names. Andrew Johnson was born in 1808 and Lyndon Johnson was born in 1908. Both were opposed for re-election by men whose names started with G.
- John Wilkes Booth shot Lincoln at the theater and hid in a warehouse.
- Lee Harvey Oswald shot Kennedy from a warehouse and hid in a theater.
- Lee Harvey Oswald and John Wilkes Booth each have 15 letters in their names. Booth was born in 1839 and Oswald was born in 1939. Both were Southerners who favored unpopular ideas.
- Oswald and Booth were both murdered before trials could be arranged.

GARFIELD/McKINLEY
Less dramatic, less numerous and much less well-known than the Lincoln/Kennedy assassination parallels are those between the other two presidents who were shot and killed while in office: James A. Garfield and William McKinley:
- Both taught school and became lawyers.

- Both were Masons.
- Both were decorated for bravery in the Civil War
- Both were Republican senators from Ohio.
- Both were killed in September, in years that begin and end with "1"—Garfield in 1881, McKinley in 1901.
- Both were succeeded by vice presidents from New York.

TRIVIATA AMERICANUS

Contrary to popular belief, seamstress-upholsterer Betsy Ross played no part in the design of the first U.S. flag. The actual designer was Francis Hopkinson, congressional representative from Burlington, New Jersey, who, on May 25, 1780, billed Congress for this and other such official designs, requesting a quarter cask of public wine as "proper and reasonable reward for the labors of fancy." The only extant proof that Betsy Ross made any flags at all is a May 29, 1777 record of payment received for flags made for the Pennsylvania navy.

Samuel Wilson (1766-1854) was a patriotic meat packer who supplied provisions to the American army during the War of 1812. Goods for the soldiers were always stamped "U.S." The story goes that when visitors asked what the initials stood for, plant workers joked

133

that they meant "Uncle Sam" Wilson. The name stuck because Wilson had a reputation for hard work and integrity.

On March 13, 1852, the first cartoon depicting Uncle Sam as the symbol of the United States appeared in a drawing by Frank Bellew in the *New York Lantern*.

Each of the following presidents was born in a log cabin: Andrew Jackson, Zachary Taylor, Millard Fillmore, James Buchanan, Abraham Lincoln and James Garfield.

Millard Fillmore

Abraham Lincoln was the first president born outside the original 13 states.

According to *The Illustrated Dictionary of Place Names*, edited by Keslie Harder (*Facts on File*, 1985), the following communities are *not* named for Abraham Lincoln:
    Lincoln, CA—Lincoln Wilson, train official
    Lincolnton, GA—Benjamin Lincoln, Revolutionary War hero
    Lincoln, MA—Lincoln, Lincolnshire, England
    Lincoln, ME—Enoch Lincoln, former governor
    Lincolnton, NC—Benjamin Lincoln

Presidents John Adams and Thomas Jefferson both died on July 4,

1826, 50 years to the day of the signing of the Declaration of Independence.

On August 1, 1858, the first street letter boxes for mail collection were installed in Boston and New York.

On August 22, 1902, Theodore Roosevelt became the first president to ride in an auto.

On June 14, 1922, Warren G. Harding became the first president to make a radio speech.

The first woman candidate for president was Victoria Claflin Woodhull, who was nominated by the Equal Rights Party in 1872 (Ulysses S. Grant won the election).

The maintenance crew at the Statue of Liberty removes some 600 pounds of chewing gum a year.

The index finger of the Statue of Liberty is eight feet long.

Vermont is the only New England state lacking an ocean coastline.

Only two states are perfect rectangles: Colorado and Wyoming.

Arizona was the last mainland state to join the Union (1912).

The biggest employer in the United States is the United States, with a payroll over 3,200,000 people long. (The *percentage* of federal employees to total employees, however, is actually less now than it was in the fifties.)

As of spring 1991, there were 14 living Vietnam veterans whose names are carved in the black granite Vietnam monument in Washington, D.C., along with those who died in the war. The error occurred because a government clerk typed a wrong number into a computer. The records for the 14 vets have been corrected, but the names on the memorial can never be erased. Said Eugene J. Toni, one of the "undead": "It's like seeing your name on a gravestone. It's a very sobering thing."

HOW IMPORTANT IS ONE VOTE?

In 1645, one vote gave Oliver Cromwell control of England.

In 1649, one vote caused Charles I of England to be executed.

In 1845, one vote brought Texas into the Union.

In 1868, one vote saved President Andrew Johnson from impeachment.

In 1875, one vote changed France from a monarchy to a republic.

In 1876, one vote gave Rutherford B. Hayes the presidency of the U.S.

In 1923, one vote gave Adolf Hitler leadership of the Nazi party.

In 1941, one vote saved Selective Service—just weeks before Pearl Harbor was attacked.

—*ELECTION JUDGE'S MANUAL* (Missouri)

THE ZODIAC
. . . what the stars are saying about you and yours . . .

We are born at a given moment, in a given place, and like vintage wines we have the qualities of the year and of the season in which we are born. Astrology does not lay claim to anything more.
—Carl Jung

All of us art of the whole, chips off the old block. Grasping a glimpse of who we are is part of the gift of astrology.
—Sidney Omarr

ARE HOROSCOPES A GOOD SIGN?
Horoscope, schmoroscope. Zodiac, schmodiac. Can the stars truly foretell our fate, or ever so neatly reveal to us the features—and probable future courses—of our personalities? Or is the whole "what-sign-are-you?" mystique scant more than a lot of superstitious crap?

Hard to say. Maybe it depends on what sign you are!

One thing for sure, if it *is* all just some sort of elaborate hoax, it's a hoax with a long and multicultural pedigree—and one whose popularity is greater than ever, as witness the continuing success of astrology books, magazines and newspaper columns.

To begin with the word: "zodiac," a 2,000-year-old Greek word, means "ring of animals." Actually, that's not the real beginning, for the idea of a zodiac was conceived as a timekeeping device hundreds of years earlier by the ancient Babylonians, Chaldeans and the Chinese. Various types of zodiacs were developed as the basic concept spread from one culture to another. An overview of some of them is presented here.

WESTERN ZODIAC
(WITH TRADITIONAL VERSES)

Aries

I AM the beginning of life, I know not fear
I leap before I look, seeking new frontiers
My fiery spirit is a rare and precious gem
I'm the best in my field—an Aries I am!

The Ram
March 21—April 19
Rules the Head and Face
Element: Fire
Ruling Planet: Mars
Birthstone: Diamond
Flower: Daisy
Color: Red
Compatible Signs: Leo, Libra, Sagittarius

Ariens are leaders, the aces of the zodiacal deck: first in love, first in war and first in the hearts of those of their countrymen not put altogether off by all this pushy thirsting for firsting. Honesty, courage and independence—such are the lofty watchwords of these compulsive children of Mars. Yet, not unexpectedly, impatience remains their foremost failing, though Ariens erring this way may be characteristically loathe to admit it. But let's face it: you could do worse than first. Arien mottoes: "I am" and "I lead."

138

Taurus

I HAVE my feet firmly planted, I don't change as a rule
My patience astounds me, though my temper's not cool
Great beauty delights me, I feast even full
My possessions are treasures, I'm Taurus the Bull!

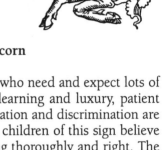

The Bull
April 20—May 20
Rules the Throat
Element: Earth
Ruling Planet: Venus
Birthstone: Sapphire
Flower: Narcissus
Color: Pink
Compatible Signs: Virgo, Libra, Capricorn

Taureans are expressively sensual lovers who need and expect lots of love in return. They are also lovers of learning and luxury, patient artists in the pursuit of beauty. Determination and discrimination are key ingredients in the Taurean mix, and children of this sign believe that anything worth doing is worth doing thoroughly and right. The obverse of this estimable trait is a tendency toward stubbornness, yet this is not so prevalent or serious as is commonly supposed. Taureans, in brief, can be the fastest of friends or the fiercest of foes—and that's no bull.

Gemini

I THINK very quickly, my tool is my wit
I'm here and I'm there, do seldom I sit
A Jack-of-All-Trades, I'm charming and fun
My life is a playground, I'm a Gemini Sun!

The Twins
May 21—June 20
Rules the Arms
Element: Air
Ruling Planet: Mercury
Birthstone: Pearl
Flower: Lily of the Valley
Color: Yellow
Compatible Signs: Aries, Libra, Aquarius

Gemini people, born beneath the sign of the twins, are volatile, change-able and gifted communicators whose personalities incline, at the odd-est of times, to do the splits. Witty and engaging, Geminis are good at getting grand projects well launched, but they are sometimes lacking in follow-through. The Gemini talent for tackling more than one major challenge at a time may lead to a perhaps unjustified reputation for double-dealing, but they're really much nicer than that—once you have perceived wherefrom, at a particular moment, they are coming.

Cancer

I FEEL very safe within my own home
I cling to my children, though times I may roam
I flow with the tide as my moods change each day
But I live in the past, that's the Cancer way!

The Crab
June 21—July 22
Rules the Breast
Element: Water
Ruling Body: Moon
Birthstone: Moonstone
Flower: Moonflower
Color: Silvery Green
Compatible Signs: Taurus, Scorpio, Pisces

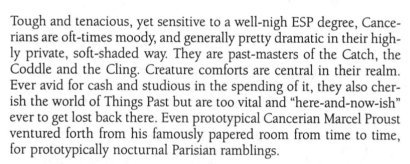

Tough and tenacious, yet sensitive to a well-nigh ESP degree, Cance-rians are oft-times moody, and generally pretty dramatic in their high-ly private, soft-shaded way. They are past-masters of the Catch, the Coddle and the Cling. Creature comforts are central in their realm. Ever avid for cash and studious in the spending of it, they also cher-ish the world of Things Past but are too vital and "here-and-now-ish" ever to get lost back there. Even prototypical Cancerian Marcel Proust ventured forth from his famously papered room from time to time, for prototypically nocturnal Parisian ramblings.

Leo

I WILL give you my heart, for I'm generous and kind
Leading the parade with my creative mind
I am King of the Jungle when let out of my cage
For the sun outshines all stars with a Leo on stage!

The Lion
July 23—August 22
Rules the Heart
Element: Fire
Ruling Body: Sun
Birthstone: Ruby
Flower: Marigold
Color: Gold
Compatible Signs: Aries, Libra, Sagittarius

Leos are regal, and regally regard praise and affection—aye, adulation even—to be their rightful, leonine lot. Courage, candor, a penchant for pleasure and more than a passing flair for the dramatic are other attributes of this mighty sign: Leos have a propensity for grandeur and high-flying style that is unique among the stars. Sensitive and caring, and skilled as a Libra or Pisces at making friends, Leo's faults are few, the principal being an occasional tendency toward arrogance.

Virgo

I ANALYZE in detail all life that I see
Putting things in order according to me
My service is endless for work is my theme
Perfection in all things is the true Virgo's dream!

The Virgin
August 23—September 22
Rules the Bowels
Element: Earth
Ruling Planet: Mercury
Birthstone: Sapphire
Flower: Hyacinth
Color: Blue
Compatible Signs: Taurus, Capricorn, Cancer

Virgo, the Celestial Virgin, is viable, but not by a helluva lot—thanks to a sometimes persnickety passion for perfection that can strain relations with those born under other signs. Mentally agile and facilely adaptable, Virgos also have a great capacity for sensuality—but a curiously sweatless sensuality that sometimes suffers from a psychic underlay of virtuous, vestal thorns. Worldliness and practicality are important Virgoan traits, yet lots of love and kindness are needed to keep the balance true. Chief bugaboo is a tendency toward egoism.

141

Libra

I BALANCE the scales, for that's only fair
I weigh one side then the other expressing great care
I seek love and harmony in all I pursue
Though making decisions a Libran can't do!

The Scales
September 23—October 22
Rules the Loins
Element: Air
Ruling Planet: Venus
Birthstone: Opal
Flower: Violet
Color: Magenta
Compatible Signs: Aries, Gemini, Aquarius

Libra, unbalanced balance that it is, constitutes a paradox: though Librans are born beneath the zodiac's only inanimate sign, they are among the most animate and avid of lovers and/or friends, charming and argumentative, serious and flirty by turns—as is their fluctuant wont. Naturally enough, they are also practical idealists, sympathetic seekers after Peace and Harmony and Justice—never quite reaching their grand goals, yet never falling so short that they think of giving up. Procrastination and moodiness are their main dangers, which, just often enough, they manage to generally skirt.

Scorpio

I DESIRE reform on all levels of life
With a penetrating force as sharp as a knife
My passion and power makes others seem weak
Intensely life's secrets the Scorpio seeks!

The Scorpion
October 23—November 21
Rules the Groin
Element: Water
Ruling Planet: Pluto
Birthstone: Topaz
Flower: Honeysuckle
Color: Purple
Compatible Signs: Cancer, Capricorn,

Supremely sexy and instinctively secretive, Scorpio is one of the heaviest of the heavenly signs. Treated right, Scorpios are delighted to treat in return. Crossed, their awesome powers tend to short-circuit into avenues of revenge and contempt, which often give rise to time-and-energy-zapping stratagems. Scorpios have an uncanny ability to keep quite cool despite any number of outward pressures and inward smolderings. Operating under the dominant idea of "I desire," the children of this clawsome sign possess the energy, pride, magnetism and willpower needed to parlay desire into fulfillment. Scorpio pitfalls are jealousy and stubbornness.

Sagittarius

I ASPIRE to greatness, my manner is grand
A natural philosopher—half horse and half man.
I'm openly honest and religiously inclined.
Good luck seems to follow the Sagittarian kind!

The Archer
November 22—December 21
Rules the Thighs
Element: Fire
Ruling Planet: Jupiter
Birthstone: Turquoise
Flower: Carnation
Color: Turquoise
Compatible Signs: Aries, Leo, Libra

The Centaur/Archer likes living life on a proverbial magic carpet, ever-ready for travel and adventure and discovery: most at home on the roam. This high flyer is bright, energetic, loyal and outspoken, a born lover of sports and the outdoors. Sagittarians find it relatively easy to glide through dark times toward the light, sometimes even helping friends along the same saving way. On the other hand, Sagittarian honesty can occasionally be brutal, and there is a tendency toward smugness—a perhaps forgivable smugness, considering the qualities involved.

Capricorn

I UTILIZE life's knowledge, for wisdom is gold
I'm old when I'm young, and young when I'm old
ambitious and patient while sowing my seeds
Through hard work and discipline, the Capricorn succeeds!

The Goat
December 22—January 19
Rules the Knees
Element: Earth
Ruling Planet: Saturn
Birthstone: Onyx
Flower: Holly
Color: Dark Green
Compatible Signs: Taurus, Cancer, Virgo

Capricorns are heavy on determination and accomplishment, but rather light on lightness. Goatlike, they traverse steep obstacles, chewing up impediments as though they were some kind of perverse new food. These frequently hoary climbers are, in fact, embodiments of the creed of "If at first you don't succeed," etc., though non-Capricorns might question whether such single-minded goal-gaining be worth the price. Sensitive enough behind their hard-bitten exteriors, Capricorns are as capable of love as almost anyone—but "it don't come easy." Infinite, weighty patience remains this sign's particular blessing—and curse.

Aquarius

I KNOW only freedom, for space won't confine
My inventive manner for helping mankind
My thoughts are original, and detached like a sage
I'm the awakening truth—I'm the Aquarian age!

The Water Bearer
January 20—February 18
Rules the Legs
Element: Air
Ruling Planet: Uranus
Birthstone: Jade
Flower: Daffodil
Color: Dark Red
Compatible Signs: Gemini, Leo, Libra

Aquarians are ever-artful strokers in the swim of life, brainy and creative and progressive, and hardly ever rippled by fate's waves: steadiness sails them through, even where strivers from other signs might have given up or, at the very least, tarried. Idealism is a large part of the Aquarian picture and those born in this period place high value on education and friendship, love a good argument and are said to have an inborn flair for such things as invention, reformation and—from time to time—downright revolution. (Norman Mailer, for one, is a pretty good example of a fully-realized Aquarius.)

Pisces

I BELIEVE in compassion, my intuition flows free
Both upstream and downstream, two fish in the sea
Receptive to all things, inspirational too
All phases of life has the Pisces been through!

The Fish
February 19—March 20
Rules the Feet
Element: Water
Ruling Planet: Neptune
Birthstone: Amethyst
Flower: Water Lily
Color: Blue—Green
Compatible Signs: Cancer, Scorpio, Capricorn

Pisces, final and perhaps most mysterious sign of the zodiac, is represented by two counterpoised fish, one swimming upstream, the other down. This duality of image vividly limns the all-pervasive Piscean involvement in every aspect of birth and death. Highly sensitive, adaptable and fond of comfort and luxury, Pisces people are peace-loving and religious, with a strong pull toward fantasy and the occult. They also possess an easygoing charm that tends to win them friends from all the other signs. Main Piscean pitfall: a tendency toward simple possessiveness and/or compound jealousy.

CHINESE ZODIAC

Some historians have linked the Chinese zodiac, for instance, to India, while others have called it a purely Chinese creation. Several legends, of varying fancifulness, trace the Chinese zodiac to the Buddha. Writer Herb Daniels of the *Chicago Tribune* relates one of these:

Once upon a time (says the legend) the Lord Buddha summoned all the beasts to a rendezvous, but only twelve came. To reward these faithful creatures through all of time Buddha decreed that each would have every twelfth month named for him. The first to arrive, the Rat, gave him name to the first year of the cycle. In order, the others were the Ox (also called Buffalo), Tiger, Hare (some say Cat), Dragon, Snake, Horse, Sheep (or Goat), Monkey, Rooster, Dog and. finally the easygoing Pig (or Boar). The cycle repeats each twelve years.... Chinese augury holds that we are marked by the nature of the animal of our birth year.... While our destiny is shaped by the year sign, we can control our lives.... We must exploit the sign's strengths and overcome the weaknesses.... We are also helped if we know the signs of others and how they affect us.

While the Western zodiac is read from east to west, as the sun seemingly travels, the Chinese zodiac reads from west to east. Some scholars have suggested that this clockwise factor might have at one time led people to use this most unique zodiac to count hours of the day (in two-hour intervals) as well as months. Your year of birth determines your Chinese zodiac sign—unless you were born before the Chinese New Year, in which case you take the sign of the preceding year. The Chinese New Year is celebrated at the first new moon after the sun enters Aquarius—sometime between January 21 and February 19. (The Chinese lunar year is divided into 12 months of 29 or 30 days; the calendar is synchronized with the solar year by the addition of extra months at regular intervals. The years are arranged in major cycles of 60 years, each successive year being named after one of the 12 animals. These cycles are continuously repeated.)

YOUR CHINESE ZODIAC SIGN

Rat	Ox (Buffalo)	Tiger	Hare (Cat)	Dragon	Snake	Horse	Sheep (Goat)	Monkey	Rooster	Dog	Pig (Boar)
1900	1901	1902	1903	1904	1905	1906	1907	1908	1909	1910	1911
1912	1913	1914	1915	1916	1917	1918	1919	1920	1921	1922	1923
1924	1925	1926	1927	1928	1929	1930	1931	1932	1933	1934	1935
1936	1937	1938	1939	1940	1941	1942	1943	1944	1945	1946	1947
1948	1949	1950	1951	1952	1953	1954	1955	1956	1957	1958	1959
1960	1961	1962	1963	1964	1965	1966	1967	1968	1969	1970	1971
1972	1973	1974	1975	1976	1977	1978	1979	1980	1981	1982	1983
1984	1985	1986	1987	1988	1989	1990	1991	1992	1993	1994	1995
1996	1997	1998	1999	2000	2001	2002	2003	2004	2005	2006	2007

Rat

You are imaginative, charming, attractive to the opposite sex and generous to those you love. You are also articulate, incisive, creative and well-suited to the "race" named for your species—but you must guard against a tendency to be quick-tempered, hypercritical and opportunistic. Careerwise, you should be happy in sales, or as a writer, publicist or critic. You get along best with a Dragon, Ox or Monkey—but avoid the Horse

Some famous Rats: Shakespeare, Mozart, Tolstoy, Washington, Churchill, Louis Armstrong, Truman Capote.

Ox (or Buffalo)

You are quiet, conservative, methodical and good with your hands. Though usually quite reserved, you can be an engaging storyteller. You can also be a most Latinous lover, but you seldom let romance divert you very far from long-range career goals. You hate artifice, so linkups with the Snake or Monkey, who strangely attract you, often end up in a malfunction mode. Rats find you fascinating and will follow you anywhere.

Some famous Oxen: Aristotle, J. S. Bach, Napoleon, Van Gogh, Charlie Chaplin, Hitler, Richard Burton.

Tiger

You are sensitive, passionate and rebellious. You have it in you to be a leader, either in the military or in business, or as a risktaker exploring strange terrain, racing cars or even fighting bulls. But you must keep a cool lid on your hot temper, and try to be less stubborn. Romance is an important ingredient in your seldom-boring lifestyle. You have an affinity for Dragons and Dogs, but steer clear of the Ox.

Some famous Tigers: Mohammed; Marco Polo; Mary, Queen of Scots; Beethoven; Karl Marx; Hugh Hefner; Marilyn Monroe.

Hare (or Cat)

You are affectionate, hospitable and industrious. Discretion is one of your long suits, as well as a related aversion to controversy. But be on guard against carrying either conservativism or sentiment to extremes. Hares, especially those of the female persuasion, are generally noted for their good taste and sophistication. You get along swimmingly with Pigs, Sheep and Dogs, much less so with Dragons and Roosters.

Some famous Hares: Confucius, Martin Luther, Queen Victoria, Einstein, Eva Perón, Orson Welles, Fidel Castro.

Dragon

You are vital and enthusiastic, and lucky in love and money. What's more, you have a winsome way of sharing your luck with others. You are also stylish, shrewd and sentimental. Your perfectionism, however, often makes you too critical and demanding. Your special callings include artist, priest or politician. Romance with a Monkey or Rooster will likely flourish, and from a Rat you can expect total devotion; for fireworks, try a Tiger.

Some famous Dragons: Joan of Arc, Sarah Bernhardt, George Bernard Shaw, Freud, Pearl Buck, Salvador Dali, Gina Lollobrigida.

Snake

You are serious, determined, wise and charming. The good news about you and money is that you're darn good at getting it; the bad news is that you're not good at sharing it. Other typical Snaky shortcomings to guard against are jealousy and possessiveness. Oxen and Roosters are your natural companions, but Tigers may well be detrimental to your health, as you may be detrimental to that of the Pig.

Some famous Snakes: Darwin, Poe, Lincoln, Princess Grace of Monaco, John Kennedy, Jackie Onassis, Bob Dylan.

Horse

You are outgoing, intelligent and incredibly hardworking. You are also self-willed and sympathetic. Your particular pitfalls are selfishness and egotism; the hope is that your innate cunning and friendliness will find or forge ways around such failings. Your chances of living happily ever after are best with a Dog, Tiger or Sheep, while with a Rat or Ox the going can get bumpy indeed.

Some famous Horses: Rembrandt, Chopin, Davy Crockett, Buffalo Bill, Mike Wallace, Neil Armstrong, Betty Ford.

Sheep (or Goat)

You are a bit of a dreamer, artistic and innovative. You are also elegant and charming, but often get off on the wrong foot with people and have a tendency to complain too much. You dislike snap decisions, but in a tight spot you can be quick, cool, even ruthless. You get along well with Monkeys, Hares and Pigs, but wavelengths go awry when it comes to Rats, Oxen and Tigers.

Some famous Sheep: Michelangelo, Cesare Borgia, Cervantes, Mark Twain, Orville Wright, Valentino, Mussolini.

Monkey

You are creative, cultured and quick of wit. Your high intelligence and magnetic personality ensure success in almost any field in which you care to cavort. Monkeyish tendencies to guard against include galloping opportunism and an overly distrustful attitude. You mingle especially well with Rats, Dragons and Snakes, but hanky-panky with Pigs can be bad news—especially for the Pigs. As for Tigers, forget it—they have little use for Monkey business of any kind.

Some famous Monkeys: Julius Caesar, Leonardo da Vinci, Harry S Truman, Charlie Parker, Elizabeth Taylor, Lyndon Johnson, Ted Kennedy.

Rooster

You are industrious, decisive and shrewd when it comes to love, business or politics. Your flashy veneer belies a conservative core. You can converse brilliantly, but you tend to be boastful and overly candid. You like to dream bold dreams, and when you set your mind to it, you have the industry to make them come true. You'd be happy as a restaurant owner, publicist, soldier or world traveler. You interface well with Dragons, Oxen and Snakes—but life with another Rooster would be nothing to crow about.

Some famous Roosters: Rudyard Kipling, Enrico Caruso, Joseph Goebbels, William Faulkner, John Glenn, Pope Paul VI, Charles Bronson.

Dog

You are honest, loyal and faithful—a person of principles, who sometimes has trouble putting feelings into words. You can also be a rather worrisome worrywart, with a tendency to faultfind to a degree the findees find uncomfortable—so lighten up! High on your career-aptitude list are businessman, activist, teacher or secret agent. You have a natural affinity with Horses and, to a lesser extent, Tigers and Hares. But wend warily amongst Roosters, Dragons and Rats.

Some famous Dogs: Socrates, Voltaire, Benjamin Franklin, Proust, Lenin, George Gershwin, Herbert Hoover.

Pig (or Boar)

You are quiet, sincere, ethical and fiscally adroit. Also sensual and loving—yet, alas, usually unlucky in love. You read avidly and are often wont to wax philosophical. Career-wise, you'd doubtless do well as an artist, entertainer or lawyer. While you combine culture and earthiness in a way that attracts interest from all the other signs, your best bet may be the Hare, while the Sheep could make a valued partner. But steer clear of Rats, Monkeys and Dragons, as they tend to take advantage of your better nature.

Some famous Pigs: Henry VIII, Bismarck, John D. Rockefeller, Henry Ford, Albert Schweitzer, Ernest Hemingway.

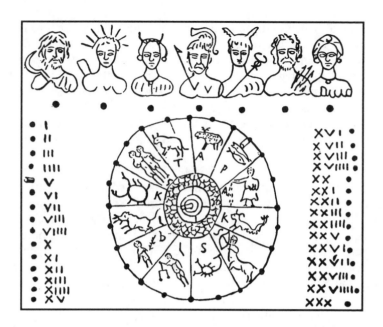

ROMAN ASTROLOGY

In this Roman "calendar stone" in the Museum at Würzburg (from Weltall und Menschheit, Vol. III), the deities presiding over the seven days of the week are pictured on the top: Saturn for Saturday; Mithra, the sun god, for Sunday; Diana, the moon goddess, for Monday; Mars, the Teutonic "Tiw," for Tuesday; Mercury, the Teutonic "Woden" or "Odin," for Wednesday; Jupiter, the Teutonic "Thor," for Thursday; Venus, the Teutonic "Frigg" or "Freta," for Friday. The circle represents the crude picture of the zodiac beginning at the top with Aries and running around to the left, each sign being accompanied by the initial of its name.

It was a Roman of old, by the way, who authored the earliest known treatise on astrology, Astronomica. He was a poet named Marcus Manilius, who lived in the reigns of Augustus and Tiberius. The five-volume Astronomica, written in the form of a Latin didactic (instructive) poem, sheds much light on the doctrines, symbolic themes, and mathematics of Roman astrology on the threshold of the Christian era. Manilius's image-laden description of the zodiac shows how pervasive was the influence of Greek mythology on the Roman mind:

Resplendent in his golden fleece the Ram leads the way and looks back with wonder at the backward rising of the Bull, who with lowered face and brow summons the Twins; these the Crab follows, the Lion the Crab, and the Virgin, the Lion. Then the Bal-

150

ance, having matched daylight with the length of night, draws on the Scorpion, ablaze with his glittering stars, at whose tail the man with the body of a horse aims with taut bow a winged shaft, ever in act to shoot. Next comes Capricorn, curled up within his cramped constellation, and after him from urn upturned the Waterman pours forth the wonted stream for the Fishes which swim eagerly into it; and these bring up the rear of the signs to be joined by the Ram.

HINDU ZODIAC

The Hindu zodiac demonstrates how densely interwoven are a culture's science, art and religion. Akin to astronomy, but enriched by fable and a yearning for the divine, Indian astrology is a unique creation that presupposes a belief in reincarnation. Another distinguishing difference is the importance of the moon as an influencing factor, as well as the belief that the sun, considered powerful but largely malefic, controls the heart, while the moon controls the mind.

151

ARABIAN ZODIAC

In the Middle Ages astrology in Persia flourished under the patronage of caliphs such as the famous Harun al-Rashid. An observatory was built in Baghdad and used by astrologers like Albumasar, whose book on the subject was one of the first published after the invention of the printing press. The 13th-century Arabian zodiac shown above was engraved on a so-called "magic" mirror, embellished with the inscription: "To the Sovereign Prince Abulfald, Victorious Sultan, Light of the World."

HEALTH MATTERS
. . . *getting well, staying well . . .*

Quit worrying about your health. It'll go away.
—ROBERT ORBEN

Always laugh when you can. It is cheap medicine.
—LORD BYRON

WHAT'S REALLY, *REALLY* IMPORTANT

Money is nice and fun is fine, but what matters most of all is the state of the brain and body involved in such fineries and funsome times. Or as my dear departed grandmother once said: "If you ain't got your health, you ain't got nothin'!" (Actually, she generally spoke a lot correcter than that, but often waxed slangful when emphasizing some truly heartfelt wad of wisdom.)

The point of all this being that this is indubitably one of the *Almanac's* two most important chapters—along with the immediately following chapter on food, inasmuch as that one is but an extension of this.

So, without further ado . . .

153

FIRST AID

Note: This and the following items on medical emergencies are intended solely as general guides to appropriate care for individuals in obvious physical distress. Because every medical emergency involves unique circumstances and conditions, it is always recommended that the advice and care of medical professionals be sought as soon as possible.

First aid is defined as the immediate, temporary care given a victim of accident or sudden illness until a physician's services can be obtained. It begins with the steadying effect on the stricken person when he or she realizes that competent hands will be giving help. The well-selected word of encouragement, the adoption of a soothing and placid manner, the telephone calls to summon help and notify relatives—these, too, are first aid.

Here follows a checklist of procedures for some commonly occurring health emergencies. In every case, if the injury or illness seems even in the slightest degree serious, a physician should be summoned at once. Avoid attempting any detailed prognosis—your task should be simply to avert any immediately pressing crisis and keep the victim as comfortable as possible until help arrives.

Animal bites—Cleanse wound with a solution of soap and water, removing all saliva, then rinse with clean running water and apply a sterile dressing. Check with doctor to determine if preventive measures against tetanus are needed.

Asphyxiation—Get victim to fresh air, if possible; at least open all windows and doors and loosen victim's clothing. Begin mouth-to-mouth resuscitation immediately.

Bleeding—Press hard on wound with sterile compress. Use part of clothing or bare hand if compress is unavailable.

Burns—If burn is minor, immerse quickly in cold water or apply ice until pain stops. Do not break blisters. If burn appears serious or if pain persists, keep victim as comfortable as possible until doctor arrives.

Chemicals in eye—Wash eye with a solution of sodium bicarbonate (a teaspoonful of baking soda to a glass of water) or plain water. Have victim close the eye, place an eye pad or piece of cotton over the lid, and bandage.

Convulsions (including epileptic)—Do not attempt to restrain victim, but protect him from injury by pushing away adjacent objects. Gently try to prevent him from biting his tongue by placing an appropriate object (such as a wrapped spoon handle) between his upper and lower teeth on one side of the mouth.

Electric shock—Cut off current, if possible. Separate person from electrical contact with some nonconducting object such as a broomstick, being sure that your hands are dry and that you are standing on a dry surface. If victim's breathing has stopped, begin artificial respiration.

Fainting—Put victim on his back and keep him recumbent until recovery is complete, otherwise he may faint again when he gets up. (A good rule of thumb is to keep victim prone for at least 15 minutes.) Open windows and loosen patient's clothing. Briefly place aromatic spirits of ammonia or smelling salts under victim's nose.

Fracture (or sprain)—Do not move victim. Immobilize and cushion affected body area with dressing and splint or splintlike object. If affected part is a foot, leave shoe on, but loosen laces to allow for swelling. Treat victim for bleeding and shock, as required.

Frostbite—Cover frozen part, but do not rub it with hand or snow. Bring victim indoors and immerse frozen part in water at body temperature, but not hot water. Handle frozen part with great care; do not apply hot-water bottle or heat lamp. Once fingers or toes are rewarmed, encourage victim to exercise them gently. Do not disturb blisters.

Poisoning—Try to obtain container or label of poison for identification purposes (often antidote will be indicated thereon). Obtain medical advice by telephone as quickly as possible. Except when strong acids, lye and other caustics, or petroleum products are involved, try to induce vomiting. If the poison or antidote is unknown, quickly administer milk and/or water in large amounts—four glasses or more with adults.

Shock—Keep victim lying down, unless there is difficulty in breathing, in which case his head and chest should be elevated. Maintain victim's normal body temperature; cover him lightly to prevent a possible chill, but do not induce sweating. If weather is hot and victim appears overheated, loosen his clothing, and, if indoors, open windows.

—AMERICAN RED CROSS

CPR

CPR, or cardiopulmonary resuscitation, can be a lifesaver when a person's heart and lungs stop functioning because of a heart attack, shock, drowning or other cause. However, it is best to have formal CPR training before attempting it as first aid. Contact a chapter of the American Heart Association or the American Red Cross for information. CPR should be used only if you have determined that both heartbeat and breathing have stopped.

**(Mouth-to-Mouth Breathing—in Cases Like
Drowning, Electric Shock or Smoke Inhalation)**

There is need for help in breathing when breathing movements stop or lips, tongue and fingernails become blue. When in doubt, apply artificial respiration until you get medical help. No harm can result from its use and delay may cost the patient his or her life. Start immediately. Seconds count. Clear mouth and throat of any obstructions with your fingers.

For Adults: Place patient on back with face up.

Lift the chin and tilt the head back. If air passage is still closed, pull chin up by placing fingers behind the angles of the lower jaw and pushing forward.

Take deep breath, place your mouth over patient's mouth, making leak-proof seal.

Pinch patient's nostrils closed.

Blow into patient's mouth until you see his or her chest rise.

—OR—

Take deep breath, place your mouth over patient's nose, making leak-proof seal.

Seal patient's mouth with your hand.

Blow into patient's nose until you see chest rise.

Remove your mouth and let patient exhale.

Repeat either method used about 12 times a minute. (If the patient's stomach rises markedly, exert moderate hand pressure on the stomach just below the rib cage to keep it from inflating.)

For Infants and Small Children: Place your mouth over patient's mouth and nose. Blow into mouth and nose until you see patient's chest rise normally.

Repeat 20 to 30 times a minute. (Don't exaggerate the tilted position of an infant's head.)

Note: For emergency treatment of heart attack, CPR is recommended.
—COUNCIL ON FAMILY HEALTH

THE HEIMLICH MANEUVER

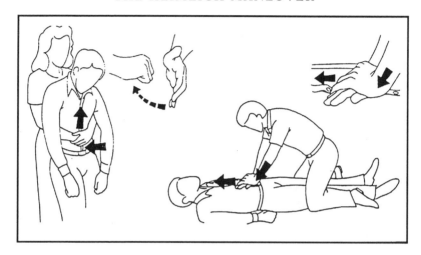

What to look for: Victim is choking on food and cannot speak or breathe; turns blue; collapses.

To perform the Heimlich maneuver when the victim is standing or sitting:

1. Stand behind the victim and wrap your arms around his waist.

2. Place the thumb side of your fist against the victim's abdomen, slightly above the navel and below the rib cage.

3. Grasp your fist with the other hand and press your fist into the victim's abdomen with a quick upward thrust. Repeat as necessary.

4. If the victim is sitting, stand behind the victim's chair and perform the maneuver in the same manner.

5. After the food is dislodged, have the victim seen by a doctor.

When the victim has collapsed and cannot be lifted:

1. Lay the victim on his back.

2. Face the victim and kneel astride his hips.

3. With one hand on top of the other, place the heel of your bottom hand on the abdomen slightly above the navel and below the rib cage.

4. Press into the victim's abdomen with a quick upward thrust. Repeat as often as necessary.

5. Should the victim vomit, quickly place him on his side and wipe out his mouth to prevent aspiration (drawing of vomit into the throat).

6. After the food is dislodged, have the victim seen by a doctor.

Note: If you start to choke when alone and help is not available, an attempt should be made to self-administer this maneuver.

—COURTESY OF NEW YORK CITY DEPARTMENT OF HEALTH

HEIMLICH VS. DROWNING

The Heimlich Maneuver for drowning victims:

• Place unconscious victim on back. Turn face to one side to allow water to drain from mouth.

• Facing victim, kneel astride victim's hips.

• With one hand on top of the other, place the heel of bottom hand on the abdomen slightly above the navel and below the rib cage.

• Press into the victim's abdomen with a quick upward thrust. Repeat thrusts until water no longer flows from mouth.

• If no response, proceed with cardiopulmonary resuscitation.

OTHER COMMON EMERGENCIES
Bruises

Symptoms:

Blue-black discoloration of skin; swelling; pain.

Treatment:

1. Reduce pain and swelling by applying gentle pressure with a cold compress soon after getting bruised.

2. If the bruise is severe, rest the affected part and elevate it if possible.

3. If you are concerned about the size or appearance of the bruise, or if pain persists, see a doctor.

Heart Attack

Symptoms:

Chest pain, unrelated to any former exertion and becoming increasingly severe; intense pressure, tightness or squeezing in the center of the chest persisting for five minutes or more; pain may spread across the chest to the shoulders, arms, neck, or jaw; sweating, nausea, shortness of breath, and faintness; patient may become unconscious; pain is not influenced by swallowing, or by a change in the victim's position; victim may perspire, skin becomes pale and cool.

Caution: Do not give alcohol, food or water; do not apply smelling salts; if the victim is under medical care, give him the prescribed medicine.

Treatment:

1. Allow the victim to sit, or prop him or her up with two pillows

or the equivalent.

2. Summon an ambulance immediately.

3. If an ambulance is not available, transport the victim, sitting up, to a hospital, or to a doctor if one is near.

4. If the patient loses consciousness, check breathing and pulse.

5. If there is pulse but no breathing, begin artificial respiration;

6. If there is no pulse, begin CPR.

Heat Exhaustion

Symptoms:

Normal body temperature; pale, moist skin; sweating; weakness; headache or dizziness; possible muscle cramps or spasms; possible nausea or vomiting; any, some or all of the above.

Treatment:

1. Immediately move the victim to a cooler area—from the sun into the shade or from heat outdoors to an air-conditioned room indoors.

2. Have the victim lie down. Loosen or remove his or her clothing.

3. Elevate the victim's feet slightly.

4. If the victim is unconscious, use artificial respiration.

5. Cool the victim as much as possible with cool cloths, a fan or an air conditioner.

6. If the victim is conscious and not vomiting, give him or her sips of juice or cool salt water (a teaspoon of salt per glass of water). If victim begins to vomit, stop fluids.

7. If symptoms persist or worsen, call for medical help.

—*U.S. News & World Report Guide to Family First Aid*

THE "FIREMAN'S LIFT"

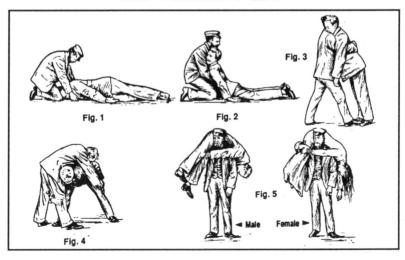

Fig. 1

Fig. 2

Fig. 3

Fig. 4

Fig. 5

◄ Male   Female ►

From *Cutler's Red Book of Ready Reference* (1903) comes this five-step guide to "A Way to Carry the Unconscious." As the accompanying caption somewhat quaintly puts it: "Because the mode illustrated above for carrying unconscious persons was first generally adopted by metropolitan fire brigades, it has become known as the Fireman's Lift. The reader can readily understand, however, that it may be applied in countless emergency cases, such as those of brain injury, sunstroke, drowning, etc. The five positions should be studied carefully, the difference in the fifth being especially noted."

10 GOLDEN RULES FOR GOOD HEALTH

1. Have a checkup every year.
2. Be a nonsmoker.
3. Drink in moderation.
4. Count each calorie.
5. Watch your cholesterol.
6. Learn nutritional values.
7. Find time for leisure and vacations.
8. Adjust to life's daily pressures.
9. Develop an exercise program.
10. Understand your physical assets and limitations.
   —THE AMERICAN HEALTH FOUNDATION.

MEDICINE-CABINET CHECKLIST

Here is a list of items prudent homemakers should have in their medicine cabinets:

Antidotes for poison
Antiseptic for cuts & scratches
Aromatic spirits of ammonia
Aspirin
Bandages & adhesive tape
Burn & sunburn lotion
Cold tablets
Cotton (sterile) & cotton swabs
Cough syrup
Eye drops
Foot care products
Insect repellent & sting medication
Iodine
Lip balm
Nasal spray
Oil of wintergreen
Petroleum jelly
Poison ivy lotion
Rubbing alcohol
Scissors (small)
Sterile gauze compresses
Thermometers (oral & rectal)
Tweezers

U.S. LONGEVITY INCREASES

Despite the onslaught of AIDS, Americans are living longer than ever—an average of 75.8 years, according to the Centers for Disease

Control and Prevention. This was a rise of 0.3 over the year before. (Worldwide, the U.S. has a way to go to match the longevity leaders: Japan, about 79 years; and Canada, France, Greece, Italy, Spain and Sweden—among others—all about 78 years.)

The overall death rate in the U.S. was the lowest ever in 1992, failing to 504.5 per 100.000 people. The infant mortality rate for the same year also reached an all-time low—8.5 deaths per 1,000 live births, compared with 8.9 per 1,000 in 1991.

Death rates for 12 of the 15 leading killers dropped in 1992, but the 33,466 deaths from AIDS represented an 11.5 percent increased over the year before. AIDS is now the eighth leading cause of death.

THE ODDS OF DYING

Some people are just dying to live dangerously. Are you? You can gauge your own chances of surviving life in the riskier lanes by checking out the following stats from the *Journal of the American Medical Association:*

Voluntary Risks

Motorcycling	1 in 50
Smoking 1 pack of cigarettes a day	1 in 200
Power boating	1 in 5,900*
Drinking 1 bottle of wine a day	1 in 13,300
Canoeing	1 in 100,000**
Skiing	1 in 430,000**
Involuntary Risks	
Influenza	1 in 5,000
Struck by automobile	1 in 20,000
Tornado (Midwest)	1 in 455,000
Earthquake (California)	1 in 588,000
Falling aircraft	1 in 10,000,000
Release from nuclear-power station	1 in 10,000,000

* Based on deaths per million participants per year.
** Based on deaths per million hours per year spent in sport

WHOLLY HOLISTIC

Feeling sad? Listless? Jumpy? Lumpy? Stuffed? Constipated? Muscle-achey? Out of breath after anything more strenuous than a walk to or from your car? Out of patience with the little pricks and arrows of life that mar your passing days?

Is *that* what's bothering you, Bunky?

Do you wish you could deal with all this *stuff* without going through the standard, compartmentalized options currently offered by the AMA-dominated medical establishment? To doctors and prescription-drug manufacturers who all too often seem more concerned with *their* bottom lines than *your* well-being?

The good news is that there *are* alternatives—the natural, environmentally-friendly options known collectively as holistic medicine, the art and science of which have been practiced quite successfully now for over 5,000 years.

Merriam-Webster's Collegiate Dictionary defines *holistic* as "relating to or concerned with wholes, or with complete systems rather than with the analysis of, treatment of, or dissection into parts (*holistic* medicine attempts to treat both the mind and the body / *holistic* ecology views man and the environment as a single system)."

At the heart of the holistic approach is the realization that we all need to start being our own physicians—at least to the extent of taking much better care of ourselves than most of us have, and keeping our contacts with the health establishment to an absolute minimum.

To do this, we need to learn simpler, less risk-laden ways to manage stress—such as yoga, meditation and exercise. We also need to eat more wisely, choosing organic foods and natural supplements like wheatgrass juice and blue-green algae. As for medicinal cures, relaxants and/or pick-me-ups, we would do well to turn first to Mother Nature's bounty of herbs before automatically accepting the prescribed chemical fixes. (For a wide range of healthful herb teas, see "Herbs to Drink" by Carol Pearson, in the next chapter, "Food for Thought—and Action.")

Other things you can do to get started on the holistic path to health:

• Visit your library, bookstore, or health-food store and check out alternative-lifestyle books, magazines and catalogs. Find out how others are making the transition from the overly-specialized, AMA-dominated world of conventional medicine to the less fragmented, more patient-friendly holistic universe.

• Get plenty of sunlight and use full-spectrum lighting indoors.

• Put nutrition at the top of your shopping list—nix the canned and frozen stuff. Eat plenty of fresh fruits and veggies, especially such pungently potent foods as onion and garlic, both effective killers of diverse bacteria, including those that cause food poisoning and skin viruses. And if you've never thought of a bag of fresh sprouts as legitimate snack food—something tasty as well as beneficial—give it a try.

• Do more of your own cooking. It's healthier than buying packaged meals and cheaper than eating out—and it provides a true sense of satisfaction when, with practice, you find your efforts translating into tasty, healthful repasts.

• Use baking soda in paste form to treat sunburn, rashes, canker sores, insect bites, bee stings and skin irritations.

- Use the leaves of the tea tree for athlete's foot, nail infections and mouth sores.
- Use exercise, stretching and deep-breathing routines to handle stress and strain. Stave off carpal-tunnel syndrome and other repetitive body-stress problems by taking regular breaks in which to alternatively flex the muscles involved.
- Wear wool and natural clothes.
- Sign up for such de-stressing, health-engendering classes as yoga, meditation, Tai Chi, cooking and herbal gardening.
- Laugh a lot. As Mary Pettibone Poole once said, "He who laughs, lasts."

Remember, only you can find the path to holistic health and harmony that's just right for you—and the only "test" in this class is the ongoing one reality administers every moment.

—CHUCK L' HEUREUX

ACUPUNCTURE

There has been much interest recently in the traditional Chinese surgical technique called "acupuncture," which involves the sticking of brass-handled metal needles into a patient's nerve centers, and thereby anesthetizing a particular body part (or parts).

The interest in acupuncture followed upon the recent report of Americans in China who witnessed major operations performed there on conscious patients who had not received any conventional anesthetic. In one case a woman undergoing open heart surgery sipped orange juice and smiled at onlookers while the surgeon held her heart in his hand.

In another case, a tumor patient had two needles in each wrist; one acupuncturist at each wrist was constantly twisting the needles, while the patient kept the doctor informed as to when the numbness began setting in, which took 20 to 30 minutes.

Asked to explain how acupuncture works, Dr. Chu Yu-kuang, head surgeon in a hospital in Wuhan, China, stated, "It is very difficult to explain exactly what happens. There are about five hundred nerve points in the body that we know we can use. We know the results we will get, but we cannot explain exactly why we get them."

COMMON COLD, UNCOMMON NUISANCE

The cold rule of three: It takes three days
to get a cold, three days to have a cold,
and three days to get over a cold.
—VERONICA CUNNINGHAM, chemist

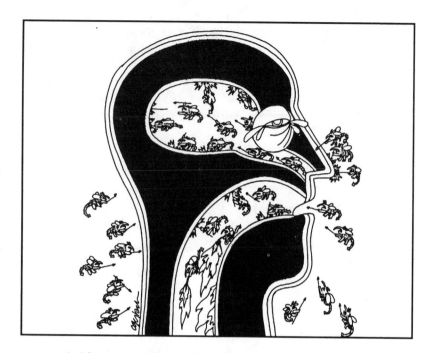

Into each life some colds may fall—2.2 a year per American adult, to be exact. That they're a genuine, certified pain in the kazoo—and most everywhere else, for that matter—goes without saying. Thanks to the common cold's very commonness, we needn't expound upon symptoms.

The only real question remaining is: Is there a cure in sight?

The bad news is: No.

The good news is: Some new approaches being offered could lead to reducing the number of colds one gets. The possibilities include developing compounds to block the proteins that produce cold symptoms and "blockading" nasal-membrane tissues where cold viruses enter the body.

Meanwhile, for what it's worth, a recent study by the Smith/Kline Beecham pharmaceuticals firm found that when it comes to coping with all the sudden wheezing, sneezing and sniffling, it makes a big difference what gender you are. To wit:

• Women, it was learned, more often blame their colds on external causes such as weather changes or breathing air after someone has coughed or sneezed, while men more often blame themselves for not having gotten enough rest, vitamins or exercise.

• Women are more apt than men to seek relief by home or over-the-counter concoctions. As for home remedies, women are more likely to choose juice, while men prefer a hot toddy.

• Women describe themselves as "crabby" when gripped by stuffy nose, sore throat and other cold symptoms, and they say their ailing mates act like grizzly bears. Men agree with both assessments.

• Among married cold sufferers, more men than women claim to act "extra nice" to their striken spouses. Both wish the other would be nicer to them while they are ill.

One large area of agreement for the sexes was that a flat-out cold cure will never be found. On that, two-thirds of both genders concurred.

So odds are we'll go right on spending nearly $2 billion a year for over-the-counter remedies that neither prevent nor cure colds and coughs—and in some cases may actually prolong them by preventing drainage of attendant fluids. But at least they beat a first-century "cure" recommended by Pliny the Younger: "Kiss the hairy muzzle of a mouse."

HOW TO GET THE BEST RESULTS FROM RX DRUGS

Here are some tips to help you use prescription drugs safely and effectively:

• If a drug is not doing what it is supposed to do for you, check with your doctor. You may need a different dosage or a different drug.

• If you have an unexpected symptom—rash, nausea, dizziness, headache—report it to your doctor immediately.

• Don't stop taking your medicine just because you're feeling better. You may prevent the drug from doing its work completely.

• Check drug labels for specific instructions or warnings, such as "Do not take on an empty stomach" or "Do not take with milk."

• Check the label, or ask the pharmacist, for storing instructions. Some drugs should be refrigerated; others must be protected from light.

- Always keep medicines out of the reach of children. Even though most prescription medicines come in child-proof containers, children sometimes can open these bottles and swallow the contents. (If you have difficulty opening such safety closures, you can request bottles with regular caps.)
- Never let another person use your medicine and never take medicine prescribed for anyone else. Your symptoms may seem the same, but you may be suffering from an entirely different problem.
- Never take medicines without checking the label to make sure you're taking the right one. Don't take medicine at night without turning on the light.
- Don't transfer medicines from the original container. These containers are designed to protect the drugs. Fancy pill boxes are not always suitable.
- Do not keep prescription drugs that are no longer needed. Destroy leftover medicines by flushing them down the toilet and dispose of containers carefully so children can't get them.
- Keep a list of all drugs you are taking to show to your doctor and your pharmacist.
- If you are taking several different drugs and have trouble remembering them and how to take them, your pharmacist may be able to provide you with a handy checklist.

—U.S. DEPARTMENT OF HEALTH AND HUMAN SERVICES

DIETARY GUIDELINES

The U.S. Departments of Agriculture and Health and Human Services recently updated their dietary guidelines—for the first time since 1938. The guidelines are used as a nutritional standard by dozens of government and private programs.

Among their recommendations:
- Eat a variety of foods.
- Maintain healthy weight.
- Choose a diet low in fat, saturated fat and cholesterol.
- Choose a diet with plenty of vegetables.
- Use sugars in moderation.
- Use salt and sodium in moderation.
- If you drink alcoholic beverages, do so in moderation.

Remember: "Food alone cures many diseases."—Hu Se-Hui, Chinese Imperial Physician (1314 A.D.)

Note: For more on eating wisely—as well as eating well—see the next chapter, "Food for Thought—and Action."

DESIRABLE WEIGHTS FOR MEN AND WOMEN

An easy rule of thumb for estimating ideal body weight, consistent with recent research by the Harvard-affiliated Brigham and Women's Hospital in Boston, which indicates that current U.S. weight guidelines are too lax and encourage obesity:

For women, 100 pounds for a height of 5 feet, with 5 additional pounds for each added inch of height.

For men, 106 pounds for a height of 5 feet, and 6 additional pounds for every added inch of height.

These ideals may vary by plus or minus 10 percent.

FIGHTING HEART DISEASE

The list of dos and don'ts for heart-healthy living and eating is not long. In their book *Take Care of Your Heart*, Dr. Ezra A. Amsterdam and Ann M. Holmes (*Facts on File*, 1984), say that the "Big Three" risk factors are cigarette smoking, high blood pressure, and high levels of cholesterol and triglycerides in the blood. U.S. Surgeon General C. Everett Koop noted that a person with those three risk factors is eight times more likely to have a heart attack than a person with none of them. Other risk factors for heart disease are diabetes, a family history of heart disease, obesity, lack of exercise, and stress.

A closer look at those risk factors for heart attack and other heart problems brings out the reasons for the association. Here's a rundown:

Cigarette smoking—The U.S. Office of Smoking and Health says there are 36 million former smokers in this country. There should be millions more. The link between smoking and heart attack and other heart diseases is established beyond a doubt. Smokers face two to four times the risk of sudden cardiac death as nonsmokers.

High blood pressure (Hypertension)—When the pressure is high, the heart has to work harder to pump blood. High pressure indicates that the arteries are either narrow or tightened. Eating habits and exercise can affect blood pressure. Overweight people run a greater risk of high blood pressure. Likewise, sodium, which causes the blood to retain liquids, can raise blood pressure in many individuals if overused. Regular exercise is linked with lower blood pressure.

Cholesterol/triglycerides—Generally, these two substances are associated with fatty foods, such as meat, milk products and eggs. These substances become the fatty deposits that cling to the walls of the arteries, eventually narrowing or blocking them.

Diabetes—Blood vessels are damaged by diabetes, and damaged blood vessels are susceptible to hardening and subsequent narrowing. Diabetes can also lead to hypertension.

Family history—We didn't get to choose our parents (if we had, we'd probably all be named Rockefeller). However, we are all subject to the genetics passed along to us, and a history of heart attacks in the immediate family can be a risk factor.

Obesity—Basically, among adults, the more weight, the higher the blood pressure and cholesterol levels.

Lack of Exercise—Regular exercise is good for the heart and most of the rest of the body. It helps to maintain proper weight, lower blood pressure, and may cut down on cholesterol levels. Lack of exercise can therefore be a definite risk factor.

Stress—Just as regular exercise protects against heart disease, so does avoiding severe stress, the National Heart, Lung and Blood Institute says. The body reacts to stress with a complicated fight/flight syndrome. The body gets ready for action, pumping adrenalin and speeding up the heart, sending more blood to the brain and muscles. The blood pressure rises; the liver dumps cholesterol into the bloodstream.

While avoiding risk factors—to the extent possible—helps prevent heart attacks, sometimes the situation has already deteriorated to a point where the heart is already affected by lack of oxygen. Arteries may have been drastically narrowed, even blocked or clotted. In such cases, a number of steps can be taken, ranging from using drugs as simple as aspirin to cleaning out and bypassing clogged arteries, to the ultimate therapy of performing a transplanted or mechanical heart operation.

The ultimate treatment for an ailing heart is replacement of the heart, with either a transplant or a mechanical heart. Bypass surgery has become almost commonplace in this country, with some 370,000 performed a year, but heart transplants and mechanical hearts are in their relative infancy.

Each year some 1.5 million heart attacks occur in this country. But the National Heart, Lung and Blood Institute reports that heart-attack deaths were down 53 percent between 1950 and 1989. It seems we're learning to have a healthy heart.

—ROGER W. MILLER, U.S. Department of Health and Human Services

HEART CHARTS

Keeping track of cholesterol, blood pressure and pulse rate is useful in keeping the heart healthy. Here are some charts that offer guidance on desirable ranges. Cholesterol counts are obtained by health professionals from blood samples. Blood-pressure readings and pulse rates can be done at home or by a health professional. These readings are usually included in routine physical exams.

Blood-Pressure Classifications
Diastolic Blood Pressure
(the lower of the 2 numbers)

Reading	Category
Less than 85	Normal blood pressure
85 to 89	High normal blood pressure
90 to 104	Mild hypertension
105 to 114	Moderate hypertension
115 or more	Severe hypertension

Systolic Blood Pressure
(the higher of the 2 numbers and with a diastolic reading under 90)

Reading	Category
Less than 140	Normal blood pressure
140 to 159	Borderline isolated systolic hypertension
160 or more	Isolated systolic hypertension

Note: These categories are for persons 18 and older.

—The Joint National Committee on Detection, Evaluation and Treatment of High Blood Pressure

Cholesterol
(in milligrams per deciliter)

Age	Moderate Risk	High Risk
2-19	Over 170	Over 185
20-29	Over 200	Over 220
30-39	Over 220	Over 240
40 and up	Over 240	Over 260

—National Institutes of Health

Exercise Pulse Rates

Age	Target Zone*
20	120-150
25	117-146
30	114-142
35	111-138
40	108-135
45	105-131
50	102-127
55	99-123
60	96-120
65	93-116
70	90-113

* "Target zone" is the pulse or heart rate in beats per minute. Exercise that sustains that target-zone level for 30 minutes should be undertaken at least three times a week. Persons over 40 who have not been

exercising regularly should consult a doctor before embarking on such a program. —NATIONAL HEART, LUNG AND BLOOD INSTITUTE

CANCER PREVENTION TIPS

Cancer—the nation's second leading killer, after heart disease—is a general term for more than 100 different diseases: lung cancer, breast cancer, stomach cancer and so on. Every cancer is a disease of some of the body's cells. The human body is made up of billions of tiny cells. Though different kinds of cells perform different functions, all cells reproduce themselves by dividing—which is how the growth and repair of body tissues take place.

If a cell begins dividing too rapidly, without any order, a mass known as a tumor builds up. A tumor may be benign (not cancerous) or malignant (cancerous). A benign tumor may grow large, but it will not spread to other parts of the body. Usually it can be removed and will not come back.

A malignant tumor, a cancer, invades surrounding tissues as it grows. Cells may break off and spread to other parts of the body, forming new tumors (metastases). In some cases, even when the original tumor is removed by surgery, the disease may come back if cancer cells already have spread.

One apparently ever-brightening hope amid all this drear has been the steady march of cancer research, which has helped push down the death rates for most major cancers. Hopefully, spurred by the recent growth of computer technology and gene-therapy research, such prospects will continue.

Meanwhile, alertness and early detection are of utmost import. The most common warning signs are:

- Change in bowel or bladder habits.
- A sore that doesn't heal.
- Unusual bleeding or discharge.
- Thickening of lump in the breast or other part of body.
- Indigestion or difficulty in swallowing.
- Obvious change in wart or mole.
- Nagging cough or hoarseness.

Note: These symptoms, it should be remembered, are *not* sure signs of cancer; they can also be caused by a number of other illnesses. However, if any of them last as long as two weeks, see a doctor. Above all, don't wait for the symptoms to become painful—it's a mixed blessing indeed, but pain is not one of the early signs of cancer.

If you're cancer-free, make it a point to stay that way by taking these tips:

- About a third of all cancer deaths may be related to what we eat—so make positive choices in your diet every day. Choose foods high in dietary fiber (fresh fruits, vegetables and whole-grain breads and cereals).

- Choose foods low in dietary fat. A diet rich in onions, garlic, leeks, chives and scallions may give some protection against stomach cancer.
- If you drink alcoholic beverages, do so only in moderation.
- Avoid unnecessary X rays.
- Know and follow the health and safety rules of your workplace.
- Avoid too much sunlight; wear protective clothing; use effective sunscreens.
- Take estrogens only as long as necessary.
- Above all, *don't smoke*—tobacco smoke causes more cancer deaths than all the other reliably known cancer-causing agents.

—NATIONAL CANCER INSTITUTE

ROBERT MERZ

THE BIG HARVEST
Now that I'm gone, I tell you: don't smoke, whatever you do, don't smoke.
—YUL BRYNNER (1920-85), actor and cancer victim, in a posthumous antismoking TV commercial

According to the American Heart Association, the three leading causes of preventable death in the U.S. are 1) active smoking, 2) drinking alcohol and 3) passive, "secondhand" smoking. The figure for total smoking deaths per year varies from source to source, but the consensus is that it's more than 400,000.

That's the bad news. The even worse news is that there's a lot more bad news:

- Smoking is the number-one cause of lung cancer, the major

171

cause of emphysema and chronic bronchitis, and one of three major risks of heart attack, accounting in fact for about a third of all heart-disease deaths and a third of all cancer deaths.

- A Boston-based research team has reported that there is strong evidence that smoking seriously disrupts the body's main line of defense, the immune system.

- Physicians at the University of Colorado School of Medicine, after exhaustive research, recently reported that secondhand smoke causes 53,000 deaths a year. According to the Environmental Protection Agency such smoke is responsible for 150,000 to 300,000 cases of bronchitis, pneumonia and other respiratory infections in children up to 18 months, while aggravating the symptoms of asthma in 200,000 to 1 million children each year.

- A recent survey by an agency of the Department of Health and Human Services found that smoking-related health-care cost at least $50 billion in 1993, twice as much as has been estimated for previous years. Moreover, the federal government and state governments pay for more than 43 percent of all smoking-attributed medical expenditures and more than 60 percent for those over age 65. (That's *your* tax money going up in smoke!)

- A recent U.S. Surgeon General's report showed that smokers who rely on pipes and cigars are not as safe as they imagine even though they rarely inhale deeply. Pipe smokers, it was noted, can develop cancer of the mouth or lip—and many pipe and cigar smokers *do* draw smoke down as far as the larynx, thereby taking their chances of developing throat cancer three to seven times greater than those who refrain from smoking of any kind.

- Smoking cigarettes that yield less nicotine and carbon monoxide than regular cigarettes does not reduce the risk of heart attack, according to a study published recently in the *New England Journal of Medicine*. Researchers, focusing on women because they make up the majority of those who smoke low-yield cigarettes, said their findings contradicted advertising campaigns suggesting that the low-yield cigarettes—known as "lights" or "ultra-lights"—are less hazardous than other cigarettes.

- Smoking is a major threat to pregnancy and the newborn baby, and while the number of smokers has declined among adults, it has increased among girls 17 to 18.

- According to a 1994 Surgeon General's report, the average age when smokers try their first cigarette is 14.5 and more than 70 percent of those who become daily smokers acquire the habit by age 18.

- About $4.6 billion a year is spent on cigarette advertising and promotion. And, as writer Ellen Goodman points out, "A good portion of that money is directed at the young, either through product placements in movies from *Roger Rabbit* to *Superman*, through sponsored events, or through the less-than-subtle creation of the Joe Camel cartoon character."

• More on Joe Camel: In 1989, a year after Joe was introduced by R. J. Reynolds, the brand's share of the teen market was 8.1 percent. By 1993, when the manufacturer's aggressive ad campaign spent $43 million, Camel's share had jumped to 13.3 percent, a 5.2-percent increase. (Among those urging the most extreme response to this sorry state of affairs is by far the least likely of spokespersons: Patrick Reynolds, heir to the Reynolds tobacco fortune, who believes "that it is moral, right and good to eliminate all advertising of cigarettes.")

• Dragging on cigarettes is also a drag on the budget. Based on an average cost of $2.70 a pack, a person who smokes a pack a day over 10 years will spend over $9,800.

• Careless use of smoking materials is the leading cause of fire deaths (28.9 percent), followed by faulty heating equipment (16.8 percent) and arson (13.6 percent). In 1991 smoking materials caused an estimated 187,000 fires and 2,300 fire deaths.

• **A note of hope:** In 1994 the Drug Abuse Advisory Committee to the Food and Drug Administration voted overwhelmingly that nicotine is the agent in tobacco that causes people to become hooked. The committee also agreed that current nicotine levels in cigarettes lead to addiction. The findings constitute an important first step toward the possible eventual regulation of cigarettes by the federal government.

• **Another hopeful note:** Although 46 to 50 million Americans still smoke, nearly half of all living adults who ever tried smoking have quit—and every year some 1.5 million more smokers quit. Also, nearly all adults who start smoking start when they are minors—so if you can get past age 20 without getting hooked, you're virtually home free.

KICKING NICOTINE: A SURE-FIRE GUIDE

There are basically two ways to quit smoking: "cold turkey" and gradually.

Neither way is easy, but personal experience and observation indicate that "gradually" is somewhat less difficult, and therefore more do-able.

Here follow some approaches popular with successful ex-smokers. Remember that successful methods are as different as the people who use them. What may seem silly to others may be just what you need to quit—so don't be embarrassed to try something new. Pick the ideas that make sense to you—then follow through.

Getting Yourself Ready

• Decide positively that you want to quit. Avoid negative thoughts about how difficult it might be. It *can* be done—and *you* can do it!

• Develop strong personal reasons besides those relating to health and obligations to others. For example, think of how much of your hard-earned cash is currently going up in smoke, both literally and figuratively, leaving you nothing in return—in fact, less than nothing, when add in the other negatives involved. Such as: the time you now waste taking cigarette breaks, rushing out to buy a pack, hunting a light and so on.

• If contemplating the "gradual" route, then set a definite target date for quitting—perhaps a special day like your birthday or anniversary. Give yourself at lest a month—but make the date sacred and don't let anything change it.

• Begin to condition yourself physically: start a modest exercise regimen; drink more fluids; avoid fatigue.

• Ask your spouse or a friend to quit with you.

Just Don't Do It

• For gradualists, start by lighting up that first cigarette later each day, while systematically cutting down on your daily total. You might try decreasing the number of cigarettes smoked each day by 20 percent a week for X number of weeks.

• Stop buying cigarettes by the carton. Wait until one pack is empty before buying another.

• Stop carrying cigarettes with you at home and at work.

• If you light up many times during the day without even thinking about it, try to look in a mirror each time you put a match to your cigarette—do you really want the world to encounter you in the guise of the nicotine-involved person looking back at you?

• Change your eating habits to aid in cutting down. For example, drink milk, which is frequently considered incompatible with smoking. End meals or snacks with something that won't lead to a cigarette.

• Don't empty your ashtrays. This will not only remind you of how many cigarettes you've smoked each day, but the sight and smell of stale butts hopefully might start getting to you.

After Quitting: Some Post-Smokum Tips

• The first few days after you quit, spend as much free time as possible in places where smoking is prohibited—for example, libraries, museums, theaters, department stores and churches.

• Drink large quantities of water and fruit juice.

• Try to avoid alcohol, coffee and other beverages frequently associated with cigarette smoking.

- If you miss the sensation of having a cigarette in your hand, play with something else—a pencil, a paper clip, a marble.
- If you miss having something in your mouth, try toothpicks. (This may lead to a toothpick-chewing habit, but you can always tackle that one later.)
- Until you are confident of your ability to stay off cigarettes, limit your socializing to healthful, outdoor activities or situations where smoking is prohibited.
- If you must be in a situation where you'll be tempted to smoke (such as a cocktail or dinner party), try to associate with the non-smokers there.
- Look at cigarette ads more critically to better understand what the tobacco companies are *really* trying to sell.
- Keep oral substitutes handy—things like carrots, pickles, sunflower seeds, apples, celery, raisins, sugarless gum and so on.
- Never allow yourself to think that "one won't hurt"—it will.
- Each month, on the anniversary of your quit date, plan a special celebration.

—Sources: NATIONAL CANCER INSTITUTE and U.S. DEPARTMENT OF HEALTH AND HUMAN SERVICES

A TOAST TO HEALTH

Alcohol is a river of danger and delight, and most of us sooner or later learn which flows to go with, and when, and how much. Moderation is achieved, we tipple more or less tidily, and our lives proceed apace.

Not so for those who drink beyond their particular limit on a regular basis—those who suffer from alcoholism, the most widely untreated (but treatable) disease in the nation and one that at some time or other affects one in every four U.S. families. (As of early 1995, the National Council on Alcoholism and Drug Dependence estimated that more than 15 million Americans drink too much.)

The evils of alcoholism are well known—damage to liver, heart and other organs; malnutrition; loss of memory; personality disorders; impaired judgment and motor skills; impotence and sterility; negative repercussions on family, friends and society; and a shortening of life by 10 to 12 years.

For most of us, the response to this formidable roster of negative possibilities need not be the dry collar of total abstinence. For alcohol *can* bring balm and joy betimes—with meals, at parties, in bars and restaurants, in the homes of friends. Again, the key is moderation. If this is for you a concept of the easier-said-than-done variety, then abstinence may indeed be indicated. But for those who *can* handle moderation, here are some suggestions from Leonard Gross's *How Much Is Too Much* (Random House, 1984):

- Don't put more than 1 1/2 ounces of liquor into a mixed drink.
- Drink slowly—it will help avoid a hangover.
- Set a sensible limit of no more than X amount a day (the X determined by such factors as your body size and the alcohol content of the drink), but don't "save up" a week's allotment and drink it all on the weekend.
- Eat something substantial when drinking; it slows the absorption of alcohol. But avoid salty foods—they make you want to drink more.
- And, finally, for the zillionteenth time, if you drink, don't drive. Moreover, if—despite all this good advice—you somehow manage to awake with a hangover, you *still* shouldn't drive. A recent report in the *Journal of the American Medical Association* indicated that on the "morning after" most people still showed decreased ability to control a motor vehicle.

Salud!

MARIJUANA: A "GATEWAY" DRUG?

"Make the most of the India Hemp Seed and sow it everywhere."
—from the writings of GEORGE WASHINGTON,
vol. 33, p. 270, Government Printing Office

Few health and social matters are as important—or as controversial—as the use and abuse of drugs. In a fear-ridden climate where perhaps well-meaning if blatantly clewless souls can feel justified in summing up the whole complex issue by frying eggs in a video pan and claiming that *that's* what (presumably *all*) drugs do to one's mind, it's clear that solving the "drug problem" must first and foremost be preceded by defining terms and drawing lines.

For instance: *Which* drugs? Heroin? Crack? Tobacco? Marijuana? Aspirin? Excedrin? Prozac? Caffeinated coffee and tea?

And when, in each case, does *use* cross over into *abuse*?

Obviously, quaffing a couple of beers or a martini or two now and then would qualify as "use," but how many quaffs equal "abuse"? States have definitions based on the alcohol content of blood, and most of us have our own inner yardsticks for taking such measures. The point is knowing the difference and modifying intake accordingly—while avoiding altogether such dangerously addictive substances such as heroin, crack and tobacco.

Setting aside the thorny issue of whether *all* drugs should or should not be made legal, it seems clear that what is needed most of all is more *education*. Basically, we must learn to differentiate more precisely *between* drugs, and to stop confusing *use* with *abuse*.

One drug that might help in this process—perhaps the most controversial drug of all—is marijuana, aka "hemp," "India hemp," "cannabis," "reefer" and plain old "pot," among other monikers. Although this herb, however named, has been widely used as medicine, rope, clothing, paper—as well as recreationally—for some five thousand years, in recent times its characteristics and effects have been hotly debated. Its advocates and detractors are incredibly diverse in the intensity of their yea- or nay-saying.

Speaking for the "defense," no less a personage than the late anthropologist Margaret Mead said: "Marijuana is safe unless taken in harmful and excessive amounts." Recent advocates include singer Willie Nelson ("The biggest killer on the planet is stress, and I still think the best medicine is and always has been cannabis"), writer Ken Kesey ("To be happy without being hysterical, smoke grass") and non-celebrity glaucoma sufferer Elvy Musikka ("I lost one eye through surgery and conventional treatment. Marijuana is helping me save what I have left.")

Among the more prominent anti-potters are former U.S. Secretary of Health, Education and Welfare Joseph A. Califano Jr. ("Legislation would sabotage significant progress we have made against illegal drugs") and former Los Angeles Police Chief Daryl F. Gates ("Occasional use of pot is treason . . . casual drug users ought to be taken out and shot"). Meanwhile, groups like the *Partnership for a Drug-Free America*, with their *Reefer Madness*-type TV ads linking marijuana use to criminally violent behavior, continue to do a great disservice to efforts to solve the *very real* problems of cocaine and heroin addiction. The true tragedy here is that when young, impressionable viewers see such blatant falsehoods about how evil and fiendish pot is, they are much less likely to take seriously the quite valid warnings about, and prohibitions against, the hard stuff.

Credibility is further undermined by anti-potters who fervently condemn marijuana is a "gateway drug" inevitably leading to addiction to hard drugs—almost always ignoring the deeper psychological and sociological reasons for addictive behavior in general. The new prohibitionists also ignore the fact that an estimated 30 million Americans a year use marijuana responsibly, with very few cases of ill effects caused by *use* (as opposed to *abuse*). In fact, after a four-year study, the National Academy of Sciences concluded in 1982 that evidence of pot's health hazards was inconclusive and that partial legalization was preferable to criminal penalties. And a recent issue of *Scientific American* quotes an official of the National Institute on Drug Abuse as saying: "Never has so much money been spent trying to find something wrong with a drug and produced so few results."

Equally at odds with the current penalty-oriented approach has been conservative sage William F. Buckley Jr.: "The blood lust by the DEA against marijuana users is being used to justify an abuse of civil rights." Or as a previous deep thinker named Spinoza once said: "He who tries to determine everything by law will foment crime rather than lessen it."

And so the debate continues . . . with little chance, in the current political climate, for the "pro"s to see their dream of legal weed come true anytime soon, or for the "anti"s to fully convince the public, beyond the proverbial reasonable doubt, that pot is a some sort of vile and demonic substance. Still, even those favorably disposed toward marijuana would do well to proceed with caution. The controversy can get heated at times, and each side needs to push back and take some very deep breaths—if only (for the time being?) of air.

A really innovative approach might be to work toward making marijuana legal again (as it was before 1937), but this time with the idea of turning it into a *true* gateway drug—one that heroin and crack addicts might use in connection, perhaps, with a program of counseling. With proper "set and setting," marijuana might thus serve as a kind of door—or *gate*, if you will—leading *away* from *all* substance dependencies, including any dependency on marijuana itself.

After all the money and effort that's been wasted trying to eradicate this apparently unconquerable herb—to say nothing of the millions in lost taxes legalization would bring—it may be worth a try.

WHITHER THE WAR ON DRUGS?

In 1991 the war on drugs cost $24 billion, with state and local governments taking the lead role, according to the federal anti-drug office. Almost four-fifths of the $15.9 billion spent by states and localities was devoted to criminal-justice activities such as incarcerating prisoners and paying for police. Federal criminal justice costs used up 79 percent of the money spent on anti-drug activities. The other 21 percent was for rehabilitation and education.

Critics have said the budgetary breakdown should be closer to 50-50 with a far greater emphasis on prevention and treatment. Meanwhile, A 1991-92 study for the California Department of Alcohol and Drug Programs found that its programs help reduce crime and lower health-care costs, saving taxpayers an estimated $1.5 billion. Most of the savings came as a result of fewer crimes committed by those in treatment.

HOW LONG DRUGS STAY IN URINE

Nicotine	24 to 48 hours
Marijuana	10 to 35 days
Cocaine	24 to 36 hours
Amphetamines	48 to 72 hours
PCP	48 to 78 hours
Valium	48 to 76 hours
Heroin	48 to 72 hours
Phenylpropanolamine	24 to 48 hours

—NATIONAL PARENTS' RESOURCE INSTITUTE
FOR DRUG EDUCATION, INC. (PRIDE)

Note: Just because you don't do drugs, don't think you can't fail a drug test—as Laurence Moore so pointedly points out in his goodie-filled collection of facts and fallacies, *Lightning Never Strikes Twice and Other False Facts* (Avon, 1994):

Professional bicycle racer Alexi Grewal was fined $500 and suspended for three months in 1992 when he failed a drug test after eating a poppy-seed muffin. The poppy seeds commonly used in baked goods are the seeds of the opium poppy, Papaver somniferum, and may contain extremely small amounts of substances that can cause a positive reaction on a morphine test. Inca tea, sold in health food stores, can lead to a false positive test for cocaine use, and cough suppressants containing dextromethorphan can result in a false positive for amphetamine use, as can diet aids that contain phenylpropanolamine.

TIPS ON PREVENTING AIDS

Here's what everyone should know to protect themselves and others from infection with the AIDS virus (human immuno-deficiency virus, or HIV):

HIV is contagious, but not in the same way that measles or chicken pox or the common cold are contagious. It is a sexually transmitted, blood-borne disease that spreads from one person to another in the following ways:

• By sexual intercourse between a man and a woman or between two men. The virus can be spread through vaginal, anal or oral sex. (Worldwide, more than 70 percent of those infected with the AIDS virus got it from heterosexual sex, while about 15 percent got it from homosexual sex; the rest got it in other ways, listed below.)

• By sharing contaminated needles or "works" used to inject drugs.

• By an infected woman to her baby during pregnancy or delivery, and possibly through breast-feeding.

• By transfusion of contaminated blood or blood components, although this risk has been sharply reduced by screening blood and blood donors and by new ways to process blood used to treat disorders such as hemophilia.

Many people infected with the AIDS virus have no symptoms and may look and feel completely well for many years. But these people can transmit the virus to others. And a person can become infected after just a single exposure to the virus.

The AIDS virus does not spread through casual social contact. In more than seven years of tracking and studying AIDS, scientists have found no evidence that HIV is spread casually through contact at school or on the job, by sharing meals or office equipment, or by handshakes or hugs with an infected person. There is no reason to avoid ordinary social contact with a person infected with HIV.

There is no risk of getting AIDS by giving blood; new equipment is used for each donor.

The AIDS virus is not spread by sexual intercourse between two people who maintain a sexual relationship exclusively with each other and who have not been previously infected.

• • •

The U.S. Public Health Service recommends that people take these precautions to reduce the risk of exposing themselves or others to the AIDS virus:

• The best protection against sexually transmitted infection by the virus is, of course, to abstain from sex or to have a mutually monogamous relationship with an uninfected person. Avoiding sex with people who have AIDS, people who have tested positive for the

AIDS virus antibody, or people at risk of infection would also eliminate the risk of sexually transmitted infection.

• Unless you're absolutely sure that your sex partner is not infected, avoid contact with his or her blood, semen, urine, feces, saliva and vaginal secretions:

Use condoms, which will reduce (but not eliminate) the possibility of transmitting the virus.

Avoid sexual practices that may cause tears in the vagina, rectum or penis.

Avoid oral-genital contact without a condom.

Avoid open-mouthed, intimate kissing.

• Do not have sex with multiple partners. The more partners you have, the greater your risk of infection.

• Do not use illegal intravenous drugs. If you do, never share needles or syringes.

• • •

If you think you may be infected, or if you have engaged in risky sexual or drug-related behavior:

• Seek counseling and a medical evaluation. Consider taking the AIDS antibody test, which would enable you to know your status and protect yourself or—if you are infected—your sex partner.

• Do not use illegal intravenous drugs. If you do, never share needles or syringes.

• Don't donate blood, plasma, body organs, other body tissues, or sperm.

• If you are a woman at increased risk, seriously consider delaying plans for pregnancy until more is known about AIDS and transmission of the AIDS virus. A pregnant woman infected with the AIDS virus has a 20 to 50 percent chance of passing the virus on to her unborn child. Women at increased risk of AIDS should take the antibody test before deciding to become pregnant.

• • •

For people who have received a positive result on the AIDS antibody test:

• See a doctor. There are medical steps you can take to protect your health. Either avoid sex or tell your prospective sex partner your AIDS test result and take the precautions listed above to protect him or her from infection.

• Inform anyone whom you may have exposed to the AIDS virus—through sex or drug use—of their potential exposure, and encourage them to seek counseling and antibody testing.

• Don't share toothbrushes, razors or other items that could become contaminated with blood.

• If you use drugs, enroll in a treatment program. Never share

181

needles or other drug equipment.

- Do not donate blood, plasma, sperm, or other body tissues or organs.
- Tell your doctor, dentist and eye doctor that you are infected with the AIDS virus so that proper precautions can be taken to protect you, them and others.
- Women with a positive antibody test should avoid pregnancy.

Persons at Increased Risk of AIDS

- Men who have had sex with another man since 1977
- People who have shared needles when they inject drugs
- People with symptoms of AIDS or AIDS-related illnesses
- Male or female prostitutes and their partners
- Sex partners of people infected with the AIDS virus or at increased risk of infection
- People with hemophilia who have received clotting factor products
- Infants of high-risk or infected mothers

How to Get AIDS Information

For more information about AIDS, call the National AIDS Hotline, 1-800-342-2437, or write or call the National AIDS Clearinghouse, P.O. Box 6003, Rockville, MD 20849; phone (800) 458-5231.
—U.S. DEPARTMENT OF HEALTH AND HUMAN SERVICES

PREVENTING ACQUAINTANCE RAPE
What Women Can Do

- State your desires and limits clearly.
- Be assertive.
- Be aware that your nonverbal actions may send messages that you do not intend to send.
- Pay attention to what is happening around you.
- Trust your intuition. If you feel afraid, say so and get out of the situation.
- Be aware that nothing you do is a guarantee against sexual assault.

What Men Can Do

- State your desires and limits clearly.
- Accept the woman's limits; listen to her and assume she means what she says.
- Do not assume that previous permission for sexual contact means she wants to have sex again.
- Understand that being turned down is not a rejection of who you are as a person. It means your partner does not want sex with you at the time.　　　　—COALITION AGAINST SEXUAL ASSAULT

MENTAL ILLNESS: SOME WARNING SIGNS

The American Mental Health Fund recently listed the following common warning signs of mental illness. Apparently, we all suffer some of these symptoms some of the time, but when the symptoms start increasing in number and/or severity, it's time to get some help.

- Marked personality change over time.
- Confused thinking; strange or grandiose ideas.
- Prolonged severe depression; apathy; extreme highs and lows.
- Excessive anxieties, fears or suspiciousness; blaming others.
- Withdrawal from society; abnormal self-centeredness.
- Denial of obvious problems; strong resistance to help.
- Thinking or talking about suicide.
- Numerous, unexplained physical ailments; marked changes in eating or sleeping patterns.
- Anger or hostility out of proportion to the situation.
- Delusions, hallucinations, hearing voices.
- Abuse of alcohol or drugs.
- Growing inability to cope with problems and daily activities.

FIVE WAYS TO MENTALLY APPLY THE BRAKES

Drive 10 mph slower. Many of us drive fast, even when we're not in a rush. Try a new route or simply notice the old one more.

Take a moment before eating. Saying grace or just sitting quietly reminds us to notice our meal instead of just wolfing it down.

Shower after work. Just for a minute or two, to "wash away" the day's work and allow you to leave it behind for the evening.

Wait a few rings before answering the phone. Many people rush to pick it up immediately, prolonging their hectic moods.

Honor the process itself. Whatever the task or activity, slow down, do just one thing, do it well, and allow yourself the sense of accomplishment without feeling the need to get it done and move on.

—STEPHAN RECHSCHAFFEN

TIPS ON BETTER SLEEP

It is said that sleep is best before midnight; and Nature herself, with her darkness and chilling dews, informs us so. There is another reason for going to bed betimes; for it is universally acknowledged that lying late in the morning is a great shortener of life. At least, it is never found in company with longevity. It also tends to make people corpulent.

—LEIGH HUNT (1784-1859)

Dr. Paul Gouin, director of the Ingham Medical Center Sleep Department in Lansing, Michigan, suggests that if getting to sleep is a problem, you may be trying too hard. He suggests not forcing sleep. Instead, you should turn on a light, leave the bedroom and do something else for 20 minutes or so, then go to sleep later. Dr. Gouin also offers the following tips on getting better sleep:

- **Wake up at a consistent hour.** A regular morning arousal time strengthens your daily cycle and leads to regular times of sleep at night.
- **Quit smoking.** Chronic use of tobacco, which damages your health in so many ways, also disturbs sleep.
- **Seek quietness.** Occasional loud noises such as airplanes, trains and traffic disturb sleep even when people are not awakened by the noise.
- **Avoid sleeping pills.** Chronic use is ineffective in most insomniacs and is potentially dangerous.
- **Avoid alcohol before bedtime.** Alcohol helps tense people fall asleep more easily, but the resulting sleep is fragmented.
- **Don't get too much sleep.** Sleep as much as you need to feel healthy and refreshed, but no more. Curtailing time in bed seems to solidify sleep; excessively long times in bed seems related to fragmented and shallow sleep.
- **Exercise regularly.**
- **Monitor room temperature.** Although excessively warm rooms disturb sleep, there is no evidence proving that an excessively cold room enhances sleep.
- **Cut out caffeine.** Caffeine in the evening hours disturbs sleep, even in those who believe it does not.

Consult your physician if you feel you have a sleep disorder. After all, one-third of our lives is spent sleeping; we might as well make it a good night's sleep.

Do see your dentist at least every six months for a general checkup and cleaning.

Don't bite pens, chew ice or other hard items like popcorn kernels, or use your teeth as tools. These habits can chip a tooth's enamel or crack the tooth itself. They may also damage fillings, crowns or other restorations.

Do wear a mouthguard when you play sports. Professional athletes wear mouthguards to protect their teeth from injury, and so should you.

Don't smoke or chew tobacco. Besides staining the teeth, tobacco contributes to gum disease and can cause oral cancer.

Do watch how much coffee and tea you drink. Excessive amounts can stain your teeth.

Don't grind or clench your teeth. Many adults take out stress on their jaws and teeth without realizing it. This habit is called bruxism and can seriously damage and wear down your teeth. Consult your dentist if you notice any of these warning signs: pain when chewing, a tired jaw when you wake up, and unexplained headaches. He or she may suggest that you wear a custom-made mouthguard at night or may prescribe other treatments.

Do get enough fluoride. Adults as well as children benefit from fluoride to help prevent decay. Ask your dentist how to get the proper amount. Common sources: fluoridated water; toothpastes and rinses (make sure they have the American Dental Association seal of acceptance); professional topical treatments; or prescription drops, gels, or tablets.

Do watch for early warning signs of oral cancer and ask your dentist how to do self-exams at home. Most oral cancers can be cured if caught early. Be on the lookout for abnormal growths; white or velvety red patches in the mouth; persistent sores or swelling; repeated bleeding; or a numb or painful area. You can also reduce your risk by avoiding tobacco and prolonged exposure to the sun; eating a balanced diet; using alcohol in moderation; and practicing good oral hygiene via regular brushing and flossing. **Some tips:**

Brushing. Brushing removes food particles and plaque from your teeth, making them look clean and freshening your breath. Brush at least twice a day with a fluoridated toothpaste that has the ADA seal. Use a brush with soft, rounded bristles and replace it every three months.

Flossing. Brushing does most of the work in keeping your teeth clean, but it can't reach plaque and food particles between teeth and under the gumline. Daily flossing will keep plaque from building up in these hard-to-reach areas.

There are two types of floss: waxed and unwaxed. Use whichever you prefer. To make sure you floss all your teeth, start behind the upper and lower molars at one side of your mouth and work toward the other side. —*Dental Health Adviser*

HEALTH-CARE BONANZA CONTINUES

The U.S. health system is still the most expensive in the world by far and the spending gap with other major countries is widening, according to a new study published recently in the journal *Health Affairs.*

The U.S. spent $3.094 per person on health care in 1992, or 13.6 percent of its gross domestic product, according to figures compiled for the Organization for Economic Cooperation and Development. Most of the other 23 countries tracked by the Paris-based OECD spent less than half as much, devoting just 8.1 percent of GDP to health.

The report said that since 1980 per-capita health spending has been climbing faster than consumer prices, growing 4.6 percent a year more than prices in the U.S.

An earlier study, by Families USA, a nonprofit advocacy group for the low-income elderly, showed that prescription-drug manufacturers made five times as much profit on their most popular drugs than the average profit from sales by *Fortune* 500 corporations. Among sample prices cited were those of Premarin, an estrogen, which increased 148 percent from 1985 to 1991, and of Lopressor, a blood-pressure pill, which increased 118 percent in the same period.

The report charges that over the same seven years manufacturers filtered more money into advertising, promotion and lobbying than research, and that the rate of increase of prescription-drug prices was about four times that of the consumer price index.

Hopefully, increased public awareness of the profit levels being realized in today's health-care biz will keep the ongoing feeding frenzy somewhat under control—but it's probably best not to stake your life's savings on it.

As Chicago columnist and social historian Irv Kupcinet once so aptly put it: "Medical costs will come down as soon as they find a cure for the common greed."

APPLYING FOR MEDICARE

Medicare is a federal health-insurance program for people 65 or older, people of any age with permanent kidney failure, and certain disabled people. It is administered by the Health Care Financing Administration. Local Social Security Administration offices take applications for Medicare, assist beneficiaries in filing claims, and provide information about the program.

Medicare has two parts—hospital insurance and medical insurance. Hospital insurance helps pay for inpatient hospital care and certain follow-up care. Medical insurance helps pay for your doctor's services and many other medical services and items.

Hospital insurance is financed through part of the Social Security (FICA) tax. Voluntary medical insurance is financed from the monthly premiums paid by people who have enrolled for it and from general federal revenues.

The specifics of Medicare—the rates and regulations involved—are so prone to change that any information that could be provided here might well be dated by presstime. For the latest lowdown, and for answers to specific questions, call your local Social Security office.

GETTING A SECOND OPINION

Most of the nine million surgical procedures performed in the U.S. each year result in desired outcomes of better health, the repair of undesirable conditions, or the control of disease. But not all surgery is necessary. Some may even be unwarranted. Some can be deferred. And many conditions may be treated just as effectively without surgery.

While physicians usually agree on whether surgery is actually unwarranted, they may not always come to the same conclusion as to whether elective surgery is the best course of action for a particular patient. In some cases the choices in a situation may weigh equally, and the preference of you, the patient, may tilt the decision toward or against surgery. In all cases you are entitled to know the range of choices open to you, to have those choices objectively considered by professionals, and to have your own preferences considered before undergoing a surgical procedure.

If your physician recommends surgery, and it is not an emergency, you may want to be sure that the recommendation is the best choice for you. You may want to get a second opinion from another physician. Medicare, as well as many private health insurance plans, encourages second opinions. Medicare will help pay for a second opinion in the same way it pays for other services of a physician.

Questions to Ask

Before agreeing to any nonemergency surgery, you should know the answers to these questions:

1. What does the doctor say is the matter with you?
2. What is the operation the doctor plans to do?
3. What are the likely benefits to you of the operation?
4. What are the risks of the surgery and how likely are they to occur?
5. How long would the recovery period be and what is involved?
6. What are the costs of the operation?
7. What will happen if you don't have the operation?
8. Are there other ways to treat your condition that could be tried first?

Ask these and any other questions you may have to get a full understanding about your surgery or treatment. Your decision may be better for it.

Finding a Specialist for a Second Opinion

If your doctor recommends nonemergency surgery, there are several ways to find a surgeon or another specialist in the treatment of your medical problem:

1. Ask your doctor to give you the name of another doctor to see. Do not hesitate to ask; most physicians will encourage you to seek the second opinion.

2. If you would rather find another doctor on your own:

• You can contact a local medical society or osteopathic or podiatric school in your area for the names of doctors who specialize in the field in which your illness falls.

• You can call Medicare's toll-free number, (800) 638-6833.

• If you're covered by Medicare, you can call your local Social Security Office (listed in the telephone directory under Health and Human Services).

• If you're eligible for Medicaid, you can call your local welfare office.

Sorting It Out

Some people do not feel comfortable letting their doctor know they want a second opinion. However, if you tell your doctor, you can also ask that your records be sent to the second doctor. In this way, you may be able to avoid the time, costs and discomfort of having to repeat tests that have already been done.

When getting a second opinion, you should tell the second doctor:

- The name of the surgical procedure recommended.
- Any test you know you have had.

If the second doctor agrees that surgery is the best way to treat your problems, he or she will usually send you back to the first doctor to do the surgery.

If the second doctor disagrees with the first, most people find that they have the facts they need to make their own decision. If you are confused by different opinions, you may wish to go back to the first doctor to further discuss your case. Or you may wish to talk to a third physician.

Paying for a Second Opinion

Medicare will pay for the second opinion at the same rate it pays for other services. Always ask your doctors, therapists or other medical suppliers if they will accept assignment of Medicare benefits as full payment.

Many private insurance companies pay for second opinions. You can contact your health insurance representatives for details. Most state Medicaid programs will also pay for second opinions.

Key Points to Remember

- You can get a second opinion whenever nonemergency surgery is recommended. Most doctors approve of patients getting a second opinion and will assist you in doing so.
- Second opinions are a way for you to get additional expert advice from another doctor who knows a lot about treating medical problems like yours.
- Second opinions can reassure you—and your doctor—that the decision to have the surgery is the correct one.
- Second opinions are your right as a patient. They can help you make a better informed decision about nonemergency surgery.
- Medicare will pay 80 percent of reasonable charges for beneficiaries enrolled in Medicare Part B who seek a second opinion. A third opinion, if necessary, will be covered the same way.
- Patients may call Medicare's toll-free number, (800) 638-6833 to locate the name of a nearby second-opinion health specialist.

—U.S. DEPARTMENT OF HEALTH AND HUMAN SERVICES

RX FOR 14th-CENTURY DOCTORS

The following list of dos and don'ts, intended for medical students in Chaucer's time, is from a book by E. S. Turner entitled *The Astonishing History of the Medical Profession:*

Tell the patient that, with God's help, you hope to cure him, but inform the relatives that the case is grave. Then, if he dies, you will have safeguarded yourself. If he recovers, it will be a testimony to your skill and wisdom.

When called to a patient, find out from his messenger as much about him as you can before you arrive. Then if his pulse and urine tell you nothing, you can still surprise the patient with your knowledge of his condition.

When feeling for the patient's pulse, allow for the fact that he may be disturbed by your arrival and by the thought of the fee you are going to charge him.

If you are asked to dinner, stay sober. During the meal, inquire frequently after the patient, lest he suspect that you have forgotten him in your enjoyment of his viands.

Do not look lecherously on the patient's wife, daughters, or maidservants, or kiss them, or fondle their breasts.

Do not disparage your fellow physicians. If you do not know them personally, say you have heard nothing but good of them.

If you find the patient dead on your arrival, show no surprise. Say you knew from the account of his symptoms he would not recover and inquire the hour at which he died. This will enhance your reputation.

ROBERT MERZ

FOOD FOR THOUGHT—AND ACTION
... a cook's tour of palate pleasures ...

Grub first, then ethics.
—Bertolt Brecht

Gluttony is not a secret vice.
—Orson Welles

MOOD FOR FOOD
This chapter, a hopefully tasty—and equally important—outgrowth of the one before, really needs no introduction. *Works for me!*

UP YOUR PYRAMID!
And right back down to the base, would be the best advice! For this pyramid is the great "Food Guide Pyramid," subtitled "A Guide to Daily Food Choices," and designed and disseminated by the U.S. Department of Agriculture. It replaces the old Basic Four food groups and illustrates the Dietary Guidelines for Americans, which were introduced in 1980 and revised in 1985 and 1990.

The hierarchy of different food groups begins at the base, with its recommended 6 to 11 daily servings of bread, cereals and pasta, and narrows toward progressively fewer servings of vegetables and fruits, then meat, eggs, poultry, dried beans and milk products and ends at a "use-sparingly" point depicting fats, oils and sweets.

Such a nutritionally naughty pinnacle may not seem logical, but its own logic *does* emerge if the idea of quantity rather than position is kept in mind. But if the pinnacle paradox still bothers you, you can imaginationally stand the pyramid on its head and climb from there up to the base. Or—*whatever!* Let's face it, eating is the one test (or one of just a few) where test taker and test monitor are one and the same. Your meals won't be graded—unless *you* do the grading.

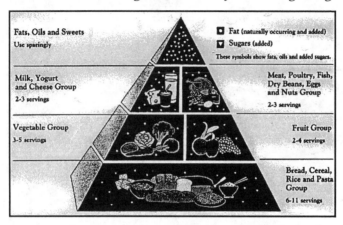

So up—or down—your pyramid, as you wish. As for the range of servings indicated in the various food groups, the choices made regarding them should reflect such variables as age, size, sex, activity level and total calorie needs. However, practically everyone should eat at least the minimum number of servings from each group.

Summing up, these are the lessons of the pyramid, along with other recommendations by the USDA and the National Cancer Institute:

- **Eat a variety of foods.**

No one food provides all the nutrients that a person needs. It is important to eat a wide variety of foods each day, such as: fruits and vegetables; whole-grain breads and cereals; lean meats, poultry and fish; dry peas and beans; and low-fat dairy products.

- **Maintain desirable weight.**

Obesity is a risk factor for many diseases, including heart disease, high blood pressure, diabetes and some cancers.

- **Avoid too much fat, saturated fat and cholesterol.**

A diet low in total fat may reduce the risk for cancers of the breast, prostate, colon and rectum. Such a diet will probably be low in saturated fat and cholesterol and may also reduce risk of heart disease.

- **Eat foods with adequate starch and fiber.**

Most Americans eat a diet low in starch and fiber. Health experts recommend that we increase the amount of starch and fiber in our diets by eating more fruit, vegetables, potatoes, whole-grain breads and cereals, and dry peas and beans. A high-fiber diet can reduce the

- **Avoid too much sugar.**

A diet high in sugar promotes tooth decay. Sugary foods are also often high in fat and calories and low in vitamins and minerals.

- **Avoid too much sodium.**

Too much sodium in the diet may contribute to high blood pressure, especially for people with a family history of high blood pressure. Untreated high blood pressure can lead to heart attacks, strokes and kidney disease.

- **If you drink alcoholic beverages, do so in moderation.**

Drinking too much can lead to many health problems. Heavy drinking is associated with cancers of the mouth, throat, esophagus and liver. Cancer risk is especially high for heavy drinkers who smoke. Alcoholic drinks are also high in calories and low in vitamins and minerals.

ROBERT MERZ

THE EBB AND FLOW OF CALORIES

Simply put, if you burn more calories than you take in, you lose weight. Even at rest, your body burns calories. As points of reference, consider that a pound of body fat contains about 3,400 calories and a single large "fast-food" burger puts about 540 calories into your sytem.

Approximate Energy Expenditure by a
150-Pound Person in Various Activities

Activity	Calories Per Hr.
Lying down or sleeping	80
Sitting	100
Driving a car	120
Standing	140
Domestic work	180
Bicycling, 5 1/2 mph	210
Walking, 1 1/2 mph	210
Gardening	220
Golf; lawn mowing with power mower	250
Slow ballroom dancing	250
Bowling	270
Fencing	300
Swimming, 1/4 mph	300
Walking, 3 3/4 mph	300
Square dancing, volleyball, roller skating	350
Ping-Pong	360
Wood chopping or sawing	400
Tennis	420
Jumping rope	550
Skiing, 10 mph	600
Squash and handball	600
Bicycling, 13 mph	660
Running, 10 mph	900

—American Red Cross

Note: Here's a good rule of thumb for knowing how many more or how many fewer calories you need to increase or decrease your weight. Multiply your present weight by 15. The result is your present average caloric intake per day. Adjust that up or down by at least 20 percent. After three months, make another prorated adjustment, remembering meanwhile to take into account the type and amount of physical exercise you are getting.

Almost No Calories Per Serving
celery sticks
lettuce
cucumbers
green peppers
mushrooms
cauliflower

35-40 Calories
1 medium peach
1 medium nectarine
1/2 grapefruit
1/2 cup skim milk
1/4 cup plain yogurt
3 saltine crackers
1/2 small banana

25-30 Calories
1 small tangerine
1/2 cup watermelon
1/4 cantaloupe
1 small tomato
1 medium carrot
1 cup popcorn

50-60 Calories
1 small apple
1 small orange
15 grapes
12 cherries
1 cup strawberries
1/4 cup cottage cheese
4 small shrimp

—FOOD AND DRUG ADMINISTRATION, U.S. DEPARTMENT OF
HEALTH AND HUMAN SERVICES

Note: To determine your present average caloric intake per day, multiply your weight by 15. Adjust that figure up or down by at least 40 percent, to effect a weight change.

OILS AND SPREADS: HOW THE FATS STACK UP

All fats and oils used in cooking contain the same number of fat grams. The differences are in the degree of saturation. Generally, any fat that's solid at room temperature is more likely to raise blood cholesterol than one that's liquid, regardless of whether it came from an animal or a vegetable. The lower the number (percent saturated), the better.

Oil	Percent Saturated
Canola	6
Safflower	9
Corn	13
Olive	14
Soybean	14
Liquid and soft-tub margarines*	14
Peanut	17
Stick margarines*	25
Vegetable shortening	25
Butter	50

* Average of several brands

EASY ON THE SODIUM

Cutting down on salt may sound difficult and distasteful—but it doesn't have to be, and the health benefits can be substantial.

Salt, or more correctly sodium (salt is 40 percent sodium), is important to the body, but too much of it can contribute to high blood pressure and other problems. Unfortunately, most of us consume too much salt: it's a taste we acquire almost from birth, thanks to the abundance of packaged and processed foods, and the widespread practice of heavily salting our food, both in the kitchen and at the table. The U.S. Food and Drug Administration offers these tips to help you cut down on your own sodium consumption:

• Use the saltshaker sparingly. Don't use it until you've tasted your food.

• Read food labels. Look for the amount of sodium in a product. See where salt or sodium is on the ingredient list.

• Look for low-salt, low-sodium or sodium-reduced products.

• Try cooking with less salt. Use spices and other seasonings.

• Give yourself a little time to get adjusted to a diet lower in sodium. Most people make the adjustment and enjoy it.

Note: One teaspoon of salt equals 2,000 milligrams of sodium.

RULES FOR LONG LIFE

• Chew perfectly what you eat.

• At meals eat, alternately, moist things after dry, fat after lean, sweet after sour, and cold after hot, to the end that the one may be corrective of the other.

• After having drunk more than once, eat dry bread or biscuit.

—*FARMER'S ALMANAC* (1793)

CHOPSTICKS

Place one stick between thumb and index finger and rest on third finger of right hand.

Place second stick above first stick, between thumb and index finger. Rest on second finger with points together.

Operate top stick up and down by raising second finger.

FOOD FLASHES

The average person eats 10 times his or her own weight in food a year.

The glue on a postage stamp contains 1/10 of a calorie.

Cannibalistic Aztecs are said to have considered the French "delicious," while deeming Spaniards "so tough as to be virtually inedible."

It takes an average of 345 squirts from a cow's udder to produce a gallon of milk.

GREAT GARLIC!

With astonishing consistency the virtues of garlic have wafted with singular vigor down the ages. Babylonians knew of its medicinal powers three thousand years ago. It was well known to the Egyptians, who used it as a mummy preservative. Their pyramids were built by slaves fed with great quantities of garlic to boost their endurance for working in the hot sun. Greek physicians used garlic in their prescriptions. Garlic was mentioned in Hindu and Sanskrit writings a thousand years before Christ, and in the Middle Ages it was believed to ward off vampires and witches. It has been mentioned in countless herbal and medical books since the advent of printing.

Perhaps the greatest esteem bestowed upon garlic was its ancient nickname, "Poor Man's Treacle," in reference to the many medicinal uses it was put to by the common people throughout the ages. Some uncommon folk of high regard also appreciated its healing properties. Hippocrates, for example, recommended it for upset stomachs, while Aristotle used it for animal bites. More recently, Albert Schweitzer used it in Africa to treat infections. It has also been found to reduce cholesterol, lower blood pressure and improve circulation.

Garlic owes much of its medicinal virtues to its extremely penetrating and tenacious odor, which exerts an inhibitory influence on some types of bacteria. It might exert an inhibitory influence on your love life, as well—so garlic with care! (Although, as far as that's concerned, famed food maven Jeff Smith—a garlic fanatic if ever there was one—flatly advises: "If your sweetheart doesn't like garlic, find someone else!")

KITCHEN TIPS

Most people have several tricks of the trade for preparing food. For those who don't (or who do and want more), here follows a sort of "starter set" of culinary lore:

• If cheese becomes dry, try soaking it in buttermilk and it will return to normal.

• Cottage cheese stored upside down lasts twice as long.

• A cracked egg can still be boiled if you rub the cracked spot with moistened salt before placing the egg into boiling water.

• When poaching eggs, add a little vinegar to the water and the whites will not float away from the yolk.

• Thaw frozen fish in milk for fresh-caught flavor.

• Before broiling fish, make three slits on each side to prevent it from bending.

• Use tongs for turning a steak instead of piercing with a fork. This will prevent loss of natural juice.

• Before carving a roast, let it "set" for 10 minutes. This will make slicing easier and more even, and more of the natural juice will be retained.

• Never allow a stew to boil—just let it simmer.

• If you've accidentally made stew or soup too salty, add slices of raw potatoes, which absorb salt quickly. Boil a few minutes and remove potato slices. Repeat until stew or soup returns to normal.

• If gravy seems flat and tasteless, peel an onion, wash it well and steep it in a cup of boiling water for 10 or 15 minutes. Add the resulting liquid to the gravy. The gravy will take on a lovely brown color *and* the flavor of the onion.

- To keep from weeping when peeling or slicing onions, place a small piece of bread between your teeth and breathe through your mouth.
- If an onion is pierced by a fork before cooking, it will retain its shape without falling apart.
- Do not peel fresh mushrooms. Instead, rinse them briefly without soaking, then dry.
- To freeze fresh mushrooms, cook them three minutes in boiling water to which salt and lemon juice have been added, rinse, then seal in plastic bags. Mushrooms will keep for several months.
- To make a garnish that will enliven almost any cold dish, add thin slices of peeled or unpeeled cucumber to a cup of vinegar that has been mixed with a cup of water and season to taste with black pepper and sugar. Chill in refrigerator before serving.
- To keep cut fruit from turning brown, sprinkle it with lemon juice.
- When making apple cider, a good rule of thumb is that it takes three apples to make a glass of cider.
- Store popcorn in the freezer, take it out as you need it and pop it frozen. This keeps moisture in and results in fewer unpopped kernels.
- Do not prepare pastry dough in a hot kitchen. It should be kept cool and placed in the refrigerator before rolling out.
- Microwave tips: Before reheating breads, wrap them in an all-white paper towel. Use the same kind of towel to cover bacon, sausage, fish or crumb-coated chicken. (If colored paper were used, the hot, moist conditions in a microwave could cause toxic dyes to bleed onto food.)

KITCHEN TIPS FOR BUSY BACHELORS

All real bachelor food is fried. If you roll the food around in flour before you fry it, you've got three of the four Unmarried Male Food Groups: fat, grease, starch and sugar. You can get the sugar, too, if you have a Mai Tai with dinner.

Don't cook steaks in the toaster, even little ones. Never serve oysters during a month that has no paycheck in it. Oregano makes everything taste like pizza.

Milk is spoiled when it starts to look like yogurt. Yogurt is spoiled when it starts to look like cottage cheese. Cottage cheese is spoiled when it starts to look like regular cheese. Regular cheese is nothing but spoiled milk.

You can cook a toasted cheese sandwich by wrapping it in aluminum foil and ironing it with a steam iron. Flambéing generally happens by accident. If you call it "Italian cheese toast," it's not disgusting to have warmed-over pizza for breakfast.

—P. J. O'ROURKE

APPROXIMATE KITCHEN MEASURES

1 cup water	8 oz.	4 medium potatoes	1 lb.
2 tablespoons butter	1 oz.	3 medium tomatoes	1 lb.
2 tablespoons flour	1 oz.	4 cups grated cheese	1 lb.
3 teaspoons soda	1/2 oz.	9 medium eggs	1 lb.
4 teaspoons baking powder	1/2 oz.	3 large bananas	1 lb.
3 1/2 cups whole-wheat flour	1 lb.	1 cup nutmeats	5 oz.
2 1/2 cups wheat flour	1 lb.	1 cup rice uncooked[*]	8 oz.
1/2 cup buckwheat flour	1 lb.	4 cups apples (sliced)	1 1/2 lb.
5 1/2 cups coffee (dry)	1 lb.	2 cups ground meat	1 lb.
6 1/2 cups tea (dry)	1 lb.	2 3/4 cups brown sugar	6-7 oz.
2 cups butter	1 lb.	1 cup granulated sugar	8 oz.
2 cups cornmeal	1 lb.	1 cup confectioner's sugar	4 1/2 oz.
2 3/8 cups raisins	1 lb.	1 cup honey, molasses, corn syrup	12 oz.

[*]Rice doubles in volume upon cooking.

CLOSE ENOUGH

- **For** 1 whole egg, for baking or thickening: **Use** 2 egg yolks.
- **For** 1 cup butter or margarine for baking: **Use** 7/8 cup vegetable, or animal shortening plus 1/2 teaspoon salt.
- **For** 1 teaspoon double-acting baking powder: **Use** 2 teaspoons quick-acting baking powder or 1/4 teaspoon baking soda if 1/2 cup of sour milk or buttermilk is substituted for 1/2 cup of whole milk.
- **For** 1 cup sour milk or buttermilk, for baking: **Use** 1 cup whole milk plus 1 tablespoon vinegar or lemon juice, or 1 cup whole milk plus 1 3/4 teaspoons cream of tartar.
- **For** 1 cup whole milk: **Use** 1/2 cup evaporated milk plus 1/2 cup water, or 1 cup nonfat dry or skim milk plus 2 1/2 teaspoons butter or margarine.
- **For** 1 cup skim milk: **Use** 1 cup reconstituted nonfat dry milk.
- **For** 1 tablespoon flour, for thickening: **Use** 1/2 tablespoon cornstarch, or 2 teaspoons quick-cooking tapioca.
- **For** 1 cup cake flour, for baking: **Use** 7/8 cup all-purpose flour.

COOKING UP ROMANCE

This suggests women have more of an effect on men if they throw away those expensive perfumes and put some pumpkin pie in the oven.
—DR. ALAN HIRSCH, of the Smell & Taste Research Foundation, on studies showing that men are sexually aroused by homey odors such as doughnuts, pumpkin pie and licorice.

10 FOODS YOU SHOULD NEVER EAT

1. Quaker 100% Natural Cereal. This overrated granola cereal contains almost 4 grams of saturated fat per half-cup serving. That's 18 percent of your daily maximum. That's as much saturated fat as you'd get from a hamburger at McDonald's! A much better choice would be a low-fat, whole-grain cereal like Kellogg's Nutri-Grain Wheat, Post Grape-Nuts, General Mills Wheaties, or Nabisco Shredded Wheat. Or look for low-fat granola by Quaker and Kellogg's.

2. Kung Pao Chicken. One average dinner-size take-out order has 76 grams of fat. That's as much fat as 17 teaspoons of oil! It also averages more than a day's worth of sodium (2,608 mg). The same size order of Szechuan Shrimp or Stir-Fried Mixed Vegetables contains one-fourth as much fat and a little less sodium.

3. Dunkin' Donuts Plain Cake Doughnut. Thanks to the hydrogenated shortening in which these doughnuts are fried, a single plain cake doughnut winds up with as much cholesterol-raising fat as a McDonald's Big Mac! If you want good-tasting pastries without the fat, give Entenmann's fat-free line a try.

4. Nissin Shrimp Cup Noodles. This soup will give you a surprisingly strong shot of fat (about 3 teaspoons' worth) and almost as much sodium (1,550 mg) as you should ideally eat in a whole day. Try Fantastic Foods Only A Pinch soups instead. A serving averages just half a teaspoon of fat and 140 mg of sodium—a much healthier alternative.

5. Movie-theater Popcorn Popped in Coconut Oil. A large bucket of unbuttered popcorn at theaters (like United Artists) that pop in coconut oil has almost three days' worth of artery-clogging fat! Add "butter" and you'll boost the cholesterol-raising fat to almost four days' worth. That's like eating *eight* McDonald's Big Macs. Even a small portion contains almost a day's worth of saturated fat. What to do? Choose a theater that uses air-popped popcorn, or at least one that pops its corn in a heart-healthy oil like canola or corn.

6. Oscar Mayer Lunchables. It would be hard to invent a worse food than these combos of heavily processed meat, artery-clogging cheese, and mostly-white-flour crackers. The line averages 5 1/2 teaspoons of fat (that's 60 percent of calories) and 1,734 mg of sodium.

7. Häagen-Dazs Exträas. Häagen-Dazs has managed to make its line of gourmet ice cream extra fatty by adding ingredients like fudge, peanut butter, peanuts, or brownies to its already-fatty ice cream. Eat a cup of Exträas Triple Brownie Overload or Peanut Butter Burst and you've downed 44 grams of fat . . . almost as much as half a stick of butter. And a cup of Exträas Cappuccino Commotion or Caramel Cone Explosion has as much artery-clogging saturated fat (20 grams) as two McDonald's Quarter Pounders with Cheese! That's a whole day's quota for many people. A cup of Mattus' Low-fat Ice Cream, on the other hand, has just six grams of fat. And only three of them are saturated. But the taste is as rich as full-fat Häagen-Dazs.

8. Campbell's Regular Soups. They're brimming with salt. Half a can contains 1,014 mg of sodium. That's about half your ideal quota for an entire day. If you're looking for more than salty water, check out Pritikin soups. A cup averages 160 mg of sodium and one gram of fat. That's a bit less fat—and far less sodium—than you'll find in Campbell's Healthy Request or ConAgra's Healthy Choice soups.

9. Taco Bell's Taco Salad with Shell. With the shell, this platter of beef, cheese, and beans has about 13 teaspoons of fat, about 4 teaspoons of saturated fat, and 838 calories. That's almost all the fat and saturated fat an adult should eat in an entire day. If you're in the mood for a fast-food salad, head to McDonald's. Its Chunky Chicken Salad contains a single teaspoon of fat and 1/4 teaspoon of saturated fat.

10. Fettucini Alfredo. An average dinner-size entrée contains an amazing 97 grams of fat—or 22 teaspoons of fat. It's like sitting down and eating an entire stick of butter! If you want a lower-fat pasta meal, try spaghetti or linguini topped with tomato sauce, red or white clam sauce, meat sauce, or meatballs.

LET IT BE MEATLESS
By Linda McCartney

My husband Paul and I stopped eating meat many years ago. During the course of a Sunday lunch, we happened to look out the kitchen window at our young lambs gamboling happily in the fields. Glancing down at our plates we suddenly realized that we were eating the leg of an animal that had until recently been gamboling in a field itself. We looked at each other and said, "Wait a minute, we love these sheep—why are we eating them?" It was the last time we did.

These days, when we have friends over for the first time, I know in advance that there will be one or two puzzled looks and glances before the afternoon's over. Eventually someone always says, "Linda, this is great food, but I didn't think you ate meat. Have you changed—or are you barbecuing it just for us?"

At this point I smile and say, "Actually, there was no meat in it at all!"

For the entire afternoon, they've been thinking that they were eating sausages, burgers, and kebabs made from meat, marinated in a really tasty barbecue sauce. In fact, they have been eating one of the most exciting developments in food this century—Textured Vegetable Protein (TVP), a meat substitute made from processed and refined soybeans. If you can't find TVP in your local health food store or supermarket, try using any soy-based meat substitute or vegetable burger. Seitan, a wheat-based product, is particularly suitable because of its meatlike texture.

These recipes for hearty winter entrees include meatless versions of English favorites such as Shepherd's Pie as well as easy-to-prepare ethnic dishes. I hope you enjoy making them as much as I do. And don't be afraid to make changes to suit your own taste. That's what cooking's all about.

Greek Beefless Stew

4 tablespoons butter or margarine
6 vegetable burgers, cubed
2 cups vegetable stock or water

2 tablespoons tomato paste
12 small onions or 4 medium onions, chopped
2 medium potatoes, chopped
4 carrots, chopped
1 teaspoon ground cinnamon
salt and freshly ground black pepper to taste

Melt the butter in a frying pan, brown the burger chunks for about 5 minutes, then place them in a deep stew pot or saucepan. Arrange the onions on top.

Add the tomato paste to the remaining hot fat in the frying pan and stir well. Gradually add the vegetable stock, stir well, and bring this mixture to a boil. Pour the sauce over the onions and burger chunks, add the carrots, potatoes, cinnamon, salt, and pepper, and stir well. Add a little more liquid if necessary.

Cover the pot and cook for 40 to 45 minutes over low heat. Serve immediately. Have plenty of fresh bread on hand.

Preparation time: 1 hour. Good source of vitamin A, vitamin C.

Shepherd's Pie

If you like a slightly stronger flavor, try adding 2 large carrots, thinly sliced, to the onion as it sautés.

1 1/2 pounds potatoes
6 tablespoons butter or margarine
1 to 2 tablespoons milk
1 large onion, chopped
1 4 1/2-ounce packet TVP mince or 6 vegetable burgers, crumbled
2 tablespoons soy sauce
1 1/2 cups vegetable stock or water (3/4 cup if using vegetable burgers)
salt and pepper to taste.

Preheat the oven to 400° F. Boil the potatoes and mash them in a bowl with 4 tablespoons of the butter and enough milk to give them a good sticky consistency. Put them to one side.

Melt the remaining butter in a frying pan and sauté the onion. Then add the TVP mince, soy sauce, and vegetable stock. Simmer for 5 to 10 minutes. Season to taste.

If you want a thicker mixture, blend a little flour or vegetable gravy mix with some vegetable stock and add to the sauté. Cook until thickened, stirring constantly. Pour the mixture into a baking dish and cover with the mashed potatoes.

Bake for 30 minutes, until the potatoes are nice and brown. For extra browning on top, just place under the grill for a few moments (make sure your baking dish will stand this treatment). Preparation time: 1 hour 15 min-

utes. Good source of vitamin A, B-group vitamins, vitamin C, potassium.

Spinach Cheese Dumplings
A wonderful tasty winter warmer—serve with a selection of vegetables.

1 pound fresh spinach
1 cup cottage or ricotta cheese
2 egg yolks, beaten
1/2 cup Parmesan cheese, grated
salt and freshly ground black pepper to taste
pinch of nutmeg
1/2 cup self-rising flour
4 tablespoons butter or margarine

Wash and trim the spinach and cook it, covered, in its own juices. Drain very well, chop finely, and allow to cool.

Mix the cottage cheese, egg yolks, half the Parmesan cheese, the salt, pepper, and nutmeg in a large mixing bowl. Add the cooled spinach and the flour and mix together.

Take a spoonful of the mixture and using a little flour shape it into a small ball. Continue in this way until all the mixture is used.

Drop the dumplings into a pot of boiling water, about 10 to 12 at a time, and cook for 4 to 5 minutes. Continue until all the dumplings are cooked.

Melt the butter. Place the dumplings on a hot serving dish and pour the butter over them. Sprinkle with the remaining Parmesan cheese and serve immediately. Preparation time: 35 minutes. Good source of protein, vitamin A, vitamin C, calcium, iron.

Madras Onion Curry
Serve with rice and condiments such as nuts, grated coconut, and chutneys.

3 tablespoons vegetable oil
1 large onion, chopped
1 clove garlic, crushed
1 tablespoon curry powder
1 4 1/2-ounce packet TVP chunks or 4 vegetable burgers, cubed
1 small apple
3 cups vegetable stock or water (2 cups if using vegetable burgers)
1 tablespoon soy sauce
1 teaspoon grated lemon rind
1 tablespoon Sucanat
salt and freshly ground black pepper to taste
1/4 teaspoon ground ginger

2 tablespoons cornstarch
2 tablespoons cold water

Heat the vegetable oil in a large saucepan and sauté the onion, garlic, and curry powder until lightly browned.

Add the TVP chunks or cubed vegetable burgers to the mixture and stir for 5 minutes over low heat.

Peel, core, and chop the apple and add it to the sauté. Now add the remaining ingredients (except the cornstarch and cold water). Stir well, cover the pan, and simmer for 10 minutes.

Mix the cornstarch and cold water together in a small bowl. Add this mixture to the curry and simmer, stirring often, until the sauce thickens.

Leave to cook, uncovered, for a further 5 minutes. Preparation time: 30 minutes.

PASTA MADE SIMPLE

The following "pasta primer" is based on data from the National Macaroni Institute, as filtered through a considerable amount of thoroughly enjoyable field research:

Pasta is thought to have been invented over two thousand years ago by either the Chinese or the Italians—or perhaps both, independently of each other. (Surviving evidence is imprecise.) In any case, it is made from a dough of semolina—the heart of high-quality hard wheat—and water. Although a great many shapes are available, the most popular in the U.S. are elbow macaroni, spaghetti, and egg noodles. (Egg solids are added to make noodles.)

Ideally, each day's menus should include foods from the basic four food groups: milk and milk products, meat and meat substitutes (including eggs and legumes), fruits and vegetables, and breads and cereals. Pasta is a part of the breads-and-cereals group and is enriched, with its nutrient content appearing on all packages.

Pasta is a valuable provider of protein and offers essential amino acids needed for optimum health and growth. It also delivers thiamine, riboflavin, niacin and iron.

Pasta is a low-fat, low-sodium, easily digested food. You can be on a diet and still indulge in it—but only if you blend in a dash or two of common sense. The key is to combine the pasta with foods or light sauces that won't add greatly to your daily calorie quota.

One of pasta's greatest advantages is that you can keep a good supply of it on hand at all times. It is a dehydrated food and—when stored in a cool, dry place—can be kept up to a year. However, once a pasta package has been opened, it's a good idea to keep the unused portion in a covered container.

Here are the basic directions for cooking pasta properly: Gradually add 8 ounces of the pasta product, along with 1 teaspoon of salt, to 3 quarts of rapidly boiling water. Add 1 tablespoon of butter or cooking oil to water to keep pasta from sticking together. Cook uncovered, stirring occasionally, the length of time determined by the thickness of the pasta—mostaccioli, for example, needing more time than spaghetti. It will take the cooking of one or two batches of pasta to get a sense of when a batch is about ready to serve, the important thing being not to overcook. The time-honored gauge is to cook only till the pasta is *al dente*—literally, "to the tooth"; figuratively, "so that it's still a little firm when you bite it."

Note: When cooking more than 8 ounces, proportions of 4 to 6 quarts of water and 2 tablespoons of salt for 1 pound of pasta are recommended. Rinse pasta *only* when making salads.

HERB BUTTER

To make herb butter or margarine, soften one stick of whichever, add 2 tablespoons of finely minced fresh herb or 1 teaspoon of dried herb, then cream ingredients together, adding several drops of lemon juice. (Suggested herbs to use: basil, tarragon, thyme, chives, dill, parsley, marjoram, rosemary.) Use on bread, baked potatoes, and other vegetables.

HERBS TO DRINK

"Ginseng," from Barton's Medical Botany (1818)

Herb teas, called "tisanes" in the herb world, are a revolution in taste. Once you try them you won't be content with the tiresome routine of coffee. For one thing, they offer a wide spectrum of tastes. Chamomile tea, for example, has a mellow flavor, like apple blossoms. Fennel tisanes have a delicate licorice taste. Lemon verbena makes a delicious grassy brew. And Linden tea, popular in France and

207

Germany, is particularly fragrant.

Herb teas are both a pleasure to drink and a valuable source of organic nutrients and vitamins—qualities that account for their universal appeal. Not only are they imbibed throughout Europe, but they are also enjoyed in India and the Mideast, where cooks traditionally serve mint teas after a meal of hot curries. And Yerba Mate, a harmless but effective stimulant rich in vitamins A and D, is a favorite South American drink.

For anyone following a health-conscious diet, herb teas are pleasant substitutes for regular coffee (which contains caffeine) and tea (which contains tannic acid). Parsley tea, for example, contains vitamins A, B and C and several important trace elements. Many herb teas have a specific medicinal action. Old-fashioned horehound tea, for example, is considered good for colds and sore throats, while elder tea, which smells and tastes like lilacs, can be helpful to asthmatics and those with skin trouble. And spicy sassafras tea makes an excellent spring tonic. Actually, most herb teas are *all-season* delights, in that they are enjoyable when served steaming hot in the fall or winter, or refreshingly iced in summer (sweetened with honey if desired).

To introduce yourself to herb teas, purchase 1/4 ounce of several different varieties. (If purchased at an herb shop or farmer's market, each package of herbs should be labeled or otherwise marked, so that you'll know what it is when you get home.) Most herb teas also come in tea bags. They can be found most readily in gourmet shops and health-food stores, while limited selections are increasingly more available at supermarkets.

Note: Equal parts of caution and common sense are needed when buying herbs and making beverages from them. First, be sure the herbs you buy are for consumption and not just "potpourri" purposes. They should also be non-chemically treated, or "bug-spray free."

Using Tea Herbs

Tea herbs are easy to use—all you need a tea bob, or a strainer and a cup, or a porcelain container with a tight-fitting lid. Herbal teas must steep longer than other teas (allow at least five minutes) to develop their full flavor and aroma .

• If you are making just one cup, cover it with a saucer. Unlined metal teapots such as those made from aluminum are not suitable because traces of the metal can contaminate the herbs.

• Infusions are made only from the leaves and flowers of herbs. These parts of the plant release their volatile oils when infused in boiling water. If they were boiled, the oils would evaporate. An infusion is made in the same manner as regular tea. Crush one teaspoon of dried herbs for each cup of water and one for the pot, or use a handful of fresh herbs. Pour boiling water over the herbs and let stand from 5 to 15 minutes, until it is as strong as you like.

• All seeds and roots and the leaves of a few herbs such as horehound, lemon balm and bee balm must be boiled to extract their volatile oils. To make a decoction, first crush the roots or seeds, allowing one teaspoonful for each cup of water and one for the pot. Boil the herbs for 15 to 20 minutes in a glass or porcelain container. Seeds, roots and bark such as sassafras may also be percolated like coffee. Decoctions are often used in preparing medicinal herbs.

• For a real hot blast, heat your teapot before adding boiling water for an infusion or pouring in a decoction—the tea won't cool off so fast. Or do as the English do: use a tea cozy to insulate your teapot.

• Herewith, a summary of the basics:

Hot tea—Pour one cup of boiling water over one teaspoon of an herb or herb mixture and steep for five minutes. Amount of tea and steeping time may be adjusted to taste.

Iced tea—Remove quart of boiling water from heat. Add four to eight teaspoons of herbs, according to taste. Let steep for about 15 minutes, then pour over a tray's worth of ice cubes in a pitcher. This method prevents the tea from becoming cloudy. *Tip:* For richer, stronger taste throughout the course of one's drink, use herb-tea ice cubes that have been prepared earlier.

Sun tea—Add four to eight teaspoons of herbs (again, according to taste) to a quart or so of cold water in a clear-glass container. Place in the sun for two to six hours. Remove herbs and chill in refrigerator and serve over ice. Fresh herbs are especially suitable for sun tea.

A Garland of Favorite Tea Herbs

Alfalfa —The seeds and leaves of this valuable herb are packed full of vitamins A, D, E and K. Alfalfa is considered to be one of the best sources of essential minerals. It also contains eight known enzymes. It makes a mild, grassy tisane that can be nicely spiked with mint.

Anise—Makes a fragrant licorice-flavored brew especially liked by children. For best results use the seeds after bruising them in a mortar and pestle. Make a weak decoction and sweeten with honey.

Bergamot—Bergamot, or Oswego, tea was first used by the Native Americans of the eastern U.S., who introduced it to the settlers. This orange-scented tisane soothes the nerves and pacifies ruffled stomachs. Bergamot is the ingredient that gives "Earl Grey" tea its distinctive taste.

Borage—The cucumber-flavored leaves of borage are great for iced tea. Rich in calcium and potassium, this brew reputedly aids those who are nervous or depressed. Also said to increase the milk supply of nursing mothers. Ideally, one should use fresh borage and float the star-shaped blue flowers in your tea.

Burdock—A superlative herb that Pechey, writing in his *Complete Herbal* (1694), said "stirs up lust." It's also supposed to help you lose weight, clear the complexion and cleanse the blood.

Caraway—For a new way to enjoy these savory seeds, bruise them in a mortar and pestle and make a mild, tonic decoction. Reputedly stimulates digestion and helps overcome nausea. *Tip:* Cool some in the refrigerator and use as an inexpensive mouthwash.

Catnip—An old-time remedy for chasing away feverish colds, nervous headaches, insomnia and various other aches and ills. It's also a pleasant tea for everyday use.

Chamomile—Makes a delicious golden apple-flavored brew once used by the Egyptians to prevent aging skin. Extremely popular in Europe, and with women having menstrual problems. *Note:* Chamomile may not be everyone's cup of tea, as it can cause allergic reactions in some people. If you're not sure, try a little bit of a relatively weak brew and see how you feel; increase density and amount consumed if and as desired.

Chicory—A common blue-flowered species of wild lettuce. Chicory tea made from the leaves reputedly tones up the system and has a mild laxative effect. The roots may be roasted and used as a coffee substitute. Many Indians of the western U.S. chew the root as a tonic chewing gum.

Dandelion—This well-known plant, generally considered a garden "pest," is actually a valuable medicinal herb, so the next time you dig it up, save the leaves and brew a tea from them. Said to be good for biliousness, with a slightly laxative effect.

Dill—A weak decoction of the seeds is reputedly a good remedy for hiccups.

Elder—Elder flowers make a great tisane that tastes very much like lilacs. Said to be good for bronchial and asthmatic complaints. Often mixed with yarrow to help ward off colds, it is also used externally as a cosmetic to clear the skin.

Fennel—A delicious tea with a peppermint-licorice taste. Great for weight watchers, it is said to help melt off the extra pounds. Also good for indigestion. Brew the seeds as a decoction.

Ginger—This spicy tea will excite and warm you on even the most chilling of wintry nights. Has a strengthening and cheering effect on the body. A great tea to serve your guests. Simply slice fresh ginger root and let it steep in boiling water.

Ginseng—A tea made from the root is highly valued as a preventative of disease and aging in the Orient. Revered by the Chinese, Japanese and Koreans for centuries, ginseng is now gaining wide favor in the U.S..

Goldenrod—A healing herb known from biblical times, goldenrod makes a sweet, highly perfumed tea. Unfortunately this plant has a bad reputation in this country because it is often confused with ragweed. The plant's Latin name, *Solidago,* means "to make whole," referring to its medicinal properties.

Gotu Kola—Considered an exotic cousin of the herb pennywort, gotu kola is almost as popular as ginseng among those seeking longevity. According to an old Sinhalese proverb, "Two leaves a day will keep old age away." A pungent tea brewed from the leaves is supposed to have an energizing effect on the brain.

Horehound—An old-fashioned remedy for coughs and colds. Promotes perspiration and in large doses has a laxative effect. Mixed with honey, it is said to clear the vision. Makes a bitter brew, so sweeten generously.

Lavender—This perfumey broth reputedly soothes the nerves and cures headaches. An exotic tasting tea best served as a mild infusion spiked with lemon.

Lemon Verbena—One of the best-tasting of herb teas, it's mild and perfumed with lemon. It is used to treat indigestion and flatulence, and has a mild sedative effect.

Marigold—A golden tea is made from the dried blossoms of the pot marigold variety called "calendula." It supposedly helps skin problems and acts as a general tonic. Often mixed with mint.

Marjoram—More delicately favored than its cousin oregano (*Origanum vulgare*), marjoram has a long and colorful history. Its scent was thought to have been the result of being touched by the goddess Aphrodite, and in the Middle Ages it was thought to be a magic charm against witchcraft.

Meadowsweet—This herb has a sweet-scented flower that was highly prized by Queen Elizabeth I, who had it strewn over the floors of her private quarters. It has been used as a remedy colic, diarrhea and the flu.

Mint—Nearly all of the 30 varieties of the mint family make excellent teas and are good substitutes for coffee. Peppermint is the strongest-tasting mint, but also well worth trying are apple mint, orange mint, pineapple mint, horse mint and spearmint.

Red Raspberry—Leaves from the red raspberry bush make an energizing and nerve-soothing tea that is also supposedly good for canker sores and sore throats.

Rose Hips—Rose "hips" make a delicious tea containing large quantities of vitamin C. Also rich in vitamins B, B_2 E and K. Mixes well with any herb. Recommended for daily use. Let steep for 20 minutes.

Rosemary—An old-fashioned tea said to be good for indigestion, colds and headaches. Many believe that it improves the memory.

Sage—A delicious Old English tea that makes a good tonic. Said to make hair grow, relieve pain in the joints, quicken the senses and aid the memory. Better than coffee for a quick pickup.

Sassafras—A traditional spring tonic dating from the colonial era, sassafras bark makes a pungent spicy brew that can be percolated like coffee. Said to cleanse the blood.

Thyme—The several varieties of thyme make refreshing tisanes. These calming brews are usually drunk after meals as a digestive aid. They also have a most beneficial effect on the mucous membranes. A tea made from lemon thyme is a rare delight.

Valerian—Even the highly skeptical, "official" pharmaceutical world hails this herb, which acts directly on the nervous system to ease pain and promote sleep. Also combats colds, measles, colic and stomach ulcers. Use in small doses as an infusion. Never boil the root. Peppermint compliments its action.

Yarrow—A powerful medicinal herb used since Achilles popularized it as a "wound" herb in ancient Greece. Also important in the medicine of Native Americans, who still value it. Considered an important blood builder, it is also used for eruptive diseases, colds and pneumonia. Considered more effective than aspirin for headaches and completely safe to use.

Yerba Mate (South American Mate)—A delicious, smoky-flavored tea popular in South America. Exhilarating and strength-giving, it is said to be useful for dieters wishing to reduce their appetite. Rich in vitamins A and D, it is more stimulating than coffee.

—CAROL PEARSON

BREWING THE PERFECT CUP OF COFFEE

Brewing flavorful, delicious coffee is easy, but like all food preparation it requires fresh ingredients and careful handling. Freshness is the heart and soul of fine coffee. To increase the freshness life of your coffee, store it in the freezer. Cold storage will increase the freshness life by a factor of four. If your coffee tastes flat, dull and lifeless it's because it is stale.

Full-flavored coffee requires the right amount of ground coffee per cup. Weak coffee tastes thin and washed out, so use enough ground coffee to brew a cup with plenty of flavor. Start with one or two tablespoons of ground coffee (or beans) per 6 ounces of water and adjust the strength to suit your taste.

Each type of coffee brewer requires an appropriate grind. Plunger brewing takes a coarse grind, drip makers a finer grind, and espresso a very fine grind. Coffee that's too coarsely ground brews up short on flavor; coffee too finely ground will brew up harsh and somewhat bitter. If you grind your own beans start on the coarse side and with each pot grind a little finer until you notice a slightly rough taste, then return to a less fine grind.

If your coffee is harsh or bitter try a coarser grind. If thin and weak brew it stronger—i.e., use more coffee per cup and check the grind.

—STEEP & BREW COFFEES AND TEAS

COFFEE SUBSTITUTE
For those who want the taste of coffee without the caffeine, here's a time-honored substitute: Infuse 1 teaspoon of ground roasted dandelion root and 1/2 teaspoon of chicory in 1 cup of boiling water.

QUEENLY BREW
"Hydromel [mead] as I made it weak for the Queen Mother. Take 18 quarts of spring-water, and one quart of honey; when the water is warm, put the honey into it. When it boileth up, skim it very well, and continue skimming it, as long as any scum will rise. Then put in one Race of Ginger (sliced in thin slices), four cloves, and a little sprig of green Rosemary. Let these boil in the Liquor so long, till in all it have boiled one hour. Then set it to cool, till it be blood-warm; and put to it a spoonful of Ale-yest. When it is worked up, put it into a vessel of a fit size; and after two or three days, bottle it up. You may drink it after six weeks, or two months.

"Thus was the Hydromel made that I gave the Queen, which was exceedingly liked by everybody."

—*THE CLOSET OF SIR KENELM DIGBY OPENED* (1669)

AN OXFORD NIGHTCAP

"Egg-posset, otherwise, in college language, Rum booze: Beat up well the yolks of eight eggs, with refined sugar pulverized, and a nutmeg grated. Then extract the juice from rind of a lemon, by rubbing loaf sugar upon it, and put the sugar, with a piece of cinnamon and a bottle of wine, into a saucepan; place it on the fire, and, when it boils, take it off; then add a single glass of cold white wine; put the liquor into a spouted jug, and pour it gradually among the yolk of eggs, etc. All must be kept well stirred with a spoon, while the liquor is pouring in. If it be not sweet enough, add loaf sugar; and lastly, pour the mixture as swiftly as possible from one vessel to another, until it yields a fine froth. Half a pint of rum is sometimes added, but is then very intoxicating, and consequently pernicious. Port wine is sometimes used instead of white, but is not generally so palatable. This beverage should be drunk about bed-time, out of wine glasses, and while it is quite hot. —Observe, that if the wine be poured boiling hot among the eggs, the mixture will curdle, and the posset be spoiled."

—Recipe, 1828

HOLY PRETZELS!

The pretzel was first contrived and eaten 1,500 years ago in a monastery in southern Europe. A monk, preparing biscuits for a Lenten meal, rolled his leftover dough into strips and twisted them into shapes resembling arms crossed in prayer. (That was the way Christians prayed in those days.)

ALL THIS AND BAKING SODA TOO

For a relatively small amount of change, you can buy a humble household tool that replaces a lot of fancy-priced ones—namely, baking soda. Its many uses include:

•Toothpaste. Mix soda with salt, for the kind of toothpaste old-time Texas dentists used to say was better than store-bought.

• Acid-indigestion tablet substitute. Just take a little soda with a glass of water. If problem persists, see a physician.

• Scouring powder. A useful cleanser, but use it with care, as it can create bad fumes if mixed with some dishwashing liquids.

• Refrigerator deodorant. An open box of baking soda in the fridge eliminates strong food odors and prevents potentially yucky taste transfers between foods. An open box of soda in the freezer will keep ice cubes and ice cream fresh-tasting.

• Sunburn ointment substitute. Spread paste of soda and water on exposed body areas.

• Kitchen-fire extinguisher. Pour baking soda onto foods that have caught fire, and the flames will go out without sputtering. (Never pour water onto burning food.)

• Car freshener. Pour 1/2 inch of soda in your car's ashtrays to eliminate stale tobacco odors and aid in putting out cigarettes and cigars. Sprinkle on carpeting and under mats to eliminate lingering pet and tobacco odors.

• Maybe even baking?

MEAT GRADING AND LABELING

The grade generally sold at retail stores.

The circle-shaped stamp you may see on the meat shows the meat was processed under U.S.D.A. inspection. It indicates meat is from healthy animals, processed under sanitary conditions.

Of the three basic grades of meat, *Prime* is fattier and costlier than the other two grades, *Choice* and *Select*.

Things are a bit more complicated when it comes to the *labeling* of meat and poultry—especially when such words as "natural" and "light" (or "lite") are involved.

According to the USDA's Food Safety and Inspection Service, the term "natural" may be used on labeling for a meat or poultry product provided the product does not contain any chemical preservative, or any artificial flavoring, coloring or other synthetic ingredient. Also, the product must not be "more than minimally processed." Minimal processing may include smoking, roasting, freezing, drying or fermenting—or other procedures "which do not fundamentally alter the raw product." (Exceptions, considered on a case-by-case basis, require a

215

supplier to modify any "natural" label "clearly and conspicuously.")

For a product to be labeled "light" (or "lite"), the following guidelines have been established:

It should have at least 25 percent less fat, salt, sodium, breading, etc., than a similar product.

If it is a product that is "unquestionably" low in calories, fat, salt, breading or sodium, "the amount of calories can be no more than 40 calories per serving and no more than 0.4 calories per gram of product. For fat and breading, the product can contain no more than 10 percent. For salt and sodium, the product can contain no more than 35 mg of sodium per 100 grams of product."

• • •

Meat labeling of another sort has recently been ordered by the Agriculture Department as part of its efforts to lower the risk of disease from salmonella, *E. coli* and other bacteria found in animals and responsible for up to 9,000 deaths a year. These labels, about the size of a credit card, say:

Some animal products may contain bacteria that could cause illness if the product is mishandled or cooked improperly. For your protection follow these safe handling instructions.

Keep refrigerated or frozen. Thaw in refrigerator or microwave.

Keep raw meats or poultry separate from other foods. Wash working surfaces (including cutting boards), utensils and hands after touching raw meat or poultry.

Cook thoroughly.

Refrigerate leftovers within two hours.

Labels on meat distributed to institutions, cafeterias or restaurants must carry the same instructions, but are to also say that food must be kept hot at 140° F or higher and that leftovers must be refrigerated immediately.

THE MEAT AND POULTRY HOTLINE

Have a question about thawing a turkey or boiling a ham? Do you wonder about the effect of power outages on refrigerated meat? Are you concerned about the way your bacon and pastrami have been handled and/or packaged lately?

Maybe it's time to call the hotline—the Meat and Poultry Hotline, that is. (See next page for numbers and times.)

The Food Safety and Inspection Service of the U.S. Department of Agriculture calls it, quite properly, "a tool for the prevention of foodborne illness." In addition to inspecting facilities and animals, engaging in research, and fielding a steady stream of inquiries, the FSIS also disseminates an equally steady stream of useful food-safety data, including the following tips:

Shopping. Grocery shop last; get food home within 2 hours. Observe use-by dates. Don't buy food in damaged containers.

Storing. Refrigerate foods you'll use quickly. Freeze raw meat or poultry you can't use in 1 or 2 days. Freezer should register 0° F.

Preparing. Wash hands before preparing food. Wash hands, utensils, cutting boards, and work areas after contact with raw products. Don't thaw or marinate food on the counter.

Cooking. Thoroughly cook raw meat, poultry, fish, and eggs to at least 160° F. internal temperature. Juices should run clear; meat should not be pink. Do not partially cook food. Have a constant heat source, and never set oven under 325° F. Microwave food in a covered dish, turning often.

Serving. Never leave perishable food out over 2 hours. Serve cooked foods hot. Use clean dishes and utensils.

Handling leftovers. Promptly refrigerate or freeze leftovers. Use small, shallow containers. Reheat leftovers to at least 165° F.

Heard it on the Hotline

To hear the latest food safety information, call USDA's Meat and Poultry Hotline
1-800-535-4555
10:00 am–4:00 pm Eastern Time

Professional home economists will answer your questions about proper handling of meat and poultry, how to tell if it is safe to eat, and how to better understand meat and poultry labels.

United States Department of Agriculture   Food Safety and Inspection Service

STORAGE LIFE OF SOME VEGETABLES

Vegetable	Optimum Storage Temperature (°F)	Expected Storage Time (weeks)
Snap beans	45-50	1-2
Melons	40-45	2-4
Cucumbers	50	1-2
Eggplant	50	1-2

Sweet potatoes	45-50	4-6
White potatoes	40-50	12-20
Pumpkins	55	8-24
Winter squash	55	8-24
Tomatoes	50	1-2

COOLING IT

Here's a table of maximum food-storage periods, at 0° F. It is assumed that you've packaged the foods properly and that they are fresh at the time of freezing.

Food	Maximum Storage Time (Months)
Beef roast	12
Steak	12
Ground beef	3
Lamb roasts	12
Lamb patties	3
Fresh pork roasts	8
Pork sausage, cured pork	2
Bacon	1
Veal roasts	8
Veal chops, cutlets	4
Cooked meats	3
Whole chickens, turkeys	12
Chicken livers	3
Chicken, turkey parts	9
Whole duck, goose	6
Cooked chicken, sliced	6
Cooked chicken pies	12
Fried chicken	4
Shrimp, fresh	12
Shrimp, cooked Creole	3
Cooked fish	3
Shucked clams	3
Berries	12
Fruit juice concentrat	12
Asparagus, beans, peas	8
Cauliflower, corn, spina	8
Ice cream, sherbet	1
Bread, rolls	3
Unbaked berry, apple pies	8
Pound cake	6

—U.S. DEPARTMENT OF AGRICULTURE

MONEY, MONEY, MONEY
. . . the whys and wherefores of gain and loss . . .

*Money is like a sixth sense, without which you
cannot make use of the other five.*
—W. SOMERSET MAUGHAM

Money is like muck, not good except it be spread.
—FRANCIS BACON

SCENE ONE: CUT TO THE CASH
Money, money, money: who's got the money?

Money, money: is it the *really* the root of all evil? Or is *not having
it* the real evil root? Or is, perhaps, having it and wanting more and
getting it but still not having enough that gives it a bad name?

Money: it may be better than barter, but do we pay too high a
price to live in a world that often worships as well as uses it? (And, if
so, what's the solution? Revolution? Evolution? Devolution? Or a
monastery, maybe?)

Good questions!

Unfortunately, they're the kind of questions that—while worth
asking—generally give rise to highly debatable, even possibly inflam-

matory answers. So let us assume, at least for here and now, that the world of money is indeed a sensible and rational universe, as we throttle down to more mundane (but still potentially fascinating) matters, such as getting and saving more of it, and spending what's left more wisely. The aim of course being to up your ante, increase your dividend and/or ring your register.

FACTS ABOUT U.S. MONEY

In the early days of the United States, before currency was issued, there were in circulation English shillings, French *louis d'ors* and Spanish doubloons, along with other units of those nations' monies. In addition, the time-tested but wildly variable institution of barter was still widespread. Corn, for example, was such an accepted medium of exchange in 18th-century America that one man used it to pay his son's tuition at Harvard. Rolls of tobacco were another colonial cash substitute. Small wonder that this patchwork state of affairs caused confusion and slowed up trade. Thomas Jefferson strongly opposed adopting the English system and urged that the basic monetary unit be called the dollar, based on the Spanish *dolar*.

This view prevailed, and the dollar was adopted in 1785 by the Congress that existed under the Articles of Confederation; the decimal system was chosen as the method of reckoning. In 1792, the U.S. monetary system was established, and the U.S. Mint began coining money at Philadelphia in 1793.

Many changes in the laws that govern coinage and the denominations themselves have been made since the original 1792 act. Coins no longer in use include the half-cent, 2-cent, 3-cent and 20-cent pieces, as well as the silver half-dime. The five-cent nickel coin (1/4 nickel, 3/4 copper) was introduced in 1866. U.S. gold coins are no longer coined or issued.

On July 23, 1965, President Lyndon Johnson signed a historic bill providing for the first major change in U.S. coinage in more than a century. Silver was eliminated altogether from the dime and quarter and substantially reduced in the half-dollar.

On December 30, 1970, President Richard Nixon signed the Bank Holding Company Act, which called for the removal of all silver from silver dollars and half-dollars.

The selection of coin designs is usually made by the director of the Mint, with the approval of the secretary of the treasury. Congress has, however, in a few instances, prescribed them. For example, as a part of the bicentennial celebration of Washington's birth, Congress declared that the likeness of the first president should appear on the quarter-dollar. Once adopted, a coin design may not be changed more often than once in 25 years without specific legislation.

The John F. Kennedy 50-cent piece, authorized by an act of Congress and approved on December 30, 1963, was released on March 24, 1964. It is one of seven "portrait coins" to be used in the U.S. coinage system.

The others are the one-cent piece, with the head of Lincoln, adopted in 1909; the five-cent piece honoring Jefferson, adopted in 1938; the 25-cent coin, with Washington's profile, first minted in 1932; the Franklin D. Roosevelt dime, introduced in 1946; the Eisenhower silver dollar, brought out in 1971; and in 1979 the silver dollar honoring famed American reformer and suffragette leader Susan B. Anthony. (The Anthony coin—or "Susie" as some call it—has become an ongoing $35,000-a-year mistake. Introduced as an alternative to the dollar bill, it was so poorly received that the U.S. Mint now spends $35,000 a year to store more than 122 million of the coins, an aggregate which would cost too much to destroy.)

The Lincoln penny was the first portrait coin of a regular series. The 100th anniversary of Lincoln's birth aroused sentiment sufficiently strong to overcome a long-prevailing popular prejudice against the use of portraits on coins. A new design was adopted in 1959, when the sesquicentennial of Lincoln's birth was observed. The familiar likeness on the obverse remains unchanged.

The design selection used for American paper currency, including the selection of portraits, is a responsibility of the secretary of the treasury, who acts with the advice of the director of the Bureau of Engraving and Printing, the U.S treasurer and others. By tradition, portraits used on present paper money are those of deceased statesmen of assured historical significance.

The first regular issue of U.S. currency, the treasury notes (commonly known as "demand notes") that were issued in 1861, carried the portraits of Alexander Hamilton (first secretary of the treasury) on the $5 denomination and of Abraham Lincoln on the $10 denomination.

Design features of U.S. paper currency having historic significance include:

• Treasury Seal: The seal imprinted on the face of paper money and on many official Treasury documents is older than the Constitution. The seal was designated by a committee appointed September 26, 1778, and composed of John Witherspoon, Gouverneur Morris, and Richard Henry Lee. Although the date of its adoption is unknown, the seal is affixed to documents issued in 1782. The design includes a shield on which appears the scale of justice; a key, the emblem of official authority; and 13 stars representing the original 13 states.

• The obverse and reverse of the Great Seal are reproduced on the backs of $1 bills. In the center of the obverse is an American eagle holding in its beak a scroll inscribed *E pluribus unum*—one out of many"—while holding in his right talon an olive branch and in his left a bundle of 13 arrows. The "13 states" theme is repeated in the stripes of the eagle's shield and in the star cluster above. On the Great Seal's reverse, above the pyramid, is the phrase *annuit coeptis*, from Virgil's *Aeneid*, meaning: "God has favored our undertaking." The phrase below the pyramid, *novus ordo seclorum*, is "A new order of the ages is created."

•. Portraits of great Americans used on the face of currency.

• Pictures of famous buildings or monuments used on the back of currency.

All notes of the same denomination bear the same portrait. Designs on U.S. currency (Federal Reserve notes) now in circulation are as follows:

Denomination and class	Portrait	Back
$1 Federal Reserve note	George Washington	Obverse and reverse of Great Seal of U.S.
$2 Federal Reserve note	Thomas Jefferson	Portrait by John Trumbull of signing of Declaration of Independence
$4 Federal Reserve note	Abraham Lincoln	Lincoln Memorial
$10 Federal Reserve note	Alexander Hamilton	U.S. Treasury Building
$20 Federal Reserve note	Andrew Jackson	White House
$50 Federal Reserve note	Ulysses S. Grant	U.S. Capitol
$100 Federal Reserve note	Benjamin Franklin	Independence Hall

The $2 bill listed above re-emerged in 1976 after a 13-year absence from the U.S. currency scene. The necessity for this denomination, however, continues to be a matter of debate. Meanwhile, notes of the higher denominations ($500, $1,000, $5,000 and

$10,000) have not been printed for many years. As they are returned to Federal Reserve banks, they are removed from circulation and destroyed. The portraits selected for these notes were William McKinley for the $500, Grover Cleveland for the $1,000, James Madison for the $5,000 and Salmon P. Chase for the $10,000.

The motto "In God We Trust" owes its presence on U.S. coins largely to the increased religious sentiment existing during the Civil War. Salmon P. Chase, then secretary of the treasury, received a number of appeals from devout persons throughout the country urging that the Deity be suitably recognized on our coins as it was on the coins of other nations.

The approved motto first made its appearance on the now-extinct two-cent coin, authorized by act of Congress on April 22, 1864, but its use has not been uninterrupted. In 1866 the motto was introduced on the double-eagle, eagle and half-eagle gold coins and on the silver dollar, half-dollar and quarter-dollar pieces. Over the following half-century it was added to the nickel, penny and dime. A law passed by the 84th Congress and approved by the president on July 11, 1955, provides that the motto shall appear on all paper currency and coins. By a joint resolution of the Congress, approved by the president on July 30, 1956, "In God We Trust" was declared to be the official motto of the United States.

In case you've ever wondered, this is what it costs the treasury department to actually *make* money:

Penny—0.8¢
Nickel—3¢
Dime—1.7¢
Quarter—7.8¢
Currency—3¢

Finally, a centsible bit of trivia: The average American has a hoard of $9.93 in pennies.

COUNTERFEIT NOTES

The advent of sophisticated color copiers has been anything but a blessing for the beleaguered Bureau of Engraving and Printing, which in 1990 alone seized $66 million in funny money. Hoping to thwart the high-tech phonies, the bureau has begun printing and circulating modified moolah containing a polyester filament about the thickness of a human hair, and imprinted with minuscule lettering—the first major change in U.S. paper currency since 1929. Visible only when held up to direct light, the thread cannot be duplicated by copiers, which use reflected light. The new currency also contains microengravings around the portrait. First denominations to be circulated: $100, $50 and $20.

The penalties in 1794 in the United States for making money by printing it on your own press included having a C branded on your forehead, having your left ear clipped, being imprisoned, and having all your property confiscated.

"KEEP THE CHANGE!"

In 1792, King Louis XVI of France was fleeing from bloodthirsty revolutionary mobs when he stopped at Vincennes to eat, offering a gold coin with his own likeness in payment. The innkeeper recognized the king and he was taken back to Paris, where the following year he and his family were guillotined.

"I REGRET I THAT I HAVE BUT ONE QUICK-PICK TO GIVE TO MY COUNTRY!"

"In colonial days lotteries were used to raise money for many institutions, such as churches, schools and forts. Perhaps the most significant lottery was one sponsored by the Continental Congress in November 1776: its object was to raise enough money to pay for the next campaign in the Revolutionary War. Agents in the different colonies sold tickets ranging in price from $10 to $40. They hoped to raise $5 million, but the lottery was not a success. The first drawing kept being postponed because not enough tickets were sold."

—SHEILA W. MARTIN, *The Colonial Spirit*

MONEY TALK

"It is hard for an empty sack to stand upright."
—Benjamin Franklin

"He who has little silver in his pouch must have the more silk on his tongue."
—Edward Bulwer-Lytton

"A wise man should have money in his head, but not in his heart."
—Jonathan Swift

"Annual income twenty pounds, annual expenditure nineteen pounds, nineteen shillings and sixpence, result happiness. Annual income twenty pounds, annual expenditure twenty pounds ought and sixpence, result misery."
—Charles Dickens (via Mr. Micawber, in *David Copperfield*)

"When you have money in your pocket, you are wise, you are handsome, and you sing well, too!"
—Yiddish proverb

"Money is a terrible master, but an excellent servant."
—P. T. Barnum

"While money doesn't mean happiness, it does mean you can be unhappy in comfort."
—Eric Sevareid

"Money is like an arm or a leg—use it or lose it."
—Henry Ford

"The answer to nine out of ten questions is money."
—Malcolm Forbes

"Expenditure rises to meet income."
—C. Northcote Parkinson

"Money doesn't talk, it swears."
—Bob Dylan

THE DOLLAR SIGN

The dollar sign has its origin cloaked in controversy. A prevailing belief is that the sign is derived from a U superimposed on an S with the bottom of the U worn off by time. This is almost surely wrong. So is the notion that it was invented by Thomas Jefferson when he proposed the dollar as the American unit of money.

One theory holds that it comes from an abbreviation of the peso. A more intriguing theory suggests that the "pillars of Hercules," symbols of strength and power, which appeared on ancient Tyrian coins, are the source of the sign. These pillars, entwined by a scroll, reappeared on Spanish "pieces of eight" and later became the symbol for both the peso and the dollar.

I think it is a graceful symbol, with ancient roots and a mysterious history, as beautiful and significant as anything else that appears in a retail ad. Besides, it helps the reader to know that the number the advertiser is whispering isn't the amount of zlotys that the purchaser is expected to pay. —WILLIAM SAFIRE

THE FINE ART OF PICKING A BANK

Consumers everywhere, pressured on all sides by the inflationary shrinkage of their dollars, are beginning to realize the value of careful comparison shopping. And many are applying the same shopping techniques to answering the question of where they should bank.

There are a lot more differences between banking institutions than what kind of inducement prizes they offer—dollar-and-cent differences that can add up impressively over the months and years.

Here's a checklist to consult while you're weighing the merits of Bank A against Bank B:

• Check the interest offered on savings certificates, as well as on regular savings accounts. Compare these figures with those of other banks. Generally speaking, the highest interest rates are offered by savings and loan associations.

• Ask yourself if the savings bank in question pay interest from the day of deposit to the day of withdrawal? If not, find one that does. Also, find out exactly when interest earnings are credited to your

226

account and make your deposits and withdrawals accordingly.

• Before opening a checking account, find out what service charges are involved. Some banks make no charge at all for accounts above a certain minimum balance—but remember to compare this economy with the interest a large balance might be earning if it were put into a savings account or savings certificates.

• Many banks offer credit cards for use in charging goods and services, and obtaining "quickie" cash advances. But beware—these cards provide an all-too-easy way to buy your way into a financial hole, often in a surprisingly short time. If you already have credit cards, pay them off and destroy all but one major card, which can be useful as an "emergency-only" tool. But don't let it tempt you into an "impulse" purchase you could really do without.

• Don't pay for banking frills you can just as well do without. Some banks offer their clients decorative blank checks in assorted colors, as well as special-finish checkbooks—at a small fee, to be sure. These luxury extras don't really add anything to the service you're buying, so why bother? Just use the standard-issue book and drafts—and pocket the difference.

• When you're traveling in a foreign land, keep in mind that a better rate of exchange on traveler's checks is usually paid by banks than by hotels or tourist offices.

"Nobody knows you when you're down and out!"

227

MAKES CENTS
One panhandler to the other: "I used to be bullish. Then I was bearish. Now I'm brokish."   —*GRIN AND SHARE IT*

HOW TO BUDGET—WITHOUT BEING A FUTZ
Don't get bugged at the idea of budgeting, no matter how fussbudgety it ofttimes seems. After all, a budget is simply a plan (of greater or lesser formality) designed to assist you in managing your money—a matter of trying to maximize the income while minimizing the outgo. It takes into consideration how much must be paid out regularly to meet your cost of living, and what you're trying to achieve in the long run. It should provide clear direction for the course ahead and reveal the best ways to spend your money.

To set up a budget, follow these basic steps:

• Put your particular financial goals in writing—everything from immediate purchases you'd like to make to the size of the nest egg you hope to have put aside three or four or more years hence. These goals will provide the motivation for your budget.

• Write down all income for the budget year and apportion it as it will come in—weekly, biweekly, monthly. Be sure to include any income from "other-than-paycheck" sources.

• Write down all your "must" expenses, those of set amounts that must be paid month in and month out: house payment, insurance premiums, taxes, school tuition, debt payments, utilities, savings. Total these and subtract from the amount of income for each budget period.

• List all other expenditures you have and expect to have during the year, but which aren't necessarily the same amounts each month: food, clothing, transportation, medical, recreation, entertainment, charity contributions, charge accounts. Always include a general miscellaneous category to cover costs that inevitably come up but that you can't anticipate. Total these expenses and compare with previous balance. If your flexible costs are more than that figure, you'll have to do some squeezing and cutting in order to get the two figures to balance out.

But remember: Just having a written budget to spread out on the kitchen table or punch up on the computer isn't the end of the job. You've got to live by your money plan. And to make it work you have to update it periodically as circumstances change.

WHAT TO KEEP FOR YOUR TAX RECORDS
Here is the potentially profitable paper that the Bank of America recommends you keep on file for the taxman.

Income records:
    Alimony income
    Business income
    Capital gains and losses
    Dividend income
    Interest income
    Pension income
    Wages, salaries, commissions
    Miscellaneous income

Deductions and credits:
    Alimony payments
    Casualty and theft losses
    Charity contributions
    Child-care expenses
    Employee business expenses
    Employee education expenses
    Energy conservation
    Interest you paid
    IRA or Keogh contributions
    Medical and dental expenses
    Moving expenses
    Home-office deductions
    Political contributions
    Property and sales taxes
    Sales taxes
    Miscellaneous deductions and expenses

General:
    Tax forms
    Tax information

THREE QUICK TIPS

Here are three pieces of traditional fiscal advice, the first of which may have to be adjusted upward for certain cities and neighborhoods:

- Don't spend over 25 percent of your gross salary on housing.
- Put 7 percent of your income into life insurance.
- Don't borrow more than 1 1/2 times your monthly salary.

TWO GREAT REASONS TO SAVE

1. Because you may be needing it soon.
2. Because you probably won't be needing it soon.

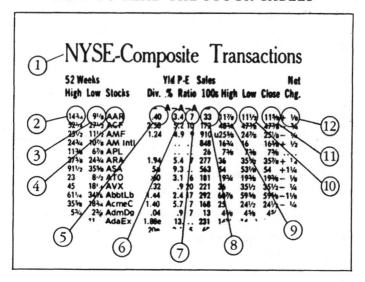

1. The composite, or consolidated, table for the New York Stock Exchange, which takes into account prices paid on that exchange and on others where a stock may have been traded that day.

2. The highest price per share paid in the past 52 weeks. Most stock prices are quoted in terms of dollars and eighths of dollars (12 1/2 cents) or in multiples of 1/8.

3. The lowest price paid in 52 weeks.

4. The company's name, usually abbreviated. In this case, AAR is the name—AAR Corp.

5. The regular annual dividend per share the company is paying based on the latest quarterly or semiannual amount.

6. The yield—the dividend divided by the current stock price, expressed as a percentage.

7. The PE ratio—the stock's price divided by the company's annual earnings per share of stock outstanding. The PE, or multiple, is one of the most widely used tools for analyzing stocks. Companies whose earnings per share are growing or expected to grow at a fast rate normally command higher multiples than corporations with slower growth.

8. The number of shares sold that day, in hundreds.

9. The highest price paid for the stock that day.

10. The lowest price paid that day.

11. The last price paid.

12. The net change in the closing price from the previous day's closing price. —*Kiplinger's Personal Finance Magazine*

HOW BONDS ARE RATED

Moody's Investors Service Inc. rates bonds according to investment risk, with "junk," or high-yield, bonds generally rated Ba or lower. Duff & Phelps Inc. and Standard & Poor's Corp. have similar rating systems.

RATING	WHAT IT MEANS	ESTIMATED YIELD (%)
Aaa	Best quality, smallest investment risk. Large or exceptionally stable margin. Fundamentally sound.	8.9
Aa	High quality by all standards. Margin may not be as strong as Aaa bonds. May be more prone to fluctuation than Aaa bonds.	9.25
A	Upper-medium quality. Protection of interest and principal adequate, but possibly susceptible to problems in the future.	9.5
Baa	Medium quality. Neither highly nor poorly protected. Security of interest and principal adequate, but not necessarily reliable over long term.	9.75 to 10, depending on industry
Ba	Speculative qualities. Futures not well assured. Moderate protection of principal and interest. Uncertain protection during bad times.	11.5 and up
B	May have only small assurance of interest and principal payments over period of significant length.	13 to 18, depending on company, industry
Caa	Poor quality. May be in default or have serious threats to payment of principal or interest.	Generally 25 and up
Ca	Highly speculative. May be in default or have other significant problems.	25 and up, depending on company, industry
C	Lowest quality. Extremely poor prospects of ever attaining investment status.	25 and up, depending on company, industry

HELP FOR INVESTORS

The Securities and Exchange Commission has set up an Office of Consumer Affairs to deal with the problems of small investors. The office will help you with complaints and questions involving securities. Write the Office of Filings, Information and Consumer Services at SEC, 450 Fifth St. NW, Washington, DC 20549.

MONTHLY MORTGAGE PAYMENTS PER $1,000

LENGTH OF MORTGAGE	RATE OF INTEREST					
	8 %	9%	10%	12%	13&	15%
10	$12.14	$12.67	$13.22	$14.35	$14.94	$16.14
15	9.56	10.15	10.75	12.01	12.66	14.00
16	9.25	9.85	10.46	11.74	12.40	13.77
17	8.99	9.59	10.22	11.52	12.19	13.58
18	8.75	9.37	10.00	11.32	12.01	13.42
19	8.55	9.17	9.82	11.16	11.85	13.29
20	8.37	9.00	9.66	11.02	11.72	13.17
22	8.07	8.72	9.36	10.78	11.51	12.99
25	7.72	8.40	9.09	10.54	11.28	12.81
30	7.34	8.05	8.78	10.29	11.07	12.65
35	7.11	7.84	8.60	10.16	10.96	12.57
40	6.96	7.72	8.50	10.09	10.90	12.54

Note: Figures shown include only payment of principal and interest.

Traditional advice: Don't pay more than twice your average annual income for a house.

CHECKLIST FOR SMART SHOPPERS
To get the most for your money and avoid consumer problems, follow these before-and-after tips:

Before you buy:
• Think carefully about what you need and what product or service features are really important to you.
• Compare brands. Ask for word-of-mouth recommendations and look for formal product-comparison reports. Check your local library for magazines and other publications that contain product comparisons.
• Plan ahead to take advantage of sales.
• Check with your local Better Business Bureau (BBB) to find out if the company is reputable.
• Check for any extra charges, such as delivery fees, installation charges and service costs.
• Read warranties to understand what you must do and what the manufacturer must do if you have a problem.
• Read contract terms carefully. Make sure all blank spaces are filled in before you sign a contract.
• Ask the sales person to explain the store's return or exchange policy.
• Don't assume an item is a bargain just because it is advertised as one.

After you buy:
• Read and follow the instructions on how to use the product or service.
• Use the product only for the purpose outlined by the manufacturer in the instructions.
• Read and understand the warranty. Keep in mind that you may have additional warranty rights in your state. Check with your state or local consumer office for more information.
• Keep all sales receipts, warranties and instructions.
• If trouble develops, report the problem to the company as soon as possible. Trying to fix the product yourself may cancel the warranty.
• Keep a file of your efforts to resolve the problem. It should include the names of the individuals you speak with and the date, time, and outcome of the conversation. Also, keep copies of the letters you send to company representatives and any replies they send to you.

—U.S. OFFICE OF CONSUMER AFFAIRS

TIPS FOR SHOPPING BY MAIL, PHONE OR TV

Today there are many ways to buy products or services. Many consumers buy items through mail order or by telephone or even from TV shopping programs. These may be convenient ways to shop, but you should be no less careful than you would be when shopping in person, and perhaps even a bit more so, inasmuch as you are dealing with *images* of goods rather than the goods themselves. So keep these tips in mind:
• Be suspicious of exaggerated product claims or very low prices, and read product descriptions very carefully—sometimes pictures of products are misleading.
• If you have any doubts about the company, check with the U.S. Postal Service, your state or local consumer protection agency or Better Business Bureau before ordering.
• Ask about the firm's return policy. If it is not stated, ask before you order. For example, does the company pay charges for shipping and return? Is a warranty or guarantee available? Does the company sometimes substitute comparable goods for the product you want to order?
• Keep a complete record of your order, including the company's

233

name, address and telephone number; the price of the items ordered; any handling or other charges; the date you mailed (or telephoned) in the order; and your method of payment. Keep copies of canceled checks and/or statements.

- If you order by mail, your order should be shipped within 30 days after the company receives your complete order, unless another period is agreed upon when placing the order or is stated in an advertisement. If your order is delayed, a notice of delay should be sent to you within the promised shipping period along with an option to cancel the order.

- If you buy a product through a TV shopping program, check the cost of the same item sold by other sources, including local stores, catalogs, etc.

- If you want to buy a product based on a telephone call from the company, ask for the name, address and phone number where you can reach the caller after considering the offer.

- Never give your credit card or social-security number over the telephone as proof of your identity.

- Postal regulations allow you to write a check payable to the sender, rather than the delivery company, for C.O.D. orders. If, after examining the merchandise, you feel there has been misrepresentation or fraud, you can stop payment on the check and file a complaint with the U.S. Postal Inspection Service, 475 L'Enfant Plaza W, SW, Washington, DC 20260.

- You can have a charge removed from your bill if you did not receive the goods or services or if your order was obtained through misrepresentation or fraud. You must notify the credit-card company in writing, at the billing inquiries/disputes address, within 60 days after the charge first appeared on your bill.

If you can't resolve a mail-order problem on your own, you can turn for help to the Direct Marketing Association, which acts as an intermediary between customers and vendors. Send a detailed letter explaining the disagreement along with copies of all correspondence to Direct Marketing Association, Mail Order Action Line, 1111 19th St. NW, Suite 1100, Washington, DC 20036.

COLLECTING STUFF

Collecting coins, currency, stamps, books, paintings, photographs, baseball cards, autographs and the like can be a surprisingly bountiful source of profit should you decide sometime to sell your lovingly gathered goodies.

How does one know which items will appreciate in value? Unfortunately, such knowledge comes only with time, familiarity and experience. Staying abreast of the market via books and periodicals is definitely recommended, especially when sizable investments are involved.

But the most important thing about collecting is not to collect anything just for the possible payoff—you should also be able to appreciate your collectibles for themselves and consider any future reward as so much gravy.

UNORDERED MERCHANDISE

You *do not* have to pay for any unsolicited merchandise, and it is illegal for the person or firm sending it to you to pressure you to return it or to send a bill. If you know of any violations of this law, or if you received unordered merchandise and are harassed with demands for payment for such, contact the Federal Trade Commission, Pennsylvania Ave. and Sixth St. NW, Washington, DC 20580.

If you receive merchandise in the mail that you did not order, federal law says you may consider it a gift and keep it without paying for it.

Only two kinds of merchandise can be sent legally through the mails to a person without his or her prior consent:

- Free samples that are clearly marked as such.
- Merchandise mailed by a charitable organization asking for contributions.

In all other instances, it is illegal to send you merchandise through the mails unless you have previously requested it.

CREDIT-CARD CHECKLIST

Credit-cards can be useful tools—or easy ways to get in financial hot water. Here are some useful do's and don't's for keeping the upper-hand when handling plastic:

- Keep a list of your credit-card numbers, expiration dates, and the phone number of each card issuer in a safe place.
- Credit-card issuers offer a wide variety of terms (annual percentage rate, methods of calculating the balance subject to the finance charge, minimum monthly payments and actual membership fees). When selecting a card, compare the terms offered by several card issuers to find the card that best suits your needs.
- When you use your credit card, watch your card after giving it to a clerk. Take your card back promptly after the clerk is finished with it and make sure it's yours.
- Tear up the carbons when you take your credit-card receipt.
- Never sign a blank receipt. Draw a line through any blank spaces above the total when you sign receipts.
- Open credit-card bills promptly and compare them with your

receipts to check for unauthorized charges and billing errors.

• Write the card issuer promptly to report any questionable charges. Written inquiries should not be included with your payment. Instead, check the billing statement for the correct address for billing questions. The inquiry must be in writing and must be sent within 60 days to guarantee your rights under the Fair Credit Billing Act.

• Never give your credit-card number over the telephone unless you made the call. Never put your card number on a postcard or on the outside of an envelope.

• Sign new cards as soon as they arrive. Cut up and throw away expired cards. Cut up and return unwanted cards to the issuer.

• If any of your credit cards are missing or stolen, report the loss as soon as possible to the card issuer. Check your credit-card statement for a telephone number for reporting stolen credit cards. Follow up your phone calls with a letter to each card issuer. The letter should contain your card number, the date the card was missing and the date you called in the loss.

• If you report the loss before a credit card is used, the issuer cannot hold you responsible for any subsequent unauthorized charges. If a thief uses your card before you report it missing, the most you will owe for unauthorized charges on each card is $50.

© Eubie Smart is a copyright of The Advertising Council, Inc.

THE FAIR CREDIT REPORTING ACT—AND YOU

If you have a charge account, a mortgage on your home, a life insurance policy, or if you have applied for a personal loan or a job, it is almost certain that somewhere there is a "file" that shows how promptly you pay your bills, whether you have been sued or arrested, or if you have filed for bankruptcy. And such a file may also include your neighbors' and friends' views of your character, general reputation, or manner of living.

The companies that gather and sell such information to creditors, insurers, employers, and other businesses are called "Consumer Reporting Agencies," and the legal term for the Report is a "Consumer Report."

If, besides credit data, the report includes interviews with a third person about your character, reputation, or manner of living, it is referred to as an "Investigative Consumer Report."

The Fair Credit Reporting Act became law on April 25, 1971. This act was passed by Congress to protect consumers against the circulation of inaccurate or obsolete information and to ensure that Consumer Reporting Agencies adopt fair and equitable procedures for obtaining, maintaining, and giving out information about consumers.

Under this law you can take steps to protect yourself if you have been denied credit, insurance, or employment, or if you believe you have had difficulties because of an inaccurate or an unfair Consumer Report.

You Have the Right:

• To be told the name and address of the Consumer Reporting Agency responsible for preparing a Consumer Report that was used to deny you credit, insurance, or employment or to increase the cost of credit or insurance.

• To be told by a Consumer Reporting Agency the nature, substance, and sources (except investigative sources) of the information (except medical) collected about you.

• To take anyone of your choice with you when you visit the Consumer Reporting Agency to check on your file.

• To obtain free of charge all information to which you are entitled if the request is made within 30 days after receipt of a notification that you have been denied credit, insurance, or employment because of information contained in a Consumer Report. Otherwise, the Consumer Reporting Agency is permitted to charge a reasonable fee for giving you the information.

• To be told who has received a Consumer Report on you within the preceding six months or within the preceding two years if the report was furnished for employment purposes.

• To have incomplete or incorrect information reinvestigated unless the Consumer Reporting Agency has reasonable grounds to believe that the dispute is frivolous or irrelevant. If the data is investigated and found to be inaccurate or if the data cannot be verified, you have the right to have it removed from your file.

• To have the Consumer Reporting Agency notify those you name (at no cost to you), who have previously received the incorrect or incomplete data, that this data has been deleted from your file.

• When a dispute between you and the Reporting Agency about information in your file cannot be resolved, you have the right to have your version of such dispute placed in the file and included in future Consumer Reports.

• To request the Reporting Agency to send your version of the dispute to certain businesses without charge, if requested within 30 days of the adverse action.

• To have a Consumer Report withheld from anyone who under the law does not have a legitimate business need for the information.

• To sue a Reporting Agency for damages if the Agency willfully or negligently violates the law; and, if you are successful, to collect attorney's fees and court costs.

• Not to have adverse information reported after seven years. One major exception is bankruptcy, which may be reported for 10 years.

• To be notified by a business that it is seeking information about you which would constitute an Investigative Consumer Report.

• To request from the business that ordered an Investigative Consumer Report more data about the nature and scope of the investigation.

• To discover the nature and substance (but not the sources) of the information that was collected for an Investigative Consumer Report.

The Fair Credit Reporting Act Does Not:

• Require the Consumer Reporting Agency to provide you with a copy of your file, although some agencies will voluntarily give you a copy.

• Compel anyone to do business with an individual consumer.

• Apply when you request commercial (rather than consumer) credit or business insurance.

• Authorize any federal agency to intervene on behalf of an individual consumer.

• Require a Consumer Reporting Agency to add new accounts to your file, however some may do so for a fee.

How to Deal with Consumer Reporting Agencies

If you want to know what information a Consumer Reporting Agency has collected about you, either arrange for a personal interview at the agency's office during normal business hours or call in advance for an interview by telephone. Some Agencies will voluntarily make disclosure by mail.

The Consumer Reporting Agencies in your community can be located by consulting the "Yellow Pages" of your telephone book under such headings as "Credit" or "Credit Rating or Reporting Agencies."

If you decide to visit a Consumer Reporting Agency to check on your file, the following check list may be of help.

For instance, in checking your credit file, did you:

• Learn the nature and substance of all the information in your file?

• Find out the name of each of the businesses (or other sources) that supplied information on you to the Reporting Agency?

• Learn the name of everyone who received reports on you within the past six months (or the last two years if the reports were for employment purposes)?

• Request the agency to reinvestigate and correct or delete information that was found to be inaccurate, incomplete, or obsolete?

• Follow up to determine the results of the reinvestigation?

• Ask the agency—at no cost to you—to notify those you name who received reports within the past six months (two years if for employment purposes) that certain data was deleted?

• Follow up to make sure that those named by you did in fact receive notices from the Consumer Reporting Agency?

• Demand that your version of the facts be placed in your file if the reinvestigation did not settle the dispute?

• Request the agency to send your statement of the dispute to those you name who received reports containing the disputed information in the past six months (two years if received for employment purposes)? A reasonable fee may be charged for this service if you have not incurred adverse action from a creditor in the last 30 days.

Note: The FDIC maintains regional offices in Atlanta, Boston, Chicago, Dallas, Kansas City, Memphis, New York and San Francisco. Check your local directory for the appropriate telephone number or call (800) 934-3342 for the address of the regional office serving you.

The Federal Agency that supervises Consumer Reporting Agencies is the Federal Trade Commission (FTC). Questions or complaints concerning Consumer Reporting agencies should be directed to the Federal Trade Commission, Correspondence Branch, Washington, DC 20580. —U.S. OFFICE OF CONSUMER AFFAIRS

CONSUMER'S HONOR ROLL

The following 20 companies have been named to a consumer's honor roll by the Council on Economic Priorities, based on eight major areas of social responsibility: corporate stewardship of the environment, opportunities for women, opportunities for minorities, workplace issues, family benefits, community outreach, charitable giving and corporate disclosure. The firms are listed in alphabetical, not qualitative, order:

Adolph Coors	Grand Metropolitan PLC
Anheuser-Busch	Hewlett-Packard
Aveda Corp.	Johnson & Johnson
Avon Products	S. C. Johnson & Son
Ben & Jerry's	Kellogg Co.
Colgate-Palmolive	Levi Strauss & Co.
Dayton Hudson	Nordstrom Inc.
Digital Equipment	Rhino Records
General Mills	Tom's of Maine
Giant Food	Warner-Lambert

Note: The products of these 20 companies—along with those of 171 other firms rated on the above criteria—are included in the book *Shopping for a Better World* (Sierra Club Books, 1994).

WRITING AN EFFECTIVE COMPLAINT LETTER

As a consumer you have the right to expect quality products and services at fair prices. If something goes wrong, there are steps you can take to resolve the problem. Generally, a good first step is to gather together all relevant paperwork—receipts, warranties, canceled checks, and the like—and contact (either in person or by phone) the person who sold you the item or performed the service.

If talking with the sales person or company representative does not resolve the problem, you will need to write a letter to the company.

Where to write:

• For a list of many corporate consumer contacts and their addresses, consult the *Consumer's Resource Handbook*, published by the U.S. Office of Consumer Affairs (single copies available free by writing to: *Handbook*, Consumer Information Center, Pueblo, CO 81009). If there is no listing there for the company, check the reference section of your local library. The following books may help you locate useful company and brand-name information:

• *Standard & Poor's Register of Corporations, Directors and Executives*
• *Standard Directory of Advertisers*
• *Thomas Register of American Manufacturers*
• *Trade Names Directory*

What to write:

• The letter should include your name, address, home and work telephone numbers, and account number, if appropriate.

• Make your letter brief and to the point. List all the important facts about your purchase, including the date and place you made the purchase and any information you can give about the product—such as the serial or model number.

- If you are writing to complain about a service you received, describe the service and who performed it.
- State exactly what you want done about the problem and how long you are willing to wait to resolve it. Be reasonable.
- Include copies of all documents regarding your problem.
- Be sure to send *copies,* not originals.
- Don't write an angry, sarcastic or threatening letter. The person reading your letter probably was not responsible for your problem, but may be very helpful in resolving it. Type your letter if possible. If it is handwritten, make sure it is neat and easy to read.
- Keep a copy of all letters to and from the company.
- Remember, if you write a letter to a Better Business Bureau, government agency, trade association or other source of help, give information about what you have done so far to get your complaint resolved.

—U.S. Office of Consumer Affairs

LONG-DISTANCE PHONE TIPS

If, having weathered the media blitz generated by AT&T and its competitors, you're still not sure who to reach out and touch, here are some pointers to help you decide:

- To compare long-distance carriers, think about when, how often and where you use long-distance service. Then compare the charges, restrictions and procedures for making calls.
- Not all carriers provide service to all areas. Make sure the one you choose provides service to the areas you call most often.
- Each long-distance carrier may have a different billing system. Some give credit for uncompleted calls, wrong numbers or calls that are unanswered.
- Ask about one-time only and regular charges. Is there a subscription fee? Monthly service fee? Monthly minimum charge?
- Judge the quality of a carrier's performance (transmission capability, service, billing and crediting). A trial period may help you decide whether the quality of phone service is adequate. Before signing up, be sure you understand the terms of the carrier's cancellation policy and the costs (if any) involved in switching to another carrier.
- Many companies now provide operator services, including directory assistance and collect calls for telephones in hotels, airports and other public places. When you dial the operator, ask which carrier is providing the service and how much you will be billed. If you prefer a different service, you may have to dial a separate access number. Check with your long-distance company to see if it provides operator services and how to use them.

25 WAYS TO TRIM ELECTRIC BILLS

1. Doors—When the heat or the air conditioning is on, an open door leads to higher operating costs. Keep doors to the outside, garage and attic firmly shut. Open and close them as quickly as possible when you go in or out.

2. Proper-sized equipment—The smallest system or unit that's adequate to heat or cool the space is the most economical. The specific conditions of your home—area, construction materials, number and size of windows, etc.—determine the necessary capacity of heating or cooling equipment. This capacity is given in the number of BTUs (British thermal units) per hour. Although oversized electric heating equipment does not reduce operating efficiency, it should be avoided to minimize your initial cost. The system should be large enough to maintain your desired inside temperature on the coldest day.

3. Unused space—Don't spend money to heat or cool space you're not using. Close off those areas. If you have room-by-room control, lower thermostats in unused rooms in winter. With a central system, close off registers in unused rooms.

4. Selecting a window air conditioner—In selecting a window unit, both the cooling capacity and the operating efficiency of the unit are important. The capacity is given in the number of BTUs removed per hour. If the rated size of the unit is too small, the unit will not cool properly. If the unit is too large for the area to be cooled, it will not operate efficiently. As a rule of thumb, you can figure that it takes about 18 BTUs per hour to cool one square foot in a normal home with regular usage. An 18,000-BTU unit, for example, can generally cool 1,000 square feet of space. A 12,000-BTU unit, 500 square feet, and so on. But note: some air conditioners use a lot more electricity than others to cool the same amount of space. So check the prospective unit's EER, an engineer's term that stands for energy efficiency ratio. To get the EER, simply divide the BTUs by the watts. The recommended EER for an air conditioner is 7 or more. Low-efficiency units have EERs of 5 or 6.

5. Economical operation—Window units are individually controlled. If the space that the air conditioner is to cool will be unoccupied for several hours, set the unit at a higher temperature or turn the unit off. Also, if you have only one window unit in the house, keep the room cool by opening and closing the door as seldom as possible.

6. Appliance use—Appliances give off heat, which your cooling system has to counteract. So, during the hottest times of the day, it is best to minimize their use. Schedule washing, drying and ironing for early morning or evening, when demands on your cooling system are less. The same goes for abnormal use of cooking ranges, lighting and TV.

7. Correct pots and pans—Matching the diameters of pots and pans to the diameters of heating elements prevents heat escaping into the air. Your range will cook more efficiently and your air conditioner will operate with less difficulty.

8. Humidifier—Cold outside air reduces indoor humidity. Just as too much humidity in summer makes you feel warmer, too little humidity in winter makes you feel cooler. Consider installing a humidifier that adds moisture and makes you feel comfortable at lower temperatures.

9. Portable electric heaters—Be sure that portable electric heaters are thermostatically controlled or limit their use to temporary spot heating. These units are not designed to be full-time heating operations.

10. Filling to capacity—A freezer or refrigerator operates more economically when filled to capacity but not overfilled.

11. Settings—A refrigerator or freezer should not be set to run colder than necessary. Follow the manufacturer's recommendations.

12. Defrosting—Defrost your freezer or freezing compartment when frost is about 1/4-inch thick. Frost decreases efficiency because your refrigerator or freezer must work harder to maintain the same temperature.

13. Inventory—Keep an up-to-date inventory of the food in your freezer. Indicate the location of each item and mark each package clearly as to its contents. When you want something, you'll know where it is. Then, you'll spend less time hunting around, and the freezer cover or door won't have to be open as long.

14. Location—A refrigerator or freezer will use less energy if located away from heating equipment and direct sunlight.

15. Using the oven more than the surface units—Oven cooking is less expensive in the long run than cooking on top of the range. Surface units stay on the whole time they are in use. An oven need only be on for part of each hour it is used. The rest of the time it can "coast" because its insulation holds in heat.

16. Warming with stored heat—You can warm foods and plates with retained oven heat and use no additional energy in the process.

17. Two for one—Bake two dishes at once. Freeze one for later use after it has cooled to room temperature.

18. Pots and pans—With covered pots and pans, you can use lower heat settings. Less heat escapes. The tighter the lid, the better. Also, utensils should have flat bottoms to make firm contact with the surface elements.

19. Cooking with small amounts of water—Use high heat to bring water to a boil, then reduce heat to simmer. Small amounts of water heat faster and consume less energy. Use 2 to 4 tablespoons of

243

water for packaged frozen vegetables and 1/2 to 1/3 cup of water for fresh vegetables. Some fresh foods that are high in water content—such as tomatoes, spinach, apples and rhubarb—can be cooked with very little water.

20. Thaw frozen foods—Whether cooked in the oven, broiler or on top of the range, frozen foods will use less energy if they are completely thawed and brought to room temperature first. For example, putting a frozen roast directly into the oven requires one-third additional cooking time.

21. Small appliances—Electric skillets, toasters, waffle irons, electric grills, popcorn poppers, electric fondues, and bean pots use less electricity than your range for specialized jobs. For example, it costs three times as much to toast bread in an oven as in a pop-up toaster. Such appliances are an economical way to prepare small meals. To be on the efficient side, always make sure the appliances are turned off when you finish using them.

22. Full loads—The automatic clothes washer goes through the same cycle for a full load or a single sock. The more you plan your wash for full loads, the more electricity and water you save. Varying the size of garments in each full load allows freer circulation and improves the cleaning action.

23. Damp dry—Damp drying saves energy and is the easiest way to prepare clothes for ironing without sprinkling. If your dryer doesn't have a damp-dry setting, you can use a shorter drying time or remove clothes before the end of the regular cycle. When the clothes are slightly damp, they are ready to be ironed.

24. Reading your manuals—Appliance manuals are rarely the most interesting reading matter in the house. The temptation is not to read them until trouble develops. But if they are read when the appliance is first brought into the house, trouble could be avoided. Manuals also give you the lowdown on the way to get the maximum benefit out of the appliance. If you put all your manuals together in a folder, you'll have easy access to them.

25. *Don't forget to turn out the lights when you leave a room!*
—COMMONWEALTH EDISON (Illinois)

SEW YOUR OWN AND SAVE

Sewing your own is an excellent way to save money while at the same time experiencing the satisfaction that comes with doing it yourself.

Veteran sewers are happily aware that they can often save up to 50 percent over comparable "store-bought" fashions by sewing their own. Their clothes are tailor-measured for one body only and garnished with the loving details of quality workmanship (matched plaids, hand-sewn hems, etc.) seldom found in off-the-rack clothes.

Even a novice sewer can save big bucks by stitching up house-hold items such as pillows, shower curtains and table linens. Check pattern books for simple patterns.

Here are a few more ways to sew up some savings:

• **Shop the large warehouse-type fabric stores for exceptional fabric bargains.** An adventuresome shopper can snatch up terrific buys at "tumble-tables" stacked with ready-cut lengths. You might even get a specially reduced price on extra yardage if the leftover piece is too small to be a salable remnant. But buyer beware: Always unfold and check the fabric for flaws or pattern imperfections. And remember, when you buy a bolt of fabric, ask for a care label with directions for washing, bleaching, ironing or dry cleaning. Make sure the care label matches the label on the bolt itself. A bolt label indicating, for example, "Care Label 2" means the salesperson should give you the care label marked "2".

• **Always wash everything (fabric, trim, zippers) before you sew.** That way, you won't wind up with a shrunken disaster that wasn't at all what you had in mind.

• **Choose children's patterns for "growability."** Raglan sleeves and simple designs can double the life of a garment. This autumn's party dress can comfortably convert to next spring's topper for a sprouting toddler. Save material scraps for emergency appliqués for ragged knees. Use leftover trim to cover up tattletale hem marks.

—CAROL PEARSON

245

HOLD THE PEPPERONI

Postal Life reports that a customer making a bulk mailing discovered his letters had picked up so much humidity they weighed more than an ounce each. Instead of immediately forking over the extra cash for the second ounce, he picked up his mail and headed for a nearby pizza parlor. There he asked the owner if he could use the oven to dry out the letters; he did so, then ran back to the post office. Sure enough, the letters all weighed less than an ounce.

PENNY-PINCHING ROMANCE

According to coin columnist Ed Rochette, writing in the *Chicago Sun-Times*, "In Shakespeare's England, pursuit of the heart was sometimes referred to as 'coony-catching.' A contemporary book on that subject, published in 1592, advised young swains to bend old pennies and give them to their sweethearts. The coins, always carried and never spent, were accepted as pledges of love and fidelity. Every reach into a change purse was a reminder of a lover's pledge. The practice of bending coins to say 'I love you' continued well into the nineteenth century."

THE ADVENTURES OF A HUGE MOUTH, BY PETER HANNAN

FIVE KEYS TO A GREAT JOB INTERVIEW

For the jobless, tough economic times translate into tough prospective employers, who are reaping the rewards of a flat-out buyer's market. And pleasing these hard-nose hirers takes more effort and concentration than ever. "They're becoming more literate about employee selection, approaching it in a logical manner, rather than a manager making a decision based on gut feeling," says Martin Yate, author of *Knock 'em Dead with Great Answers to Tough Questions* (Bob Adams, 1991).

The result, he says, is new intensive and carefully structured interviews rife with treacherous, calculated volleys of questions designed to reveal your true behavioral traits and predict your ability to succeed in the job you're seeking.

How best to handle this often hoary challenge? Yate offers the following five keys to a great job interview. (Mastering them won't automatically win you that job—the kind of competition you're up against at any given moment must be taken into account—but seriously failing in one or more of these areas will certainly dampen your chances.)

1. Before the interview, try to anticipate the traits the interviewer will be probing to find, and strategize ways to portray them in your answers.

2. Make sure you know what the first and most pressing projects or challenges will be for the job you're seeking, and directly address ways to attack them. This allows the employer to perceive you as a problem-solver and form a mental picture of you functioning in the job.

3. Never answer a question that hasn't been asked. And if you aren't sure what the optimum answer is to a question that is asked, rather than risk rambling on about something in which the interviewer has little interest, ask that the question be qualified. For example, if you're asked, "Tell me about yourself," respond with, "Would you like to hear something about my personal or my work history?" In answering, use a story that illustrates why you are a good candidate for the job.

4. Expect stressful, curveball questions and statements designed to determine your poise. A woman interviewing for a network anchor spot, for example, was told that she obviously wasn't ready for the job. She stormed out, Yate says. Instead, she should have smiled and responded with "Why do you say that?" putting the ball back in the interviewer's court.

5. Watch body language. A closed appearance—crossed arms, fidgeting, crossed legs—will contradict your positive verbal communication. Lean forward slightly in your chair, which indicates interest. Bring a pad and pen to occupy your hands.

COMPELLING EXPLANATIONS

It is widely accepted that a poorly written, ungrammatical resume is employment suicide. And according to Accountemps founder Robert

Half of Menlo Park, California, so are the some of the reasons he's heard for people leaving their last jobs:

- "The boss said the end of the world is near."
- "Was met with a string of broken promises and lies, as well as cockroaches."
- "Fired because I fought for lower pay."
- "I was working for my mom until she decided to move."

YOU'RE DEHIRED: A LITANY OF EUPHEMISMS
Terms used by corporations when firing employees:

Outplacement
Downsizing
Right-sizing
Force reduction
Work-force adjustment
Indefinite idling
Redundancy elimination
Involuntary separation
Skill-mix adjustment
Work-force imbalance correction
Chemistry change
Negotiated departure
Redeployment
Destaffing
Dehiring
Degrowing
Dismissal
Axed
Canned
Let go
Deselected
Decruited
Excessed
Transitioned
Vocational relocation
Release
Selective separation
Coerced transition
Executive culling
Personnel-surplus reduction
Career assessment and reemployment
Fumigation

—EXECUTIVE RECRUITER NEWS

ANTI-PANIC POINTERS
FOR THE RECENTLY DOWNSIZED

From *Woman's Day's* money guru Jane Bryant Quinn comes the following advice for the newly unemployed, obviously applicable to men as well as women:

• Apply for unemployment insurance and any other benefits you may be entitled to immediately. Then use your income only for the basics—food, shelter, utilities, transportation, insurance, job-hunting.

• Explain the situation to your creditors, then send them $10 good-faith payments every month. Some might carry you for a while. Others will dun you, but your priorities are to keep the lights on, the mortgage paid, and food on the table.

• If you have any stock-owning mutual funds, convert them to cash. If a CD matures, put the cash into a money-market deposit account so it will be accessible.

• If you can't pay cash-value life-insurance premiums, don't let the policy lapse. Either borrow against the cash value for the premiums, use the cash to buy a smaller paid-up policy, or switch to a cheaper term policy.

• Try to keep up with health insurance.

GOING INTO BUSINESS: 10 TACTICS FOR SUCCESS

1. Learn as much about your proposed business as you can.

2. To the best of your ability project sales and potential profits for the first year or—preferably—three years.

3. Accept the fact that starting a business always takes more money than you anticipate.

4. Study successful competitors carefully.

5. If you're going into retail, remember the realtor's motto: location, location, location.

6. Decide what kind of image you want to create with your service, product, packaging, pricing, ads, personnel, decor, vehicles, etc.

7. Keep complete and accurate records for tax purposes, for your bank and, most important, for your own guidance.

8. Hire good, experienced help and find a competent lawyer, accountant, banker, insurer and promoter.

9. Learn what, where and when to buy and how to gauge inventory.

10. Allow for all expenses—including your living costs, possible losses, "shrinkage," costs such as fringe benefits and taxes—before figuring your potential profit.

—Roy Hoopes

KNOW THE SCORE

The Service Corps of Retired Executives has 13,000 volunteer counselors around the country but is constantly recruiting. It seeks successful retired businesspeople who have had experience in their own companies or in small to large corporations. As SCORE president Bob Bertelsen, a former 3M Company executive, says, "The business principles used to run a large corporate division are not much different from those used in a small business."

SCORE came into being in September 1964, when the Small Business Administration announced signing up more than 1,100 retired executives to help small businesses learn to achieve greater sales and profits. The original emphasis was on assisting "struggling small businessmen eager for help," said then-SBA administrator Eugene P. Foley. But over the years the emphasis has shifted to advising and counseling would-be entrepreneurs before they risk entering a tough, competitive marketplace.

SCORE counselors come from all business fields, though not everyone who has been in business is qualified. Volunteers take a 90-day orientation course and, says former SCORE president Harry Matzen, "Some are upset when we reject them."

What SCORE wants are men and women with successful business experience who are intelligent, know how to listen and are comfortable with other people. Women and minorities are especially urged to sign up. Oddly enough, former chief executive officers and presidents are not ideal candidates. "CEOs are used to delegating authority, not doing it themselves," says Matzen. Instructors are also needed to teach basic business principles in SCORE workshops. The work hours are flexible; most volunteers work one or two days a week.

Bertleson encourages retired businesspeople to come out of retirement for at least a few days a week; that's how he began counseling. "After you've painted the house, fixed up the yard and taken a few trips, you find out retirement is better if you're doing something—especially something worthwhile."

For more information call SCORE/SBA at (800) 634-0245, or write SCORE, 409 Third St. SW, Washington, DC 20024.

—Roy Hoopes

SOCIAL SECURITY—AND YOU

Social Security gives you two things: monthly benefits and insurance protection. Most people know something about Social Security, but few know the extent of the monthly benefits they will eventually receive when they retire. And many people do not realize that, while they are working, they have insurance protection for themselves and their families should they die or become severely disabled.

To learn more about what Social Security has to offer, check through the following questions most asked.

When Can I Receive My Retirement Benefit—and How Much?

The normal retirement age today is 65. That is the age when you are eligible for full retirement benefits. But you can start receiving reduced benefits as early as age 62, and your spouse can receive them at the same age. If your child is under 16 or disabled, is receiving Social Security benefits, and is in your care, you can receive spouse's benefits regardless of your age.

The amount of your benefit depends on how old you are, when you apply, and your *lifetime* earnings on which you paid Social Security taxes. Other earnings and other types of income are not used to figure your Social Security benefit.

I am in my twenties and have just started working full-time. What does Social Security provide me?

As you work and pay Social Security taxes, your family is also becoming eligible for monthly benefits should you die.

The monthly benefits paid to your family, should you die, are called survivors benefits. They are paid to:

• Widows or widowers. Benefits are paid at age 60, at age 50 if disabled, or at any age (including widows and widowers who are divorced) if they have responsibility for a child who is under 16 or disabled and is receiving benefits.

• Surviving children under age 18 (under 19 if in high school) or at any age if they are disabled.

• Parents of a worker who dies if the parents are 62 or older and were dependent on the worker.

I Have Heard About the Social Security Disability Program. What Does It Mean to Me?

You should understand two things about the disability program. One is that you will have this valuable protection soon after you start working. There are different coverage requirements for younger workers than for older ones, but generally you need to have paid Social Security taxes for five of the 10 years before you become disabled.

Another thing to remember is that "disability" is defined in the law very strictly. Sometimes people believe they qualify for disability benefits, but they actually do not. In order to qualify for disability benefits, a person's condition has to be expected to last for a year or result in death. The condition also must be so severe that it prevents people from doing their previous work and, considering their age, education, and work experience, stops them from doing *any* kind of substantial work.

The disability protection you are earning while you work and pay Social Security taxes can be substantial.

Is There More to Social Security Than Retirement Benefits?

Yes. Take a minute to think about it. If you are a worker, how well would your family get along if you became disabled or died?

If you have worked long enough under Social Security—and most workers have—you could count on a continuing cash income for yourself and your family if you became disabled, and your survivors would receive monthly cash benefits if you should die.

Part of the FICA taxes withheld from your pay are for Medicare. When you become 65, you will be eligible for Medicare even if you keep on working. Also, you are eligible for Medicare if you have been receiving disability benefits for two years or have permanent kidney failure.

How Do I Receive Benefits?

The first step is to call your local Social Security office as soon as possible after you decide to claim benefits. Your application can be taken by phone, or you can schedule an appointment to talk to a Social Security representative. Also, someone from the office can come to see you if you are hospitalized or unable to leave home because of a disability.

How Do I Become Eligible for Social Security?

For a worker and a family to receive monthly cash benefits, the worker must have earnings *credits* for a certain amount of work under Social Security. Almost every kind of job, as well as self-employment, fits in this category.

When a person has a certain amount of credits, he or she is fully insured and can receive monthly benefits at retirement age.

No one can be fully insured with less than six credits (1 1/2 years of work), and a person who has credit for 10 years of work can be sure that he or she will be fully insured for life for retirement or survivors benefits. Having enough credits means only that certain kinds of benefits can be paid—it does not determine the amount.

Is Social Security in Your Future?

This is one of the most frequently asked questions about Social Security. Some people are always concerned about the future of Social Security. But the fact is, today, the program is on a very sound financial footing. The Social Security taxes paid this year exceed the benefits that will be paid, and this is expected under present law for the next 40 years, at which time a sizable reserve fund is expected to exist. So the solvency of the program extends into the next century.

As you learn more about Social Security for you and your family, you should also know more about the size and scope of the entire program. It really does affect almost all of us:

• In a recent year, 126 million people—more than nine out of every 10 workers (and their employers) in this country—paid nearly $250 billion in Social Security taxes.

• Currently, about 40 million people receive Social Security benefits every month—about one out of every six persons in this country—and three million of these beneficiaries are children.

• Those beneficiaries were paid about $330 billion in a recent year. That's more than $18.1 billion each month or almost $600 million every day.

Social Security Can't Do It All

Although Social Security is a good program for our country, and probably will be for you personally and for your family, it should not be your only source of income when you retire. In addition, you should not count on Social Security to provide complete disability or survivors coverage for you or your family. Instead, Social Security should serve as a *foundation* upon which you can build a total package of protection. Ideally, it should be supplemented with pensions, savings, insurance and other investments.

When to Contact Social Security

Probably the first time you will want to be in touch with the Social Security Administration is to obtain a Social Security number. Often this is done by your parents, or you may have applied yourself. Of course, if you do not have a number, be sure to call or write the local Social Security office to obtain one.

Here are other times to contact the Social Security office:

• Every few years, you should ask for a copy of the record of your earnings upon which Social Security taxes were paid and the amount of Social Security taxes.

• If you are unable to work because of an illness or injury that is expected to last a year or longer.

• If you are 62 or older and plan to retire.

• If you are within three months of 65, even if you do not plan to retire.

• If someone in your family dies.

• If you or someone you know has limited income and is 65 or older or blind or disabled, there is a Federal program called SSI (supplemental security income) that Social Security administers but is paid for by general taxes, not Social Security taxes.

—SOCIAL SECURITY ADMINISTRATION,
U.S. DEPARTMENT OF HEALTH AND HUMAN SERVICES

P.S. A TIP FOR THE ROAD

If you haven't done it yet—or if you haven't done it lately—make a copy or two of everything in your wallet except the cash and put the copies in a safe place (not on your person). If you ever lose your wallet, the copies will save a big chunk of your ever-valuable time, money and energy.

HOME IMPROVEMENT
. . . how to putter like a pro . . .

*Have nothing in your houses that you do not know
to be useful or believe to be beautiful.*
—WILLIAM MORRIS

Measure twice, cut once.
—ANONYMOUS

BE YOUR OWN DECORATOR
A house, we all know, is not necessarily a home. Nor vice versa, as
tents and igloos—and especially apartments—so vividly attest. A

home is a place where you and your partner and/or possessions intermingle in order or chaos, beauty or ugliness—and many differing combinations thereof, according to occasion and energy and whim. Furnishing and decorating one's abode need not cost the proverbial kingly ransom—if one shops smartly and takes a do-it-yourself approach wherever possible.

Here follow some tried-and-true ideas that can help you make your surroundings more beautiful, while being as gentle as possible to your budget.

• **Let your calendar be your guide.** As much as possible, plan major purchases for your home or apartment to coincide with the big annual furniture sales most large stores hold. (*Note:* Linen sales are generally held in January and June, furniture sales in February and July.)

• **When stymied by exposed pipes and radiators, play them up, not down.** If it is not feasible to hide an unsightly heating or plumbing element, paint the annoying item in colors that harmonize with that particular room's decor. Make a virtue of necessity.

• **Buy unfinished pine furniture.** Finish to taste—stain, varnish, paint or antique. You'll save some money, and you'll have the satisfaction of giving your pieces exactly the look you want.

• **Keep as many plants as possible without crowding.** Put them on windowsills or shelves, or hang them from the ceiling. (For more on greening your scene, see the next chapter, "Gardening—Indoors and Out.")

• **Spruce up your mantelpiece (or similar display-type area) with seasonal foliage you've gathered yourself.** For example, at autumn time, take a trip into the woods (or forest preserves), and collect ears of bright-hued "Indian corn," sprigs of berries, cattails, milkweed stalks, and the like. Use these raw materials to create natural-looking displays, with or without the aid of a vase. In winter, pine branches and cones may be used, and similarly suitable items may be substituted in spring and summer.

• **Use bricks and boards for shelves to hold TV and audio equipment, books and knickknacks.** The beauty of this is that the boards needn't be attached to the bricks—so no carpentry at all is involved here. Just set the boards atop the bricks, with or without other bricks and boards atop those. You can alter your shelving arrangement quite easily this way, as you add or subtract possessions.

• **Use wooden food crates as plant stands or as containers for books or CDs.** Wire and plastic milk crates are also suitable for these purposes. A wooden crate's appearance can be readily improved by sanding and painting (or varnishing) to taste, while a wire or plastic crate is perhaps best spray-painted.

• **Decorate with sheets.** All you need here is a dose of imagination combined with some basic stitching know-how. For instance, you can buy inexpensive, colored, pre-hemmed sheets up to 108 inches wide and stretch them over a ceiling or wall, cutting to fit. Or you can laminate them onto window shades—using iron-on laminating cloth for this purpose. Or you can transform them into bargain-price tablecloths, curtains, cushion covers, or bedspreads. (*Tip:* After you've turned a sheet into an economical substitute bedspread, consider using a second sheet to make a dust ruffle to cover the box spring.)

• **Adorn walls with inexpensive prints and posters.** Frame, or have framed, items that you want to keep for a long time.

• **Fashion wall-hangings from colored cording, twine or yarn.** For general techniques and specific patterns, consult a book or pamphlet on the art of macramé.

• **Make masks for use as mantelpiece decorations or wall-hangings.** Pablo Picasso and other noted artists, ancient and mod, have done well making and displaying masks, and so can you, if on a somewhat more modest scale. The masks may be of many styles, many materials. Wood and grass, for example, can be used to fashion an African mask. Other possible materials: metal, cardboard, butcher paper and papier-mâché. If grass is not available or desired for use as hair, then try string, wire, straw, raffia or simple strips of colored paper. Make your fabricated faces happy or sad or quizzical or grotesque or whatever, then paint the finished product according to taste. In short, unmask your imagination!

• **If you use wallpaper, be careful to keep it from clashing with other elements of your decor.** If the wallpaper has a particularly busy pattern, pictures should not be hung over it.

• **Use seashells for ashtrays.** Or glue them artfully together into mantelpiece and coffee-table sculptures.

• **Turn a large wooden telephone-cable spool into a table.** You can find these spools from time to time in industrial neighborhoods or at construction sites. Sanded and either painted or varnished, they make sturdy, rustic pieces of furniture for indoor or outdoor use. (*Tip:* If a new tabletop is wanted, put it on over the old one—don't try removing the old one or else the center slats that form the spool's core will become "unsprung" and very difficult to put back together the way they were.)

• **A tablecloth-covered barrel makes a great occasional table.** Extra storage space is an added bonus.

• **Spruce up and paint old thrift-shop camp and storage trunks.** Then use them to store linens and other such items.

• **Use an old picnic table (and benches) as an ultranatural**

dining-room set. Paint these pieces brightly and give your mealtime setting a blast of pizzazz.

• **Make bright paper objects and hang them from the ceiling or on the walls.** Try your hand at fashioning fanciful kites from kite paper and lightweight wooden strips. Or create birds and boats and the like from stiff, colored stock, using as your guide a book on decoupage, or on the Japanese art of origami. The objects may be suspended separately by thin strings or wires, or incorporated into a mobile.

• **Give doors and dressers a fresh look by putting on new knobs and accessories.** Such minor changes can often make a big decorating difference.

• **Collage over that "blah," eyesore refrigerator.** If your fridge gives you visual indigestion, then try covering it with magazine and newspaper clippings, photographs or parts thereof, swatches of fabric, or anything else you can think of that you can paste or tape down. Just keep Matisse in mind; after all, he did some mighty spiffy things with nothing more than a few hunks of colored paper and a pair of scissors—and you can, too. Of course, a refrigerator isn't all that can look good collaged. As a general rule, any relatively small surface is fair game for the collager's art. For a whole wide wall, however, a cover of paint or a hanging or somesuch is perhaps more appropriate—but remember, *you're* the artist, and therefore the ultimate judge in such matters.

• **Add lighting drama with canister lights.** They can be used to shine a beam up from the floor through the branches of a large plant or behind a favorite piece of furniture.

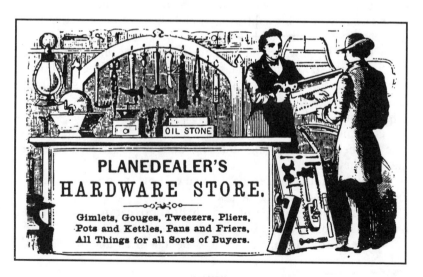

A BASIC TOOLBOX

Claw hammer—Get a fairly hefty one having a head weight of about 14 ounces or so (a forged-steel head is generally preferred). Don't get the "cheapo" variety that may "lose its head" when put to a really heavy-duty test; a quality hammer is a wise household investment. Later on, you can add some special-duty hammers to your arsenal, for example: a small-headed magnetic tack hammer (for work in tight spots on carpeting or upholstery); a plastic-faced hammer (for work on metal surfaces); a rubber mallet (for driving dowels or pounding tight-fitting joints).

Several screwdrivers—Include, in your assortment, at least one Phillips screwdriver, identifiable by its unique cross-shaped tip. If your budget allows, a hollow-handled spiral ratchet screwdriver is suggested, since it works much easier and faster than the standard, "unpowered" type.

Several pairs of pliers—Besides an all-around pair of "slip-joint" pliers, you'd do well to include a pair of needle-nose pliers (for working with delicate objects or in tight, hard-to-get-at places) and a pair of wire-cutting pliers.

Multibladed jackknife—Worth checking out, when jackknife shopping, is the line of red-handled Swiss Army knives. They're exceptionally well crafted and come in many models, each with its own set of special blades.

One or more handsaws—If you get only one, make it a crosscut model, generally the most useful. You can add a ripsaw, jigsaw, hacksaw and powered band saw later, should the need arise.

Cordless drill (rechargeable)—More expensive, of course, than the hand-operated type, but well worth the extra money, in terms of time and effort saved. This is another of those items on which one should not skimp. (For all-around home use, a small drill accommodating bits up to 1/2 inch is recommended, along with an assortment of attachments—sander, polisher, circular saw, and so on).

Plane—A plane is what you need for such tasks as smoothing rough lumber, trimming boards to size, and shaving doors and storm sashes so that they open and close properly. A "block" plane is the most commonly used type, and a recommended starter for any collection.

Adjustable wrench—A 10-inch model is suggested for general use. Indispensable for any kind of work involving plumbing.

Crowbar—Great for pulling nails and other purposes.

Assortment of chisels—All would-be chiselers should have more than one (preferably three or four, but at least two), both small-bladed (about 3 inches) and standard length (about 6 inches). Remember: *Never* drive a chisel with a conventional claw hammer—

doing so may split or "mushroom" the chisel's handle, unless a special steel-headed chisel is used. Instead, use a wood or rubber mallet, or a plastic-faced hammer.

Pair of heavy-duty kitchen shears—For best results, get the nickel-or chrome-plated kind, made of hot-forged or stainless steel. With better quality shears, one of the blades usually will have a serrated edge.

Steel "button-control" measuring tape—One of the most essential of your tool-kit components. And it's fun to push the little button and have the metal tape zap and clatter back into the spool. A 16-foot tape is traditional. Serious handypersons might want to opt for a folding "zigzag" carpenter's rule.

Large aluminum square—This L-shaped helper can be used to measure things, and for lining up a perfect right angle.

Liquid carpenter's level—Use one of these to check that your handiwork doesn't sag or tilt. Sometimes getting that little bubble centered may drive you slightly bananas, but it *does* help to raise the quality of your work another notch above rank-amateur status.

Two or three C-clamps—These jobbies are always handy to have around for many kinds of light and medium work, though not as good, of course, as a single rugged bench-mounted vise. Best of all would be to have one heavy bench vise and a few C-clamps besides.

Ice pick—Get a good, sturdy one; great for punching holes—and even for chipping ice.

Soldering iron—Also, naturally, a spool of solder and a can of soldering paste.

Spatula and small box of patching plaster or spackle—These are good to have around for minor wall-plastering jobs, where the costly procedure of calling in a professional plasterer may not be warranted. You can use an old coffee can to do your mixing in.

Assorted files—Indispensable for many shaping, smoothing, and sharpening jobs. Get the sizes and types best suited to the kinds of work you'll be doing most.

Assorted nails, tacks, screws, nuts and bolts.

Assorted pieces of sandpaper—Keep a good selection on hand, from coarse grade to emery paper.

Assorted tubes of glue—Wood glue, "instant" glue, "all-purpose" glue, and so on.

Wood filler and putty.

MEASURING SCREWS

Here's a handy guide to help you buy the right size and type screw you want:

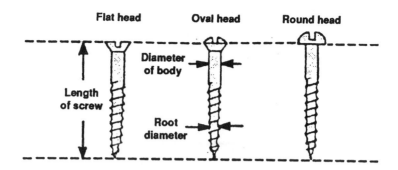

Flat head   **Oval head**   **Round head**

TWO BY FOUR MAKES *WHAT?*

Once upon a time, lumber used to be sold "rough-cut," with the task of planing it smooth left to the buyer. It was also a time when a two-by-four actually measured 2 inches by 4 inches. Nowadays, when lumber is sold ready-planned and smooth on all sides, the pieces you take home are smaller than their names would lead you to believe—the difference reflecting the amount of wood lost in the process.. For instance: a two-by-four now measures 1.5 inches by 3.5 inches, a four-by-four measures 3.5 inches by 3.5 inches, and a two-by-twelve is 1.5 inches by 11.25 inches.

NAIL NOTES

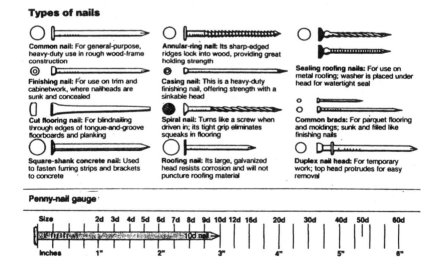

Types of nails

Common nail: For general-purpose, heavy-duty use in rough wood-frame construction

Finishing nail: For use on trim and cabinetwork, where nailheads are sunk and concealed

Cut flooring nail: For blindnailing through edges of tongue-and-groove floorboards and planking

Square-shank concrete nail: Used to fasten furring strips and brackets to concrete

Annular-ring nail: Its sharp-edged ridges lock into wood, providing great holding strength

Casing nail: This is a heavy-duty finishing nail, offering strength with a sinkable head

Spiral nail: Turns like a screw when driven in; its tight grip eliminates squeaks in flooring

Roofing nail: Its large, galvanized head resists corrosion and will not puncture roofing material

Sealing roofing nails: For use on metal roofing; washer is placed under head for watertight seal

Common brads: For parquet flooring and moldings; sunk and filled like finishing nails

Duplex nail head: For temporary work; top head protrudes for easy removal

Penny-nail gauge

261

HINTS FOR THE HANDYPERSON

- A shoe bag with pockets, hung above your workbench, can make a great place to keep tools.
- Before storing seldom used tools, spray then with silicone lubricant, then wrap each in aluminum foil.
- To avoid smashed fingers, use a bobby pin to hold a tack or nail in place as you hammer.
- When pulling a nail out of wood with a claw hammer, put a magazine under the hammerhead. This will give you better leverage, while protecting the wood surface.
- To keep your screwdriver from slipping while in use, rub some chalk on the tip of before inserting it into the screw.
- A screw will go in easier if you first push it about three-quarters of the way into a bar of soap.
- If a wood screw has gotten loose, remove it and stuff the hole with steel wool. Then screw in the screw, which ought to go in with much of its original tightness.
- For a more permanent mounting, wet a nail or screw before driving it in. When it rusts, it will bond tighter to its surrounding materials.
- To make sure that a bolt stays right, put on a second nut and tighten it against the first one
- To hold glued objects in place as they dry, use a spring-type clothespin or clamp-type pants hanger—or, if they're not weight-bearing, hold the objects in place with masking tape.
- If you have to measure something long with a tape measure and

you're alone, secure one end of the tape with masking tape

• To make sure your work is on the level—when you can't locate the level you *should* have in your toolbox—fill a glass measuring cup half full and use that.

• Wasted space at the bottom of a closet can be turned into extra storage space if you construct a boxlike frame to hold a storage drawer

• To gain extra storage space, take a low box or discarded drawer and attach casters to it This movable bin can then be filled with out-of-season items and kept under a bed.

• If a door won't stay open when you want it to, its hinges may need adjusting. Remove the pin from the top hinge and strike the pin gently with a hammer to bend it slightly. Repeat with other hinge pins if necessary.

• For sticking doors, squirt graphite into the keyhole, then work the graphite into the lock by inserting the key and turning it.

• To make it easier to carry a piece of plate glass or an unwieldy sheet of sharp-edged metal, slit a length of garden hose down the middle and use the halves as grippers.

• To safely remove a broken windowpane, glue newspapers to both sides, let it dry, then gently chip away the putty. The pane should come out without showering glass about.

• To remove wood rot from lower corners of window and door frames, cut out defective areas with a sharp knife and glue in fresh pieces of wood, then treat with wood preservative.

• To clean refrigerator condenser coils that have become clogged with dirt, use the wand attachment of a vacuum cleaner. (The coils are under or in back of the refrigerator; check them when the refrigerator cools poorly or fails to defrost. To reach under-unit coils, first remove the motor-compartment grill.)

• If you have trouble removing a buildup of soap and minerals from the ceramic tile around your bathtub, try using vinegar.

• To unclog a drain, first try using a plunger. If still clogged, pour a handful of baking soda into the drain, then add a half cup of white vinegar. Cover drain tightly for several minutes, then flush with cold water. If drain is *still* clogged, call a plumber.

• To lessen the danger of falling off a wooden stepladder, keep the climbing up and down to a minimum by inserting small hooks into the side of the ladder—then use the hooks for hanging needed tools, rags and so forth. Jar lids nailed to the top of the ladder will hold nails and screws and such.

• Candles will burn longer if kept in the refrigerator several hours before using.

• To remove candle wax from a wooden table without damaging

the surface, harden it with an ice cube and it will lift off. Clean the surface with a cloth moistened with paint thinner or mineral spirits (petroleum solvent).

• To remove candle wax from a rug or carpet, harden it with an ice cube, then break or scrape off as much as possible. All or most of the remaining wax can be absorbed by putting several layers of paper towel over the spots and applying a moderately hot iron. Use mineral spirits to remove any wax still remaining.

• To remove gum from a rug, harden the gum with an ice cube, then crush it with pliers and rub it out. Sponge any remaining stain with cleaning fluid. Repeat if necessary.

• To remove furniture indentations in a rug, separate the crushed fibers with a screwdriver or knife, then steam the indentation for a minute or two with a steam iron held a few inches above the area. Repeat until indentation is gone.

• To remove a cigarette burn from a hardwood floor, use a knife and sandpaper to take off the burned wood. Then, for a shallow depression, apply two costs of varnish. If the depression is deep, fill it with a matching wood filler, then sand and varnish.

• If you wish to find a wall stud and have an electric razor, run the razor gently along the wall. When it passes a stud, the tone of the buzzing will change.

• If you want your chain link fence to provide more privacy, slide venetian-blind strips diagonally between the links.

THREE HOME REPAIRS MADE SIMPLE

Home improvement and interior decoration are excellent pursuits that can greatly enhance your lifestyle and peace of mind. But of even greater importance is the foundation upon which these pursuits depend—home maintenance. This is the nitty-gritty of everyday life that intrudes at the damnedest times, demanding attention—and expense. Of course, when faced with pesky home-maintenance problems, the temptation is to do what any red-blooded American would do—ignore them. Unfortunately, all that usually does is make the problems worse. Leaky pipes, after all, don't fix themselves; they just get leakier.

Luckily, there is help to be had, along with the assurance that many home repairs are surprisingly easy to perform, if you just break each job down into separate steps and make sure you have everything you need on hand and in good order before starting in on the first step. A good idea would be to make the first step of all the procurement of some clearly written, easy to follow "literature," starting perhaps with whatever relevant government booklets are available. One such booklet, prepared by the Extension Service of the U.S. Department of Agriculture, is *Simple Home Repairs . . . Inside*, which offers up a bounty of home-repair basics. (For price and availability, write to Superintendent of Documents, U.S. Government Printing Office, Washington, DC 20402.)

Presented here are excerpts covering three common home-maintenance tasks: repairing a leaky faucet, patching holes in wallboard or plaster, and repairing screens:

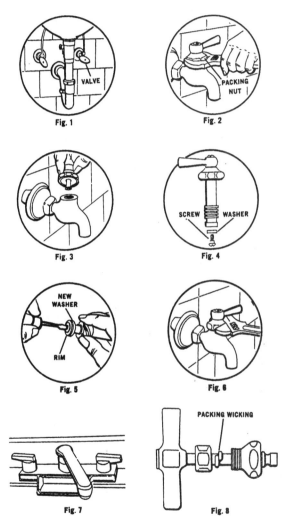

REPAIRING A LEAKING FAUCET

Your problem:
- Leaking faucets waste water.
- Dripping faucet may cause a spot in the sink.
- Constant dripping is annoying.

What you need:
- A box of assorted-size washers, unless you know the size.
- A screwdriver.
- An adjustable wrench.

How-to:

1. Turn off the water at the shut-off valve nearest to the faucet you are going to repair. Then turn on the faucet until the water stops flowing. (Figure 1 on preceding page)

2. Loosen packing nut with wrench. (Figure 2) (Most nuts loosen by turning counterclockwise.) Use the handle to pull out the valve unit. (Figure 3)

3. Remove the screw holding the old washer at the bottom of the valve unit. (Figure 4)

4. Put in a new washer and replace screw. (Figure 5)

5. Put valve unit back in faucet. Turn handle to the proper position.

6. Tighten the packing nut. (Figure 6)

7. Turn on the water at the shut-off valve.

Faucets may look different, but they are all built about the same. Mixing faucets—which are used on sinks, laundry tubs, and bathtubs—are actually two separate units with the same spout. You'll need to repair each unit separately. (Figure 7)

Is water leaking around the packing nut? Try tightening the nut. If it still leaks, remove the handle and loosen the packing nut. If there is a washer under it, replace the washer. If there's no washer, you may need to wrap the spindle with "packing wicking". (Figure 8) Then replace packing nut and handle, and turn water back on at the shut-off valve.

Your reward:
- Lower water costs.
- Spots in sink prevented.
- You save money by doing the job yourself.

Patching Holes in Wallboard or Plaster
Your problem:
- There's a hole in the wall.
- There's a crack in the wall.

What you need:
- Choose one of the two types of patching compounds: *Spackling compound* is convenient for small jobs but is more expensive. It can

be bought as a powder or ready-mixed. *Patching plaster* can be bought in larger packages and costs less. Both spackling powder and patching plaster need to be mixed with water.

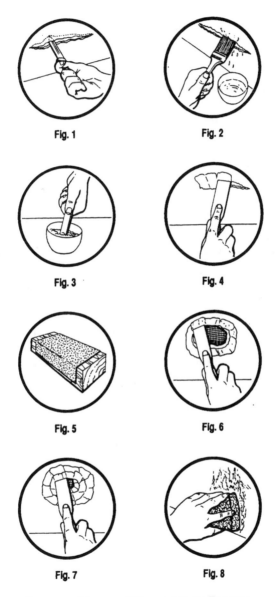

Fig. 1

Fig. 2

Fig. 3

Fig. 4

Fig. 5

Fig. 6

Fig. 7

Fig. 8

PATCHING HOLES IN WALLBOARD OR PLASTER

- Putty knife.
- Knife.
- Sandpaper—medium grit.
- Old cloth or a paint brush.

How-to:

1. Remove any loose plaster. With a knife, scrape out plaster from the back edges of the crack until the back of the crack is wider than the front surface. (Figure 1 on preceding page)

2. Thoroughly dampen the surface of the crack with a wet cloth or paint brush. (Figure 2)

3. Prepare patching compound according to directions on package. Mix only a small amount the first time. (Figure 3)

4. You can fill small holes with the patching mixture. Be sure to press the mixture until it completely fills the hole. Smooth the surface with the putty knife. (Figure 4) After the patch has dried, you can sand it. Wrap the sandpaper around a small piece of wood. This makes the surface even. (Figure 5)

5. Larger holes or cracks should be filled step-by-step. First, partly fill the hole. Let the patch dry. This gives a base for the final fill. Add a second batch of compound. Let dry. Sand until smooth. (Figure 6)

6. You may need to fill in behind large holes with wadded newspaper. Start patching by working in from all sides. Let dry. Apply another layer around the new edge. Repeat until the hole is filled. After the patch has dried, sand until smooth. (Figure 7)

Note: If the walls have a textured surface, you'll want to make the patch match it while the plaster is still wet. You might need a sponge or comb to do the texturing. (Figure 8)

REPAIRING SCREENS

Your problem:
- Insects come in through holes in screens.
- Small holes tend to become larger.
- New screens cost money.
- Help is hard to get.

What you need:
- Screening or ready-cut screen patches.
- Shears.
- A ruler or small block of wood with a straight edge.
- Fine wire, or nylon thread.

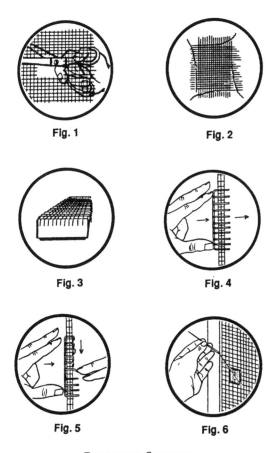

Fig. 1

Fig. 2

Fig. 3

Fig. 4

Fig. 5

Fig. 6

REPAIRING SCREENS

How-to:

1. Trim the hole in the screen to make smooth edges. (Figure 1)

2. Cut a rectangular patch an inch larger than the hole.

3. Remove three outside wires on all sides of patch. (Figure 2)

4. Bend the ends of the wires. An easy way is to bend them over a block or edge of a ruler. (Figure 3)

5. Put the patch over the hole from the outside. Hold it tight against the screen so that the small, bent wire ends go through the screen. (Figure 4)

6. From inside, bend down the ends of the wires toward the center of the hole. You may need someone outside to press against the patch while you do this. (Figure 5)

Mending You can mend small holes by stitching back and forth with a fine wire or a nylon thread. Use a matching color. (Figure 6)

Your reward:
- Keeps insects out.
- The house looks better.
- You save money by doing the job yourself.

SHOPPING THE THRIFTS

If you've never shopped in consignment or thrift shops, you've missed some real shopping fun. Here are some tips to get you started:

- Make a list before you go. Need a table for the patio? A toy box for the tots? A picture for the living room wall?
- Carry the measurements of your doorways , stairways and hallways for opening size and turning space. You don't want to buy an armoire that's too big to get into your house or apartment. Take a tape measure with you to check the dimensions of furniture before you buy it.
- Check the phone book under "Consignment Service" and "Thrift Shops" for addresses and phone numbers. Make a list of shops you want to visit, arranging them in geographic order to save driving time and gas. Call ahead for days and hours the shops are open to save the aggravation of driving some distance only to find the place closed.
- "Buy when you see it," veteran thrift shoppers say. Merchandise turns over quickly in these stores and the great find may not be there another day.
- To stay within a modest budget when visiting consignment or thrift shops, buy only those pieces of furniture that do not need reupholstering or refinishing. However, if you can afford to have a good find refurbished, do it. Older pieces of furniture are often better constructed than new, and the money you spend can be worthwhile.

—KNIGHT-RIDDER NEWSPAPERS

FRAME-UPS AND HANG-UPS

O.K., you feel you've got an eye for art—for photos and for posters and/or prints and/or paintings—and now you're hung up about framing same, or about where and how to hang them up. Well, unhang your hang-up with these tips from Bette Frank Rosenberg, home-fashions director for Spiegel Inc.:

- Don't limit yourself to centering hung objects over the sofa. It's O.K. to break out of the boundaries occasionally.
- Group photographs on the fireplace mantel, combining them with interesting art.
- Set a framed picture on a windowsill or lean it up against a wall.
- Accent your art or photo groupings with architectural details

270

such as ormolu trim, fragments, clocks or wall shelves.

• If you have a big staircase, take some small photos and run them up, as long as they're out of the way.

• Set up a family photo gallery wall in a hallway. Use clear frames so the art stands on its own.

• You can mix frames and styles, but keep one thing in mind in decorating eclectically. You need a point of view, a single decorative force: color, style, something to pull it all together and give it focus.

• Don't forget to accent your art with the right lighting: track, recessed, or lights that can be hung on the pictures. An important piece of art becomes even more so when properly lit.

SHELVING SYSTEMS

The many attractive and easy-to-install shelving systems that have been put on the market in recent years have helped homeowners and apartment-dwellers to increase storage and display space by making use of otherwise unused wall areas. Suitable for storing everything from books to television sets, the systems are also used for supporting small cabinets, drop-leaf desks, and other wall-hung furniture. The components are sold in almost all hardware and department stores, as well as at many lumberyards.

Although some companies' shelf brackets and wall standards are interchangeable, many are not, so it is generally wise to buy matching standards and brackets from the same source. The larger companies produce them in a variety of finishes, and wall standards are available in sizes ranging from 12 inches to 12 feet in height. Shelf-support brackets vary from 4 to 14 inches in length.

For books, shelves should be 8 inches wide, although 10-inch shelves will look better and will more satisfactorily hold oversize books. If ready-made shelves are used, then brackets can be bought to fit.

The vertical wall standards can be spaced from 24 to 36 inches apart, depending on the load the shelves will carry. For books and other closely packed, heavy articles, 24 inches should be the maximum, but for display shelving spacing of 32 to 36 inches is permissible. The easiest way to install standards on most interior walls is to attach them directly to the studs with long screws. Since studs are usually 16 inches apart, a standard can be fastened to every other stud (giving a 32-inch spacing). However, when studs are not located in the place where standards are to be installed, then expansion bolts, toggle bolts, or anchors of some kind must be used. Most of these devices require that a hole be drilled beforehand, although some that are designed for drywall installations can be simply hammered into place. A screw is then tightened to anchor the device in the wall and permit attaching the standard. Properly installed, one of these fasteners will support any load that the shelves are capable of supporting.

To be sure shelves are level when installed, standards must be properly aligned. After determining the correct height for the top of the first standard, attach it to the wall with the top screw only. Before this screw is tightened, allow the standard to swing so that it lands plumb. (For best results, a level should be held alongside to check this). Then mark the remaining screw holes with a pencil and swing the standard out of the way to drill the holes for the wall anchors.

PAINTING POINTERS

• Prepare all surfaces properly. Most people find this preliminary step to be the most difficult and boring part of any painting project—but, unfortunately, it's also one of the most important, since even the best paint will prematurely peel and flake when applied to a surface that has not been well prepared. All surfaces should be thoroughly cleaned and rinsed, and old paint should be completely removed by scraping, sanding or wire-brushing.

• Use masking tape to cover areas you don't want painted that are adjacent to those you do. The extra time you put into this step you'll save later, at cleanup time.

• Always buy the best grade of paint you can afford. Buying lesser-quality paint to save money is to practice a false economy, since such paint has a shorter life span.

• Fit the paint to the purpose. For instance, whether to use water-thinned acrylic latex paint, alkyd resin paint, oil-based paint, or enamel depends on whether you are painting an interior or exterior surface, the kind of wear that is expected, and so on. Discuss your particular painting needs with your dealer—and get a second opinion, if necessary. A bit of research early on will pay off in the long run.

• To keep loose brush bristles from coming off in the paint, run a comb through the brush before you start painting.

• To keep paint from peeling off concrete or sheet metal, apply a coat of vinegar to the surface before you begin.

• To keep your brush or roller free of excess paint as you work, draw it across a wire fastened midway across the opening of the paint can. (Attach wire by punching small nail holes in opposite sides of the rim of the can.)

• When painting baseboards, you can keep carpeting from getting in your way by pressing it down with a dustpan as you paint.

• To continue using a stairway while you're painting it, paint every other step on one day and the rest on the next.

• To help you keep track of how much paint you have on hand,

and what colors, paint a stripe around the outside of the can at the level of the remaining paint. Do this every time a paint job is finished, and you'll always be able to make a quick and easy paint inventory.

• Plastic milk or bleach jugs make excellent containers for left-over latex paint. Clean them first, then fill and cap tightly. Shake well before reusing. (**Caution:** Be sure to relabel all beverage jars with their new contents, and store away from children.)

• For a small amount of leftover paint, pour it into a glass jar and seal tightly. Use it for touching up nicks and scratches, or for painting incidental items.

• After a paint job, all masking tape should be removed as quickly as possible, certainly within eight hours. If allowed to remain in place beyond that time, it will dry and become very difficult to remove—in which case, a contact-cement solvent or petroleum solvent is recommended (the latter being available at a service station).

• To open a painted-shut window, run a putty knife or similarly bladed tool between the sash and the window frame, tapping the knife with a small hammer if necessary. Hold a block of wood sagest the sash, then use hammer to tap block lightly.

• To remove paint or varnish from chrome hinges and door pulls, simmer the for a few minutes in baking soda and water, then wipe off the solution.

• If you must stop work on a latex-paint job before it's finished, store your brush or roller inside a plastic bag, pushing the air out and tying the end shut

• To clean a roller, put it in a quart milk carton with water or other solvent (depending on the paint used), crimp the ends shut, give the carton a few shakes, then let it sit for a couple of hours.

• Never allow brushes to rest on their bristles in a can of solvent, as they will bend and lose their shape Put solvent in an empty coffee can or similar container having a plastic lid, cut an X in the lid, then push the brush handle up through the slits so that the brush will hang in the can rather than rest on the bottom.

FIRE-SAFETY TIPS

One home improvement you shouldn't overlook is the installation and maintenance of fire-prevention devices—they'll increase both your home equity and your peace of mind.

Herewith, a checklist based on recommendations by the National Safety Council

• Protect your home with at least one good quality smoke alarm near each sleeping area and one on each level of a house. Check the batteries each month.

• Don't disconnect a smoke alarm at any time. If minimal smoke from household cooking sets off the alarm, fan the device. Some detectors have reset buttons to quiet false alarms.

• Check for electrical fire hazards, such as overloaded outlets or frayed wiring. Avoid running electrical wires or cables under carpeting or against upholstery. Also, to prevent overheating, make sure there is enough "breathing room" around TVs, stereos, computers and such kitchen devices as toasters and toaster ovens. To keep from blowing a fuse—or worse, overheating a cord—don't use more than one high-wattage device (such as a toaster or an iron) at one time. (When purchasing such equipment, aim for the lowest wattage acceptable for the job.)

• Don't smoke in bed or any where you might fall asleep (most fires occur between 10 P.M. and 6 A.M.). Smoking is the leading cause of fatal residential fires.

• Keep fire extinguishers handy on each floor, as well as one in the kitchen, workshop, basement and garage. The safety afforded, and the peace of mind achieved, is well worth the investment involved.

• Don't leave the kitchen unattended when cooking with grease, oil or fats.

• Don't store flammable liquids or use them near any heat or ignition source, such as hot-water tanks or furnaces.

• Prepare and rehearse an escape plan and be sure every family member knows the possible escape routes. Establish a pre-arranged reunion spot outside.

• Keep cigarettes, matches or lighters away from children.

WHEN YOU HIRE SOMEONE ELSE TO DO IT

Spring and summer are periods when both home-improvement efforts gear up and itinerant and/or shoddy workers approach consumers to offer assistance at prices usually substantially lower than established companies can afford to quote. While itinerant workers can be sincere about doing a good job—such as a student seeking summer employment—many are simply seeking a mark, and their cheap price is aimed at the consumer wanting something for nothing.

To avoid being ripped off by perpetrators of home-improvement frauds, follow these guidelines:

• Remember that a price quotation means nothing unless you know exactly what is being provided for that price.

• Know the salesperson's name and the name and address of the company he or she represents.

• Check the reputation, dependability and responsibleness of the contractor before you sign anything.

• Obtain and check references from the company—get satisfactory responses.

• Avoid any salesperson who tries to high-pressure you into signing a contract.

• Get more than one bid (with identical specifications) for each job you want performed.

• To protect yourself in case of an accident, get a certificate evidencing a contractor's liability-insurance-coverage limits, policy term and number, and company.

• If your contract includes a long-term guarantee, you have reason to believe the company will be in existence during the term of the guarantee. Get any guarantee or warranty in writing, and make sure it answers these questions:

1) Is the whole job guaranteed, or only certain materials?

2) Who pays labor charges if only materials are covered?

3) Does the dealer or manufacturer make good on the guarantee?

• Ask your contractor if any of the work will be subcontracted. If so, get a waiver on any and all liens as proof that the contractor has paid for the materials used on your job.

• Know exactly how much the entire job will cost, including interest and service charges, and be certain you can make the payments. Check all possible sources for financing—your bank, savings and loan association, or other lending institutions.

• Insist on a written contract including the contractor's name; all oral promises made by the salesperson; color and size of materials to be used; and specific dates for the project's beginning and completion. Read and understand the contract completely before signing it—and keep a complete, readable copy signed by the salesperson.

• Beware of people wanting advance payment or cash, rather than requesting that a check or money order be sent to the company itself.

• Never sign a completion certificate until all work mentioned in the contract has been done according to that agreement; be careful not to sign such a certificate along with the sales order. Sign such a certificate only after you have been assured the contractor has paid for all labor and materials used.

• If you sign a contract in your home, remember that you have three business days during which you may cancel the contract. Such contracts can be canceled without penalty by your sending a signed and dated notice to the company within the time allotted. Send any such notice by certified mail, requesting "return receipt requested."

—BETTER BUSINESS BUREAU

GARDENING—INDOORS AND OUT
...of green thumbs and rosy harvests...

ROBERT MERZ

*God Almighty first planted a garden. And, indeed, it is
the purest of human pleasures.*
—FRANCIS BACON

More things grow in the garden than the gardener sows.
—SPANISH PROVERB

TO GARDEN IS TO DIG

To garden is to dig, and to dig is to get your hands or gloves dirty,
which can be strangely satisfying to a gardener—generally a life-
affirming sort who has either managed to retain a bit of the child
about him or her, or else has had the good sense to go back in mind-

time to reclaim some measure of animal wonder and fun.

For many are the joys of gardening, as young and old gardeners alike through the ages have attested. After all, its history is as old as our own: before there were farming and agriculture, there was that mini-agriculture we today call gardening, the growing and cultivation on a relatively small scale of herbs, fruits, vegetables and the like.

Over time, farming and agriculture have flowered into great mechanized industries, yet there still abides the art and craft of personally cultivating plants—that superb antidote for the often barbaric hurry of modern civilization. For puttering about in one's garden, whether small or large, indoors or out, can be a great balm and solace.

So it's not surprising, these frazzlesome days, that gardening has become more popular than ever. What's more, it can be a boon for body as well as mind, often providing its outdoor practitioners with all the fresh air and exercise a body can stand. Gardening can also satisfy one's urge to organize, cultivate and enjoy beautiful and/or useful objects, whether roses or radishes, orchids or onions. And growing your own food *can* save you money—never a hard side-effect to endure.

A garden, above all, is a flexible resource that reflects its owner's personality and preferences. You can specialize in particular herbs, fruits, vegetables or flowers, or you can mix them however you like (within, of course, limits dictated by geography and soil and such).

A garden can be a small or large expanse behind or alongside the house you call home, or a room or hallway or alcove in your apartment—or maybe just a windowsill or two upon which sit but a smattering of plants. The space you have at your disposal is your gardening "canvas" as it were: with time, energy, imagination—and a modest expenditure of money—who knows what grand or miniature masterpieces might grow there?

Take, for example, the great French painter, Claude Monet, who lived in—and made incredibly luminous paintings of—his garden at Giverny, France. The garden was dominated and made glorious by flowers and included a water-lily pond, which inspired many of his most memorable works. At the age of 84, Monet said:

> My garden is a slow work, pursued with love, and I do not deny that I am proud of it. Forty years ago, when I established myself here, there was nothing but a farmhouse and a poor orchard. . . . I bought the house and little by little enlarged and organized it. . . . I dug, planted, weeded myself; in the evenings, the children watered.

Happily, such joys are universal, and outdoor gardening of one type or another can be enjoyed in all but the world's harshest climates, while indoor gardening can be enjoyed just about anywhere.

Americans today can trace their own ever-growing interest in gardening through every stage of their country's history, dating back to the early settlers who grew food first for survival, then for profit. Many who were not full-fledged farmers were at least part-time gardeners, tending their private fields or patches as time permitted, with or without the help of other hands. Then, too, there were the areas called "commons," where people shared grazing and planting space. Some colonial statesmen—most notably Washington and Jefferson— were able to maintain extensive gardens that provided a refreshing counterbalance to the cares and frustrations of public life. As Washington confided to a friend in a letter of April 7, 1797:

> *I am once more seated under my own vine and fig-tree . . . and hope to spend the remainder of my days . . . which in the ordinary course of things (being now in my sixty-sixth year) cannot be many, in peaceful retirement; making political pursuits yield to the more rational amusement of cultivating the earth.*
>
> *Freed, as I now am, from the toils, the cares, and responsibility of public occupations, and engaged in rural and agricultural pursuits, I hope (aided by the recollection of having contributed my best endeavors to promote the happiness of that country which gave me and my ancestors birth) to glide peaceably and gently on the shades of retirement, and with good will to all men, until my time shall be no more. In doing this I promise myself more real enjoyment than in all the bustling with which I have been occupied for upwards of forty years of my life, which, as the wise man says, has been little more than vanity and vexation.*

Of course, not even the finest of gardens can filter out all the vanity and vexation that may find their way into *your* life, but growing things— whether outdoors or in—*can* be of help in soothing a ruffled mind.

For more of us, the problem is finding the space. But the odds are (with some perseverance and ingenuity on your part) you *can* find some space *somewhere* under the sun or under your roof for at least salad fixings, or a few of the smaller fruits or flowers. So whether you think of gardening as an art form, as a supplemental food supply, or as simply a good, dirt-under-the-fingernails way to pass the hours, the time to get started is *now*. Even if outdoor plans must wait for the right season, it's never too soon to get a notepad and some seed catalogs and start giving shape to your garden dreams.

Or, as Voltaire once so memorably put it: "We must cultivate our garden."

279

Early-19th-century drawing of a so-called "pepper-pot" garden house or toolhouse, from Benson J. Lossing's The Home of Washington and Its Associations (Townsend, 1865). These structures, dubbed the "new necessaries" by avid colonial gardener George Washington, also served as "seed-houses" or, more rarely, as schoolhouses.

TOOLS AND STUFF

Most likely, you won't need *all* of the following, and just as likely not everything you'll need has been included—but it's still a good checklist for getting started:

Heavy-duty work gloves—Obviously, only if you're going to be doing some heavy-duty garden work.

Waterproof kneepad—See above.

Brimmed hat—Can also double as informal, *non*gardening attire.

Scoop—For soil, peat moss, compost, etc..

Spades/shovels—Whatever you choose to call them, you might want to get a couple of different-sized ones, for light and heavy digging jobs.

Fork—You might want to consider having both a digging fork and a plain old kitchen fork to your gardening arsenal; both are great for breaking up clods of soil.

Hoe—Perfect for making furrows in which to plant seeds.

Trowel—Ideal for setting out transplants.

Dibble—Great for making holes in the ground for seeds, bulbs or plants.

Mattock—This somewhat neglected tool, akin to an axe or a pick, is handy for digging and grubbing.

Pruning shears—The thing about pruning shears is to keep them sharp; dull blades leave ragged cuts that may not heal.

Rake—You might also want to include a toy rake or back scratcher.

Watering can—Be sure to buy one that, when filled, is sufficiently comfortable to lug.

Garden hose—If you have a lawn, may want a hose with a jar attachment for applying insecticides and/or herbicides.

Oscillating sprinkler—Be sure to get one you can adjust to the size of your lawn or garden.

Rubber syringe—For pinpoint watering.

Stakes, string, etc.—For staking out your garden, keeping rows straight and making trellises and such.

• • •

Note: As for how much you should spend on your particular garden equipment, only you and your budget can say. Here's what Carolyn Ulrich, the *Cultivated Gardener* columnist, has to say on the subject:

> *Nobody can garden without tools, and nobody should garden without the best quality tools he or she can afford. There has been much talk lately about American vs. English garden tools, with the point being made that Americans buy cheap and expect breakage, while the English spend more on tools that last a lifetime. It's not that Americans can't make quality products, but there has been a tendency to concentrate quality manufacturing on equipment for landscape contractors rather than home gardeners. Hence, the prevalence of English names where quality spades and forks are sold to the gardening public.*

LAWN LORE

It is assumed, for the purposes of this item, that you have already struggled mightily with the momentous philosophical question of whether to keep your lawn neatly trimmed or let it have a natural, "unkempt" look—and have opted for the former. Or, possibly, you aren't aware of (or don't give a fiddler's fig about) the ongoing Great Lawn Controversy that flares up from time to time—you just happen to like a well-tended lawn. Either way, the following tried-and-true lawn lore should prove helpful:

• Check soil for imbalances in nutrients and pH level (acidity and alkalinity) with a do-it-yourself kit or by sending a soil sample to the county extension office. Excessive acidity is a common problem, so you may have to add lime. The EPA recommends "top-dressing" your lawn every year with a thin layer of rich topsoil, peat moss, bone meal or other soil builder.

• Whether you're seeding bare ground or thin areas, it's best to use a "blend" or "mix"—a blend being a combination of varieties of the same grass, a mix being a combination of grasses. With blends or mixes, a disease striking one variety won't wipe out the entire lawn. Kentucky bluegrass is the most popular type of grass in northern states because of its rich color and thin blades.

• Contrary to popular belief, the best time to plant grass seed in most areas is from August 15 to September 20—not in autumn. Later planting results in loss of new grass.

• All grass varieties need lots of light. Selectively remove tree limbs where necessary. For shady areas, use a special mixture containing fescue grasses.

• Newly planted lawns should be watered daily and carefully with a fine spray. For a mature lawn, a thorough watering once a week is much more beneficial than a light watering administered every day or every few days. You shouldn't even begin the job unless you're prepared to thoroughly drench the ground, wetting the soil at least an inch below the surface—a too-light watering will cause the roots of grass to turn up and become shallow. Also, don't water in bright sunlight or your grass will scorch and brown. The best time to water is early morning, when the water-evaporation factor is minimal.

• To combat weeds, insects and diseases, don't automatically reach for herbicides, pesticides and fungicides—too much of which can throw a lawn's ecology out of balance. Eliminate weeds by digging them up, and if you *must* use a pesticide, do so sparingly—spot-treating problem areas and carefully following label directions. According to EPA spokesman Al Heier, "Children and animals shouldn't be allowed to roll around in the grass moments after it's been applied. If it's enough to kill a weed or an insect, it's toxic."

• If you see that weeds are growing up through mulch or gravel, cover the area with plastic and put the mulch on top.

• As a general rule, mow high rather than low—no shorter than about 2 1/2 inches in the spring and 3 inches in the summer, and never cut more than a third of the grass blade at a time. Too-close mowing, especially in hot weather, weakens the turf and makes it susceptible to weeds and diseases; it also tends to dry out grass roots and

282

lowers drought resistance, which can cause yellowing or browning. If you let the lawn go so that the grass is tall, trim a third off, wait a few days then mow again. The final mowing of the fall should be a little shorter—about 2 inches—to reduce winter-fungus problems.

• To keep grass from sticking to mower blades, spray blades with vegetable oil.

• Thatch (matted grass clippings) should not be allowed to accumulate to a depth of more than a half inch.

• If crabgrass seems to be getting a foothold, apply a "postemergent" herbicide in time to eliminate it before it goes to seed. Herbicides are also available for such other lawn weeds as ground ivy, knotwood and chickweed, as well as the ubiquitous dandelion. (An adjunct to the aforementioned Great Lawn Controversy is the Great Dandelion Controversy—this pivoting on the question of whether said plant is a weed to be murdered on sight or a flower, however modest, to be valued for itself. Those deciding "weed" might do well to ponder Ralph Waldo Emerson's definition of same: "A plant whose virtues have not yet been discovered." To those still determined to rid their lawn of all traces of this flowering menace, a tip on how to keep the seeds from blowing all over: use a vacuum cleaner on a long extension cord to vacuum the seed heads.)

• Prevent soil compaction by aerating or coring in early spring. (You can rent a gasoline-powered aerator that removes cores of soil two or three inches long and a half-inch in diameter. These can be left on the ground to decompose in a week or two.)

• Use only enough fertilizer to maintain a normal growth rate. Folk wisdom has it that the best times to fertilize lawns are St. Patrick's Day, Memorial Day, the Fourth of July and Labor Day, but most specialists recommend two applications a year, one in the spring and one in the fall. Use natural, organic fertilizers rather than synthetic, chemical ones. Organics, which cost a little more, are better for the environment and release their nutrients slowly, thereby reducing the risk of "burn."

ANNUAL/PERENNIAL/BIENNIAL

Plants are of three types based on how they reproduce.

The **annual** type, such as the tomato and the impatiens, dies with the onset of winter; you have to save the seeds for replanting in spring. Annual flowers bloom all summer and are generally more vivid than perennials.

The **perennial** has a longer-term reproductive cycle, requiring one to two years to develop its flowers, which usually last less than a month. However, they can seed many times—for generations—saving you the job of yearly replanting. Perennials include columbines, forget-me-nots, peonies and tulips.

The **biennial**, such as the cabbage and the pansy, last but two years. The first year, they spend just growing; the next, they bloom, seed and die. But many feel that what biennials lack in longevity, they make up for with the visual delights proffered by their flowers.

PERENNIAL FLOWER GUIDE

Variety	Sun or Shade?	When in Bloom	Height
aster	sun	August to frost	2-4 ft.
bachelor button	sun	midsummer to fall	1-2 ft.
buttercup	sun	May-June	1-1 1/2 ft.
carnation	sun	summer-fall	15-18 in.
chrysanthemum	sun	September-October	2-4 ft.
columbine	shade	May-June	1 1/2-2 ft.
delphinium	sun	June-July	1-4 ft.
forget-me-not	shade	May-July	8 in.
foxglove	part shade, part sun	June-July	2-3 ft.
hollyhock	sun	June-July	5 ft.
iris, common	sun	May	2-3 ft.
iris, dwarf	sun	April-May	8 in.
lily of the valley	shade	May	8-10 in.
mint	part shade, part sun	June-August	6 in.
pansy	part shade, part sun	summer	8 in.
peony	sun	May-June	2-3 ft.
sweet pea	part shade, part sun	July-August	2-5 ft.
sweet william	sun	June	15 in.
violet	shade	spring-fall	6 in.
verbena, hardy	sun	July to frost	8-12 in.
yucca	sun	June-July	3-4 ft.

BIG-MOTHER MELON

Besides being the birthplace of President Clinton, Hope, Arkansas, is the "Watermelon Capital of the World." When local boosters there recently offered a $10,000 prize to any local resident who could raise a 200-pound watermelon by a certain day, Ivan Bright, 65, came within ounces and hours of winning—but his melon didn't reach full growth till two days past the deadline. Still, Bright was not overly gloomy, thanks to $500 in prize money for his near-win—and to being able to sell seeds from his mammoth melon for $100 a dozen.

GROWING INSIDE

Planning and tending one's very own garden, all might agree, are wondrously worthy and satisfying pursuits, except perhaps for one minor detail—most of us don't have one. For we mainly live in apartments these days, perhaps from time to time gazing wistfully from our windows at a house-owning neighbor's herb and/or flower garden, or vegetable patch.

But you really needn't wait—not if you downscale your garden dreams a bit and bring them indoors. Chances are, with a little imagination, you can find—or create—enough space for a few plants at least. Remember, indoor gardening is not just greenhouses and conservatories, it's any biosphere set up independently of the earth proper—any area in the attic, basement or garage; any spare room or windowsill or patio or porch; anywhere, in fact, where plants can be comfortably situated and provided with light, water, nutrients and a favorable atmosphere.

Even jars and glasses can be used as growing sites, as you may recall from classroom science projects. And some of your garden can just go hang—in plain or fancy pots or baskets or buckets suspended from ceiling skyhooks. (Flowers and ferns are particularly well-suited "hang-ups.")

Almost all the benefits the outdoor gardener enjoys can be enjoyed by the indoor gardener as well. Though the scale is smaller, the same fun and satisfaction can be had, and you can also save and/or make some money growing your own herbs. (For using herbs as delicious and/or medicinal potables, see "Herbs to Drink" in the "Food for Thought—and Action" chapter.)

Another plus for indoor gardening is its ability to help you through times when other activities aren't going so well. Cold, snowy days are brightened for those with plants to take care of. And it doesn't take long to get started.

Once your site or sites have been established, the next step is to build a biosphere. Here you can enjoy the main compensating advantage indoor gardening has over out: the ability to create the ideal conditions for your particular plants, to come as close to cultivational perfection as your knowledge and diligence permit, simply by setting up, then adjusting and readjusting, the various elements of your miniature universe.

As for your basic gardening medium, soil will be the choice of almost everyone—but you may wish to at least look into such alternatives as hydroponics or water gardening. As *Time* magazine explains:

> In the simplest hydroponic systems the plant roots are anchored in gravel or perlite through which the gardener periodically shoots water and inorganic solutions. . . . The indoor gardener is spared the necessity of messing with loam in the home and if careful can avoid the danger of bacterial infection around his plants
>
> Indoors or out, growing plants in water permits far more intensive cultivation than geoponics, or earth gardening. Since the roots do not spread out in search of nourishment, six times as many plants can be raised in the same space needed for earth farming.

Whatever the medium *you* choose, here are some "inside" growing tips:

• If you're growing in soil you have a choice of buying prepared mixes or making your own mixture with equal parts soil, peat moss, and perlite. If you use dirt from the ground, remember to test it (or have it tested) for acidity. If it contains too much acid, add lime.

• Be sure your pots and/or other containers are big enough for the plants they contain. Repot any that start looking crowded, doing so as gently as possible to minimize transplant trauma. Soil that has gotten too compacted to permit adequate drainage or admit needed oxygen should be replaced.

• Unless you have a rooftop or glass-roofed balcony or patio or somesuch, getting sufficient light to your plants may require installing a fluorescent light fixture or two. A good idea is to suspend such fixtures from pulleys, so that they may be easily raised or lowered as your plants require. As for bulbs, the ordinary workshop type will work fine, though you may want to try the more expensive "grow" lights at least once, to judge for yourself if the results justify the additional expense.

• An excellent fluorescent-light setup can be put together from two 48-inch, two-bulb industrial fixtures, four pulleys, various hooks, cords (or chains), electric cables, aluminum foil (strategically placed to reflect as much light as possible onto the plants)—and a timer, so that your plants get just the amount of light they need. Place fixtures side by side to amplify each other's output. Most herbs do well with about 12 to 14 hours of light a day.

• Whether you are starting plants indoors for later transplanting outside or growing plants in their permanent places, once the growing medium has been decided on, it's time to start thinking seed. If preplanted kits are not used, you can sow a greater variety of seed by ordering from seed catalogs or buying it at garden stores. Specific instructions are usually printed on the seed packets themselves.

• When you're ready to sow your seeds, you should first put sterilized soil or inorganic planting mix into trays of peat pots, then place a few seeds in each pot and press them lightly into the soil. Water each pot carefully with a rubber syringe. Keep the trays in full sun or directly under lights.

• Seed germination can be facilitated by building a simple indoor "greenhouse" from a clear plastic storage box (such as a sweater box) placed in sun or under lights. When the lid is on, the moist conditions inside the box are ideal for germinating seeds. If a plastic storage box is not available, pots and flats may be covered with sections of glass or clear plastic strips to stabilize moisture and temperature (70° to 75° F is ideal). Remove coverings when seeds start to sprout.

• For indoors-to-out transplanters, March opens the indoor seed-planting season, a preparation for when the seedlings can be transferred outside once the ground is warm. Fine, slow-growing seeds should be started promptly. Faster-germinating seeds should be started in early April. If you've used peat pots for starting your plants, when the weather is right they can be set out in the garden—pots and all.

- Author Bessie Buxton tells of an effective, if somewhat unorthodox method of fertilizing indoor plants. "An old-fashioned method of fertilizing pot plants is to thrust match heads into the soil. They contain sulfur and phosphorus, both of which are used by plants. These chemicals are in animal fertilizers and in bone meal, so do not used both fertilizers and matches."

- Should you inadvertently overfertilize, you can minimize the damage by immediately rinsing the soil with clear water. Put the plant in the sink or a bucket and water heavily to flush out the fertilizer.

- One often-overlooked factor in the well-being of indoor plants is their need for humidity. Most need a lot of it, and it can sometimes be hard to come by, particularly in an apartment in winter, when the heated air becomes excessively dry. If practical, installing a humidifier as part of your overall heating system is the ideal solution—but a cheaper, easier way to go is to get portable units and place them near your plants. Still another way to heighten general humidity is to group potted plants in a large, deep tray with an inch or so of pebbles at the bottom and to keep the water level in the tray just below the pots. As the water evaporates, it moisturizes the air around the plants.

- Generally speaking, plants in hanging baskets will dry faster than their nonhanging counterparts, so water them often. This frequent watering will in turn require frequent light fertilization, as nutrients are leached from the planting mixture A soluble plant food applied every other week is recommended.

- To keep potted plants on a window ledge from falling off, fasten curtain-rod holders on the outside of the window frame, one on each side of the window, three or four inches up from the windowsill.

- In Victorian times, it was customary to fill an empty fireplace with growing potted plants—not a bad idea today if you should have a fireplace. And if it's a nonworking fireplace, you've got a fine, year-round garden spot.

WHEN SETTING OUT PLANTS

1. Water soil well before disturbing the plants.
2. Keep plants wet.
3. Loosen soil before putting plants in seedbed.
4. Water soil before and after setting plants.
5. Press soil firmly about roots.
6. If possible, shade the plants for a few days.

SOME REALLY, REALLY LATE BLOOMERS

Some 2,000-year-seeds taken from an ancient tomb in central China recently stunned the scientific world by sprouting into plants bearing tomatoes. Archeologists exploring a Han dynasty tomb found several mysterious carbonized objects, which they covered with boiled and sterilized blankets. A month later, they lifted the blankets to discover that the remains had germinated, producing about 40 green buds. That the plants were tomatoes became obvious when they continued to grow and bore fruit.

TOMATOES, PEPPERS ARE GARDEN FAVORITES

According to the National Gardening Association, the five most common garden vegetables, in order, are tomatoes, peppers, beans, cucumbers and onions. The leader of this veggie parade just might have been the pepper, were it not for the fact that in 1893 the U.S. Supreme Court declared that the tomato is a vegetable rather than a fruit. (Technically, the tomato is a fruit but is commonly considered a vegetable because of its uses.)

Vegetables	No. of Days Before Picking	Vegetables	No. of Days Before Picking
beans, snap bush	45-60	okra	55-65
beans, snap pole	60-70	onions, bulb	80-120
beans, lima bush	65-80	onions, seed	90-120
beans, lima pole	75-85	parsley	70-90
beets	50-60	parsnips	120-170
broccoli	60-80	peas, English	55-90
brussels sprouts	90-100	peas, southern	60-70
cabbage	60-90	peppers	60-90
carrots	70-80	potatoes, Irish	75-100
cauliflower	70-90	potatoes, sweet	100-130
celery	125	radishes	25-40
cucumbers	50-70	soybeans	120
eggplant	80-90	spinach	40-60
garlic, cloves	140-150	squash, summer	50-60
lettuce, head	70-75	tomatoes	70-90
lettuce, leaf	40-50	turnips, greens	30
mustard	30-40	turnips, roots	30-60

Woman watering a rosemary plant, from a book by J. Schott (1518).

HARVEST OF HINTS

Before you can be led down—or, for that matter, up—the garden path, there has to be one. As for ingredients, popular options include flat rocks, pebbles, planks, wood chips, grass, plain soil and shredded leaves.

To help you design a flower bed or vegetable patch with a curve or two, use a garden hose heavy enough to stay put, but light enough to move around easily until you get just the right shape for the space. Chain or string will also work, though not as well.

Household-hinter Mary Ellen, writing in her *Best of Helpful Hints, Book II* (1981), offers the following sure-fire old-seed test: "Count out about fifty seeds, placing them between two layers of wet newspaper covered with a plate after five days, count the number of seeds that have germinated to determine how thick they will have to be spread. If half are no longer good, use twice as many as you normally would."

According to folklore, everything that produces fruit *above* the ground should be planted in the new moon, while everything that produces food *under* the ground should be planted in the dark of the moon.

If you're out of containers and potting soil, try starting seedlings in eggshells half filled with compost When transplanting, put the shells and all in the ground.

Try to give seedlings the best light possible, so they don't get too spindly or "leggy," a condition of botanical ineptitude caused by the seedlings growing taller than they should, in their effort to get more light.

If you have a choice, plant in the evening or at the start of a spell of cloudy weather. Don't tamp soil down around roots with hands or feet—just "settle" it by watering. Wait a few days before fertilizing.

For budding herbalists, the Herb Society of America advises: "Like flowers and vegetables, herbs will survive in a poor soil, but they need good soil, with humus and fertilizer, to grow best. Barn manure, compost, and wood ashes are especially beneficial. If your soil is very poor, use a commercial fertilizer such as 5-10-5, according to the directions on the package, to bring the plants along fast. Herbs may be grown with great success with mulches. During the summer a mulch such as salt marsh hay, buckwheat hulls or Dutch peat moss may be spread between the rows. This prevents weeds from growing and keeps the soil moist."

Very tiny flower seeds can be mixed with sand and sown from a saltshaker.

A good watering rule to remember is that no water at all is better than a shallow sprinkling, which can cause roots to rise to the surface and dry out, often killing plants in the process. For most plants, you should provide the equivalent of an inch of rain a week during the growing season.

When planting melons or cucumbers, put a tablespoon of moth flakes in some lime and add to soil near each plant, making sure that the mixture is covered with soil. To keep the bugs away, plant a couple of onion sets or cloves of garlic nearby.

Lure snails and slugs to their doom with small saucers of beer. They'll stop off for a friendly nip and glug their way to death. (It's the beer's yeast that drives 'em to drink.)

POINTERS ON PETS

. . . not all animals are beasts . . .

*Animals are such agreeable friends—they ask no
questions, they pass no criticisms.*
—George Eliot

Pets are the four-legged flowers of our lives.
—Ed Asner

PETS: PRO AND CON

There are many good and glowing things to be said of pets—and perhaps a fair number of not so good and glowing. High on the positive side is the fact that they're *generally* warm and cuddly (naturally we're not talking pets of the piscine or reptilian persuasion). And they're *generally* loving and loyal. And time- and money-consuming. And frequently messy.

Pets can also be ingratiating, annoying, comforting, dangerous, incredibly expressive and maddeningly "dumb"—the latter being really a compliment in the sense that pets can convey so much meaning without words, it's sometimes frustrating not to be able to carry "conversations" with them even further. You speak, with varying modulations, and they reply with their assorted noises and movements—and sometimes the *felt* communication is so strong it's eerie.

However, while millions of us have taken pets into our hearts and homes, millions of others have no use whatever for them, and are far from shy in voicing this view. In fact, most landlords these days will not rent you an apartment if you're a "pet person." In the cities, many a verboten Morris has had to be moved on the sly into a non-pet pad, and often will go undetected, while Fido—being Fido—is almost impossible to smuggle in.

So what's the big attraction? For one thing, it's mutual. You provide your darling or darlings with the basic necessities, and they in turn provide you with some psychic necessities you might not be getting, or getting enough of, from your fellow humans.

Indeed, pets are famous as tonics for the all-too-frequent feelings of depression and isolation many of us experience in today's hyped-up, rapidly changing world. Moreover, pets—especially dogs—can be trained to help the handicapped in various ways. And with the help of pets to teach them trust, autistic people have achieved amazing behavioral breakthroughs, as have hard-core criminals, who previously felt little more than hostility. A recent prison study found that, thanks to pets, there was a decrease in the amount of medication inmates required. Said one convict of his pet bird: "I fell in love with the bird, and it got me started talking to other people. I really got along fine after that."

Of course, the benefits of living with a pet or pets are not all in the mind: they can actually make you physically healthier as well. Studies have shown a clear connection between pet ownership and increased longevity, as well as fewer instances of heart disease and high blood pressure—the latter being easy to understand when you consider that the simple act of *speaking* to other people raises one's blood pressure. It has also been found that pet owners undergoing serious operations have a better survival rate than their petless counterparts. And we have all heard or read accounts of pets who, by one means or another, saved their owners' lives.

If there is a dark cloud in this rosy portrait of pet-human bonding it is that there are many more companion animals, or would-be pets, than there are homes for them—every year in the U.S. more than 12 million unwanted, homeless dogs and cats are "put to sleep." Most are less than 18 months old, and about 90% are healthy and adoptable.

Strays on the street face particularly bleak possibilities, ranging from starvation to impoundment to traffic-related injury or death. When stray dogs are caught, they are brought to pounds, where they quickly become statistics counted only by the ton.

Some of the luckier strays are brought to places like the Citizens for Animal Protection, a humane shelter in Houston, where they have an opportunity to be adopted. But shelters run out of cages. According to the U.S. Census Bureau, six times more animals than people are born every hour, and already there are pets in over half the households in the country.

Overpopulation in the pet world is caused primarily by the pet-breeding "mills" that supply the large retail pet stores, by the hobby breeders who are cranking out pure-bred dogs, and by people who just let their cats and dogs roam free and breed indiscriminately. (And letting an animal have "just one litter" before spaying in some cases makes it a worse pet, due to habits formed while protecting its litter.)

Another factor contributing to overpopulation is the lack of commitment on the part of some owners—those who get a pet, then at some point decide it's too much trouble and abandon it.

There are two things we can all do to begin solving the pet-overpopulation problem:

• If you are thinking about getting a pet, be aware that it entails a lifelong commitment. Ask yourself if you can provide the time, energy and money the pet will take. Above all, resist acting on a whim. Pets are something more than animated hobbies, to be shunted aside when the novelty fades.

• If you *do* get a pet, have it spayed or neutered as soon as possible.

But, you may ask, will spaying a pet make it fat and lazy?

Not necessarily. Sometimes female dogs and cats will put on a little weight, especially the first three or four months after they've been spayed—but you can counter this by closely watching their diet and keeping it lean, both fatwise and portionwise.

As for the fear that neutering a dog will take away its spirit, that too is largely groundless. As one pet-shelter worker put it: "Neutering a male dog just takes away its instinct to breed, but it does not change the character or the personality of the animal. It's very much like gelding a racehorse." Or as author Michael Fox of the Humane Society Institute notes:

"The negativity about castrating male dogs is generally coming from the male owner, because somehow he has his own sexual identity—whatever—involved with his dog. He would not think twice about neutering a tomcat."

In the vanguard of the fight against pet overpopulation are the roughly 3,500 animal shelters in the U.S. that care for strays and abandoned pets. They are constantly trying to place these unfortunate animals in responsible homes and will be glad to spay or neuter an adopted pet for a reasonable fee scaled to the owner's income. So if you decide to get a pet or pets, go first to an animal shelter, where there are animals that really need a home. It's a much more caring and thoughtful path to pet ownership than patronizing the breeders, especially the large commercial breeders.

"Tell me, do you think the mice will win the series?"

PETS IN THE CITY

Apartment tenants who keep pets, and those tenants who are probably violating their leases by keeping pets, may be able to avoid crises with the landlord by following a few simple rules:

• Pets should be on a leash when taken in or out of an apartment house. Do not use a leash that gives the animal too much headway because it will be more difficult to control the pet.

• A pet should be walked away from buildings and close to the street curbing. Litter should be disposed of properly.

• A dog should not be left alone for long periods or over weekends. Barking, lonely dogs may be brought to an animal pound during an owner's absence.

• If you hire a dog walker or other type of pet sitter, ask for references. When in doubt, try someone else.

• To avoid "high-rise pet syndrome"—pets accidentally falling from high windows—install screens or guards on any windows you leave open. Also, do not allow pets on terraces or rooftops.

THE DAY OF THE CAT

Although the dog long held claim to the title of top American pet, today that honor belongs to the *generally* less demonstrative, less bothersome—and much more mysterious and subtle—cat.

Reliable pet censuses are hard to come by. Reputable sources differ widely in this area but a reasonable estimate is that household cats outnumber household dogs roughly 60 million to 50 million, as the cat population continues its strong upward trend.

Is this ascendancy of the cat yet another sign of the strife and stress of modern times? A time when jammed-up schedules no longer permit a daily walk or two with Fido? A time of trying to get your beloved animal friend past the portals of an increasing number of anti-pet landlords, many of whom may be adamant when it comes to dogs, but who just *might* be swayed when it comes to a quiet, litter-trained cat or two? Or is it something in the psyche of the modern pet owner that finds an increasing affinity with the cat?

The reasons are indeed numerous—including the fact that cats are equally at home in an apartment as outdoors and need little special care. They are instinctively clean animals, taking quickly to using a litter tray, and—if provided a scratching post—they can be taught to spare your furniture the necessary fury of their claws. (Some may disagree, but most true "cat people" feel that cats should definitely not be declawed, that doing so constitutes too great a physical alteration and renders them defenseless against other animals.)

Cats *do* require a certain amount of loving attention, but usually on a smaller time-and-energy scale than dogs. There is also the matter of spaying and neutering. Females left to their natural ways can produce dozens of kittens in a lifetime and in periods of heat cry with annoying shrillness, while tomcats turn feisty and spray a most pungent and odoriferous substance indeed, one that is virtually impossible to remove from furniture or carpets. But that's really the worst of the bad news; the good news is that most animal shelters will alter pets on a sliding fee scale, pegged to the owners' income.

If you are considering a cat as a pet, consider also that many feline fanciers think that having two cats instead of one is well worth the additional expense. Cats need a certain amount of semi-aggressive play—nothing dangerous for an alert owner, but a need that can more readily be met by another cat. But be advised that if you *do* opt for two cats instead of one, you should probably get them at the same time. If you get one now and try to bring a second one into your household later, the first one is likely to protest vehemently. Ultimately, this is something you alone must judge, based on your knowledge of your cat's personality and on your informed appraisal of the new cat you're thinking of adopting.

Meanwhile, whether or not you are considering adopting a cat or cats, you may be intrigued by their truly incredible and often unfathomably bizarre history—a history marked by deification, slaughter and assorted mayhem, as the following tales and tidbits attest:

• According to E. Laurence Palmer's *Fieldbook of Mammals* (1957):

Very likely first domestication was in Egypt about 1300 B.C., but some records point to about 2400 B.C. Cats are not mentioned in the Bible and were probably not domesticated in Europe until the beginning of the Christian era. They were venerated in Egypt, where the city of Bubastis was dedicated to cat worship. To this city 700,000 persons came in one year to worship cats. . . . In medieval Europe cats were feared, hated, associated with the devil, darkness, sin, and witches; in England, they were tortured by roasting in cages before slow fires. Few animals have been more hated, worshiped, petted, abused, and feared by mankind than have cats.

• John Voight, writing in *Cat Fancy* magazine, tells how the infamous Black Plague resurrected the feline image from "the animal from Hell" to the savior of European civilization:

When Europeans began to destroy their innocent cats, they left themselves no protection against the newly invading Asiatic black rat and Black Plague. Europe suffered heavily for its crime against the cats. Three-fourths of the entire population died of the plague. When the cats showed their ability in destroying the Asiatic vermin, people's opinions changed. Both the church and the state ceased their senseless killing of the cats. Men slowly came to see the cat not as an agent of evil, but as an agent of good.

• In ancient Egypt, shaved eyebrows were an owner's sign of mourning for his or her deceased cat.

• According to the *Natural History* (1767) of Count de Buffon (as translated by William Smellie): "The wild cat existed in America before its discovery by Europeans. A hunter brought one of them to Christopher Columbus, which was of an ordinary size, of a brownish gray colour, and having a very long and strong tail." As for De Buffon's opinion of cats, it reflected the traditionally negative pre-Victorian attitude: "The cat is an unfaithful domestic, and kept only from the necessity we find of opposing him to other domestics still more incommodious, and which cannot be hunted; for we value not those people, who, being fond of all brutes, foolishly keep cats for their amusement."

• From Judy Fireman's *Cat Catalog* (Workman, 1976) comes the following romantic footnote to the ongoing saga of cat-human relations, this a Spanish tale centering on the words for cat and cat door—*gata* (female cat), *gato* (male) and *gatera* (cat door):

The gatera was cut into the door of old Spanish homes to provide the cat with easy passage in and out of the house. It also provided many a young man with a door to his lady's heart. Young

Spanish suitors sometimes conducted courtships by talking through the cat door. When the girl's balcony was too high up for courting conversations, the boy and girl would lie on the floor on either side of the door and flirt through the hole.

• The old English proverb, "The dog for the man, the cat for the woman," appears to be quickly passing out of date, as growing numbers of men have taken to living with cats. Pat Meehan, adoption director for the Humane Society of New York, says: "We're getting lots of men looking for cats—young men, old men, married and single." Publishing executive and cat owner Roger Straus III feels that feline companionship is instructive for men: "It teaches them humility and how to land on their feet."

• Members of the Cat Fanciers' Association were stoutly assured of their patriotism during a 1976 meeting in Washington, D.C., when welcoming Congressman Gilbert Gude (R-Maryland) told them: "Tyrants hate cats. Genghis Khan and Napoleon and Mussolini are said to have hated cats. Who loved cats? Thomas Jefferson loved cats. There were cats at Mount Vernon because George Washington liked them too, as did Abraham Lincoln." (P.S.: President Rutherford B. Hayes received the first Siamese cat ever sent to America; the exotic creature became a White House favorite.)

• Cats snooze two-thirds of the time but always remain alert to sounds.

• All cats purr—sometimes audibly, sometimes not—but exactly how they do so remains a mystery. A cat can make many different purring sounds, usually signifying contentment and affection, but sometimes also pain—the latter expressed by purring that's harsher and sharper than normal.

• It takes an average of three pounces for a cat to catch a rodent.

CAT TIPS

• If your cat is a picky eater, try sprinkling its food with a little oil from a can of tuna.

• If your cat should refuse liquid medicine, hint-sharer Mary Ellen suggests spilling some on its fur—whereupon he or she will instinctively lick it off.

• A cardboard box, open on one side, makes a fine makeshift cave for Morris or Tabby to hunker down in and peer out of. First put a relatively flat cushion on the bottom, then put one or two of your cat's toys inside, then sprinkle a bit of catnip on a small area of the cushion—and his or her curious nature will do the rest.

• To make a catnip toy, wrap some nip in tissue paper and tie it up in an old sock or piece of cloth.

• For another low-rent but time-tested toy, crumple some aluminum foil into a small ball—cats love to use these as hockey pucks, or stand-in mice. However, you may want to supervise such play, to be sure that none of the foil is ingested. Also, don't let a cat play with rubber bands, string, yarn or feathers, all of which can cause death if swallowed.

BRITAIN'S FIRST CAT BEATS MURDER RAP

Great Britain's first cat, Humphrey, is innocent of charges that he murdered a nest of baby robins, Prime Minister John Major recently told the nation.

"I can tell you beyond any doubt at all that Humphrey is not a serial killer," Major proclaimed during a TV newscast. "Humphrey has been very unjustly accused. There was a small nest of robins just outside the Cabinet room. I am afraid they are dead, but it is natural causes."

DOG TALES

Stone Age tribes may have had hunting dogs before 10,000 B.C.—canines that most likely descended from the lighter-built southern Asian races of the wolf, with admixtures from other wolf races.

• • •

The saluki is the oldest known breed of domesticated dog. Excavations of the Sumerian Empire, estimated at 7000-6000 B.C., have produced carvings resembling the saluki. The saluki can run 50 miles an hour and was used by Arabs to catch the swift gazelle.

• • •

Although better known for their worship of cats, ancient Egyptians also felt much the same way about dogs—as witness their pharaoh-like mummification of the bodies of salukis. As writer Robert Rosenblum notes in his book, *The Dog in Art: From Rococo to Post-modernism*

(Abrams, 1988), "[The Egyptians personified] Sirius as the ever-faithful dog-star, since every year it benevolently signaled with its appearance the flooding of the Nile and the need to move the cattle to higher land," while the Hebrews "could vilify dogs, associating them with forbidden unclean animals and with pagan idolatry." Attitudes toward dogs moderated somewhat in the postclassical world, as "the extremes of deifying or abominating dogs were tempered by more terrestrial and practical attitudes, in which dogs could be integrated into human life not only as workers who played a major part in the hunting of animals for sport or food, but as loving, loyal, and unselfish companions."

• • •

The Pekingese were the sacred dogs of the emperors of China and were owned only by royalty. Unlawful possession of a Pekingese was punishable by death. Pekes were unknown to the outside world until 1860. The first Pekingese in Europe were five dogs brought from China after they had been removed by the British from the women's apartments in Peking's Summer Palace, during the so-called Boxer Rebellion of 1889-1900.

• • •

According to the Reader's Digest *Book of Facts* (1987), the idea of using dogs to help blind people stemmed from a chance incident at a German hospital during World War I:

> *A doctor walking in the grounds with a blinded soldier was called away and left his pet German shepherd (Alsatian) to look after his patient. Impressed by its response, the German doctor began training dogs to guide the blind.*
>
> *In the early 1920s a wealthy American, Dorothy Eustis, had set up a kennel in Vevey, Switzerland, to breed and train German shepherds for the army and police. Hearing of the German experiments, she hired former German Army dog trainers and eventually set up the Seeing Eye center in New Jersey, where German shepherds and other breeds learned to guide the blind.*

• • •

Rick Kogan of the *Chicago Tribune* tells the following four-star canine tale, set in the Ambassador East Hotel's "Pup Room," a place where visitors to the ultra-posh Pump Room checked their dogs before making the scene (the dogs being paw-printed on arrival and provided Bow Wow Burgers):

> *One night a dog belonging to Alfred Hitchcock's daughter Pat was distraught at being left in a coatroom basket while his owners*

dined. The dog, Phillip (named for the Duke of Edinburgh), played dead. Kay Harley, "Mistress of the Hounds" (i.e., coatroom attendant), tried frantically to revive the dog. Hitchcock was summoned and the dog sprang immediately to life. "I wish some of my actors were as convincing," said Hitchcock.

• • •

Man bites dog—and lives! (Albeit $33 poorer.) In 1986 a man admitted in court in Bristol, England, that he bit his dog on the ear after it had made a mess in the house. Stuart Smale, 19, of Bristol, said in court that he became angry after his dog, Jade, misbehaved. Smale said he threw the dog out of the house after biting its left ear. The court forbade Smale from keeping a dog for a year and ordered him to pay $33 in veterinary costs.

• • •

The American Kennel Club, which keeps a regular account of such things, reports that the "top dog" since 1983 has been the cocker spaniel, followed in recent years by Labradors and poodles. In fact, the club named the cocker not just the dog of the decade but of all time—noting that dogs that become hugely popular tend to be cute, adaptable to a wide variety of conditions, and trainable. The cocker gets very high marks in the first two categories, but the scoring varies widely in the last. Most learn quickly, but some are too high-strung, or too ornery, to really get with the routine; these and other random quirks are considered the unavoidable by-products of inbreeding. (P.S.: Hottest breed by far is the rottweiler, crashing into the top 10 of dogdom at number 6—up from 44 just a decade earlier.)

• • •

The people at the Dog Museum of America, located in St. Louis, marked the museum's fifth year recently with a resolve to be taken more seriously and to expand the scope of its exhibits, which till now have consisted mainly of paintings and sculptures of dogs. Since its founding in 1986, the museum has been the subject of mocking commentary and worn-out jokes about dogs, a situation new director Susan Brown intends to correct by turning it into a true "teaching museum." Projected new attractions include an exhibit on the history of humans' long relationship with dogs.

• • •

According to *New Woman* magazine, you can tell what a man's like by the dog he keeps. A man with an Irish setter, for instance, would like a woman who is a wild, flaming beauty "with a minimum amount of introspection." Owners of small breeds, such as Chihuahuas or Mexican hairless, should be avoided if you are someone "who does not like someone watching over you, or if lavishly demonstrative people give you claustrophobia." Men who own "gun dogs"—such as Labradors or golden retrievers—are often conservative, good with children, and fond of the great outdoors. But a note of caution about owners of German shepherds: they "tend to impose their personality on their surroundings."

MATCHING DOG TO CHILD

The puppy whose mournfully winsome gaze through the pet-shop window melts your child's heart could turn out to be the worst possible pet choice—and mistakes can be tragic for both child and dog.

For such an important decision as adopting a dog, your family should first sit down and thoroughly discuss the effort dog ownership will require and the potential problems involved. Even if your child is very responsible, you still must be prepared to provide a certain amount of supervision, as well as temporary care of the animal during the child's more serious illnesses.

The first question to consider is, how much do you know about dogs? If the answer is "not much," it's a good idea to go to or otherwise contact a library, animal shelter or veterinarian for booklets on characteristics, sizes and suitability of various breeds of dogs as house pets, as well as on how to train a puppy. While reading about breeds, it might be advisable to translate "very alert" as jumpy and bouncy, "ideal hunting dog" as one that will be pointedly unhappy in a three-room apartment, and "150 pounds when grown" as almost a zoo specimen.

Just because children are small, you needn't restrict yourself to a small dog. Personality and disposition are more important factors in choosing a pet for children. Golden retrievers, for instance, can be much gentler with youngsters than some smaller breeds.

If space and or dog walkers are scarce, and if the child or children involved are not too overly rambunctious, a "toy" dog—such as a pug, poodle or Chihuahua—can be the answer. Such a dog can be trained to use kitty litter and travels happily in a shopping basket.

If you're short on space but cool to the subcompact "Kewpie dogs," the medium-sized breeds—like the basset hound, bulldog or cocker spaniel—offer a possible compromise, inasmuch as they are neither so small as to be overwhelmed by a child nor large enough to be a danger.

Dogs like the German shepherd and the pit bull are not advised for households with small children. A 1989 study of dog-bitten children (published in *Pediatrics* magazine) found that pit bulls are more likely to attack children without any provocation than any other type of dog. The dogs likeliest to bite were German shepherds, followed by pit bulls, rottweilers, Dobermans and terriers. But 94 percent of the pit-bull attacks were unprovoked, compared with 43 percent unprovoked attacks by German shepherds. In more than three-fourths of the cases the dogs were known to the children, whose average age was 8. The two physicians who conducted the study recommended "measures [that] would lead to early identification of a potentially dangerous dog and restrict ownership."

YES, VIRGINIA, THERE ARE OTHER PETS

While cats and dogs continue to reign in the world of pets, there are many other companion animals that brighten our travails and share in some of our fun. Among these are such time- and tot-tested favorites as hamsters, gerbils, goldfish, parakeets and canaries.

Cat and/or dog owners may feel such fauna to be sorely lacking in personality—but telling that to a "bird" person, aquarium-gazer, or youngster with his or her very own hamster will almost certainly result in some spirited words of dissent. "Personality," after all, is a commodious word not given to exactly definable parameters—and who's to say that none whatsoever is detectable in the face of a fish or the nod and bob of a cockatoo?

If *your* particular preference in pets runs to the exotic, but you're not quite sure how exotic you *want* to get—or how exotic the law *allows* you to get—then research should be your first priority. Keep in mind that rustic pets, such as chicks and rabbits are not always easy to maintain in a nonrustic setting where they may require hard-to-find food or special living arrangements. For information on popular exotics such as ferrets, parrots and Vietnamese pot-bellied pigs, start with your neighborhood library, then check the pet shops. Meanwhile, from Robb Deigh of *U.S. News & World Report* come the following cautions:

> *Federal and state laws put some exotic beasts off limits to most people. You can't own ultraexotic animals like tigers and chimpanzees unless you're an experienced handler or licensed breeder. In some states, you'll need a permit even for local critters like skunks and raccoons. State offices of the U.S. Fish and Wildlife Service have information on ownership restrictions.*
>
> *In amateurs' hands, exotic animals often suffer severe health problems. Deprived of the entire kill and fed only muscle meat, big cats and birds of prey can develop brittle bones.*
>
> *Behavior can be vexing, too. "If you want an animal that acts like a dog, get a dog," says [Pat] Hoctor, who breeds cats and primates and won't sell to private individuals.*

A more serious drawback to owning exotic pets may be the negative impact their sale can have on animal populations. According to Susan Lieberman, a wildlife expert with the Humane Society, up to 80 percent of parrots destined for shipment to the U.S. from South America, Asia, Africa and other areas die when captured or in transit. Moreover, says Lieberman, the space requirements of exotic animals "usually are huge. Social patterns and diets are complex. And you may not even be able to tell when they're sick."

305

Another factor when considering an exotic pet is the additional expense that may be involved. Tropical fish ain't cheap, nor are pythons or boas—or aquariums or special cages. At Casa de Pets, an exotic-animal shop in Sherman Oaks, California, prices were recently flying from $195 for an umbrella cockatoo to $22,000 for a black palm cockatoo, while $500 would have gotten you a lion cub.

If, despite the generally higher tariff and the special problems involved, you're still more inclined toward getting an exotic pet than a domestic one, you might at least consider getting a small one rather than a large. They're much more manageable—and far less likely to create friction with landlords and neighbors.

LEAPIN' LIZARDS!

"My dad hates them. He won't allow me to enter his house with a lizard. I'm, like, married to lizards. I'm sorry to have to say this, but there is lizard prejudice."

> —HARRY LIZARDLOVER, of Los Angeles, who changed his last name from Schiff, on the 30 lizards he keeps as pets.

VISITING THE VET

Here are a few basic tips to make sure you and your pet get the most out of a visit to the veterinarian:

• Call your veterinarian's office to make an appointment. It's common courtesy and will save you time. (Also, the doctor may want you to bring along a stool or urine sample or to prepare the pet in some other way for the visit.) Tell the receptionist exactly what's wrong so the doctor can schedule enough time for the visit.

• Write down a detailed history of your pet's illness and any questions you want to ask. The more information you can provide, the more easily your veterinarian can diagnose the problem and begin

306

proper treatment.

• It's also a good idea to write down the veterinarian's instructions for home care. If you don't think your schedule or situation will permit you to follow the instructions, let the veterinarian know. Another treatment plan can usually be arranged.

• Ask questions if you don't understand. Professional advice is worthless if you don't understand it.

• When your pet is being examined, don't be upset if you can't be at its side; it will be well treated. There may be times, on the other hand, when the veterinarian will ask you to hold your pet to keep it calm during treatment. If the animal tends to be a biter, snapper or scratcher, warn the doctor (or the assistant) before he or she finds out the hard way.

> —BILL RADOS AND CATHERINE W. CARNEVALE, U.S.
> Department of Health and Human Services,
> Public Health Service, FDA

"TRACER" IMPLANTS GAINING FAVOR

A growing trend among dog and cat owners is the implanting of a flea-sized computer chip in a pet to allow a scanner to identify it if it gets lost. The procedure, called "chipping," is said to be relatively painless:using a large hypodermic needle, the tiny device is planted under an animal's skin between its shoulder blades. The chip involved is imprinted with an ID code that is activated by a special laser scanner available to veterinarians and animal-control officers.

The scanner, similar to those used at checkout counters, is passed over the animal's neck and shoulders. An implant causes a beep to sound and a 10-digit code to appear on a computer screen—a code revealing the pet's owner, address and phone number, along with any special medical instructions. The implant costs about $40, plus a small annual fee for data storage.

So far, the tracer-implant system has been slow to catch on in the U.S., largely because scanners can't read all of the several competing brands of chips currently in use. In Spain's largest cities, however, where a coordinated technology is in place, the chip implants are virtually mandatory, exceptions being made only for owners decide instead to get a "tattoo" for their pet. But a tattoo costs more and requires that an animal be anesthetized, which is not the case with chipping process—thus making the latter option far more popular.

"The whole object is not only to make it nationwide, but also Europe-wide and then universal," said Dr. William Hutchinson, a Scottish vet working in Madrid. Hutchinson said the chips do not infect or otherwise irritate the animal and will outlast even the most durable dog or cat. He hopes the chips will someday help trace such data as an animal's genealogy and health record.

The original purpose of the Madrid law—like those in such cities as Barcelona, Bilbao and Pamplona—was to monitor rabies vaccination rates and keep tabs on the pet population. The system is currently used on a voluntary basis in several other countries including Britain, Ireland, Belgium and Norway.

In the U.S., despite the lack of industry standards, the system is being used by a few community groups, shelters and vets in New York City and northern California. Hopefully, as more and more dog and cat owners become aware of the system and its benefits, pressures to find a mutually compatible technology will force a solution—just as they so dramatically have in other segments of the computer industry.

SHIPPING OR SCHLEPPING A PET

Shipping or schlepping a pet is, at best, a headache and a half. To minimize the inevitable trauma, plan well ahead. Begin by making a real or mental list of things to do:

• If you don't already have one, buy a pet carrier—but first check with your airline or railroad as to applicable rules and restrictions: what size the carrier must be, how many pets you can bring with you, and so on. Most airlines offer "correct" carriers for sale. (**Note:** Buses are definitely *not* recommended as a means of pet transport.)

• Clearly tag both pet and carrier.

• Put a couple of the pet's familiar toys in the carrier.

• Before a projected long car ride with a cat, try taking it for a short spin or two to see how it adjusts. (Although the cat should be kept in its carrier during the ride, the carrier can be opened occasionally to allow you to pet the cat.) If things go smoothly, or with just a modicum of stress, it augurs well for the longer trip ahead. Otherwise, you may want to opt instead for boarding your cat in a kennel, or leaving it in the care of a trustworthy sitter until you return.

• Stop feeding your pet eight hours before a trip. Stop providing water two hours before.

• Take along your pet's favorite food. Animals being rudely uprooted—even for a brief time—may have trouble adjusting to unusual grub.

• Don't forget to pack whatever medicines your pet may need. If you're traveling by car with your dog to shore areas from New England to Florida, or Florida to Texas, or around the Great Lakes, Pittsburgh veterinarian Laurence Gerson advises taking along medicine to ward off heartworm disease, which is transmitted mainly by mosquitoes. "If your vacation calls for camping in wooded areas, especially around the East Coast, says Gerson, "make sure you protect your animal from Lyme's disease, which is carried by ticks and fleas. There are sprays for Lyme's disease."

• If traveling by plane, try to book direct flights and be sure to ask your airline ahead of time about requirements for boarding (such as health and vaccination certificates). Consider giving a pet facing an air trip a vet-prescribed tranquilizer an hour or two before flight time. Test the drug beforehand to be sure the animal's behavior is what is intended; some tranquilizers can produce hyperactivity in sensitive dogs or cats.

• If possible, arrange to fly with your pet at other-than-peak times, as delays can spell extra stress for all involved.

• If you stop and get out of your car while traveling with your pet, do not leave it locked inside without sufficient ventilation.

• From William H. A. Carr's *Basic Book of the Cat* (Scribner's, 1963) comes this ingenious method of keeping a cat from freaking when moving to a new house or apartment:

> *Put the cat in its carrying case before the movers begin taking the furniture out of the house. Then release the cat in the new house in one closed room which contains some furniture to which the cat is accustomed. After the rest of the furniture is moved in, the cat can be led out to wander through the rest of the house, exploring. If the cat continues to show distress in its new home, try smearing butter on its paws and legs. The cat will be so distracted by its need to lick them clean of the awful stuff that it will forget all about its unhappiness over the move.*

• Pets that are away from home, or those being pet-sat while you are away, take comfort in being able to snuggle up to an article or two of your clothing.

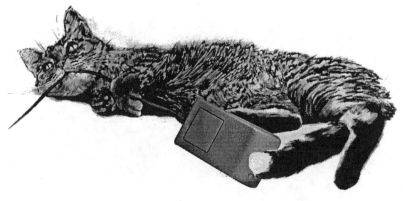

ART—FOR LIFE'S SAKE

. . . myriad Muse-ings old and new . . .

Art, were I called on to define the term, I should call it "the reproduction of what the senses perceive in nature through the veil of the soul."
—EDGAR ALLAN POE

Art is much less important than life, but what a poor life without it.
—ROBERT MOTHERWELL

ART: WHO, WHAT, WHY AND WOW

Some artists and art appreciators say that art must be a voice, while the whispers and winks of others smugly proclaim it to be their own special secret—which they may or may not deign to share. Still others—quite often the majority, in fact—say simply: *"Who the hell cares???"*

To all of which *we* say: Fair comment.

For art is about as controversial as anything gets, beginning with just what *is* and *isn't* art. As most of us know from experience, one person's music can be another person's noise, and one person's sculpture is another's garbage . . . or urinal . . . or worse. And arguments can get heated indeed when we discuss with others movies or books we've recently seen or read—as witness, for example, the often fiercely dueling thumbs of Siskel and Ebert.

But none of this need be fatal, although backers of plays and movies and other such costly enterprises may suffer financially when critical thumbs resemble nothing so much as middle fingers. It is probably small solace that thus is the nature of their chosen territory. For in the infinitely varied and amorphous world of art, controversy is an inescapable ingredient—and about all anyone can confidently agree on is that virtually any aspect of art may be endlessly debated, without ever reaching anything approaching a clear-cut, final consensus.

Of course, that's just *our* opinion. Meanwhile, some random slants to get things going . . .

"My first acting teacher said all art is one thing—a stimulating point of departure. That's it. And if you can do that in a piece, you've fulfilled your cultural, sociological obligation as a workman. What you're supposed to do is keep people vitally interested in the world they live in. . . . You push that boulder up [the Sisyphean mountain], it rolls down. You push it up again. Man's dignity is in the trip down the mountain, returning to his labors. This is where artists are supposed to be of use, to make people, not necessarily happy, but enrich their vitality."—JACK NICHOLSON

"Literature, music, and art have the same effect on us as dreaming. If we don't dream, doctors say, we go mad and die. In a way, if we go without literature and music and art, we also go mad. We need the things of the imagination to resolve the uncertainties we live with."—NICOLAS VON HOFFMAN

"This world is kind of basically an unbearable situation, and art is there to help you with it, to help you pull your load along a little more easily."——LINDA RONSTADT

"In art, it can't be done only until someone does it."—ROBERT PINSKY

"The imitator is a poor kind of creature. If the man who paints only the tree, or flower, or other surface he sees before him were an artist, the king of artists would be the photographer. It is for the artist to do something beyond this: in portrait painting to put on canvas something more than the face the model wears for that one day; to paint the man, in short, as well as his features."—JAMES MCNEILL WHISTLER

"Art's obscured the difference between art and life. Now let life obscure the difference between life and art."—JOHN CAGE

"Art, like morality, consists in drawing the line."—G. K. CHESTERTON

"Less is more."—LUDWIG MIES VAN DER ROHE

"I shut my eyes in order to see."—PAUL GAUGUIN

"There is an amusing story about realism and Picasso. A sailor once complained to him that his paintings were not realistic, and then took out a tiny snapshot of his child for the painter to see. Picasso squinted seriously at the snapshot and handed it back to the father, merely saying, 'Small, isn't she?'"—SYDNEY J. HARRIS

"A primitive artist is an amateur whose work sells."—GRANDMA MOSES

"I do not take drugs—I *am* drugs."—SALVADOR DALI

"You see on television when somebody wins a prize, $2,000 or something, she starts jumping up and down. You can't be happy without jumping. That's dance. That's human nature. And as long as people are happy, they will keep on dancing."—GEORGE BALLANCHINE

BRAD HOLLAND

The Italian Coalition

WORLD'S OLDEST STATUE DISCOVERED

Archeologists in Iraq recently discovered the world's oldest statue—a stone four feet high, covered with plaster molded into the shape of a human. The stone man, dating to 11,000 years ago, was fashioned by a people who were emerging from the Stone Age into the Neolithic world of early farming. It is 30 centuries older than the world's previously known oldest statue.

Probably of religious significance, the statue was located inside a prehistoric house, one of the earliest sophisticated buildings ever discovered by archeologists. Investigations have shown that the house had beautifully finished clay-coated, lime-plastered walls and floor.

So far excavations at Qermez Dere, 300 miles northwest of Baghdad, have unearthed three buildings containing seven standing stones, four of which retain traces of the lime plaster that once covered them. However, only one of these shows evidence of having been shaped into the likeness of a human.

Excavations, directed by archeologist Trevor Watkins of Edinburgh University, have revealed that each building appears to have had at least one standing stone inside it; one house had three. The plaster-covered human-shaped stone has what appear to be shoulders and the stumps of arms and part of a neck. The head apparently has broken off.

The three houses were mainly subterranean in their construction. The clay- and lime-coated walls and floor were finely made and spotlessly kept. The roofs would probably have been flat and made of wood, reeds and mud.

Evidence unearthed by the archeologists shows that the prehistoric inhabitants lived by hunting wild cattle, horses, gazelle, sheep, goats, foxes, hares and birds, and by harvesting wheat, barley and lentils—and a poisonous plant called bitter vetch, which needed to be leached in water for 24 hours to detoxify it. Their culture appears to have developed at least 112 centuries ago and is more than twice as old as Pharaonic Egypt and Minoan Crete and almost three times as old as Stonehenge.—SCRIPPS-HOWARD NEWS SERVICE

LIGHT SHED ON BURIED ARMY

Chinese archaeologists recently reported the discovery of the names of 85 sculptors who created the thousands of clay warriors buried some 2,000 years ago with the first emperor to unite China.

The imperial tombs containing 8,000 terra-cotta soldiers and horses, 100 chariots and numerous bronze weapons, were discovered in 1974 near the ancient capital of Xian, but the identity of the creators had been a mystery. But now the head of the excavation team,

Yuan Zhongyi, said he has found the names of 85 craftsmen—either potters in the imperial court or folk craftsmen—hidden in their work.

The engravings have been found in the armpits and underneath the long military coats of the more than 7,000 soldiers excavated so far. No two soldiers in the terra-cotta army are alike. They were found in the tombs of Emperor Qin Shihuang, who ruled from 221-107 B.C.

The three excavated pits containing the unearthed figures are one of China's main tourist attractions.—ASSOCIATED PRESS

ART IMITATES DEATH

A night watchman was making his rounds at an art museum in Fort Lauderdale recently, when he spotted someone in the museum window. It was a casually dressed gray-haired woman, sitting in a black metal chair and reading a magazine. The guard tapped on the glass to get her attention.

No reaction.

When he tapped again and still got no reaction, he ran to a phone and dialed 911.

Firemen quickly arrived. "We could see that she wasn't breathing," said Lieutenant Don Bartling. Bartling, who knew something about art, also could see that they were staring at an exhibit, albeit a very realistic one. "You can see the veins in her hands and legs," he said.

The guard, who was not identified, apologized.—JON HILKEVICH

WEIRD ART NEWS

In November 1993, sculptor Rachel Whiteread, 30, won the coveted Turner Prize as the best British artist of the year during a show at the Tate Gallery in London. During that show, she was also voted worst British artist by the K. Foundation, whose prize money—about $60,000 in pound notes nailed in clumps to a board—was twice the amount of the Turner Prize. . . . In June 1994, Beijing police raided a performance art show that consisted of the artist Ma Liuming, naked, cooking potatoes in a pot along with a watching and an earring, and then burying the potatoes, Liuming and 10 audience members were detained by the authorities. . . . "Conceptual artist" Ronnie Nicolino was continuing, in spring 1994, to collect brassieres in a whistle-stop tour of Western states, toward a goal of stringing 10,000 bras across the Grand Canyon to symbolize, he said, "the chasm between human nature and America's obsession with breasts." He now has over 2,000, but prospects of his getting permission to rig the Grand Canyon are still dim.—CHUCK SHEPHERD

JOHANN, WOLFGANG, OR LUDWIG—WHO'S NUMBER ONE?

"An unexpected discovery of Mozart is occurring in our time. A shift is taking place within the Bach-Mozart-Beethoven triad. The nineteenth century put Beethoven in first place; at the beginning of the twentieth century there was a tendency to reserve this place for Bach; and now Mozart is mentioned more and more as number one. But the triad itself is "eternal"; one can hardly speak seriously about a fourth candidate for this company. Perhaps it is still too early to analyze the meaning of the shift. Although it *is* possible to assert that if you are searching for man in music, then your composer is Beethoven; if music for you is a means of communion with God, you will hardly bypass Bach; but if you want music from music, then the name Mozart acquires for you a special significance." —VLADIMIR MARKOV

"Bach elevates us, Mozart delights us, Beethoven deepens us; all bring us closer to the wellsprings of life."—SYDNEY J. HARRIS

HAYDN SONATAS ARE FINALLY FOUND

Six lost piano sonatas written by 18th-century composer Franz Joseph Haydn were recently found in Germany.

The sonatas came to light when an elderly woman in Munster showed the manuscripts, which she had owned for some time without realizing their importance, to a local music teacher who submitted them to experts.

Professor H. C. Robbins Landon, a leading Haydn scholar and musicologist who authenticated the sonatas, hailed the discovery as "the greatest musicological coup of the twentieth century."

Scholars have long known that sonatas dating the middle of Haydn's life—probably 1766-69—were missing because the composer compiled a catalog that listed the first few bars of each piece.

The manuscripts are not in Haydn's hand but copies, made in Italy around 1805. They are believed to have been among the first sonatas written by Haydn for the fortepiano, a forerunner of the modern piano.

The sonatas were published in 1994.—REUTERS

THE EVERYDAY MUSIC QUIZ

Q: What's difference between a violist and a dressmaker?
A: A dressmaker tucks up frills.
Q: What's the difference between a clarinet and an onion?
A: Nobody cries when you chop up a clarinet.
Q: Why do drummers always have trouble entering a room?
A: They never know where to come in.
Q: What do lead trumpet players use for birth control?
A: Their personalities.—ANN NONIMUS

REJECTERS' SLIPS

If at first you don't succeed, so what? Take heart from the fact that Beethoven's *Fidelio*, Puccini's *Madame Butterfly*, and Stravinsky's *The Rite of Spring* all flopped on opening night. And when the Beatles auditioned for Decca Records, they were turned down cold.

Why? Because, as one Decca executive put it, "We don't like their sound. Groups of guitarists are on the way out."

OPERA ON THE COUCH

These days so much bad behavior has been occurring in the audiences of opera houses that it is notable that some folks would be probing the behavior on the other side of the footlights.

Psychiatrists Eric A. Plaut and Stuart L. Keill recently did just that in a paper presented at a meeting of the American Psychiatric Association, looking at the psychic profiles of some of opera's great—and not so great—characters.

Among the findings were that Guiseppe Verdi's *Otello* had a "prototypical paranoid disorder" and Richard Wagner's *Tannhauser* had "a pattern of unstable and intense interpersonal relationships."

The cruelest cuts, however, were reserved for protagonists in Richard Strauss's *Elektra*: "Everyone is either psychotic, autistic or, at best, borderline," the psychiatrists said.

DIZZY ATMOSPHERE

A bent silver trumpet that the late jazz great Dizzy Gillespie used in thousands of performances between 1972 and 1985 was recently donated to the Smithsonian Institution, joining about 2,500 other musical instruments in the Smithsonian collection.

The unique trumpet, its distinctive bell turned upward at about a 45-degree angle, was the result of an accident with another horn that Gillespie left on a music stand at a party in the early 1950s: a dancer backed into the horn, apparently ruining it.

However, when Gillespie tried playing it, he found he liked what he heard because the upturned bell allowed sound to reach his ear more quickly than it would on a normal trumpet. He had the silver horn specially bent to reproduce that quality.

THE JOY OF SAX

The first person to play a saxophone, naturally, was the Belgian inventor who patented it in 1946, Antoine Joseph Sax, known as Adolphe, who created such a horn specifically for French martial music by Hector Berlioz. Today some two thousand people worldwide play classical music on the sax. There is no estimate available for those who use the sax to play jazz.

A BRIEF CONCORDANCE

Excluding two-letter prepositions and "an," I imagine *me* is the most used two-letter word in Songdom. "I" (leaving out indefinite article "a") is doubtless the most used one-letter word (and everywhere else, for that matter). "You" (if definite article "the" bows out) is the most frequent three-letter word. "Love" probably gets the four-letter nod (referring strictly to songs that can be heard in the home). In the five-letter stakes I would wager that "heart" and "dream" photo-finish in a dead heat. As for words of more than five letters, you're on your own.—IRA GERSHWIN (*LYRICS ON SEVERAL OCCASIONS* / VIKING, 1973)

FOUR SEASONS, UMPTEEN NAMES

The pop-rock group the Four Seasons (aka Frankie Valli and the Four Seasons) took its name from that of a cocktail lounge in a New Jersey bowling alley. Before that, the group had gone through a slew of musical monikers, including:

The Variety Trio	Frankie Valle and the Romans
The Variatones	Billy Dixon and the Topics
Frankie Vallie and the Travelers	Village Voices
Frankie Love and the Four Lovers	

"Music must rank as the highest of the fine arts—as the one which, more than any other, ministers to human nature."—HERBERT SPENCER

"The flute is not an instrument with a good moral effect. It is too exciting."—ARISTOTLE

"Wagner has his moments, but has bad half-hours."—CLAUDE DEBUSSY

"Wagner's music is better than it sounds."—BILL NYE

"Opera is when a guy gets stabbed in the back and, instead of bleeding, he sings."—ED GARDNER

"Rock 'n' roll clouds the senses and hypnotizes the brain."—LITTLE RICHARD

"I think rock 'n' roll is all frivolity—it *should* be about pink satin suits and white socks."—MICK JAGGER

"Let's face it, I wasn't a bad-looking stud. But that's not it. It's the music. . . . A lot of women just flip. You call Mick Jagger good-looking?"—ARTIE SHAW, swing-era bandleader and one-time co-king (with Benny Goodman) of the clarinet

"I'll play it first and tell you what it is later."—MILES DAVIS

"I'm a devout musician."—CHARLIE PARKER (on being asked his religion)

"Only sick music makes money today."—FRIEDRICH NIETZSCHE

ROBERT MERZ

CZECH IT OUT!

The lyrics to the following 19 songs, among others, appeared in *Reading Material for the Graduation Exam*, a study guide published in the Czech Republic for high-school students preparing for their oral graduation exam in English. The lyrics were interspersed with the guide's basic English lessons:

"Blowin' in the Wind" / Bob Dylan
"Bridge over Troubled Water" / Simon and Garfunkel
"Enter Sandman" / Metallica
"Good Night, Irene" / Pete Seeger
"The Happiest Days of Our Lives" / Pink Floyd
"A Hard Day's Night" / The Beatles
"Here Comes the Sun" / The Beatles
"Me and Julio Down by the Schoolyard" / Paul Simon
"Scarborough Fair" / Simon and Garfunkel
"The Show Must Go On" / Queen
"The Sounds of Silence" / Simon and Garfunkel
"Strawberry Fields Forever" / The Beatles
"Woman" / John Lennon
"Yellow Submarine" / The Beatles

THE GOLD SINGERS

As of March 1995, the Recording Industry Association of America, which certifies recordings as gold or platinum sellers, had listed the following groups and solo artists as having received the highest number of gold-album certifications (awarded to albums selling 500,000 or more copies domestically):

The top gold-getting groups and the number of their certifications: the Rolling Stones, 34; the Beatles, 27; Kiss and Rush, 20 each; Chicago, 19.

Male solo artists: Elvis Presley, 61; Neil Diamond, 31; Elton John, 28; Bob Dylan, 22; Kenny Rogers and Frank Sinatra, 21 each.

Female solo artists: Barbra Streisand, 36; Linda Ronstadt, 17; Reba McEntire, 16; Olivia Newton-John and Dolly Parton, 13 each; Tanya Tucker, 12.

THE SUPER SINGLES

According to Joel Whitburn, who used *Billboard* magazine charts to compile his book *Top 1,000 Singles*, these were the eight all-time best-selling singles of the rock era (1955-90):

1. "Don't Be Cruel"/"Hound Dog" / Elvis Presley
2. "Singing the Blues" / Guy Mitchell
3. "Physical" / Olivia Newton-John

4. "You Light Up My Life" / Debby Boone
5. "Mack the Knife" / Bobby Darin
6. "All Shook Up" / Elvis Presley
7. "Bette Davis Eyes" / Kim Carnes
8. "Hey Jude" / The Beatles

BEHAVE THYSELF!
(10 COMMANDMENTS FOR AUDIENCE MEMBERS)

1. Thou shalt keep thy mouth shut.
2. Thou shalt not spoil the ending for others.
3. Thou shalt not play the critic; keep thy opinions to thyself.
4. Thou shalt not sing along.
5. Thou shalt not consume noisily.
6. Thou shalt not go to concerts if thou art ill and apt to cough.
7. Thou shalt not overadorn thyself with baubles, bangles, beads or too much cologne.
8. Thou shalt not walk around during the show.
9. Thou shalt not be late.
10. Thou shalt respect thy neighbor's right to enjoyment as thine own.—BRYAN MILLER

TAPE RECORDING AND THE LAW

If you: 1. Record yourself, friends, parties or famous personalities (in person), 2. Copy phonograph recordings or prerecorded tapes, 3. Tape programs off the air, 4. Tape live performances, Do NOT: Sell or distribute your recordings unless you obtain permission to do so from the following, wherever applicable:

1. The persons involved.
2. The performers and person, company or agency to which they may be under an exclusive service contract.
3. The copyright owner of the subject matter of the performance, if it is a work protected by copyright.
4. The program's broadcaster and producer.
5. The manufacturer of the recording.

PHOTOGRAPHY—A SNAP FOR BUFF OR PRO

According to the *Wolfman Report*, which follows the photographic industry, in 1992 some 17 billion photographs were taken in the U.S., up from 11 billion only a decade earlier—and as you read this the figure is X billion higher and counting.

Unquestionably, then, photography is truly the "people's art" of the machine age—or, as Oliver Wendell Holmes put it, a "mirror with a memory." It offers the serious shooter of artistic ambition a great challenge to be met with tools selected from a dazzlingly wide array, yet it is accessible enough in its basics to give satisfaction to millions of amateurs interested in nothing more than freezing memorable moments.. Snapshots, moreover, can sometimes through accident or design reach the realm of art, giving the shooter a sense of creative accomplishment as well as another chunk of time to stick in the scrapbook.

Once past the box stage, virtually every piece of camera equipment has its own dos and don'ts, and instructions should be read carefully before use. Report any defect to your dealer at once.

Lenses are the eye and heart of photography, and a thorough study of the market is advised before buying. A high-speed lens is a must for available-light work, but don't be afraid to experiment with different lenses for special effects. For example, close-ups taken with a wide-angle lens can produce some strange and often dramatic results. Lenses should be kept clean with a soft, dry, lintless cloth. Keep the lens covered, except when actually shooting. On the beach or on the water, protect your camera from sand, mist, and sea spray by keeping it covered in a waterproof plastic bag.

Equally as important as camera and lens is, of course, film, so it pays to shop wisely for the best film you can afford to do the particular job you have in mind. Don't be a creature of habit, getting the same "old faithful" film type simply because it's the one you always get. Grab a bag of types and brands you've never tried before. Chances are you'll wind up with one or two new "old faithfuls." Remember, if the day is overcast and the scene shaded, use a fast film with a high ASA number. For bright, sunny days, use a medium-fast film that allows for greater variations of aperture and shutter speed while still being able to "freeze" fast action.

Always store unexposed film in a cool, dry place—never in a glove compartment or car trunk.

Double-check focus and lighting before snapping the shutter.

Whenever possible, shoot with the camera rested on a tripod or something solid, such as a ledge or table.

Never shoot directly into the sun—the glare may spoil your shot. The sun should be over your shoulder and at such an angle that you don't cast unwanted shadows across the field of vision. Be sure important subjects are in the center of the viewfinder, never near the edges. Also, don't aim the camera at a light-eyed person's face or the subject will have red eyes. Turn the camera slightly or use a flash extender to keep the bulb farther from the lens.

Vary your point of view—try new perspectives. Take some shots standing and others kneeling. For instance, shoot a parade or other such occasion at ground level, then move to a high window overlooking the event.

Have exposed film processed as soon as possible.

Note: For travel-photo tips, see the "Notes for the Road" chapter.

REEL RIFFS

According to the *Chicago Tribune's* "Inc." column, "A lot of stars and producers won't admit that they're clients of Peter Hurkos, but the psychic makes a very nice living as a 'script consultant' to some of Hollywood's hottest movie types. His service: passing his hand over scripts and reporting on the vibes he's getting."

Dennis, Davis & Associates, reports that Gerard Depardieu used 100 false noses during the filming of *Cyrano de Bergerac*.

Donald Duck made his film debut in a 1934 cartoon entitled *The Wise Little Hen*.

Stuntmen making the movie *Smokey and the Bandit* wrecked 50 cars.

Charlie Chaplin once entered a Charlie Chaplin look-alike contest in Monte Carlo—and came in third.

"Acting really isn't a very high-class way to make a living, is it? Nobody ever won a Nobel Prize for acting. You have to remember that Shirley Temple could do it at the age of four." —KATHERINE HEPBURN

"I am a typed director. If I made *Cinderella*, the audience would immediately be looking for a body in the coach."—ALFRED HITCHCOCK

"Metaphor has left art and gone into current events. How do you write *Pat and Mike* after the Bobbitts?"—MIKE NICHOLS

"He wrote me sad Mother's Day stories. He'd always kill me and tell me how bad he felt about it. It was enough to bring a tear to a mother's eye."—CONNIE ZASTOUPIL, on her son, Quentin Tarantino

11 ALL-TIME HIGHEST-GROSSING FILMS

Title	Year	Box Office*
1. *E.T.: The Extra-Terrestrial*	1982	$399.8
2. *Jurassic Park*	1993	357.1
3. *Star Wars*	1977	322.7
4. *The Lion King*	1994	312.5
5. *Forrest Gump*	1994	309.5
6. *Home Alone*	1990	285.6
7. *Return of the Jedi*	1983	263.7
8. *Jaws*	1975	260
9. *Batman*	1989	251.2
10. *Raiders of the Lost Ark*	1981	242.4
11. *Ghostbusters*	1984	238.6

*As of March 1995, actual domestic (U.S. and Canada) grosses in millions, adjusted for inflation. (Source: Entertainment Data Inc.)

FLICKS FOR THE AGES

The following 25 motion pictures were the first to be selected by the Librarian of Congress for inclusion in the National Film Registry. (Further additions have since been made, and more are planned.)

The Best Years of Our Lives. 1946; William Wyler, director; received Academy Award for Best Picture

Casablanca. 1942; Michael Curtiz, director; received Academy Award for Best Picture

Citizen Kane. 1941; Orson Welles, director

The Crowd. 1928; King Vidor, director

Dr. Strangelove (or. How I Learned to Stop Worrying and Love the Bomb). 1964; Stanley Kubrick, director

The General. 1927; Buster Keaton, director

Gone with the Wind. 1933; Victor Fleming, director; received Academy Award for Best Picture

The Grapes of Wrath. 1940; John Ford, director

High Noon. 1952; Fred Zinnemann, director

Intolerance. 1916; D. W. Griffith, director

The Learning Tree. 1969; Gordon Parks, director

The Maltese Falcon. 1941; John Huston, director

Mr. Smith Goes to Washington. 1939; Frank Capra, director

Modern Times. 1936; Charlie Chaplin, director

Nanook of the North. 1922; Robert Flaherty, director

On the Waterfront. 1954; Elia Kazan, director; received Academy Award for Best Picture

The Searchers. 1956; John Ford, director

Singin' in the Rain. 1952; Gene Kelly and Stanley Donen, directors
Snow White and the Seven Dwarfs. 1937; Walt Disney, director
Some Like It Hot. 1959; Billy Wilder, director
Star Wars. 1977; George Lucas, director
Sunrise. 1927; F. W. Murnau, director; received Academy Award
for Best Picture
Sunset Boulevard. 1950; Billy Wilder, director
Vertigo. 1958; Alfred Hitchcock, director
The Wizard of Oz. 1939; Victor Fleming, director

CITIZEN KANE REVISITED

A little over half a century ago, on May 1, 1941, a movie premiered
at the RKO Palace Theater in New York that would change American
film forever—*Citizen Kane.* Produced, directed and co-written by
Orson Welles, this kaleidoscopic saga of the rise and fall of a megalo-
maniacal newspaper publisher, based loosely on the life of William
Randolph Hearst, startled audiences with its surrealistic images, syn-
copated editing, intricate script, daring special effects, eccentric camera angles and unorthodox sound engineering. In one stroke, Welles
had demolished the sacred conventions of the Hollywood studio picture and redefined the technical dimensions of film for decades to
come.

Film critics instantly recognized Citizen Kane's genius. Bosley
Crowther of the *New York Times* called it "the most surprising and cin-
ematically exciting motion picture to be seen here in many a moon."
John O'Hara of *Newsweek* said it was the best picture he had ever
seen. Wrote Cecelia Ager in *PM* magazine, "It's as if you never really
saw a movie before."

Although the American public and the Hollywood establishment
were initially lukewarm to *Citizen Kane* (it lost money at the box office
and won only one Academy Award, for best screenplay), its frequent
showings on TV and in art cinemas during the 1950s and 1960s
rekindled interest in the film. Since 1962 it has topped *Sight and
Sound* magazine's list of the "Ten Best Films of All Time."
Why do Americans love this movie so much?

Surely the film's technical virtuosity accounts for much of its
appeal. "This is the best electric train set a boy ever had," exulted the
25-year-old Welles when he first toured the RKO studios prior to
making *Citizen Kane.* He and cinematographer Gregg Toland quickly
put every switch, lever and gadget on that "train set" to imaginative
use, creating a film that explodes before our eyes with innovative
techniques: deep-focus photography that imitates the human eye in
holding all objects in focus at once; tracking shots in which the cam-

325

era moves constantly toward the subject as if probing or investigating; varied camera angles that suggest the multiple viewpoints from which the story is told; exceptionally long takes juxtaposed with sequences of lickety-split montages; the use of miniature sets, painted backdrops, and films within films; "pan" sound, which picks up simultaneous conversations; lightning sound mixes in which characters finish sentences spoken by others in the previous scene; and idiosyncratic lighting, which suggests the shadowy, elusive quality of Kane himself.

Several of the film's scenes have become icons of American film—the enigmatic, whispered "Rosebud"; the shattering of the snowstorm paperweight; Bernstein's magical reminiscence about seeing a girl with a white parasol on the ferry; the failure of the Kane's 10-year marriage condensed to a 3-minute montage of their breakfasts together; the camera rising through opera house rafters for a stagehand's pungent critique of Susan Alexander's debut; Jedediah Leland, as an old man, repeatedly asking his interviewer for a good cigar; Susan forlornly assembling a jigsaw puzzle in sterile Xanadu; Kane's maniacal demolition of Susan's bedroom; the climactic revelation of "Rosebud's" identity.

But if *Citizen Kane's* genius lay only in its cinematic wizardry or its memorable moments, the film would today be appreciated only by a few movie buffs. In their preoccupation with the film's technical achievements, analysts have often overlooked the fundamental reason for its enduring greatness—its profound exploration of the dark underside of the American Dream.

Above all else, *Citizen Kane* tells the story of a man who through luck, ambition, and sheer force of will achieves everything that American culture defines as success—wealth, power, influence, social status and fame. But in his obsessive pursuit of these outward goals, he loses his fundamental integrity, self-respect and, most of all, the love and friendship of other people. Like other archetypal heroes of American fiction (Captain Ahab and Jay Gatsby come most immediately to mind), he climbs to the pinnacle of power only to discover the abyss of his own soul.

At the end of the film, Kane is reduced to a lonely old man rattling around in an empty castle, incarcerated in a prison of his own making. He has committed the fundamental, fatal American sin—embracing unlimited power, material success and radical individualism, while abandoning the human values of integrity, community and love. Like America itself in the second half of the 20th century, he is forced to confront the painful realization that his omnipotence is only an illusion.

Fifty-some years after its release, *Citizen Kane* endures, not simply because of its astonishing technical breakthroughs, but because of its prescient warning about the loss of our national soul. It's worth noting that Welles' original title for his film was, quite simply and quite appropriately, *American.* —ROBERT S. KYFF

OF LIFE AND ART

About four and half months before John Wilkes Booth killed President Lincoln, the three Booth brothers (John Wilkes, Edwin and Junius Brutus, Jr.) appeared together in Shakespeare's *Julius Caesar*—in which a country's leader is assassinated. (Edwin played the part of Brutus; Junius Brutus, Jr., was Cassius; and John Wilkes played Mark Antony.)

NO KIDDING

Five characters and the actors who first played them:

1. Columbo—Bert Freed (TV, 1961)
2. James Bond—Barry Nelson (TV, 1954)
3. Amos Burke—Dick Powell (TV, 1961)
4. Sam Spade—Ricardo Cortez (film, 1931)
5. Sherlock Holmes—Maurice Costello (film, 1905)

ONE-MINUTE CONFESSIONS

The following revelation is brought to you courtesy of TV news/feature princess, Katie Couric:

"Basically, I try to be as charming and ingratiating as I can without making myself vomit."

And from Kylie Travis as witchy Julie of *Models Inc.*:

"I resisted being a calculating viper as long as I could."

TV TOLL

A large-scale study of American television watching, supported by the National Institute of Mental Health and released in 1990, found that it takes more skill and concentration to eat a meal than to watch TV and that the longer people watch, the more drowsy, bored, sad, lonely, irritable and/or hostile they become.

SELLING THE KIDS

Almost 20 percent of children's TV programming consists of nonprogram material, most of it advertising, according to a recent study by the Children's Advertising Review Unit of the Council of Better Business Bureaus.

The average child, the study said, watches 3.5 hours of TV daily and "would be likely to see a somewhat limited array of products, dominated by toys, cereals and sugared snacks and drinks."

The group examined 604 hours of TV programming during February and March 1990 in seven areas, and found that stations affiliated with one of the major networks aired an average of 10 minutes of advertising an hour, while independent stations aired 9.4 minutes and cable channels 6.5.

Concerns about excessive commercialization of children's programming prompted the Federal Communications Commission to adopt a limit on advertising of 10.5 minutes an hour on weekends and 12.5 minutes an hour on weekdays.

YET ANOTHER REASON TO LIMIT TUBE TIME (OR, THE FATTING OF JUNIOR)

Television may be fueling a near-epidemic of obesity among American children because it drives metabolism dramatically lower, even below that found in youngsters who are simply resting, say researchers at Memphis State University and the University of Tennessee in Memphis.

"Television viewing has a fairly profound lowering effect on metabolic rate and may be a primary mechanism for the relationship between obesity and amount of television viewing," the researchers reported in a recent issue of *Pediatrics*.

"Excessive television viewing may place a child at high risk for obesity," considering the lower metabolism and the high-fat snacks that often accompany the hours many children spend in front of the tube, they added.

The Memphis study is said to be the first to explore TV's effects on metabolism, the process by which the body turns food to tissue or energy.

The researchers said childhood obesity has become a near-epidemic in the U.S., afflicting as many as one of out of every four youngsters. About 30 percent of adult Americans are so affected.

According to a 1985 survey, U.S. children aged 6 to 11 watched about 26 hours of TV every week, as much time over a year as they spend in school.

The mechanism that drives metabolism lower during TV watching remains unknown. The metabolic rate that was measure in the study is an indication of how much energy the body is expending. Energy taken in but not used often winds up being stored as fat.

—REUTERS

328

THE BIRTH OF THE BOOK

An international team of archeologists digging in the ruins of an ancient city in one of Egypt's most remote oases recently discovered what it believes are the origins of the modern book. The find consists of two complete notebooks with pages made of wood, thought to be the first to be found intact anywhere in the world. Even the books' leather bindings were located.

For years, scholars have searched for evidence of how today's book came to evolve from the parchment scroll and to be bound in sets of eight leaves per set. Now they think they know.

Dr. Colin Hope, a research fellow at Melbourne University, uncovered the books while excavating in the ruins of the city of Ismant, about 500 miles from Cairo in the western Sahara. Ismant was buried by shifting sand dunes 1,700 years ago. The people are thought to have simply walked away, leaving most of their possessions—including the two books—behind. Hope is a member of an international archeological team working in el-Dakhleh. The project is one of the largest in the world, and, after 10 years, it has begun to make some startling finds.

Dr. Geoffrey Jenkins, who is also a researcher at Melbourne University, is translating the books and editing them for publication. Jenkins said the wooden tablets represented a transition from the irregularly formed, perishable papyrus book and the beginnings of the parchment book—and that the eight-leaved signature or set, of which all modern books are made, clearly stemmed from this period. "Here is evidence that the eight leaves had become standard," he said. "In the first century, texts were written in scrolls. These tablets help us understand how the eight-leaved book finally moved from the friable papyrus, which could not successfully be bound in eighths, to the more sturdy parchment, which was made up in eight leaves, sewn together and bound."

One of the books is a piece of homework by a village schoolboy who copied out a text by the Greek philosopher Isocrates, a contemporary of Aristotle. The other is a farm account book with an extraordinary record of transactions involving many of the villagers. Hope and Jenkins have fixed the date of the books at around 360 A.D. By studying the handwriting, Jenkins was able to identify it as similar in style to other Greek writing elsewhere in Egypt at this time. Commodity prices mentioned in the farm account book have also helped confirm the date. Jenkins said the Isocrates text was 500 years older than the earliest known version.—GEOFFREY MASLEN

"Courting the Muse?"

WRITING—AS WRIT

Writers, writers, writers. They seem as common as the dandelion these desktop-highway days—and about as apt to receive encouragement from the world at large.

The world at large, after all, is having enough trouble trying to keep up with the writing that's already around, so why should it do anything to add to so massive a backlog?

Sound, very sound, one might deem such reasoning—but where, then, does that leave your average foolhardy, dedicated writer, that hard-laboring, eternally hope-driven drone who writes not necessarily to fill a public need but rather to satisfy a private obsession.

Most likely at the typewriter or computer, alone with his or her creative—and sometimes not-so-creative—pangs. And if you are among the beleaguered lot, you may well be wondering just where your next bit of encouragement is coming from.

Well, have you tried the Holy Bible lately? For sprinkled through the venerable pages of that good book are all sorts of ancient balms and words of wisdom for those of the scribbling persuasion, to wit:

"Write the vision, and make it plain." [Habakkuk 2:2]

"What thou seest, write in a book." [Revelation 1:11]

"But refuse profane and old wives' fables." [1 Timothy]

"Evil communications corrupt good manners." [1 Corinthians 15:33]

"For the ear trieth words, as the mouth tasteth meat." [Job 34:3]

"Publish, and set up a standard; publish, and conceal not." [Jeremiah 50:2]

However, lest you be *too* encouraged by all this, keep in mind these biblical cautions:

"Let thy words be few." [Ecclesiastes 5:2]

"Of making many books there is no end; and much study is a weariness of the flesh." [Ecclesiastes 12:12]

BOOK NOTES

"Books are a guide in youth and an entertainment for age. They support us under solitude and prevent us from becoming a burden to ourselves. They help us to forget the crassness of men and things, compose our cares and passions, and lay our disappointments asleep."
—JEREMY COLLIER

In the floor of London's Westminster Abbey is a tiny stone marking the burial place of noted poet and Shakespeare contemporary Ben Jonson. Because he was too poor to pay for the normal grave space, he was buried standing up.

"The English naval officer and diarist Samuel Pepys (1622-1703) had a vast collection of eye-popping pornography: hundreds of his 'little French books' survive to this day, and many of them make the sweaty offerings of the local porno palace look tame by comparison. On the other hand, American writer Henry Miller, who gained notoriety for such once-banned classics as *Tropic of Cancer* and *Sexus*, kept his eyes pure of all but a few specimens of literary erotica—such naughty wonders, for example, as Sir Richard Francis Burton's translation of the *Thousand and One Arabian Nights* and Petronius's *Satyricon*. Today Pepys would be working for the Joint Chiefs of Staff, while Miller would be on the run from Jesse Helms."—GREGORY MCNAMEE (*Small Press*)

"I love being a writer. What I can't stand is the paperwork."
—PETER DE VRIES

The first novel ever to be written on a typewriter was *The Adventures of Tom Sawyer*, in 1875. It was typed on a Remington by Mark Twain himself, who, however, wished to keep the fact a secret. He didn't want to write testimonials or answer any questions about the "newfangled thing."

"A book should serve as the axe for the frozen sea within."
—Franz Kafka

331

"It's hard not to write satire."—JUVENAL (c. 60-130)

"Everywhere I go, I'm asked if I think the universities stifle writers. My opinion is that they don't stifle enough of them."—FLANNERY O'CONNOR

"There's no clear boundary between experience and imagination. Who knows what glimpses of reality we pick up unconsciously, telepathically."—NORMAN MAILER

"*Anyone* can become a writer—the real test is *staying* a writer."
—HARLAN ELLISON

"[Maxwell] Perkins's boss Charles Scribner (1854-1930) was a gentleman of the old school. Reading the manuscript of *The Sun Also Rises*, the conservative publisher grew concerned about the four-letter words Hemingway used. As he read, he recorded these words on a daily calendar, leaving it on his desk, when he went out to lunch. While she straightened his desk that noontime, his rather prudish secretary came across the calendar. It was headed "Things To Do Today," with the words '*piss . . . shit . . . fuck*' listed below."—ROBERT HENDRICKSON (*The Literary Life*)

"As for you, fellow independent thinker of the Western Bloc, if you have anything sensible to say, don't wait. Shout it out loud right this minute. In twenty years, give or take a spring, your grandchildren will be lying in sandboxes all over the world, their ears to the ground, listening for signals from long ago. In fact, kneeling now on the great plains in a snootful of gray dust, what you do you hear? Pigs oinking, potatoes peeling, Indians running, winter coming?"—GRACE PALEY (opening of the short story "Faith in the Afternoon")

THE WRITER AND HIS ASTERISK

> A writer owned an Asterisk,
>   and kept it in his den,
> Where he wrote tales (which had large sales)
> Of frail and erring men
> And always, when he reached the point
>   Where carping censors lurk,
> He called upon the Asterisk
>   To do his dirty work.
> —STODDARD KING (1913)

ALBEE DARNED

Playwright Edward Albee claims he won't conduct college courses because he can teach everything in half an hour and would have nothing left for the rest of the semester. Here's his advice to Johns Hopkins students during a drama workshop:

"Have the major speeches by the major characters given onstage and not off. Have the climax toward the end. Know what everyone else has written. But don't always read masterpieces, read some failures, too. If anything, it's encouraging. And that's about it. I taught you everything I know about writing in about twenty-six minutes."

CRITIC CRITIQUE

"Critics are like eunuchs in a harem: They know how it's done, they've seen it done every day, but they're unable to do it themselves."
—BRENDAN BEHAN

LEAVE YOUR CANON AT THE DOOR

At a recent meeting of the Modern Language Association, members were informally polled as to what or who was in and what/who was out. Among the responses:

In	Out
Virginia Woolf	Beowulf
gay and lesbian studies	grammar
Afro-Atlantic syncretic narrative	textual editing
the 18th-century novel	the 19-century novel
ambiguity	closure
Hemingway as androgyne	Hemingway as male chauvinist

333

Andrew Marvell	John Donne
heterodoxy	orthodoxy
cross dressing	elbow patches
South American writers	Scandinavian writers
electronic culture	the written word
Jacques Derrida	Paul de Man
Troilus and Cressida	*Julius Caesar*
Columbia University	Harvard University
the literature of polemic	long poems that rhyme

"Let's not spoil a good thing."

MASTERS OF WAR

Come you masters of war
You that build all the guns
You that build the death planes
You that build the big bombs
You that hide behind walls
You that hide behind desks
I just want you to know
I can see through your masks

You that never done nothin'
But build to destroy
You play with my world
Like it's your little toy
You put a gun in my hand
And you hide from my eyes
And you turn and run farther
When the fast bullets fly

Like Judas of old
You lie and deceive
A world war can be won
You want me to believe
But I see through your eyes
And I see through your brain
Like I see through the water
That runs down my drain

You fasten the triggers
For the others to fire
Then you set back and watch
When the death count gets higher
You hide in your mansion
As young people's blood
Flows out of your bodies
And is buried in the mud

You've thrown the worst fear
That can ever be hurled
Fear to bring children
Into the world
For threatening my baby
Unborn and unnamed

You ain't worth the blood
That runs in your veins

How much do I know
To talk out of turn
You might say that I'm young
You might say I'm unlearned
But there's one thing I know
Though I'm younger than you
Even Jesus would never
Forgive what you do

Let me ask you one question
Is your money that good
Will it buy you forgiveness
Do you think that it could
I think you will find
When your death takes its toll
All the money you made
Will never buy back your soul

And I hope that you die
And your death'll come soon
I will follow your casket
In the pale afternoon
And I'll watch while you're lowered
Down to your deathbed
And I'll stand o'er your grave
'Til I'm sure that you're dead

—BOB DYLAN

PEACE
There is a point at which earth
and sky partake of one another
by more than metaphor.
It is the point on the horizon
of the mind at which both
vanish in beginning.

—AARON MILLER

Bicentennial Commemorative

FANCIFUL HUMORS
. . . beaux jests and bits of wit . . .

*Hanging is too good for a man who makes puns; he
should be drawn and quoted.*
—FRED ALLEN

Start off each day with a smile and get it over with.
—W. C. FIELDS

RX FOR MELANCHOLY
One evening in 1808, a gaunt, sad-faced man entered the offices of
Dr. James Hamilton in Manchester, England, and claimed that he was
sick of life. He said that nothing amused him anymore, and there
seemed to be no alternative but to kill himself.

The doctor diagnosed the complaint as melancholia caused by
overwork and prescribed a remedy: "Go to the circus that's in town,"
he said, "and see Grimaldi the Clown. Grimaldi is the funniest man
alive—he'll cure you!"

"But Doctor," said the sad man, "*I* am Grimaldi!"
—TRADITIONAL ANECDOTE
(re famed clown Joseph Grimaldi, 1779-1837)

YOU KNOW IT'S GOING TO BE A BAD DAY WHEN—
You call Suicide Prevention and they put you on hold.

You arrive at your office and find a *60 Minutes* news team waiting there.

You want to put on the clothes you wore home from last night's party—and there aren't any.

Your horn goes off accidentally and remains stuck as you follow a group of Hell's Angels on the freeway.

You turn on the news and they're showing emergency routes out of the city.—ANN NONIMUS

DUELING WISDOMS

Funny thing about ageless, tried-and-true gems of folksy wisdom—often enough, they constitute memorable distillations of hard-worn experience and insight. And sometimes they just out-and-out *suck*.

Either way, no problem—picking and choosing is easy as cream. The *real* problem with homilies and adages and such is when you get come across two of equal stature and acceptance—but that directly contradict one another.

Consider, for instance, the following:

"Out of sight, out of mind." / "Absence makes the heart grow fonder."
"Two's company, three's a crowd." / "The more the merrier."
"Birds of a feather flock together." / "Opposites attract.
"When in Rome, do as the Romans do." / "To each his own."
"A bird in the hand is worth two in the bush." / "Nothing ventured, nothing gained."
"You can't teach an old dog new tricks." / "It's never too late to learn."

STANFORD CHAPARRAL

"Well anyway, I got their goddamn cheese!"

340

Adams's Laws: (1) Women don't know what they want; they don't like what they've got. (2) Men know very well what they want; having got it, they begin to lose interest.—A. W. ADAMS

BBB Law of "Caveat Emptor": If a deal or offer sounds too good to be true, it usually is.—BETTER BUSINESS BUREAU

Bernstein's Law: A falling body always rolls to the most inaccessible spot.—THEODORE BERNSTEIN

Clopton's Law: For every credibility gap there is a gullibility fill.—RICHARD CLOPTON

Dolan's Law: If a person has had any connection with Harvard University or the state of Texas, he will find a way to make that known to you during the first 10 minutes of your first conversation.—MARTY DOLAN

Ettore's Law: The other line moves faster.—BARBARA ETTORE

Fuchs's Law: If you actually look like your passport photo, you aren't well enough to travel.—SIR VIVIAN FUCHS

Gualtieri's Law of Inertia: Where there's a will, there's a won't.—*MURPHY'S LAW, BOOK THREE*

Lee's Law of Business Competition: Always remember to keep your swash buckled.—GERALD LEE STEESE

Magary's Law: When there is a public outcry to cut the deadwood and fat from any government bureaucracy, it is the deadwood and fat that do the cutting, and the public's services that are cut.—JOHN T. MAGARY

McKeon's Law of the College Catalog: The university catalog is much like the campus—it lies about the university.—THOMAS J. MCKEON

Moore's Law of Irresistible Forces: Trailer parks attract tornadoes.—DAVID E. MOORE

Nachman's Rule: When it comes to foreign food, the less authentic the better.—GERALD NACHMAN

Neudel's Law: Any person hired by a bureaucracy to respond to public complaints has no power to remedy them. *Corollary*: The only people worth talking to in a bureaucracy are the ones who never deal with the public.—MARIAN HENRIQUES NEUDEL

Peterson's Law: Trucks that overturn on freeways are filled with something sticky.—DONNA PETERSON

Runyon's Law: The race is not always to the swift, nor the battle to the strong, but that's the way to bet.—DAMON RUNYON

Soderquist's Paradox: There are more horse's asses than horses.—*1,001 LOGICAL LAWS*

Weed's Law: Never ask two questions in a business letter. The reply will discuss the one in which you are least interested and say nothing about the other.—Brian J. Weed

WEBSTER'S FUNABRIDGED:
A GLOSSARY OF DIFFERENITIONS

"Define your terms!" is a fine and classic imperative, and perhaps never so important as now, in these days of exploding data and media-merging superhighways of communication. As for the definition of "definition," in the case of *this* particular set of definitions, it well might be that a better term would be "*diff*erenitions." (As in, "A rose by any other . . .")

Obviously, *these* meanings are not those of the Webster named Noah. The only school in which you can discover *their* truths firsthand is that universal alma mater, ol' Hardknocks U., as attended and recorded for us by light-hearted humorists and sour cynics alike. Not surprisingly, the results of their labor represent something of a "mind" field, so to speak—so step lightly . . .

Note: The original sources of these "differenitions" are indicated in brackets immediately following the entries. Those uncredited are, of course, the work of the ever-indefatigable Ann Nonimus. All entries are as originally writ or spoken, except that in some cases the bridging verb *is* has been replaced by a colon.

Advertisement: What gets people on the brandwagon. [*Dell Crossword Puzzles*]
Archeological Expedition: Bone voyage. [*The Complete Pun Book*]
Autumn: When Mother Nature goes through a change of leaf. [*2,500 Jokes*]
Bankruptcy: Life after debt. [*White's Law Dictionary*]
Bellydancing: Navel maneuvers. [Helen Daley]
Braggart: A person who, every time he opens his mouth, puts his feats in. [Maria Nelson]
Conservative: A statesman who is enamored of existing evils, as distinguished from a liberal, who wishes to replace them with others. [Ambrose Bierce]
Cynic: A man who, when he smells flowers, looks around for a coffin. [H. L. Mencken]
Deficit: What you have when you haven't as much as when you had nothing. [*Toastmaster's Guide*]
Dentist: A prestidigitator who, putting metal into your mouth, pulls coins out of your pocket. [Ambrose Bierce]
Diplomacy: To do and say / The nastiest thing in the nicest way. [Isaac Goldberg]
Death: The ultimate negative patient health outcome. [William L. Roper]
Egotism: Usually just a case of mistaken nonentity. [Barbara Stanwyck]
Egotist: A person of low taste, more interested in himself than in me. [Ambrose Bierce]
Experience: A comb life gives you after you lose your hair. [Judith Stern]

342

Expert: Someone who can take something you already knew and make it sound confusing. [*Farmer's Digest*]

Fanatic: One who can't change his mind and won't change the subject. [Winston Churchill]

Fashion: A form of ugliness so intolerable we have to change it every six months. [Oscar Wilde]

Gardening: A root awakening. [Gordon Gammack]

Ghosts: Unsubstantiated roomers. [Angie Papadakis]

Gigolo: A man who sells himself to the highest biddy. [*2,000 More Insults*]

God: The John Doe of religion. [David Tucker]

Hula: Welcome waggin'. [Frank Tyger]

Inflation: When your nest egg is no longer anything to crow about. [*It Takes All Kinds*]

Klutztrophobia: Anxiety over being clumsy. [Shelby Friedman]

Lawyer: One skilled in circumvention of the law. [Ambrose Bierce]

Lexicographer: A writer of dictionaries, a harmless drudge. [Samuel Johnson]

Locomotive: Crazy reason. [Dora Wood]

Love: An ocean of emotion surrounded by expanses of expenses. [*Sunrise*]

Mallennium: A thousand years of shopping. [Troy Dickson]

Man: The only animal that blushes. Or needs to. [Mark Twain]

Mediokra: Second-rate vegetable. [Kenneth C. Snelling]

Military Intelligence: A contradiction in terms. [Groucho Marx]

Nostalgia: Life in the past lane. [*Laughing Matter*]

Paristroika: Economic restructuring in France. [William D. Tammeus]

Passport: A document treacherously inflicted upon a citizen going abroad, exposing him as an alien and pointing him out for special reprobation and outrage. [Ambrose Bierce]

Philosopher: A man up in a balloon, with his family and friends holding the ropes which confine him to earth and trying to haul him down. [Louisa May Alcott]

Politician: An arse upon which everyone has sat except a man. [e. e. cummings]

Prejudice: A vagrant opinion without visible means of support. [Ambrose Bierce]

Procrastination: The art of keeping up with yesterday. [Don Marquis]

Queen: Often, a crone on a throne. [Alberto Young]

Religion: Philosophy that takes itself too seriously. [Bob Perlongo]

Rescind: The first thing Adam and Eve did after they were expelled from paradise. [G. Angela De Rose]

Sex: The thing that takes up the least amount of time and causes the most amount of trouble. [John Barrymore]

Sins of Omission: The ones we haven't gotten around to yet. [*Modern Maturity*]

Suspended Animation: When you're not allowed to watch cartoons. [Cory Greeson]

Television: A medium, so called because it is neither rare nor well done. [Ernie Kovacs]

Workaholic: Someone who says, "Thank God it's Monday!" [Jerry Banks]

The personnel director of an Inglewood, California, aerospace company had to fill out a government survey form that asked, among other things, "How many employees do you have, broken down by sex?" After a moment's consideration he wrote, "Liquor is more of a problem with us.—UPPER & LOWER CASE

A PLETHORA OF JOKES, QUIPS, CARTOONS AND PUNS

"I hate my mother-in-law," said the cannibal.
"Then just eat your vegetables."

"Lead us not into temptation. Just tell us where it is; we'll find it."
—SAM LEVENSON

Patient: "Doc, what should I take for a bad cold?"
Doctor: "Don't refuse any reasonable offer."—HUMOR ON PARADE

"Thank you, but I have other plans."—PAUL FUSSELL (in response to "Have a nice day!")

Warning to All Personnel: Firings will continue until morale improves.

"I don't work out. If God wanted us to bend over, He'd put diamonds on the floor."—JOAN RIVERS

Q: "Why is there so much ignorance and apathy in the world?"
A: "I don't know—and I don't care!"

Employer: "We can pay you $250 a week now and $300 a week in six months."
Applicant: "Great! I'll be back in six months."—FAMILY LINES

"A hooker came up to me and promised to do anything for fifty dollars. I told her to paint my house!"—HENNY YOUNGMAN

"A pun is the lowest form of humor—when you don't think of it first."
—OSCAR LEVANT

"The only reason I would take up jogging is so that I could hear heavy breathing again."—ERMA BOMBECK

Letter to advice columnist Dorothy Dix: "My husband keeps telling me to go to Hell. Have I a legal right to take the children?"

Among the many humorously incorrect translations collected by Richard Lederer in his book *Anguished English* are these signs:
   In a Paris hotel elevator: Please leave your values at the front desk.
   In a Bangkok dry cleaner's: Drop your trousers here for best results.
   In a Swiss mountain inn: Special today—no ice cream.
   In an Acapulco hotel: The manager has personally passed all the water served here.

"My doctor gave me six months to live, but when I couldn't pay the bill he gave me six months more."—WALTER MATTHAU

MOTHER GOOSE & GRIMM

I'VE FALLEN IN LOVE WITH A SIX-PIECE DINING ROOM SET.

"What if everything is an illusion and nothing exists? In that case, I definitely overpaid for my carpet.—WOODY ALLEN

"A man is only as old as the woman he feels."—GROUCHO MARX

"For three days after death hair and fingernails continue to grow, but phone calls taper off."—JOHNNY CARSON

"What makes Teflon stick to the pan?"—GALLAGHER

"The other day I went into McDonald's—they told me I don't *deserve* a break!"—RODNEY DANGERFIELD

Doctor to gymnast: "Don't worry, we'll have you back on your head in no time."—GRIN AND SHARE IT

A problem child was being brought into the principal's office with unusual regularity. One day the principal showed her annoyance: "This makes the fifth time I've had to punish you this week. What have you to say for yourself?"

"I'm sure the hell glad it's Friday!"

"I may be schizophrenic but I always have each other."—BOB HERGUTH

"What's short, green and comes with little wheels?" actor Gene Wilder asked photographers at a recent Amsterdam press conference. Everyone gave up.

"Grass," said Gene. "I lied about the wheels."

One truck-stop waitress to another: "I'm so hungry I could eat here!"
—*American Legion*

Q: What is brown, has two humps, and lives at the North Pole?"
A: "Rudolph the Red-Nosed Camel."

One frog to another: "Time's sure fun when you're having flies!"
—*Orben's Comedy Fillers*

Guidelines for Bureaucrats
1. When in charge, ponder.
2. When in trouble, delegate.
3. When in doubt, mumble.—JAMES H. BOREN

"At least we get to keep the shirts."

"Why is it that when you send something by ship, it's cargo, and when you send it by car, it's a shipment?"—LARRY ANDERSON

"Stuffed deer heads on walls are bad enough, but it's worse when they have streamers in their antlers, because then you know they were at a party when they were shot."—ELLEN DEGENERIS

Ever notice that the only places where they wait on you hand and foot are where they charge you an arm and a leg?—*READER'S DIGEST*

Actress Tallulah Bankhead once visited a family with a particularly spoiled, obnoxious teenage son. "We just don't know what to make of him," said his mother.

"Well," suggested Bankhead, "how about a nice rug?"
—*THE ENGLISH*, DAVID FROST AND ANTHONY JAY

Bill: "Why does a hummingbird hum?"
Jill: "Because he doesn't know the words!"

Q: What lies at the bottom of the ocean and twitches?"
A: "A nervous wreck."—*HEALTH* (CANADA)

"I bought some powdered water but I don't know what to add."
—STEVEN WRIGHT

PASTIMES AND DIVERSIONS

... fun and games to go or stay ...

The great God Ra Whose shrine once covered acres
Is filler now for crossword-puzzle makers.
—KEITH PRESTON

If you must play, decide upon three things at the start:
the rules of the game, the stakes and the, quitting time.
—CHINESE PROVERB

THE ALL-TIME GREATEST PUZZLE

Puzzles come and puzzles go, and a rare few come and go again and again, challenging and beguiling one generation after another. Such, apparently, has been the fond fate of the puzzle known to unpuzzlers and would-be unpuzzlers alike as the Smith-Jones-Robinson classic, which the *Reader's Digest* has called "a masterpiece of its kind" and, in fact, "the all-time greatest puzzle." Most who seek to solve it reportedly fail, the *Digest* pointing out that in one group of 240 people trying it, only six came up with the solution.

But we are assured that there is no "catch" in it, and that the answer has been worked out by many people in 5 or 10 minutes. The thing to keep in mind is that *every fact* is important and must be considered:

On a train, Smith, Robinson and Jones are the fireman, brakeman and engineer, but NOT respectively. Also aboard the train are three businessmen who have the same names: a Mr. Smith, a Mr. Robinson and a Mr. Jones.

1. Mr. Robinson lives in Detroit.

2. The brakeman lives exactly halfway between Chicago and Detroit.

3. Mr. Jones earns exactly $20,000 per year.

4. The brakeman's nearest neighbor, one of the passengers, earns exactly three times as much as the brakeman.

5. Smith beats the fireman at billiards.

6. The passenger whose name is the same as the brakeman's lives in Chicago.

Who is the engineer? (Answer on page 369.)

ASK MARILYN

Marilyn vos Savant, the aptly named syndicated savant who is listed in the *Guinness Book of World Records Hall of Fame* for "Highest IQ," recently received the following intriguing puzzler from one of her legions of readers:

There is a racetrack 1 mile around. If you drive around the track the first time at 30 mph, how fast will you have to go around the second time to average 60 mph for both times around? (Answer on page 369.)

UNMAZING

A prehistoric Scandinavian stone maze

The maze at Chartres Cathedral, 13th century

352

Mazes—with their often maddeningly hard-to-find centers and exits—have been with us, in one form or another, from the time of Babylon and ancient Egypt. Twelfth-dynasty pharaohs, for instance, constructed on Lake Moeris a mammoth mortuary temple and administrative temple of some three thousand rooms, with a bewildering subterranean maze that only the souls of the entombed king-gods were thought capable of negotiating, along their sacred journey to the Land of the Dead.

The mania for mazes has continued through the ages, from the stone labyrinths of the Scandinavians, to the patterned-floor mazes of medieval French cathedrals, to the formal English-garden mazes of the 17th and 18th centuries, with their ingeniously intricate paths and high hedges. As for the four specimens presented above, alas they can give but a hint of the diversity and ingenuity of the maze maker's sometimes scary art. For more, one can only suggest a journey through the frequently mazelike innards of a well-stocked bookstore or library.

WORDY GURDY

1. Impertinent mouth (1)
2. Challenge 1934 heavyweight champ (1)
3. Say nay to NATO's former cousin (2)
4. The devil made this TV Uncle do it (2)
5. One weaving loose pants gathered at knee (2)
6. What Jimmy and Gary use to hold up socks (1)
7. Clodlike marine puffer (2)

Every answer is a pair of rhyming words (like FAT CAT) that fit in the squares. The number after the clue tells how many syllables there are in each word. (Answers on page 369.)—RICKY KANE Reprinted by permission of UFS, Inc.

UPS AND DOWNS
A hiker can average 2 miles per hour uphill and 6 miles per hour downhill. Going uphill and down, and if he spends no time at the summit, what will be his average speed for an entire trip? (Answer on page 369.)—C. R. WYLIE, JR., *101 Puzzles in Thought and Logic*

WORD GAME

Word game challenges you to find as many words as you can, as quickly as you can, in one master word.

EVERYDAY

Everyday: EV-ree-day. Ordinary.

Can you find 27 or more words in EVERYDAY?

Average mark: 20 words.

Time limit: 35 minutes.

Here are the rules:

1. Words must be four or more letters long.

2. Words that acquire four letters by the addition of an *s, such* as "bats" and "cats," are not used.

3. Only one form of a verb is used. For example, either "pose" or "posed," but not both.

4. Proper nouns are not used.

5. Slang words are not used.

(Answer on page 369.) Reprinted by permission of UFS, Inc.

WHO SPEAKS?

Riddles—rhymed and un—have always been with us. Can you solve the following traditional verse-puzzler?

> King I am none,
> Yet a crown I wear,
> Watch have I none,
> Yet the time I declare.

(Answer on page 369.)

ANIMALS FOR SALE

You have exactly $100 to spend on exactly 100 animals. The following animals are available in unlimited numbers: cows, $10 each; goats, $2.50; chickens, 50 cents. How many of each must you buy? (Answer on page 369.)

FAMOUS AMERICAN NAME-FINDER PUZZLE

On the list at the side of the following chart are the names of 24 well-known Americans, including two—Benedict Arnold and John Wilkes Booth—who are more *infamous* than famous.

In any case, the idea in this puzzle is to find all 24 names in the diagram and to circle each name as you find it. The names always read in a straight line, but may appear forwards or backwards, either across, up, down or on a diagonal. The same letter may appear in more than one word.

To help get you started, Whitney has already been circled. Good

```
T H G N I V R I E L B H Y I S W
C H Y G V D W Z A(Y)L O T S E W
R E B N T A Y N M E W L O B T I
S C G U D R T N B N S X T N A Y
L I U A C R F U L T O N B H E R
T Y M C R H G N J I L S C H G R
U S R L C G A O L H S T Y A W E
G B U A W R N N S(W)E O L M D P
A D R Y T E N R A H U W H I M J
R T F N S L D K I N G E S L T R
R W E B S T E R G E R H Y T M E
A M D V G T R N W H E R M O A D
F L O I N D R O L R C G Y N M B
E W N R L E H Y M C F H L I N D
B I O O S L R A G H N W T G Y M
L U N V T E N C H E O R N O X I
E R R M N T S M O N R O E L O L
A C T R N F I L L M O R E E L B
```

ADAMS
ARNOLD
BOONE
BOOTH
BUCHANAN
BURR
CLAY
FARRAGUT
FILLMORE
FULTON
HAMILTON
HOWE
IRVING
JONES
LIND
MONROE
MORSE
PERRY
SHERMAN
STOWE
WEBSTER
WEST
WHITNEY
YOUNG

—N. M. MEYER, *Nostalgia Crossword Puzzles*

HOW OLD IS ANNIE?

Mary is 24 years old. She is twice as old as Annie was when Mary was as old as Annie is now. How old is Annie? (Answer on page 369.)

SOME CREATIVE CALCULATIONS

Tired of punching up numbers on your pocket calculator as you attempt to balance your checkbook? Put aside the bank statement and canceled checks for a few minutes, take your calculator and solve the following for some entertaining—if somewhat insignificant—moments. (**Note:** To read your results properly, you must turn your calculator upside down.)

1. GREETING: Square root of 196.
2. DISTRESS: (152 - 124) x 5.
3. SNAKE SONG: 471 x 265 + 410,699.
4. SMALL ISLAND: 31 x 11 x 11.
5. WHY YOU SAY "YESSIR": (30,000,000 - 2,457,433) x 2.
6. A RUN IN YOUR: 60^2 - 96.

7. UNWELCOME MAILBOX GUESTS: 5,016 x 11 + 2,542.
(Answers on page 369.)

A TRIO OF TEASERS

Fish Story

I just wanted to make my family a simple seafood dinner, but by the time I finished asking everyone which fish they'd like, I had enough for bouillabaisse. My daughter, a fencer, asked for swordfish, my husband, a Yankee fan, insisted on catfish, and my son, the tennis player, wanted lobster. Worse yet, they've invited a few friends. Can you guess what kind of fish these folks are likely to choose?

1. A faultfinder
2. An ironworker
3. A beekeeper
4. A carpenter
5. An astronomer
6. A mariner
7. A beach bum
8. A porno star
9. A jockey
0. A gambler

—Lola Schancer

A Great Catch!

Can you tell what is very unusual about this sentence?

I DECIDED DICK COBB HOOKED COD.

—Sidney Kravitz

A Basket Case

Is it possible to put nine eggs in four baskets so that there is an odd number of eggs in each basket?

(Answers on page 369.)

1,089 NUMBER PLAY

Follow these steps exactly and the final answer will always be 1,089:

1. Write any number containing three different figures, from left to right, on a sheet of paper.

2. Beneath that number write the same figures in reverse.

3. Subtract the smaller number from the larger. If the result has two figures, add a zero in front of it.

4. Reverse the number resulting from the subtraction.

5. Add the numbers in steps 3 and 4.

15,873 NUMBER PLAY

Yet another "magic" number is 15,873. To see what this amount can amount to, first multiply it by any single number from 1 to 9. Then multiply that total by 7.

The inevitable, and very strange, result will be an amount made up of numbers that are all the same as the single number you first multiplied 15,873 by.

WHO'S LAUGHING NOW?

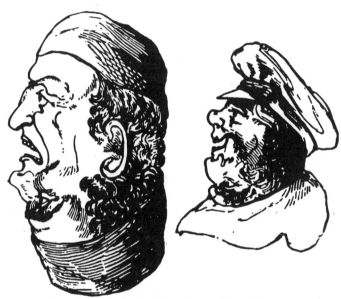

It may not be who you think. (Turn the book upside down and see.)

INCREDIBLE NINE

Nine has always been known as the mind-boggler of numerology. Within this trick-laden jokester lives a whole world of wondrous order. For example, here's a really different way to multiply by 9: Reduce by 1 the number to be multiplied (up to 10) and write it down, then after it write the number needed to make two digits that add up to 9. For instance, take 8 x 9. Reduce 8 by 1 to make 7. After it write 2, the number needed to make 9. Ergo, 72.

Or perhaps you prefer the "hands up" method. With this one, you start by holding your hands up, palms in. You begin with the number you're multiplying by 9: Count that many fingers from the left and bend down the finger you finish counting with (thumbs count as fingers). The fingers to the left of the held-down finger con-

357

stitute the first digit of your answer, and the fingers to the right are the second digit.

Nine is also very persistent, the salt of the mathematical sea. For example, multiply 9 by any number and ultimately the sum of the digits in the answer will always be 9. Thus: 6 x 9 = 54; 5 + 4 = 9. Or, when larger numbers are involved: 526 (for instance) x 9, which comes to 4,734. Then add: 4 + 7 + 3 + 4 = 18; then 1 + 8 = 9.

Or take any two-digit number and reverse the digits. Then subtract the lesser number from the greater. The result will always be 9 or a multiple thereof.

Here's one final nifty niner: Have someone write down the numbers 1 to 9 in order, omitting only 8—in other words, 12,345,679. Then have the person select any digit in this sequence and multiply it by 9. The result should then be multiplied by the original sequence. The answer will always be a nine-digit sequence of the number selected. For example, take 7. First multiply it by 9 to get 63, then multiply 63 by 12,345,679—and get 777,777,777!

PALINDROMES, ANYONE?

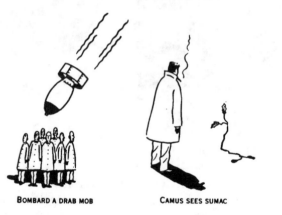

BOMBARD A DRAB MOB   CAMUS SEES SUMAC

STEVEN GUARNACCIA

Palindromes are fun! Palindromes are fascinating! Palindromes can be a pain in the ol' wazoo to try and devise!

But just what, you may ask, is a palindrome?

Well, you might think of a palindrome as mirrored language, in that it consists of a word, phrase or sentence that reads the same both forward and backward. (This applies only to actual letters and words—by convention, and though purists may argue otherwise, punctuation needn't strictly follow the forwards-and-backwards rule.) And if you don't think that's much of a challenge, just try it! Meanwhile, here are some nifty classics to get your brain cells working:

Pupils slip up.

Revolt, lover!

Too hot to hoot

Draw, O coward!

Madam, I'm Adam.

Ma is a nun, as I am.

Never odd or even.

Naomi, did I moan?

Step on no pets.

Was it a rat I saw?

Pull up, Bob, pull up!

Was it Eliot's toilet I saw? (According to Robert Hendrickson, in his fascinating anthology *The Literary Life and Other Curiosities*, this "possibly apocryphal palindrome is said to have been uttered by an American publisher on visiting Faber and Faber," the English publishing house for which T.S. Eliot worked as an editor.)

Dennis and Edna sinned.

Otto did gnu dung, did Otto?

Able was I ere I saw Elba. (This is the famous "Napoleon Palindrome.")

Egad! Alas! A salad age!

Egad, a base tone denotes a bad age.

A man, a plan, a canal—Panama!

Go hang a salami—I'm a lasagna hog.

Live dirt, up a sidetrack carted, is a putrid evil.

And, finally, here's a fairly recent example of the palindromic art, said to have been overheard in the office of Alan Williams, editorial director of Viking Press:

A slut nixes sex in Tulsa!

A VERY TASTY POEM—ALMOST

Wordsmith and puzzlemaster Willard R. Espy, in his book *The Game of Words*, has left two words out of the following poem—10- and 8-letter words respectively, which the reader is asked to supply, using the poem's context as a guide. Can you "unasterisk" them?

FRUITS IN SEASON
Two melons had an argument:
A lover's quarrel, too.
One melon said, "I **********";
The other, "********!"
—W. R. E.
(Answer on page 369.)

359

THE MAGIC SQUARES

4	9	2
3	5	7
8	1	6

6	3	10	15
9	16	5	4
7	2	11	14
12	13	8	1

The innate magic of certain numbers, or combinations of numbers, has intrigued mathematicians and amateur number buffs for many a moon. As a popular armchair pastime, numerical noodling ranks right up there. The above grids are prime examples of the power of numbers to mystify and amaze. Both grids work on the "eternal bingo" principle, wherein the same result is reached whether the numbers are totaled vertically, horizontally or diagonally. The result with the smaller grid is always 15, while the larger grid's constant total is 340.

How many eternities of trial and error, you may ask, were needed to arrive at these singular arrangements? Don't ask.

RANK OF HANDS IN STRAIGHT POKER
(NOTHING WILD)

1. STRAIGHT FLUSH, the highest possible hand. All five cards of the same suit and in sequence, as the 6, 7, 8, 9 and 10 of diamonds. The highest-ranking straight flush is the A, K, Q, J and 10 of one suit, called a ROYAL FLUSH.

2. FOUR OF A KIND, as four aces or four sixes. It does not matter what the fifth unmatched card is.

3. A FULL HOUSE is three cards of one rank and two cards of another rank—for example, 8-8-8-4-4.

4. A FLUSH is five cards of the same suit, but not all in sequence.

5. A STRAIGHT is five cards in sequence, but not all of the same suit.

6. THREE OF A KIND ranks next.

7. TWO PAIR—for example, Q-Q-7-7-4, ranks next.

8. ONE PAIR beats any hand containing no pair.

9. Below the rank of hands containing one pair are all the no-pair hands, which are rated by the highest card they contain, so that an ace-high hand will beat a king-high hand, and so on.

POKER: AVERAGES IN THE DEAL

When playing a hand of poker with nothing wild, the odds of being dealt a valueless hand are even. The odds of being dealt *some*thing are as follows:

ONE PAIR: 1.37 to 1
TWO PAIRS: 20 to 1
THREE OF A KIND: 46 to 1
STRAIGHT: 254 to 1
FLUSH: 508 to 1
FULL HOUSE: 693 to 1
FOUR OF A KIND: 4,164 to 1
STRAIGHT FLUSH: 72,192 to 1.
ROYAL FLUSH: 649,739 to 1

Note: There are 2,598,960 possible poker hands.

POKER: AVERAGES IN THE DRAW

Chances against making (without joker):

If player is holding:

ONE PAIR, drawing three cards	
Two Pair	5 to 1
Threes	8 to 1
Full House	97 to 1
Fours	359 to 1

ONE PAIR, AND AN ACE KICKER, drawing two cards	Aces up ....7½ to 1
	Another pair .....17 to 1
	Threes ....12 to 1
	Full House .....119 to 1
	Fours ....1,080 to 1

TWO PAIR, drawing one card	Full House ......11 to 1

THREES, drawing two cards	Full House ....15½ to 1
	Fours ....22½ to 1

THREES, AND ONE OTHER CARD, drawing one card	Full House .....14½ to 1
	Fours ....46 to 1

If player is drawing:

ONE CARD TO A FOUR
STRAIGHT, Both ends open ....Straight ....5 to 1

One end or interior open .....Straight ....11 to 1

Four Flush ....Flush ....4¼ to 1

Four Straight Flush, both ends open ....Straight Flush ....22½ to 1

One end or interior open .....Straight flush ....46 to 1

If player is holding 1 ace and drawing 4 cards, the odds are 3 to 1 against making a pair of aces and 14 to 1 against aces up (a pair of aces and another pair of anything).

TRUMPING FATHER TIME—WITH BRIDGE

Everyone goes on and on about exercise today. Of the body, that is. But what about exercise of the mind? One answer might be contract bridge.

So you never thought to put bridge in the category of a mental calisthenic? Join the club. But a recent study conducted at Scripps College in Claremont, California, suggested that the game might be just that—an excellent way to increase working memory and reasoning. "There is reason to believe," say authors Louise Clarkson-Smith and Alan A. Hartley (both Ph.D.'s), "that bridge can enhance cognitive performance."

Fifty bridge-players were compared to 50 nonplayers (both groups were between ages 55 and 91) in tests measuring working memory, reasoning, reaction time and vocabulary. Distinct differences were noted between the groups in memory and reasoning, but none were noted in either vocabulary or reaction time—elements not exercised while playing bridge.

The authors also point out that there are different levels of bridge play. Some people use the game as a means to a social end; they keep up a running conversation during the game and make little or no attempt to keep track of the cards. Then there are the really serious players who keep mental records of what each player has bid and the cards played. They are "continually forming mini-hypotheses and modifying them as new information is obtained," say authors Clarkson-Smith and Hartley. No wonder it takes a lifetime to perfect the game!

Now, before you pull yourself too comfortably up to the bridge table, consider another study by the same researchers on the relationship between physical exercise and those same cognitive abilities. You guessed it: The group that exercised performed significantly better on measures of reasoning, working memory and reaction time—all of which reflect brain function. (Remember? Bridge had no effect on reaction time.)

The results, say Clarkson-Smith and Hartley, support the theory that "exercise may help to forestall degenerative changes in the brain associated with normal aging."

The research participants were 62 men and women ages 55 to 88 who exercised vigorously, and 62 sedentary individuals in the same age range. Variables such as education and medical conditions were taken into consideration.

"So play bridge, do crossword puzzles, or take up computers," says Clarkson-Smith. "All of these activities may slow the rate of normal decline. But if you want to keep a really sharp mind, don't ignore physical exercise."—*Modern Maturity*

LET'S PLAY CHESS

Chess is a game for two players, one with the "White" pieces and one with the "Black"—no matter what colors your set actually uses. At the beginning of the game, the pieces are set up as pictured above. (See diagrams below to identify pieces.)

These hints will help you remember this setup:
1. Opposing Kings and Queens go directly opposite each other.
2. The square in the lower right corner is a light one ("light on right").
3. The White Queen goes on a light square, the Black Queen on a dark square ("Queen on color").

The Pieces and How They Move

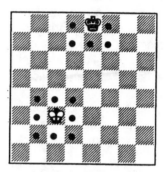

The King

The King is the most important piece. When he is trapped, his whole army loses. The King can move one square in any direction — for example, to any of the squares with dots in this diagram. (An exception is castling, which is explained later.) The King may never move into check — that is, onto a square attacked by an opponent's piece.

The Queen

The Queen is the most powerful piece. She can move any number of squares in any direction — horizontal, vertical, or diagonal — if her path is not blocked. She can reach any of the squares with dots in this diagram.

White always moves first, and then the players take turns moving. Only one piece may be moved at each turn (except for "castling," a special move that is explained later). The Knight is the only piece that can jump over other pieces. All other pieces move only along unblocked lines. You may not move a piece to a square already occupied by one of your own pieces. But you can capture an enemy piece that stands on a square where one of your pieces can move. Simply remove the enemy piece from the board and put your own piece in its place.

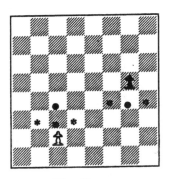

The Pawn

The pawn moves straight ahead (never backward), but it captures diagonally. It moves one square at a time, but on its first move it has the *option* of moving forward one or two squares.

In the diagram, the squares with dots indicate possible destinations for the pawns. The White pawn is on its original square, so it may move ahead either one or two squares. The Black pawn has already moved, so it may move ahead only one square now. The squares on which these pawns may capture are indicated by an ✳.

If a pawn advances all the way to the opposite end of the board, it is immediately "promoted" to another piece, usually a Queen. It may not remain a pawn or become a King. Therefore, it is possible for each player to have more than one Queen or more than two Rooks, Bishops, or Knights on the board at the same time.

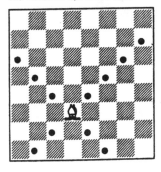

The Bishop

The Bishop can move any number of squares diagonally if its path is not blocked. Note that this Bishop starts on a light square and can reach only other light squares. At the beginning of the game, you have one "dark-square" Bishop and one "light-square" Bishop.

The Knight

The Knight's move is special. It hops directly from its old square to its new square. The Knight can jump over other pieces between its old and new squares. Think of the Knight's move as an "L." It moves two squares horizontally or vertically and then makes a right-angle turn for one more square. The Knight always lands on a square opposite in color from its old square.

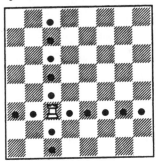

The Rook

The Rook is the next most powerful piece. The Rook can move any number of squares vertically or horizontally if its path is not blocked.

Special Moves

The diagrams below show what happens:

Before Kingside Castling   After Kingside Castling

Before Queenside Castling   After Queenside Castling

Castling

Each player may "castle" once during a game if certain conditions are met. Castling is a special move that lets a player move two pieces at once — his King and one Rook. In castling, the player moves his King *two* squares to its left or right toward one of his Rooks. At the same time, the Rook involved goes to the square beside the King and toward the center of the board (see illustrations at left).

In order to castle, neither the King nor the Rook involved may have moved before. Also, the King may not castle out of check, into check, or through check. Further, there may not be pieces of either color between the King and the Rook involved in castling.

Castling is often a very important move because it allows you to place your King in a safe location and also allows the Rook to become more active.

When the move is legal, each player has the choice of castling Kingside or Queenside or not at all, no matter what the other player chooses.

En Passant

This French phrase is used for a special pawn capture. It means "in passing," and it occurs when one player moves a pawn two squares forward to try to avoid capture by the opponent's pawn. The capture is made exactly as if the player had moved the pawn only one square forward.

In the diagram, the Black pawn moves up two squares to the square with the dot. On its turn the White pawn may capture the Black one on the square marked with the ✱. If the White player does not exercise this option immediately — before playing some other move — the Black pawn is safe from "en passant" capture for the rest of the game. But new opportunities arise with each other pawn in similar circumstances.

About Check and Checkmate

The main goal of chess is to checkmate your opponent's King. The King is not actually captured and removed from the board like other pieces. But if the King is attacked ("checked") and threatened with capture, it must get out of check immediately. If there is no way to get out of check, the position is a checkmate, and the side that is check-mated loses.

You may not move into check—for example, move into a direct line with your opponent's Rook if there are no other pieces between the Rook and your King. Otherwise, the Rook could "capture" the King, which is not allowed.

If you are in check, there are three ways of getting out:

1. Capturing the attacking piece.

2. Placing one of your own pieces between the attacker and your King (unless the attacker is a Knight).

3. Moving the King away from the attack.

If a checked player can do none of these, he is checkmated and loses the game.

If a King is not in check, but that player can make no legal move, the position is called a *stalemate* and the game is scored as a *draw*, or tie.—U.S. CHESS FEDERATION

CHESS FOR YOU

"The exact facts about the origin of the game of chess are murky. But it is generally accepted that a version of the game was played in India as early as A.D. 500. It spread to Persia, where it acquired the name, *chess*, from the Persian word for king, *shah*. Arabic peoples learned the game when they conquered Persia in the seventh century and carried it with them into Europe when they invaded Spain in the tenth century. There is also reason to believe that the game was introduced into Europe by traders and travelers returning from the Byzantine world. . . . As long as anyone can remember, the pieces used have been called chess*men*. But in this day and age of aroused feminine consciousness, it is necessary to set a wrong to right. The *queen* has been a part of the action for over 900 years. She is also, without question, the most powerful piece on the chessboard. It behooves us to revise the name and make amends for centuries of neglect; hence, chess*people*." —MARION MULLER

"Chess is a great game. No matter how good one is, there is always somebody better. No matter how bad one is, there is always somebody worse."—I. A. HOROWITZ

"In the opening a master should play like a book, in the mid-game he should play like a magician, in the ending he should play like a machine."—RUDOLPH SPIELMAN

"I like to coax my opponents into attacking, to let them taste the joy of the initiative, so that they may get carried away, become careless and sacrifice material."—VICTOR KORCHNOI

"If I win, it was a sacrifice. If I lose, then it was a mistake."—GEORGE KOLTANOWSKI

WHAT'S HIS ANGLE?
The stogie-smoking artist above has good reason, perhaps, to admire his handiwork. Not only has he drawn a handsome holiday greeting for you, but he's done so with such self-satisfied cleverness that it's obvious that only the equally clever can read it. Can you? (Answer on page 369.)

PUZZLE ANSWERS

THE ALL-TIME GREATEST PUZZLE

The brakeman, who lives halfway between Chicago and Detroit, also lives near Mr. _____, who earns three times as much as he does. Mr. _____ can't be Mr. Robinson, as Mr. Robinson lives in Detroit. He can't be Mr. Jones, as Mr. Jones's $20,000 a year isn't evenly divisible by three. Therefore the brakeman's neighbor must be Mr. Smith.

The passenger whose name is the same as the brakeman's lives in Chicago. He can't be Mr. Robinson, as Mr. Robinson lives in Detroit. He can't be Mr. Smith, as Mr. Smith is a neighbor of the brakeman, who lives halfway between Chicago and Detroit. Therefore he must be Mr. Jones.

Therefore the brakeman's name is also Jones.

Smith beats the fireman at billiards, so the fireman must be Robinson.

Therefore the engineer is Smith.

ASK MARILYN

It's impossible to accomplish. To average 60 mph for two trips, you'd have to drive around the track twice in two minutes, but you already used up those two minutes when you drove around the track at 30 mph.

WORDY GURDY

1. FLIP LIP; 2. DARE BAER; 3. VETO SEATO; 4. GUILTY MILTIE; 5. BLOOMER LOOMER; 6. CARTERS GARTERS; 7. OAFISH BLOWFISH.

UPS AND DOWNS

Three miles per hour.

WORD GAME

eared	eyre	rayed	yard	deer
eery	vary	read	yare	dray
evade	veer	ready	year	dyer
ever	veery	reed	dare	aery
every	very	reedy	dear	aver
eyed	rave			

WHO SPEAKS?

A rooster.

ANIMALS FOR SALE

Four cows, six goats and 90 chickens ($40, $15 and $45).

WHAT'S HIS ANGLE?

The message, "Happy New Year," can be read if you tilt the page away from you, sighting first along the artist's left shoe toward the upper right-hand corner of the drawing, then along the artist's right shoe toward the upper left-hand corner.

FAMOUS AMERICAN NAME-FINDER PUZZLE

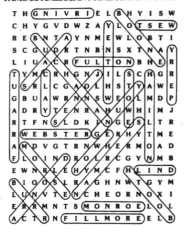

HOW OLD IS ANNIE?

Annie is 18.

SOME CREATIVE CALCULATIONS

1. HI
2. SOS
3. HISSES
4. ISLE
5. HOHOHO
6. HOSE
7. BILLS

Now that you are reminded of *why* you are balancing that checkbook, get back to work!

FISH STORY

1. Carp
2. Smelt
3. Stingray
4. Sawfish
5. Starfish
6. Sailfish
7. Sunfish
8. Blue fish
9. Sea horse
10. Fluke

A GREAT CATCH!

Hold it upside down in front of a mirror and it will read exactly like the original.

A BASKET CASE

Take a large basket with three small baskets inside it. Put three eggs in each of the three small baskets and you'll have an odd number of eggs in all four baskets!

FRUITS IN SEASON

Two melons had an argument:
A lover's quarrel, too.
One melon said, "I cantaloupe";
The other, "Honeydew!"

SPORTS AND SPECTACLES
... of stars and stats ...

I always turn to the sport page first. . . . They record people's accomplishments; the front page, nothing but man's failure.
—EARL WARREN

Professional sports add something to the spirit and vitality of a city. They are a reflection of the city's image of itself. I don't simply believe that: I know it. A winning team can bring a city together, and even a losing team can provide a bond of common misery.
—BILL VEECK

THE TRIUMPH OF SPORTS

Flash—Sports is *not* taking over the world!

It only seems that way, and not just because of the squadrons of sports-widow wives across the land who get a trifle miffed at times playing second fiddle to a flock of jocks. It's also the dazzlesome status of said jocks, the mighty rewards they reap. We shout and rave and cringe and implore as they gambol and toil before us, our passionate loyalty constantly being tested, our rasping throats once again in dire need of truly cold liquids.

The "widow" may never understand, but her "rivals" are the Roman gladiators of our day—the idiotically well-paid icons of a jaded age, their every grin and shuffle a potential 30-second spot. These, after all, are the celebs' celebs, and homage—we seem to feel—is only their due.

But consider: in every contest our heroes enter, they risk defeat, injury and—not least—scorn. Any wonder, then, that to the victors belong suitably heroic spoils? Oh, we may sometimes grumble at the injustice of it all—the vast per-hour gulf between what *we* make and what *they* make—but, deep down, at some instinctual level, we well understand how the larger as well as the more specific game is played.

Hell, if *we* were Michael Jordan, we'd want umpteen millions as well!

Truth is, as popular as sports have become, they are getting even more so all the time. According to a recent *Sports Illustrated* poll, fully 73 percent of Americans profess an interest in sports, up two percentage points from an *SI* poll taken five years earlier. The poll also found that pro football is still the nation's most popular sport (with a 60 percent rating), while baseball continues to lose ground (52 percent). Among the other findings: 60 percent of us believe pro athletes are overpaid, and we are split evenly as to whether Pete Rose should be in baseball's Hall of Fame.

There's not much mystery as to why sports have become so incredibly successful, considering the sublimation and emotional release involved: conflict, after all, is an integral part of existence in this rough, imperfect world, and how wonderful when there are clear-cut rules and more or less clear-cut winners and losers whom we can either identify with or wholeheartedly detest and deride.

Lewis H. Lapham, writing in *Harper's*, recently underscored the apparently primal significance of sports in American life:

Given a nation in which so many cannot read and so few take even a cursory interest in history, it is the lexicon of sports that binds together the text of a common memory. The box score and the portrait on the bubble-gum card take the place of Shakespeare and Vermeer. JFK and FDR vanish into the oblivion of old campaign slogans, but Ruth and Dempsey and Grange remain vividly in mind, still reminding us of who we were and who we might become.

The playing field is the holiest of American grounds because it is the place where time past retains the light of time present. The ghosts sit in the stands of all the American arenas—the gridiron, the court, the racetrack, and the ring . . . Wars come and go; the family business fails; the bank forecloses the mortgage on the farm; and the child dies in a spring flood. But inside the park the world is as it was at the beginning—as green as the grass of childhood, as safe as mother and home.

If you're the kind of fan whose only sports reading is statistics, statistics and more statistics, you may find in the present chapter a certain slimness of pickings. That's because this is an *occasional* rather than an *annual* almanac, which makes it virtually impossible to provide all the vast ranks of statistics that sports have generated over the years and continue to generate—even as we speak.

However, you *will* find a selective smattering of sports facts, figures and trivia, along with yarns and vignettes about some of the colorful and often implausible people behind the data.

So let the games begin . . .

FOOTBALL—GAME OF BASICS

Is football America's number-one sport?

By some valid measures, yes. By others equally valid, the honor might as deservedly go elsewhere. For instance, horse racing is the champ in terms of greatest number of spectators annually—a category in which football runs second.

Perhaps the best answer is, "Who cares?" Because (unless you're a Heisman Trophy judge or a wire service ranking the college squads) such concerns are almost always irrelevant—the game itself being what counts. And when it comes to football, it's a game of the most basic of basics.

For what could be more basic than two hulking, foul-oath-muttering aggregates of humanity fighting over territory and resorting without qualm to as much violence as the rules allow in their pitched pursuit of victory? As the legendary Green Bay Packer coach Vince Lombardi once so bluntly put it: "Football isn't a contact sport, it's a collision sport. *Dancing* is a contact sport."

Football is also a sport of high and low drama, with heroes and fools, violence and artistry, mighty deeds and godawful goof-ups. A lot, in fact, like life. Watching the game in person or on TV is therefore an understandable joy and fascination for millions of people, who are thus able to share the attendant toils and spoils without

373

undue bodily harm—beyond, perhaps, injuries suffered during the occasional beery brawl among differently-opinioned onlookers.

As supplement to all this more or less orderly turmoil, we offer the following features and facts:

• Football, a kicking cousin of such sports as soccer and rugby, can trace its heritage back to various games played in ancient Greece and Rome. In the U.S., the word "football" refers only to the American game, while in the rest of the world it usually means soccer. There are also Canadian, Australian and Gaelic versions of football.

• Walter Chauncey Camp, the "Father of American Football," was a prominent Yale athlete who, eight years after his 1880 graduation, became coach of the university's football team, as well as a prime influence on the sport's development, virtually inventing the forward pass. (When, in an 1876 game against archrival Princeton, Camp threw that first, desperate pass—for a touchdown, no less—there were no rules to cover the situation, so referee C. B. Bushnell persuaded the teams to put it to a coin toss, which Yale won. Only later was it learned that Bushnell was a Yale undergraduate.) Another Camp contribution to the game was the establishment in 1889—with Caspar W. Whitney—of the annual practice of choosing an All-American college football team.

• Two other football legends who played major roles in shaping the course of the game were Amos Alonzo Stagg (1862-1965) and Knute Rockne (1888-1931). If Walter Camp is football's "Father," then Stagg is the game's "Grand Old Man." As athletic director at the University of Chicago from 1892 to 1933, he coached the football team to 314 victories and 5 undefeated seasons, and served (1904-32) on the football-rules committee. Rockne was coach at Notre Dame from 1918 to 1931 and is credited with revolutionizing the game by stressing the forward pass, a tactic largely neglected since its introduction by Camp. Under Rockne, Notre Dame became college football's most illustrious team, winning 105 games, losing 12 and tying 5. Like Stagg, Rockne also had five undefeated seasons. Of the many stars he nurtured, the most famous were star halfback George ("The Gipper") Gipp, and the so-called "Four Horsemen" who for a time made up his backfield—quarterback Harry Stuhldreher, fullback Elmer Layden and halfbacks Don Miller and James Crowley. Gipp, portrayed on film by Ronald Reagan, died a premature and legendary death in 1920, his last words to Rockne being a request that, if the team ever got in a really tight spot, he ask the guys to go out and "Win one for the Gipper!"—a scenario that came to pass eight years later. Unfortunately, Rockne too met an early demise, in an airplane crash in 1931.

• The first Rose Bowl game was played in Pasadena, California, in 1902. It has been played there annually since 1916.

• The practice of players of athletic games wearing numbers on their jerseys began in 1913 in a football game between the Universities of Chicago and Wisconsin.

• Depending on which authorities you go by, the first professional football game was played either in West Racine, Wisconsin, in October 1894 or in Latrobe, Pennsylvania, in August 1895. In any case, it was not until 1920, with the establishment of the American Professional Football Association at Canton, Ohio, that pro football became organized along modern lines. In 1922, after several reorganizations, the association was renamed the National Football League.

• Harold "Red" Grange—the consummate college halfback whom they called "The Galloping Ghost"—made every All-America team in his three seasons at the University of Illinois (1923-25), scoring 21 touchdowns and gaining 3,367 yards running and another 643 passing. He went on to a successful pro career, and in 1963 was one of 17 charter inductees into the Pro Football Hall of Fame. Grange's on-field philosophy was simple: "If you have the football and eleven guys are after you, if you're smart, you'll run."

• Roy Riegels, a center for the University of California Bears, was the sensation of the 1929 Rose Bowl. When a Georgia Tech player fumbled, the ever-alert Riegels was there to pick it up—and gallop 67 yards toward the goal line. Unfortunately, it was the *wrong* goal line, and Riegels got to within a yard of it before being tackled by a teammate. The next play resulted in a safety, and California wound up losing by a score of 8-7. Ever since, our would-be hero has been known as Roy "Wrong Way" Riegels.

• On December 17, 1933, the Chicago Bears beat the New York Giants 23-21 in professional football's first championship game.

• Quite possibly the dullest game in the history of pro football was one played in 1940 by the Chicago Cardinals and the Detroit Lions. The game, which took place in a heavy snowstorm, started off slowly, then tapered off. "Highlights" of the boring fiasco included a period in the final quarter during which the teams traded eight straight punts without a single intervening scrimmage play. When it was all over, a combined total of 30 yards had been gained from scrimmage, and the score still stood at 0-0.

• The 1954 Cotton Bowl was the setting for one of the strangest spectacles in football history—the sight of an unhelmeted player getting up from the bench while a play was in progress and running out onto the field to tackle the other team's halfback. The halfback, who got credit for the 95-yard run he would otherwise have made, was

Rice's Dick Moegle. The tackler, whose sudden mindless impulse secured for him a place in the game's more dubious annals, was Alabama's Tommy Lewis. (Rice won the game, 28-6.)

• The shortest touchdown pass in football history was thrown by Dallas quarterback Eddie LeBaron in a 1960 game against the Washington Redskins. LeBaron's toss to his left end went for all of 2 inches.

• On June 8, 1966, the National and American Football Leagues merged. On August 5, 1967, the Denver Broncos became the first AFL team to beat an NFL opponent in an exhibition game, with a 13-7 win over the Detroit Lions. The first Super Bowl victory by an AFL team came in 1969, in the third such showdown, when the New York Jets upset the Baltimore Colts, 16-7. Before the game, in the face of scoffers (and oddsmakers who had declared the Colts 18- to 20-point favorites), the outspoken, media-genic Jet quarterback Joe Namath had brazenly "guaranteed" that his team would win.

• In 1987 Joe Montana of the San Francisco 49ers set a record for consecutive passes completed (22). In 1989 Montana set a record for most passing yardage in a Super Bowl (357) as he led his team to a 20-16 win over the Cincinnati Bengals. (The regular-season mark is 554 by Norm Van Brocklin, Los Angeles Rams, in a game against the New York Yankees on September 18, 1951.) Other notable pro passing achievements include most touchdown passes completed, career (342, Fran Tarkenton, Minnesota Vikings and New York Giants); most passing yards gained, season (5,084 in 1984), and most passes completed, season (378 in 1986), Dan Marino, Miami Dolphins; and most TDs in consecutive games (47, Johnny Unitas, Baltimore Colts).

• On January 3, 1983, in a game against the Minnesota Vikings, Dallas quarterback Tony Dorsett made the longest run from scrimmage (99 yards) to score a TD. Other NFL record rushers include Chicago Bears running back Walter Payton, who holds the records for most rushing yards in a game (275, against Minnesota, on November 20, 1977) and in a career (16,726), as well as most TDs rushing, career (110). The record for most TDs rushing in a season, is 24, by John Riggins, Washington Redskins, while the mark for most rushing yards gained, season, is 2,105 in 1984, set by Eric Dickerson, Los Angeles Rams.

• The longest pro punt ever punted was 98 yards, by Steve O'Neal, New York Jets, 1969. The longest field goal was 63 yards, Tom Dempsey, New Orleans Saints. The record for most consecutive field goals is 24, Kevin Butler, Chicago Bears, 1988-89.

• The record for most points scored by a player in a game is 40 (6 TDs, 4 points after) by Ernie Nevers, Chicago Cardinals, against the Chicago Bears, on November 28, 1929. The record for most points scored in a career is held by George Blanda, various teams, with 2,002 (9 TDs, 943 points after and 335 field goals).

• The NFL uses more elastic bandaging tape than any other group in the world. Wrapping players to help avoid injury can take up to 125 miles of tape, per team, per season.

THE MRS. PLAYED PRO FOOTBALL

Pat Palinkas only had to walk onto a pro football field to make history: as a place-kick holder she was the first and only woman ever to play in a men's pro football game.

Like many minor-league professional sports franchises, the Orlando Panthers of the Atlantic Coast Football League were looking for a gimmick to spruce up the attendance for the 1970 season. The Florida team looked hard—but not far. The Panthers decided to utilize a woman player in their August 15 game with Bridgeport, Connecticut. Their candidate for the manly chore was 27-year-old housewife Pat Palinkas, whose husband just happened to be the Panther place-kicker.

Pat had held the football on the kicking tee in the past while her husband practiced, so the Panthers were not exactly introducing the game to a neophyte. The team announced that she would enter the roster and would hold for her husband.

Funny, right?

Well, one of the Bridgeport players didn't think so. As Pat lined up the ball after the Panthers' first touchdown, in swooped defensive lineman Wally Florence, who had been trying to eke out a living in football after starring at Purdue University seven years before.

When Pat fumbled the center's passback, the 235-pound Florence crushed her into the ground, soiling her brand-new No. 3 jersey. At 5' 6" and 122 pounds, Pat was at once both the smallest and sorriest player in pro football.

Pat held for two more kicks which were good as the Panthers won, 26-7.

377

If Pat was sore, Florence wasn't sorry.

After the game, he told newsmen who had gathered for the historic event: "I tried to break her neck. I don't know what she's trying to prove. I'm out here trying to make a living and she's out here prancing around, making a folly out of a man's game."

End quote.

And nearly the end of Pat Palinkas' career. She retired shortly thereafter.—JIM BENAGH

SUPER BOWL RESULTS

	Year	Winner	Loser
I	1967	Green Bay Packers, 35	Kansas City Chiefs, 10
II	1968	Green Bay Packers, 33	Oakland Raiders, 14
III	1969	New York Jets, 16	Baltimore Colts, 7
IV	1970	Kansas City Chiefs, 23	Minnesota Vikings, 7
V	1971	Baltimore Colts, 16	Dallas Cowboys, 13
VI	1972	Dallas Cowboys, 24	Miami Dolphins, 3
VII	1973	Miami Dolphins, 14	Washington Redskins, 7
VIII	1974	Miami Dolphins, 24	Minnesota Vikings, 7
IX	1975	Pittsburgh Steelers, 16	Minnesota Vikings, 6
X	1976	Pittsburgh Steelers, 21	Dallas Cowboys, 17
XI	1977	Oakland Raiders, 32	Minnesota Vikings, 14
XII	1978	Dallas Cowboys, 27	Denver Broncos, 10
XIII	1979	Pittsburgh Steelers, 35	Dallas Cowboys, 31
XIV	1980	Pittsburgh Steelers, 31	Los Angeles Rams, 19
XV	1981	Oakland Raiders, 27	Philadelphia Eagles, 10
XVI	1982	San Francisco 49ers, 26	Cincinnati Bengals, 21
XVII	1983	Washington Redskins, 27	Miami Dolphins, 17
XVIII	1984	Los Angeles Raiders, 38	Washington Redskins, 9
XIX	1985	San Francisco 49ers, 38	Miami Dolphins, 17
XX	1986	Chicago Bears, 46	New England Patriots, 10
XXI	1987	New York Giants, 39	Denver Broncos, 20
XXII	1988	Washington Redskins, 42	Denver Broncos, 10
XXIII	1989	San Francisco 49ers, 20	Cincinnati Bengals, 16
XXIV	1990	San Francisco 49ers, 55	Denver Broncos, 10
XXV	1991	New York Giants, 20	Buffalo Bills, 19
XXVI	1992	Washington Redskins, 37	Buffalo Bills, 24
XXVII	1993	Dallas Cowboys, 52	Buffalo Bills, 17
XXVIII	1994	Dallas Cowboys, 30	Buffalo Bills, 13
XXIX	1995	San Francisco 49ers, 49	San Diego Chargers, 26

Note: With its victory in Super Bowl XXIX, the San Francisco 49ers became the first team in NFL history to win five Super Bowls, pulling ahead of the Dallas Cowboys and the Pittsburgh Steelers, which each have four championships. In the same game, 49ers quarterback Steve Young's six TD passes broke the previous Super Bowl record, set by his San Francisco predecessor, Joe Montana, in 1990.

COLLEGE FOOTBALL CHAMPS

The National Collegiate Athletic Association (NCAA) recognizes as the unofficial national college football champion the team so chosen each year (after the regular season and before the bowl games) by polls of the Associated Press (of writers) and *USA Today*/Cable News Network (of coaches). (Prior to 1992, the coaches' poll was conducted by United Press International.) Where the polls differ, both teams are recognized; the AP poll winner is listed first.

1937	Pittsburgh	1966	Notre Dame
1938	Texas Christian	1967	Southern California
1939	Texas A & M	1968	Ohio State
1940	Minnesota	1969	Texas
1941	Minnesota	1970	Nebraska and Texas
1942	Ohio State	1971	Nebraska
1943	Notre Dame	1972	Southern California
1944	Army	1973	Notre Dame and Alabama
1945	Army	1974	Oklahoma, Southern California
1946	Notre Dame	1975	Oklahoma
1947	Notre Dame	1976	Pittsburgh
1948	Michigan	1977	Notre Dame
1949	Notre Dame	1978	Alabama and Southern California
1950	Oklahoma	1979	Alabama
1951	Tennessee	1980	Georgia
1952	Michigan State	1981	Clemson
1953	Maryland	1982	Penn State
1954	Ohio State and UCLA	1983	Miami (FL)
1955	Oklahoma	1984	Brigham Young
1956	Oklahoma	1985	Oklahoma
1957	Auburn and Ohio State	1986	Penn State
1958	Louisiana State	1987	Miami (Florida)
1959	Syracuse	1988	Notre Dame
1960	Minnesota	1989	Miami (FL)
1961	Alabama	1990	Colorado and Georgia Tech
1962	Southern California	1991	Miami (FL) and Washington
1963	Texas	1992	Alabama
1964	Alabama	1993	Florida State
1965	Alabama and Michigan State	1994	Nebraska

HEISMAN TROPHY WINNERS

The Heisman Memorial Trophy is awarded annually by New York City's Downtown Athletic Club to the nation's outstanding football player, as determined by a consensus of sportswriters and sportscasters.

1935	Jay Berwanger, Chicago	1949	Leon Hart, Notre Dame
1936	Larry Kelley, Yale	1950	Vic Janowicz, Ohio State
1937	Clinton Frank, Yale	1951	Dick Kazmaier, Princeton
1938	Davey O'Brien, Texas Christian	1952	Billy Vessels, Oklahoma
1939	Nile Kinnick, Iowa	1953	Johnny Lattner, Notre Dame
1940	Tom Harmon, Michigan	1954	Alan Ameche, Wisconsin
1941	Bruce Smith, Minnesota	1955	Howard Cassady, Ohio State
1942	Frank Sinkwich, Georgia	1956	Paul Hornung, Notre Dame
1943	Angelo Bertelli, Notre Dame	1957	John Crow, Texas A & M
1944	Leslie Horvath, Ohio State	1958	Pete Dawkins, Army
1945	Felix Blanchard, Army	1959	Billy Cannon, Louisiana State
1946	Glenn Davis, Army	1960	Joe Bellino, Navy
1947	Johnny Lujack, Notre Dame	1961	Ernie Davis, Syracuse
1948	Doak Walker, Southern Methodist	1962	Terry Baker, Oregon State

1963	Roger Staubach, Navy	1979	Charles White, Southern California
1964	John Huarte, Notre Dame	1980	George Rogers, South Carolina
1965	Mike Garrett, Southern California	1981	Marcus Allen, Southern California
1966	Steve Spurrier, Florida	1982	Hershel Walker, Georgia
1967	Gary Beban, UCLA	1983	Mike Rozner, Nebraska
1968	O.J. Simpson, Southern California	1984	Doug Flutie, Boston College
1969	Steve Owens, Oklahoma	1985	Bo Jackson, Auburn
1970	Jim Plunkett, Stanford	1986	Vinny Testeverde, Miami (FL)
1971	Pat Sullivan, Auburn	1987	Tim Brown, Notre Dame
1972	Johnny Rodgers, Nebraska	1988	Barry Sanders, Oklahoma State
1973	John Cappelletti, Penn State	1989	Andre Ware, Houston
1974	Archie Griffin, Ohio State	1990	Ty Detmer, Brigham Young
1975	Archie Griffin, Ohio State	1991	Desmond Howard, Michigan
1976	Tony Dorsett, Pittsburgh	1992	Gino Torretta, Miami (FL)
1977	Earl Campbell, Texas	1993	Charlie Ward, Florida State
1978	Billy Sims, Oklahoma	1994	Rashaan Salaam, Colorado

ON THE BALL

It weighs just five ounces and measures between 2.86 and 2.94 inches in diameter. It is made of a composition-cork nucleus encased in two thin layers of rubber, one black and one red, surrounded by 121 yards of tightly wrapped blue-gray wool yarn, 45 yards of white wool yarn, 53 more yards of blue-gray wool yarn, 150 yards of fine cotton yarn, a coat of rubber cement, and a cowhide (formerly horsehide) exterior, which is held together with 216 slightly raised red cotton stitches. Printed certifications, endorsements, and outdoor advertising spherically attest to its authenticity. Like most institutions, it is considered inferior in its present form to its ancient archetypes, and in this case the complaint is probably justified; on occasion in recent years it has actually been known to come apart under the demands of its brief but rigorous active career. Baseballs are assembled and hand-stitched in Taiwan (before 1984 the work was done in Haiti, and before 1973 in Chicopee, Massachusetts), and contemporary pitchers claim that there is a tangible variation in the size and feel of the balls that now come into play in a single game; a true peewee is treasured by hurlers, and its departure from the premises, by fair means or foul, is secretly mourned. But never mind: any baseball is beautiful. No other small package comes as close to the ideal in design and utility. It is a perfect object for a man's hand. Pick it up and it instantly suggests its purpose; it is meant to be thrown a considerable distance— thrown hard and with precision. Its feel and heft are the beginning of the sport's critical dimensions; if it were a fraction of an inch larger or smaller, a few centigrams heavier or lighter, the game of baseball would be utterly different.—ROGER ANGELL

MYSTERIES OF THE CURVE

Hitting a baseball is not easy. A 90-mile-per-hour fastball completes its trip to the plate in less than half a second. That gives the batter only a quarter of a second to decide whether to swing and another quarter of a second to guide the bat to an area that the baseball passes in a little more than a hundredth of a second. But most hitters can only follow the ball two-thirds of the way to the plate; after that, it's guesswork. Most batters guess wrong seven out of 10 times, largely because of 216 stitches of red cotton thread joining the two hourglass-shaped pieces of cowhide that form the cover of a baseball. These stitches, raised ever so slightly above the smooth spherical shell, are what makes the last, unseen third of a pitch treacherous. They make the curveball curve, the sinker sink, and the slider slide.

For a long time there was some question whether the curveball curved at all. In 1870 Fred Goldsmith placed three poles along a chalk line from the mound to home plate. He then threw a ball which traveled to the right of the first pole, to the left of the second, and then to the right of the third. Still there were unbelievers. Seventy-one years after Goldsmith's demonstration, *Life* magazine, which commissioned strobe light photographs of a curveball, concluded, "Possibly there is an infinitely small side movement of the ball in flight. If so, these repetitive-flash pictures fail to show it."

Perhaps *Life*, looking for a sideways motion, missed the point: A major league curve breaks downward, not sideways. "The ball has to break down," says Ray Miller, pitching coach for the Baltimore Orioles, "or it's not an effective pitch. The hitting area of a bat is three inches wide and eight inches long. A ball that breaks horizontally is just going to hit another part of the bat." Any miscalculation of the flight path up or down means a grounder or a pop-up, and a curveball that breaks down is going to help produce that miscalculation.

To make the ball curve downwards, a pitcher puts topspin on it, snapping his fingers over the ball. As the ball spins, the raised stitches carry a layer of air with it. The bottom half of the spinning layer moves with the wind created by the ball's flight, but the top half moves against the wind. This means the air on the bottom will be moving faster than the air on the top. The difference in velocities puts greater pressure on top, pushing the ball down.

The late Lyman J. Briggs, director of the National Bureau of Standards, found that the stitches also affect the distribution of air around the ball, making some of the air that would normally go over the top go under the bottom. Because the bottom air has farther to go to get around the ball than the air going over the top, it must travel faster. It exerts less pressure, and the ball drops.

A pitch, of course, can curve in any direction, depending on the orientation of the spin. An overhand curve will break downward, but a sidearm curve will break horizontally (as in Goldsmith's demonstration). Most pitchers throw the curve with a three-quarters delivery, producing a break both downward and sideways. A pitcher's natural motion can also put spin on a fastball. An overhand delivery can make it rise, and a three-quarter throw can make the ball sink.

In the 1940s a few pitchers were experimenting with a pitch that did not move much; some disparagingly called it a "nickel curve." It is now known as a slider or "fast curve," and it has been largely responsible for the slow decline of batting averages during the 1950s and '60s, leading up to a 1968 season in which only six batters hit over .300, and Carl Yastrzemski won the American League batting title with .301. Soon afterward the pitcher's mound was lowered and the strike zone made smaller. A 45-degree spin is put on the ball with a delivery somewhat like that of a spiraling football pass. It looks like a fastball, but the spin makes the slider tail away at the last minute.

A few pitchers use neither speed nor spin to get their outs. When a knuckleballer jams the ball against his fingertips and throws it towards the plate, no one, least of all the batter, is sure of the gyrations it will perform on its way. Contrary to sandlot philosophy, an ideal knuckler is not a ball without any spin. Mechanical engineer Robert Watts found that a spinless ball moves very little, but a ball that spins a quarter of a revolution on its way to the plate can curve in and out as much as a foot. The slight spin shifts the orientation of the stitches in the "wind," which changes the distribution of the air around the ball as it flies. The shifting flow of air pushes the ball in different directions. "If the ball spun any more than a quarter turn, the forces would cancel out and you'd be in big trouble," says Watts.

A good knuckler is hard to hit, but its awkward grip makes it a tough pitch to master. So some pitchers just add water to produce an instant knuckler. A bit of spit on the fingers makes the grip slippery. The ball is released like a watermelon seed popped between the fingers, a delivery that gives it very little spin and a lot of movement.

Though the spitball was outlawed in 1920, it still enjoys an underground popularity, keeping alive, some say, pitchers whose careers would have evaporated long before. In 1968 a prohibition on putting the hand to the mouth was issued, so the pitch became a Vaseline-ball, the co-conspiring substance being easily hid under the bill of a cap or on a pant leg.

A cruder, and also illegal, method of doctoring the ball is nicking or scuffing the surface. The ways of tampering with the ball are varied. One pitcher was caught with a flesh-colored bandage on the index finger of his glove hand, from which the business end of a thumbtack protruded. Nearby was a piece of emery cloth.

A scuffed ball behaves like a Wiffle Ball. The damaged side of the ball is put opposite the way a pitcher wants it to break. Then he throws an average fastball. The scuffs catch the air and create drag that forces the ball in the opposite direction.

Though science has explained some aspects of the art of pitching, there are still a few mysteries to argue about during the seventh-inning stretch of the world series this fall. One dispute, considered closed by physicists but open by most people who have batted against a major league pitcher, is not whether or how a ball curves but where.

Batters swear a curveball looks like it's going in a straight line and then drops down at the last instant. Sliders, they say, break even more precipitously. Scientists say the movement must be constant. "If there were no gravity, a curveball would travel in a complete circle," says Watts. "What they call a break is an optical illusion." If curves do break sharply, as yet no one has come up with a good explanation how the pitches could suddenly change direction. But when they do, there will be pitchers and batters eager to listen.

"I'm very interested in how pitches work," says Scott McGregor of the Orioles. "Of course, with bases loaded in the bottom of the ninth, I don't think about it much."—WILLIAM FOSTER ALLMAN

MAJOR LEAGUE BASEBALL: SELECTED STATS

Highest batting average, season: .438, Hugh Duffy, Boston Braves, 1894 (since 1900: .424, Rogers Hornsby, St. Louis Cardinals, 1924).

Highest batting average, career: .366, Ty Cobb, Detroit Tigers.

Most years batted over .300: 23, Ty Cobb, Detroit Tigers.

Last player to hit .400 or more: Ted Williams, .406, Boston Red Sox, 1941.

Most career hits: 4,256, Pete Rose, Cincinnati Reds.

Most career home runs and RBIs: 755 and 2,297, Hank Aaron, Atlanta Braves. Others in the home-run Top Ten:

Babe Ruth	714
Willie Mays	660
Frank Robinson	586
Harmon Killebrew	573
Reggie Jackson	563
Mike Schmidt	548
Mickey Mantle	536
Jimmy Foxx	534
Ted Williams	521

Most RBIs, season: 190, Hack Wilson, Chicago Cubs, 1930.

Most career runs: 2,245, Ty Cobb, Detroit Tigers.

Most career strikeouts: 2,597, Reggie Jackson, various teams.

Most career complete games and victories by pitcher: 751 and 511, Cy Young, various teams.

Most career shutouts pitched: 110, Walter Johnson, Washington Senators.

Most consecutive games won by pitcher: 24, Carl Hubbell, New York Giants, 1936 (16) and 1937 (8).

Last pitcher to finish every game he started in one season: Ted Lyons, Chicago White Sox, 20 games in 1942.

Most All-Star Game victories by pitcher: 3, Lefty Gomez, New York Yankees.

First pitcher with glasses to pitch no-hitter: Bullfrog Dietrich, Chicago White Sox, 1937.

Most career double plays, shortstop: 1,553, Luis Aparicio, Chicago White Sox.

Most career double plays, second base: 1,706, Bill Mazeroski, Pittsburgh Pirates.

Most stolen bases, season: 130, Rickey Henderson, Oakland A's, 1982.

First player to steal home twice in one game: Joe Tinker (of "Tinker to Evers to Chance" fame), Chicago Cubs, June 28, 1910.

Youngest player: 15 years, 10 months, 11 days; Pitcher Joe Nuxhall, Cincinnati Reds (started career in 1944).

Most consecutive games played: 2,130, Lou Gehrig, New York Yankees.

New York Yankee immortal Joe DiMaggio holds one of the most amazing records in baseball history—hitting safely in 56 straight games in 1941, a record many feel may never be broken. In fact, it is such a landmark accomplishment, all you need to say in referring to it is "the streak" and most baseball fans will know immediately what you're talking about.

It was a streak that only some spectacular fielding by Cleveland Indian third-baseman Ken Keltner kept from reaching 57, as he twice turned hot shots into putouts. What happened next has had what-iffers what-iffing for decades now: DiMaggio promptly went on another hitting rampage, this time a 16-game streak that invites the inevitable speculative question: what if Keltner had performed just a little less spectacularly that night? If he had, DiMaggio's incredible streak would have been an even more incredible 73 straight games!

The Yankees, that vintage year of 1941, walked off with the pennant, a full 17 games ahead of the second-place Boston Red Sox, and in the World Series beat their arch-rival Brooklyn Dodgers in five games. DiMaggio was named the American League's Most Valuable Player, beating out Boston's Ted Williams. (All Williams did that year was hit .406; he remains the last player to have batted .400 or more.)

A moving P.S. to the tale of the DiMaggio and his famous streak is provided by Daniel Okrent in his book, *Baseball Anecdotes* (Oxford University Press, 1989). About a month and a half after the streak had ended, at Washington's Hotel Shoreham, Yankee pitcher Lefty Gomez was taking an unusually long shower, when his roommate DiMaggio urged him to hurry or "all the steaks will be gone." As Okrent relates:

Gomez got out of the shower and told Joe to relax. On their way out, Lefty said, "I just remembered something. I have to stop by Selkirk's room." DiMaggio said he would go ahead to the dining room and order, but Gomez insisted he come with him. "It'll only take a minute," he said.

When DiMaggio walked into George Selkirk's room, there were 40 men—Yankees and sportswriters—with champagne glasses raised for a toast. Gomez presented DiMaggio with a silver cigar humidor which pitcher Johnny Murphy had ordered from Tiffany's. On the cover was a relief likeness of DiMaggio in mid-swing, on one side was the number 56 and on the other side was the number 91, signifying each hit he had during the streak. And there was an inscription: "Presented to Joe DiMaggio by his fellow players on the New York Yankees to express their admiration for his consecutive-game hitting record, 1941."

THE AMAZIN' METS OF 1969

Cinderella lives! And if you can't believe that, consider precisely what was accomplished on October 16, 1969, at Shea Stadium when the New York Mets became the World Champions of baseball.

In their seven previous seasons of existence—from 1962 through 1968—the Mets' record was an almost stainless portrait of disaster: five times in the cellar, and twice only one notch out of it. They regularly piddled away games in orgies of ineptitude and were considered baseball's patsies—laughable losers who were saved from abandonment at the box office only by their high style and the campy, comic aura they exuded. Brothers in suffering, the Mets and their devoted fans seemed resigned to a fate of lovable failure.

Then came 1969. In July men walked on the moon. On September 10 a similarly unprecedented event took place on earth: the Mets copped first place in the National League's Eastern Division from the Chicago Cubs, who had held it continuously since opening day. As one-time Met manager Casey Stengel put it: "The team has come along slow but fast."

Talk of the Mets being the "Children of Destiny" began to be bandied about. Phrases such as "Miracle Workers," "The Impossible Dream," and "Mets' Magic" were also frequently heard. On his way to becoming his league's Manager of the Year, Mets pilot Gil Hodges seemed more and more to be a man with an irrepressible mission, though many skeptics continued to scoff. Some still scoffed after the Mets swept the Atlanta Braves three straight in the league playoffs, setting the stage for one of the most startling and dramatic World Series of all time. Coming back from 1-0 behind in games, the underdog Mets won it all four straight from the Baltimore Orioles. Naturally, they had to come from 3-0 behind to take the last game—leaving Oriole manager Earl Weaver with some rather harsh pre-series words to eat: "Destiny, intangible momentum? You're not going to sell me that line. This is baseball, not a circus. We have the best team in baseball because we have pitching, power, and defense. It's that simple. And we'll prove it in the World Series."

What Mr. Weaver had not counted on, of course, was that unpredictable, indomitable "something" in the soul of the Mets that never bothered to read the statistics or the odds-makers' careful reports.

THUS SPAKE BERRA—OR DID HE?

Lawrence ("Yogi") Berra, the bad-ball-hitting New York Yankee catcher who went on to a second career as a manager, has also gained fame for his often strange and colorful sayings. Over the years, however, truth and legend have intermingled to produce Berraisms ranging from the genuine to the partly genuine to the flat-out phony.

Herewith, a sampling of sayings considered authentic (except where otherwise noted):

"I want to thank all those who made this night necessary." (At a "Yogi Berra Night" at Sportsman's Park in his birthplace of St. Louis; it was 1947, his first season as a Yankee.)

"You can see a lot just by observing."

"If the world were perfect, it wouldn't be."

"It's wonderful. It keeps the kids out of the house." (On the merits of Little League baseball.)

"If you can't imitate him, don't copy him." (To a young player trying, with scant success, to emulate the batting style of a veteran player.)

"He's a big clog in their machine." (On comparing a player on his team to Tony Perez and the Cincinnati Reds or Ted Williams and the Boston Red Sox.)

"He must have made that before he died." (About Steve McQueen in the movie *The Magnificent Seven.*)

"What the hell is wrong with him now?" (To his wife Carmen, when she said she had taken their son Tim to see *Doctor Zhivago.*)

"Thanks. You don't look so hot yourself." (On a hot day, on being told by New York Mayor John Lindsay's wife Mary that he looked "nice and cool" in his summer suit.)

"Nobody goes there anymore. It's too crowded." (About a popular Minneapolis restaurant.)

"It gets late early out there." (For this one, Yogi provides a remarkably sensible explanation, from his 1989 autobiography, *Yogi: It Ain't Over . . .* , written with Tom Horton: "I said that when I missed a ball in the sun. I was playing left. It was 1961, against the Reds. What I meant was that because of the shadows in Yankee Stadium at that time of year, it was tough to see the ball even early in the game.")

"We were overwhelming underdogs." (On the 1969 New York Mets, who late in the season overtook the Chicago Cubs for the National League Eastern Division title. Pitching star Nolan Ryan, who like Berra was on that fabled squad, thought this Berraism particularly wise. As Yogi relates: "He really liked the way I put it. He said that is *exactly* what we were. He said if I had gone to college, they would have made me talk clearer, but not better.")

"Why buy luggage? You only use it when you travel." ("I thought that made sense when I said it, but I don't think so anymore.")

"I really didn't say everything I said."

"I don't do them on the phone." (Reply to someone with whom he was speaking on the telephone who had asked him for a Berraism.)

Two pseudo-Berraisms (they sound rightly wrong—or is it wrongly right?—but Yogi denies ever having said them):

"It's déjà vu all over again."

"Always go to other people's funerals; otherwise they won't go to yours."

As for the oft-quoted, "If you come to a fork in the road, take it," Yogi doesn't recall saying it, but he also doesn't quite rule it out: "I really don't know about that one."

BASEBALL FLUBS, JORDAN FLIES

You don't hear it much anymore, but once upon a time there used to be bandied about a fairly popular put-down phrase, "flubbing the dub." As in, "You stupid *jibroney*, you really *flubbed the dub* that time!" (Don't even *ask* about "jibroney"—some things are just better left unsaid.)

In any case, it's a phrase that seems tailor-made for the professional baseball strike that began in early August 1994 and ended in early April 1995, a strike that wiped out the 1994 World Series, soured countless fans on at least the professional version of the sport, and—not incidentally—triggered the flight of super-duper superstar Michael Jordan from the fields of his diamond dreams.

It was a characteristically high-profile flight that might not otherwise have come to pass, given His Airness's well-known grit and determination. Who knows how much further those qualities might have taken him in his second sport, or how much more time he might have devoted to trying? But the prickly pros of baseball decided the matter for him—and thus the ex-Bull became a renewed-Bull, as one sport's loss became another's unexpected blast of fresh air, with a capital A.

Perhaps Jordan's flight from the mess that pro baseball has become was the event that brought home the stark, undeniable fact that this time pro baseball had really *flubbed the dub!* As in: struck out, balked, dropped the ball, missed the tag, forgot to touch the friggin' base.

As in: How the blazes can it expect fans to care very much about a lot of fan-indifferent, greedo millionaires who obviously have missed the whole point of what baseball should be and once was. Of course, it's natural for *business* aspects to enter in and counterbalance to *some* degree the *game* aspects of the sport, and there *have* been business-related problems in the past.

What's unnatural in the present is the depressing *degree* to which the business aspects have predominated, and to which a mood of negativity has been generated by all parties to the wrangle—in a phrase, the degree to which pro baseball has just flat-out *flubbed the dub!*

But that's O.K.—Jordan's back and, as a whole, the world of sport remains healthy a place to live in or visit.

THE EVOLUTION OF BASKETBALL

March 11, 1892—The first public contest took place at the School for Christian Workers, Springfield, Massachusetts, with the students beating the instructors 5-1 before a crowd of 200.

March 22, 1893—The first women's game was played at Smith College, Northampton, Massachusetts. The female players wore bloomers, so no male spectators were allowed to watch.

1894—Soccer balls were replaced by laced basketballs manufactured at the Overman Wheel Company in Chicopee Falls, Massachusetts. Also that year, the first backboards were erected to keep spectators from interfering from the balconies.

1897—Five-man teams became accepted after games with up to 50 players on a team became unmanageable.

1899—Players were allowed to alternate hands while dribbling. (Previously a player could switch only once.)

1901-08—Players could not shoot for the goal after dribbling, but had to pass to a stationary teammate.

1903—Court boundaries were required to be straight. (Some early courts jogged around pillars, stairways, and other obstructions.)

1906—After years of climbing up to remove the ball from the peach basket and after trying a contraption to eject the ball, the bottom of the basket was finally removed.

1907-08 season—The Buffalo Germans began a string of 111 straight wins.

1921—Basket ball became one word: basketball.

1923-24—"Designated foul shooter" was eliminated; person fouled had to take the foul shot.

January 7, 1927—The Harlem Globetrotters, organized by Abe Saperstein, played their first exhibition game in Hinckley, Illinois.

1929—The "cage" was eliminated; use of rope or chicken wire around the court was discontinued.

1932—The center jump after each score was eliminated; ten-second rule (for advancing ball past midcourt) went into effect.

1944-45—Goaltending declared illegal.

1956—The foul lane was widened from 6 to 12 feet.

1960—The Minneapolis Lakers moved to Los Angeles, California, giving professional basketball coast-to-coast coverage for the first time.

1971—Size of women's teams was reduced from six to five players.

1974—Moses Malone signed with the Utah Stars of the American Basketball Association to become the first professional basketball player to go directly from high school to the pro ranks.

January 5, 1986—Game called because of rain. (A leaking roof in the Seattle Coliseum forced an NBA game to be canceled.)

March 1, 1987—The Boston Celtics became the first NBA team to win 2,000 regular-season games.

1989—President Ronald Reagan sent $10,000 worth of basketball equipment to Burundi.

March 24, 1990—41,046 fans attended the Indiana High School Championship in the Hoosier Dome.—CHRISTINE SCHULTZ
(Reprinted with permission from the 1991 *Old Farmer's Almanac*, published in Dublin, New Hampshire.)

SOME OF THE ORIGINAL RULES FOR "BASKET BALL"

• The ball may be thrown in any direction with one or both hands.

• The ball may be batted in any direction with one or both hands (never with the fist).

- A player cannot run with the ball. The player must throw it from the spot on which he catches it.
- If either side makes three consecutive fouls it shall count a goal for the opponents (consecutive means without the opponents in the meantime making a foul).
- A goal shall be made when the ball is thrown or batted *from the grounds* into the basket and stays there, providing those defending the goal do not touch or disturb the goal. If the ball rests on the edges and the opponent moves the basket, it shall count as goal.
- When the ball goes out of bounds, it shall be thrown into the field of play by the first person touching it. He has a right to hold it unmolested for five seconds. In case of a dispute the umpire shall throw it straight into the field. The thrower-in is allowed five seconds. If he holds it longer it shall go to the opponent. If any side persists in delaying the game the umpire shall call a foul on that side.
- The time shall be two fifteen minutes, halves, with five minutes' rest between. —JAMES NAISMITH, *Rules for Basket Ball* (1891)

NBA MOST VALUABLE PLAYERS

1956	Bob Pettit, St. Louis	1976	Kareem Abdul-Jabbar, Los Angeles
1957	Bob Cousy, Boston	1977	Kareem Abdul-Jabbar, Los Angeles
1958	Bill Russell, Boston	1978	Bill Walton, Portland
1959	Bob Pettit, St. Louis	1979	Moses Malone, Houston
1960	Wilt Chamberlain, Philadelphia	1980	Kareem Abdul-Jabbar, Los Angeles
1961	Bill Russell, Boston	1981	Julius Erving, Philadelphia
1962	Bill Russell, Boston	1982	Moses Malone, Houston
1963	Bill Russell, Boston	1983	Moses Malone, Philadelphia
1964	Oscar Robertson, Cincinnati	1984	Larry Bird, Boston
1965	Bill Russell, Boston	1985	Larry Bird, Boston
1966	Wilt Chamberlain, Philadelphia	1986	Larry Bird, Boston
1967	Wilt Chamberlain, Philadelphia	1987	Magic Johnson, L.A. Lakers
1968	Wilt Chamberlain, Philadelphia	1988	Michael Jordan, Chicago
1969	Wes Unseld, Baltimore	1989	Magic Johnson, L.A. Lakers
1970	Willis Reed, New York	1990	Magic Johnson, L.A. Lakers
1971	Kareem Abdul-Jabbar*, Milwaukee	1991	Michael Jordan, Chicago
1972	Kareem Abdul-Jabbar, Milwaukee	1992	Michael Jordan, Chicago
1973	Dave Cowens, Boston	1993	Charles Barkley, Phoenix
1974	Kareem Abdul-Jabbar, Los Angeles	1994	Hakeem Olajuwon, Houston
1975	Bob McAdoo, Buffalo		

*During the 1971 season and part of the next Kareem Abdul-Jabbar was known by his birth name, Lew Alcindor.

SPORTS SHORTS

The game of golf, which most authorities say originated in Scotland (though it *may* have been Holland), was introduced to colonial America by the Scots—but it was not until 1888 that the first club devoted to the sport was formed, the St. Andrews Golf Club of Yonkers,

New York. In 1894 the leading golf clubs got together to form the U.S. Golf Association and to establish two annual championships, the U.S. Amateur and the U.S. Open, to determine the sport's amateur and professional champions. Today the principal pro groups are the Professional Golfer's Association (PGA) and the Ladies Professional Golfer's Association (LPGA).

Players who have won the most tournaments on the PGA tour, through 1994:

1	Sam Snead	81
2	Jack Nicklaus	70
3	Ben Hogan	63
4	Arnold Palmer	60
5	Byron Nelson	52

• During the 1949 British Open, Harry Bradshaw drove a ball into a beer bottle, breaking off the top part. Opting to play it "as it lay" rather than take a penalty by removing it, Bradshaw smashed the bottle with his club, sending the ball about 30 feet.
• The record for most LPGA championships (based on annual tour earnings) is eight, by Kathy Whitworth, from 1965 to 1973.
• On July 22, 1979, 67-year-old Sam Snead shot a 66, becoming the first golfer to shoot lower than his age.

Tennis—described by Billy Jean King as "A perfect combination of violent action taking place in an atmosphere of total tranquility"—is a relatively recent offshoot of the ancient game of court tennis. It was introduced at a lawn party in Wales in 1873 by Major Walter Clopton Wingfield, who called it "Sphairistike"—but the name was as much a failure as the game was a success, and it soon began to be called "lawn tennis" instead, by which name it is still also known. In 1874 the game was played in the U.S. for the first time at the Staten Island Cricket and Baseball Club.

Standardization along modern lines came about 1880, and in the following year the U.S. Lawn Tennis Association was founded and conducted the first national championships at Newport, Rhode Island. (In 1975 the word "Lawn" was dropped from the group's title.)

The international Davis Cup matches began in 1900, but it was not until 1926 that professional tennis began and not until 1968, with its acceptance at Wimbledon, England, that it was fully recognized. The Wimbledon tournament, established in 1877, remains the sport's premier event. Since 1978 the U.S. championships have been held in Flushing Meadows, New York.

• The youngest player ever to win a championship at Wimbledon was Charlotte "Lottie" Dod, who in 1887, at 15 1/2, won the women's amateur singles title.

• In 1973 fried onions were banned from Wimbledon, reportedly because some blue bloods in the center-court stands were offended by the smell.

• On July 8, 1984, John McEnroe took only 80 minutes to defeat Jimmy Connors for the Wimbledon men's singles title (6-1, 6-1, 6-2).

If you've ever wondered why a score of zero in tennis is referred to as "love," rest assured that it has nothing whatever to do with love. "Love" in this context derives from the French word "l'oeuf," which means "the egg"—as in "goose egg."

Ice hockey was developed in Canada, where it is the national game. In 1893 Baron Stanley of Preston, a Canadian governor-general, donated a trophy to be awarded to the annual winner of the nation's amateur hockey championship—the so-called Stanley Cup. The cup's first winner (in 1894) was the Montreal Athletic Association, which edged the Osgoode Hall team of Ottawa. An Ottawa newspaper reporter wrote of the historic event: "There were fully 5,000 persons at the match, and tin horns, strong lungs, and a general rabble predominated. The ice was fairly good. The referee forgot to see many things."

• In the annals of sports-related frustration, the experience of the St. Louis Blues hockey teams of 1968-70, surely deserves a favored niche. Three straight times they skated and fought their way to the playoffs—and three straight times they were zapped, four games to none. (Twice in a row by the Montreal Canadiens, then by the Boston Bruins.) The Blues' record of 12 consecutive losses in Stanley Cup play still stands, so prodigious a feat of failure that it may never be broken.

Soccer by other names—"football" or "Association Football"—has been played by official rules since 1848. The name itself, coined by Englishman Charles Wreford Brown in 1863, has no relation to the verb "sock," though the rough-and-tumble nature of the game might understandably lead one to think so.

• On July 13, 1930, 13 nations took part in the first World Cup in soccer at Montevideo, Uruguay. In 1994 Brazil became the first country to win the cup four times (the other times being 1958, 1962 and 1970). The next winningest countries are Italy and West Germany, with three cups each—Italy in 1934, 1938 and 1982, and West Germany in 1954, 1974 and 1990.

• In recent years soccer has become increasingly popular in the U.S., with the national team drawing an average of about 40,000 spectators over a three-game stretch in spring 1991. Alan Rothenberg, head of the U.S. Soccer Federation, said, "Around the country, people are going to have to take note of the sport with crowds this big. Otherwise, they will find a revolution going on right under their noses." In 1994, for the first time ever, the U.S. was the host country of the World Cup matches.

Horse racing is at least 3,000 years old and took place in colonial America. England and Canada have been in the forefront of the development of the sport in its present form.

• The first Kentucky Derby was won on May 18, 1875, by a horse named Aristides. The Derby has been won a record five times by two jockeys—Eddie Arcaro and Bill Hartack.

The famed Hialeah racetrack was opened for business on January 25, 1925, by the Miami Jockey Club, but by May the state legislature had outlawed gambling. Biding its time till the betting winds shifted, the track began selling postcards of horses. If the horse on your card won, you could sell it back to the track at a price pegged to the winning odds. In recent years the horse-racing industry has been hurt by riverboat casinos and other forms of legalized gambling. Purses are smaller, and many track owners are looking to diversify or get out of the business altogether.

On May 6, 1954, Roger Bannister became the first person to run the mile in under four minutes, with a time of 3:59.4.
• Weird-news reporter Chuck Shepherd tells the following tale of college sprinters Kevin Braunskill of North Carolina State and James Trapp of Clemson, who were suspended from competition in February 1991: "The two were on the award stand after Braunskill had won the 200-meter race when Trapp took a swing at Braunskill; Braunskill retaliated by hitting Trapp over the head with his first-place plaque."

The fastest pit stop in Indianapolis 500 history was made on May 30, 1976, by Bobby Unser—four seconds.

Boxing immortal Joe Louis holds the record for the longest reign of a heavyweight champ—11 years, 252 days (1937-49). Before fighting light-heavyweight champ Billy Conn on June 18, 1941, Louis said: "He can run, but he can't hide."

- In what is perhaps boxing's greatest comeback, featherweight Willie Pep, severely injured in a plane crash, came back to win 26 straight fights and retain his world title.
- The record for most career knockouts is 145, by light-heavyweight Archie Moore (1936-63).

GIRLS AND WOMEN IN SPORT: TEST YOUR IQ

To test your women-in-sports IQ, try this quiz prepared by the National Association for Girls and Women in Sports.

1. In 1986, she became the first African-American female elected to the International Olympic Committee. She is the IOC's first black member from a country without a majority black population.
    a. Anita DeFrantz
    b. Jackie Joyner-Kersee
    c. Althea Gibson
    d. Debi Thomas

2. According to a recent survey by the Amateur Athletic Foundation of Los Angeles (1988), women hold what percent of all sports leadership roles? (Included are positions in the Olympic movement, college sports, sports media and major U.S. professional sports.)
    a. 12%
    b. 5%
    c. 1%
    d. 18%

3. At Jennifer Capriati's first professional tennis tournament, officials clocked the speed of her serve. How fast was it?

a. 53 mph
b. 72 mph
c. 94 mph
d. 103 mph

4. In 1990, which of the following sports had the highest percentage of female coaches at the college level?

a. Basketball
b. Tennis
c. Field hockey
d. Gymnastics

5. In 1985, Elizabeth Balsley and Jacqueline Lantz, both 16 and from the New York area, showed their pioneering spirit when they successfully challenged the long-standing practice of excluding girls from trying out for traditionally boys-only contact sports. Which sport did they try out for?

a. boxing
b. rugby
c. ice hockey
d. football

6. Who was the first woman to win a NASCAR (stock car) race in its 40-year history?

a. Janet Guthrie
b. Shwana Robinson
c. Lyn St. James
d. Lori Johns

7. The first women's Olympic cycling race was won by Connie Carpenter Phinney, who beat silver medalist Rebecca Twigg by only inches in the 72.5 kilometer race. When did this race take place?

a. 1924
b. 1956
c. 1976
d. 1984

8. Since 1970, what country has won the most Women's World Figure Skating Championships?

a. USA
b. East Germany
c. Soviet Union (CIS)
d. Canada

Answers: 1A; 2B; 3C; 4C; 5D; 6B; 7D; 8B.—NATIONAL ASSOCIATION FOR GIRLS AND WOMEN IN SPORTS

NOTES FOR THE ROAD
... *know before you go* ...

Travel is fatal to prejudice, bigotry, and narrow-mindedness—
and many of our people need it sorely on these accounts.
—MARK TWAIN

When traveling, take twice the money and half the clothes
you think you will need
—BETSY WACKERNAGEL

"HIT THE ROAD, JACK!"

Most of us live lives narrowed by purpose and repetition: we are happy (or not) in our familiar surroundings, we are performing well (or poorly) in our particular places, and there is a kind of comfort in the enveloping sameness—regardless of how our fortunes may, at the moment, be waxing or waning.

Still, no matter how smug and snugly in our homey abodes we may get, every now and again we are seized—sometimes even zapped—by the itch to switch, as a rut-weary voice within whispers or shouts (depending on how long it's been): "Hit the road, Jack!"

And off we go—as soon as work and home and other schedules can be aligned—maybe to a coast, maybe north, maybe south, maybe even to a foreign shore or two or three.

As a scenario—so far, so good. But when it comes to real life, it's important to insert an extra step in there somewhere, a certain time (brief or long, again *depending*) dedicated to research and preparation. For wherever—and however distant—your wanderlust wills you to stray, you should first mentally prepare yourself for adventure and try to let go of the need for a totally planned and orchestrated sojourn. Above all, try to think of yourself as a soon-to-be "traveler" rather than "tourist" (in the pejorative sense in which that word is often used).

There is a difference. A traveler has a penciled-in plan that's easy to revise, while a tourist has a detailed itinerary for each and every day—and woe be it to anyone or anything that may interfere! A traveler gives the host state's or country's menu a fair try, while a tourist will seek out vittles just like those he or she had at home.

Not that there's anything wrong with being a "tourist" in the neutral sense of the word—that is, as one who "tours," or makes "a journey for business, pleasure or education in which one returns to the starting point." (Tourism, after all, is a mostly honorable field of endeavor for both visitor and visited—a $344-billion-a-year industry that is the nation's third largest; it also ranks among the top three industries in 46 states, and is the second largest employer in the country.)

So tourism, schmourism—whatever the word, whatever the emphasis your way of going gives it, you may also be interested in some related data herein gathered: on camping and boating and biking, on auto upkeep, on planes and trains, even on moving your household. May these road notes ease your way, whether the road be highway or path, truck or track, water or air.

MODERN CAMPING: COMFORT VS. FREEDOM

Camping is enjoying unprecedented popularity throughout the country, but not all its devotees are purists who insist on roughing it completely. More than three million campers prefer to combine outdoor living with a certain amount of creature comfort by traveling and camping in a variety of special vehicles tailored to their budgets and preferences.

The key conveniences that appeal to owners of mobile camping units include ease of cooking, adequate storage space, and minimum packing and setting-up requirements. Owners of mobile camping vehicles also mention such comfort factors as adequate protection from weather and insects, good sleeping accommodations, clean quarters, privacy. and roominess. Most camping trailers are compact, sealed units that, when opened, support a tent and provide sleeping accommodations for four. The higher-priced units include such features as a stove, sink, refrigerator, heater and toilet.

But campers who are purists about their avocation look askance at the practice of bringing along the proverbial kitchen sink, as it were. They'd rather take only what they can carry without its being a strain, thereby gaining mobility and increasing the likelihood of finding honest, off-the-beaten-path adventure. As a U.S. Forest Service booklet notes: "Backpacking offers freedom found in no other type of wilderness travel. You can venture into wilderness country with your home on your back and know the joys of stopping when and where you will without thought of schedules or definite destinations." Nearly 15 million acres of wildlife areas can be traveled only on foot or by horseback.

Backpacking is enjoying a bright new era largely because of the extensive amount of ultralight hiking and camping equipment that has been developed. But budgeting is important—this streamlined gear *can* be costly.

Experienced backpackers, through trial and error, have developed many little techniques to keep pack weight to a near-absolute minimum. Here are a few ideas designed to help you start "thinking small":

- Bring a small, rather than full-sized, towel.
- Wrap food in plastic bags, rather than in paper or cardboard.
- Take scouring pads with built-in soap, thus eliminating a bar of soap and dishcloth.
- Bring a multibladed jackknife in place of the separate tools such a knife combines.
- Keep your pack to a maximum of 25 pounds. For the luxury of taking any more than that, you pay a premium in bother and fatigue. This doesn't mean, however, that you should leave behind anything you really need. And when you start sorting out the needs from the luxuries, don't forget to include in the first category a flashlight and spare batteries. (*Tip:* In packing the flashlight, *reverse* the cells so they won't burn out if the switch is accidentally snapped on in transit.)

SLEEPING UNDER THE STARS

There comes a time in the life of just about every camping adult when an air mattress is essential to a good night's sleep. (Youngsters can adjust their bones to the hard earth and awake refreshed.)

Fortunately, the equipment companies have come out with light and durable air mattresses for backpacking and most backpackers use them. They come in different lengths, again saving ounces. A mattress that measures from the shoulders to just below the hips is all that is necessary for comfort. It is a good idea to put some gear under the feet and legs for warmth.

Mattresses are made of plastic, nylon or rubber. Prime considerations in selecting one are weight and durability. Most people blow up their air mattresses too much. A good test is to sit on the mattress. You should feel the ground, but only slightly. Deflating the mattress is simple—before rising, take out the plug or valve and let your body weight help push out the air.

Backpackers usually carry sleeping bags, and a favorite indoor sport on a long winter night is to compare the relative merits of the many types on the market. Weight, warmth, bulk, waterrepellency and cost are important factors to evaluate in selecting a sleeping bag. Consider the materials used for both the outer lining and for the insulation. Decide how much warmth is needed and buy accordingly. Look for stitching and shape in a bag. Stitching is needed to prevent bunching of the filling, but should not go clear through the outer and inner cloth of the bag.

Mummy bags that taper at the foot are popular, but consider foot room. Bags having a zipper all down one side and across the foot are easier to get into and out of; with these types of bags, warmth can be regulated by unzipping a little or a lot. These bags are usually rectangular in shape and can be spread out like a comforter. Moreover, two can be easily zipped together; a feature to be considered. (Some people make their own sleeping bags with comforters and long zippers.)

Mummy bags come with a built-in hood for warmth. Others have a flap that comes up over the head, providing shelter against rain and drafts. Head protection is particularly important if no tent is used.

A final word about sleeping bags—air them out completely after using. A sleeping bag that's not been aired long enough gets unpleasantly musty.

THE BEAR FACTS

Although national park campgrounds are planned with certain safety factors in mind, there are no man-made fences to separate you from wildlife. Some animals will root through garbage cans and your picnic leavings, but others will approach boldly for a handout. Do not be deceived apparent tameness is sometimes only an illusion. Most park animals are wild, the "friendly looking" black bear included.

Because of their protected status within parks, many bears lose their fear of man and acquire a taste for his food. Instinctively a hunter, the bear may become aggressive when teased with tidbits from a car window or a picnic table. If the supply of goodies runs out, it may try to seize more by force. The result—a badly clawed arm, or worse. For your protection, park regulations prohibit the feeding or molesting of bears.

If you camp away from designated campsites, here are a few things to remember to keep the bears away:

- Do not throw aside or bury garbage and food containers.
- Combustible trash should be burned. Burn in cans and other noncombustible containers, except glass, to destroy food smells. Then remove cans from the cold ashes, flatten them and take them to trash receptacles at the trailhead.
- Store foodstuffs (preferably in airtight containers) out of reach of bears. Food can be suspended by ropes between trees.
- If previous campers have left a dirty camp, give yourself a few moments to rant and rave about their inconsiderateness—then, for your own protection, clean up the mess.
- Use dry, prepackaged foods and avoid greasy, pungent foods such as bacon and ham. Packs and sleeping bags should be kept clean and free of food smells. As a precaution, sleep some distance from your campfire and cooking area.

WHEN LIGHTNING STRIKES

In case of a lightning storm, get off exposed peaks or ridges, avoid lone tall trees, and stay away from bodies of water. Stay far from any natural "lightning rods," and don't make one of yourself. If it is impossible to get into the protection of brush or trees, sit down and wait for the storm to pass.

THE TIME OF THE BIKE

There are now about 90 million bicycles in use in this country—a figure representing an ongoing upward trend, as people become increasingly aware of biking's many benefits: the money you save on fuel, the relatively painless exercise you get, the environmental advantage biking has over driving on short trips. (Sixty-three percent of all auto trips are under five miles in length, and these trips—which are just the ones bike-riding could replace—cause the most air pollution.)

Biking's incredible upsurge in popularity, however, has brought a corresponding increase in accidents involving bikes. There are currently about a million such accidents annually. Of these, the National Safety Council estimates that 80 percent are caused because the bike rider did not follow "the rules of the road."

Here are some tips for improving your own bicycle safety:

• Be sure your bicycle is safety-equipped and kept in good running order—tires inflated properly, moving parts regularly lubricated, etc.

• Adjust seat and handlebars to assure maximum riding comfort.

• Know and follow the rules of the road—obey traffic signals, give clear hand signals, ride in a straight line to the right of traffic, ride single file, and never ride against traffic.

• Be constantly alert for cars that travel to your front, back and sides.

• Don't weave in and out of traffic.

• Never pass on the right.

• Be on the lookout for potholes, oil slicks, water puddles, wet leaves and other such biking hazards.

• Never ride more than one person to a bike—unless, of course, you have a bicycle built for two.

• When riding at night or other times of poor visibility, wear bright, reflective clothing and use your headlight.

• Don't wear earphones while riding—it helps to hear traffic as well as see it.

• Wear a helmet when riding in all but very light traffic.

• Be aware of local ordinances affecting bikers. Some communities, for example, allow biking on sidewalks, others don't.

• Use bikeways or bike paths whenever possible. There are now over 20,000 miles of these nationally, and local, state and federal agencies plan to add many more paths, especially in and around cities.

• Keep your bike secure with a good U-lock through the rear wheel, the frame and around a sturdy post. If you have a quick-release front wheel, secure it with a cable or take it with you.

• The New York Police Department offers the following suggestion, which can come in very handy if, despite your having taken the above precautions, your bike is stolen: record the serial number and keep it in a safe place, along with the sales receipt and a photograph of the bike.

WHAT IT TAKES TO GET JAMMED

Gary Washburn, who writes on transportation matters for the *Chicago Tribune*, poses the burning question (as in when you're doing a slow-traffic burn): How many cars does it take to slow traffic down to 20 mph, not counting accidents and gapers' blocks?

Answering his own question, Washburn explains:

• If there are 12 vehicles (averaging 25 feet long) per mile in a lane of the expressway, then they can travel at 55 mph or higher.

• If the number of vehicles increases to 30 within the same space, the traffic flow slows to 40 mph, allowing enough space between vehicles to stop safely if an accident occurs.

• At 67 vehicles per mile, per-lane traffic slows to 20 mph. Any more than 67 vehicles per mile is stop-and-go.

IMPROVING YOUR CAR'S EFFICIENCY

Getting the best possible performance from your car depends on three factors: the blending of the gasoline, the mechanical condition and tune of your engine, and the selection of the proper gasoline grade or octane rating.

Blending

The oil companies blend gasoline to meet the needs of your particular region and climate. Special blends are provided for cold weather, hot weather, and high and low altitudes. Some brands may perform better in your car than others, but you can be reasonably sure that the gasoline you buy in a given area is blended to meet local conditions.

Tuning

You should have your car tuned at regular intervals as recommended in the owner's manual. It is especially important that the carburetor, distributor and spark plugs are in precise adjustment for maximum performance, efficiency and pollution control.

Selecting the Right Gasoline

When selecting gasoline it is important to choose a brand and grade with an octane rating high enough to prevent "engine knock." This phenomenon is one of the most troublesome problems you may encounter with your car. It occurs when, instead of burning smoothly, a portion of the gasoline/car mixture explodes spontaneously and prematurely in the cylinders. Knocking decreases power and fuel economy and can damage engine parts if allowed to continue.

Engine knock can be caused by overheating, a badly adjusted carburetor, incorrect timing, or by deposits in the cylinder head or on top of the pistons. A common cause is the use of gasoline with an octane rating too low for your engine. Here is a simple procedure that will help you select the octane rating your particular car needs:

• Have your car tuned by a competent mechanic to exact factory specifications. When shopping for a good mechanic, check with friends and neighbors to see if they know one who is a specialist on your make of car. If you have your car serviced at a large agency, get acquainted with the service manager and see if you can have the same person see to your car every time.)

• Wait until the gas is low, then fill up with the brand you usually buy, specifying the grade (premium, regular or other) as recommended by the owner's manual. Drive a few miles until the engine is warned up, come to a complete stop, then accelerate hard.

• If the engine knocks or pings on the gas with the recommended rating, use up the tank and refill with the next higher grade. Repeat the acceleration test. If the engine does not knock, this is the octane you need. If it does knock on this higher octane, see your mechanic. You have mechanical trouble.

• If the engine does not knock or ping on the gas with the recommended octane rating, use up the tank and refill with the next lower grade or octane. Repeat the acceleration test. If the engine knocks, this lower grade is inadequate for your car's needs, and you should go back to the higher octane. If the engine does not knock, you probably can use this lower grade safely.

• Remember, changing conditions can change octane requirements. As your car ages, its tendency to knock usually will increase. Heavy loads or low humidity may have the same effect. To be safe, if your car is in good mechanical condition but is knocking, use the next higher octane.

Other Additives

Antiknock compounds are not the only additives you may need in the gasoline. The other principal additives include:

Anti-icing compounds, which prevent the buildup of ice—for example, in carburetors.

Antifreeze agents, which help prevent ice formation in fuel lines.

Antioxidants, which prevent gum formation.

Metal deactivators, which prevent unwanted chemical reactions between gasoline and metal.

Antirust compounds, which protect fuel systems against corrosion.

Detergents, which help keep carburetors and fuel systems clean.

Ignition-control compounds, which reduce deposits in cylinders or on pistons, and on spark plugs, and help to prevent premature ignition or misfiring.

If you want to be sure what additives are in your gasoline, ask your dealer or distributor.

Checklist for Better Performance

After you have selected the gasoline with the octane rating and additives you need, you can do a number of things to improve performance and save gas:

• Be sure that a careful service record is kept on all repairs, so that the mechanic knows what work has been done before, and when.

• Follow the recommendations in the owner's manual for major and minor service and tune-ups.

• Check tire pressure and treadwear pattern periodically. Too low tire pressure increases rolling resistance, causes increased treadwear and reduces gas mileage. If the tires wear unevenly, gas mileage will also drop.

• If you drive a good deal, consider using radial tires. They can improve gasoline mileage about 3 percent over conventional belted or bias ply tires.

• If possible, avoid pressing the accelerator all the way down when climbing hills and long grades. It wastes gas.

• Avoid excessive high speed or jerky driving; learn to drive as smoothly and steadily as traffic and road conditions allow.

• Turn off the engine if you stop more than a minute. Restarting uses less gasoline than a minute's idling.

• Use the brake rather than the accelerator to hold the car in place on a hill.

• Jumpy starts and fast getaways can burn over 50 percent more gas than normal acceleration.

• Avoid weaving, spurting and lane changing in heavy traffic. Such practices waste fuel.

• Look ahead and pace yourself to minimize stops at traffic lights and jam-ups.

• Slow down. Excessive speed is the greatest waster of gas. For best mileage do not exceed 50 mph.

• Limit use of air conditioners and other fuel-eating accessories.

• If you get a sudden drop in gas mileage, check with your mechanic. Trouble is brewing, and the sooner you have it fixed, the less it is likely to cost you.

- Make fuel economy a consideration in any new car purchase.
- Reduce the number of unessential auto trips through careful trip planning.
- Use mass transit, car pools or bicycles when feasible.

—U.S. DEPARTMENT OF TRANSPORTATION
OFFICE OF PUBLIC AND CONSUMER AFFAIRS

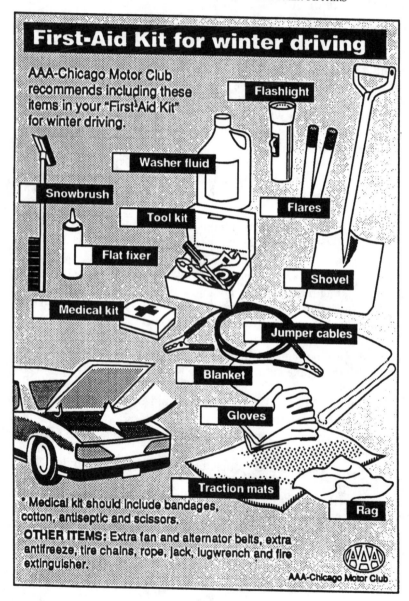

First-Aid Kit for winter driving

AAA-Chicago Motor Club recommends including these items in your "First-Aid Kit" for winter driving.

Flashlight

Washer fluid

Snowbrush

Flares

Tool kit

Flat fixer

Shovel

Medical kit

Jumper cables

Blanket

Gloves

Traction mats

Rag

* Medical kit should include bandages, cotton, antiseptic and scissors.

OTHER ITEMS: Extra fan and alternator belts, extra antifreeze, tire chains, rope, jack, lugwrench and fire extinguisher.

AAA-Chicago Motor Club

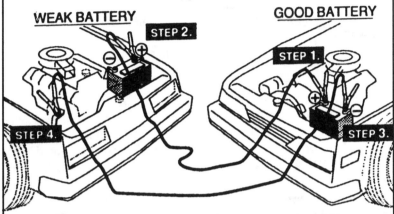

How to jump-start your car safely

The AAA-Chicago Motor Club warns that jump-starting a car with a weak battery can be dangerous if proper procedures are not followed. ■ Before attaching booster cables, make sure both cars are in "park" and not touching each other. ■ Turn off the ignitions and all electrical accessories. ■ If the "dead" battery has water cell caps, remove them and place a damp cloth over the openings.

WEAK BATTERY   STEP 2.   **GOOD BATTERY**   STEP 1.

STEP 4.   STEP 3.

- ■ **STEP 1.** Connect one end of the positive cable to the positive terminal of the good battery.

- ■ **STEP 2.** Attach the other end of the positive cable to the positive terminal of the disabled battery.

- ■ **STEP 3.** Connect one end of the negative cable to the negative terminal of the good battery.

- ■ **STEP 4.** Attach the other end of the negative cable to a good ground, such as a bolt on the engine or other unpainted, metal surface of the disabled car, as far from the battery as possible.

- ■ **START** the healthy car's engine and let it run for several minutes before starting the disabled car. *To remove the cables, reverse the order above.*

AAA-Chicago Motor Club

CAR-RENTAL CHECKLIST

• Before you reserve a car, know what model and options you want or need and how much you are willing to spend. In that way, you are less likely to feel pressured into making a hasty or expensive decision that you may regret later. (Be aware that each car-rental company may have its own vehicle classification system. The terms "compact," "mid-size" and "luxury" sometimes differ among companies.)

• Call several car-rental companies and get price estimates. Many companies have toll-free numbers, and many offer weekly and weekend specials. Watch the newspaper and magazine ads and ask about advertised specials. If your business or vacation plans permit flexibility, you may be able to save money by renting a car when you can get a price break. Be sure to ask about any restrictions on special offers, including "blackout" dates, when an advertised special price is unavailable.

- Determine where you will pick up and drop off the car and if these locations are without special fees.
- If you are considering a rental for more than four days, ask about the weekly rate. The daily rate for rentals of more than four days, but less than seven, is often higher than renting a car at the weekly rate.
- Ask about mandatory additions to the quoted price, such as mileage rates and caps, fuel charges, airport surcharges, and taxes.
- Ask about charges for an optional collision damage waiver (CDW), personal-accident insurance (PAI) and personal-effects coverage (PEC) or personal-effects protection (PEP). Find out if your own auto-insurance policy covers rental cars and the conditions of the coverage.
- Ask about other optional charges, such as additional-driver fees, underage driver fees, out-of-state charges, and equipment-rental fees.—U.S. FEDERAL TRADE COMMISSION

PRE-VACATION CHECKLIST

From Chief Ed Sindles, of the Round Lake Beach (Illinois) Police Department, come the following four tips on how to maximize your peace of mind as you prepare to go on vacation:

- Arrange to have the mail and newspaper held or picked up by a neighbor.
- Put the lights and a radio on a timer.
- Arrange to have a neighbor keep an eye on the house.
- If possible, leave a car in the driveway or have a neighbor park in the driveway.

A DESTINATIONAL SHORTLIST

Here follow the 10 "absolute-must" U.S. travel destinations that every American should see, according to the April 1995 issue of *Glamour* magazine. The destinations are listed alphabetically:

Beverly Hills, California
Charleston, South Carolina
Glacier National Park
The Grand Canyon
Louisiana plantations outside New Orleans

Manhattan
San Francisco
The U.S. Capitol
Walt Disney World
Yellowstone National Park

TOP 10 TRAIN TRIPS

From James Russell, in the January/February 1995 issue of *Eco-Traveler,*
comes the following list of the 10 most scenic train trips in North America:

1. Copper Canyon (Chihuahua to Los Mochis), Mexico
2. Canadian Rockies (Vancouver to Edmonton via Jasper)
3. North Vancouver to Prince George, British Columbia
4. Agawa Canyon (Sault Ste. Marie to Canyon, Ontario)
5. Pacific Coast scenery (Seattle to Los Angeles)
6. San Francisco to Denver
7. Seattle/Portland to Chicago
8. New York to Montreal
9. The Alaska Railroad (any route)
10. New York/Washington to Cincinnati

BEATING THE TRAVEL-PHOTO BLAHS

Most people strike out on vacation with a taste for new foods, new
environments and new experiences, but the spirit of adventure often
flees the moment they pick up their cameras.

Most of us invariably return with travel pictures of family mem-
bers centered in front of changing backdrops—Old Faithful one year,
Cinderella's Castle at Disney World the next, and the Empire State
Building the year after that.

It doesn't take just more equipment to get better shots—that can
help, but the real cure for the snapshot blahs is a fresh point of view.
A few tips from some contemporary experts and a little inspiration
from a couple of past masters can give travel photographs a whole
new look at life.

"The earth looks very good indeed; the forms of nature—once
they are integrated on the magic rectangle of the film—satisfy me
completely," Ansel Adams wrote in a letter to photographer Minor
White in 1947. "A long line of rising land is so much in itself; the hint
of clear air and the organic life of clouds—well, I guess that's for me
from now on." The comments succinctly describe the ethereal landscapes Adams made at his beloved Yosemite National Park and other
wilderness sanctuaries.

Some 60 million people will visit the national parks this year, toting millions of cameras with them. But capturing those organic

411

clouds that Adams wrote of with such rapture—clouds that so enhance a landscape—can mean staying out to photograph when other tourists are running for cover.

"Don't let bad weather dampen your photography," advises Tom Gray, assistant chief of the division of audiovisual arts with the National Park Service. His job takes him around the country shooting motion pictures, videos and stills for the Park Service. "When the weather turns from bad to good or good to bad—that's when the clouds are best. I carry an umbrella to shoot while it's raining," he says.

A camera bag or even a plastic bag is ample protection for a camera in the rain, Gray says. "I ended up getting in the bag with the camera one time. I carry big garbage bags." He suggests shooting in the early morning or late afternoon for the most prized landscape light, a light that casts dramatic shadows as the sun glows low in the sky. In addition, he suggests favoring either earth or sky when photographing dramatic vistas such as those at the Grand Canyon. "Don't cut the picture in half with canyon and sky," he says.

What about shooting wildlife, a trophy picture every amateur photographer likes to bring home from vacations to the national parks?

While photographing a deer from a hiking trail sounds idyllic, practicality actually favors shooting the picture from a car window, Gray notes. "Out in the open, deer won't let you walk any closer than 150 to 200 feet. You need a 300-mm lens on a 35-mm camera to shoot that," he says. "Deer will let you get within 30 to 40 feet in a car. In my car, I got in so close to elk in the Rocky Mountains that I couldn't focus with a 300-mm lens." A tripod between the seats supported his camera.

Trying to lure animals closer with hand-held food is one of the don'ts of wilderness photography, Gray says. "Safety should always be a concern."

Amateur photographers insist on placing their families against the backdrop of the mountains or some other scenic spot, he says. "By the time they move back enough to get the scene, the people are going to be too small to recognize." Instead, says Gray, "Move in close for family shots, placing subjects off center."

The experts advise capturing the larger scene in a panoramic shot without people. Whether the vista is of a national park or Disney World, the trick often is to isolate the subject from the crowds. "That's feasible almost anywhere in the park with a little imagination," says Robbie Pallard, who has taught photo seminars at Disney World and is senior photography librarian for the Magic Kingdom's image bank of two million negatives and slides. "We have a rose garden off Main Street and people don't go there very much. It's perfect for a photograph with an unobstructed view of the castle."

While landscapes are enhanced with the dramatic interplay of sun and shadow, Pallard recommends taking people shots in the shade: "You get a more even tone, and people aren't squinting into the sun." Flash can be used outdoors to fill in shadows, such as those on a face.

Pallard also recommends ISO 400 film for vacations, fast enough to stop the action of even the most restless toddler. Even with fast film, he recommends a tripod for clear nighttime shots of scenics such as fireworks. In a pinch, brace against a trash can or a fence to hold the camera steady, he says.

Photos with the Disney characters are, of course, a must at Disney World, as Donald Duck, Minnie Mouse and their friends wander the park. "One of the most oft-asked questions is, 'Where can I have my photo taken with Mickey Mouse?' We've set up Mickey's Starland, where you can go to photograph in his dressing room," Pallard says. "It was set up in 1989 for Mickey's sixtieth birthday, and it was so popular we kept it."

City scenes, with their dizzying array of signs, traffic, pedestrians and buildings, often have tourists scurrying for the tops of skyscrapers where they can get a more ordered view of the great urban canyons. But the photographer shooting from the observation decks of a town might want to heed Berenice Abbott's comments on her famous skyward view of the Flatiron Building in New York City. "I did this building two ways. One version was from a height, in a building up the street," she notes in the 1982 book *Berenice Abbott: American Photographer*. But she concludes, "There is no doubt in my mind that this building looks better from street level and I was careful in picking the precise location to set my camera." The pedestrian's-eye view is even bolder in her photograph "Canyon, Broadway and Exchange Place," where the skyscrapers utterly enfold the viewer.

How-to photography books offer a wealth of travel tips, everything from what gear to take to what settings to shoot at. But art books, such as the one of Abbott's work, can inspire a world of picture-taking ideas for the photographer who already has the basics down pat.

Tourists should check on special restrictions that may apply to indoor photography in places such as museums. Many art museums prohibit the use of flash, for instance, because curators consider the constant additional light harmful to their collections. "One flash doesn't deteriorate a painting, but if our four million visitors a year use flash, the paintings would fade before our eyes," says Matthew Austin, spokesman for the Metropolitan Museum of Art in New York City.

A tripod again becomes an almost essential accessory under such circumstances, and the Met is among the museums that require a tripod pass.

Most vacationers can get by with a single camera bag even with a tripod, considering the highly portable and lightweight models available. That's a far cry from the wagonload of equipment needed by early expedition photographers who pioneered the art of travel photography.

William Henry Jackson, photographing the Western wilderness for the U.S. government in the 1870s, hauled his gear on pack animals, including the tent he used for a makeshift darkroom. He had glass-plate negatives instead of film, and these had to be coated with emulsion, loaded into a cumbersome view camera, and used while still wet. In Jackson's hands, however, the technique resulted in some of the most breathtaking landscapes ever made.

Englishman Francis Frith, traveling to Egypt and the Holy Land in the 1850s, photographed both the ancient ruins and the village life surrounding them. Popular rumor among the Egyptians was that his canvas-covered wagon darkroom really housed a harem.

While few tourists toting cameras can spark such interest today, they can take a few measures to ensure respectable vacation snapshots:

• Develop photographs on location, when possible. Considering the prevalence of overnight and same-day photo finishing, it's easy to determine results on the spot and reshoot if necessary.

• Have camera bags handchecked at airports. One run through an X-ray machine probably won't fog film, but the effects of radiation are cumulative and will take their toll after a few trips through airports.

• On car trips, keep the camera bag in the trunk or on the floor. Temperatures on a sunny back window of a car can rise much higher than those recommended for film storage.

• Have the camera loaded, open and ready to use. A special sunset or encounter with a deer may not last long enough for you to load film and fuss with equipment.

• For a classic look, shoot a roll of black-and-white film.

—ABIGAIL FOERSTNER

WHEELCHAIR TRAVELERS WELCOME HERE

Herewith, a checklist of top U.S. attractions described in Fodor's *Great American Vacations for Travelers with Disabilities* as being "entirely accessible" to wheelchair travelers:

1. U.S. Capitol, Washington, DC
2. World Showcase (except Norway), Epcot Center, Walt Disney World
3. Sea World, San Diego

4. Caesars Palace, Las Vegas
5. Universal Studios, Hollywood
6. Radio City Music Hall, New York City
7. Viewmobile sightseeing trains, Niagara Falls
8. Pike Place Market, Seattle
9. Faneuil Hall, Boston
10. Trail to Yosemite Falls, California

NINE WAYS TO MAKE YOUR MOVE

Moving is never easy. It always costs more and takes longer than you thought it would.

Having said that, here are nine tried-and-true things you can do to keep the ansgt to a minimum and the karma-flow to the max:

1. Well before your move, begin giving away, selling or recycling as much as you can stand to part with. We all have way too much stuff, anyway. As someone surely must once have said, another sign of riches—besides the well-known yardsticks of goodies and gold—is how much of such stuff you can do without. Having things also means having to keep them up and sometimes store them. Of course, you need X number of things for the business of living, and Y number for pleasure—it's up to you where to draw the line.

2. Weigh all options before deciding to move-it-yourself. If your normal schedule is a very busy one, and if you have a great many things to move, it may be a false economy to try to do it on your own or with a couple of friends. You have weigh the value of the time and energy involved against the possible dollars saved. You just may find the best bargain is buying someone *else's* time and energy—to say nothing of the cost and trouble of arranging for and operating the vehicle or vehicles used.

3. **If you opt to hire a moving company, shop around for one with a good reputation for skill and dependability.** Ask family, friends and neighbors about movers they've used and how they compare.

4. **If you *do* hire a moving company, minimize the cost by doing as much of the packing as possible.** This will also help keep breakage to a minimum—thanks to the extra measure of care and concern you bring to the task. When you begin packing, be sure you have sufficient quantities of proper packing materials on hand, including cartons, rope, twine, tape, and so on. If you're packing stuff you intend to move yourself, be careful not to put too many heavy things—such as books—in big cartoons; they be hard to lift and otherwise handle, and could increase the chances of an accident.

5. **Another way to minimize the cost of hiring a mover:** Book time in the middle of the week, during the middle part of the month—since that's the lowest demand time, and therefore usually booked at reduced rates. You may not have control over the time of year of your move, but if you do, avoid the summer, which is the busiest season for the moving business.

6. **If you're doing your move yourself, remember to lift objects with the legs, so to speak, keeping your back straight.** It's often better to make an extra trip, than to try to load yourself down with more than you should be trying to carry. Obviously, this will be a judgment call only you can make on an item-by-item basis.

7. **Whether you hire someone or decide—despite our above cautionary noises—to move it yourself, one of the most important keys to a smooth and successful move is to start working on it *well in advance* of the actual day when the vehicle or vehicles are present for loading.** If you're hiring, you should get on your mover's schedule at least a month and a half in advance. And whether your hiring or moving it yourself, that's also a good time to get the whole process started—sorting, winnowing, packing, address changing, and so on. Once you've begun, you'll be amazed at how quickly the time flies, how much more there is to do from how you remembered it *last* time you moved!

8. **After a move made by a moving company, if any items were lost or damaged, file your claim with the company as soon as possible, providing as much documentation as you can.** You

should always have a comprehensive inventory of at least the more valuable items moved. It would also help greatly to have, say, photographs of those items—showing how they looked *before* the movers moved them.

9. To make future moves a little easier and less prone to mishap, keep the original cartons and molded filler materials for electronic equipment.

NOTES FOR AND FROM ABROAD

Here are the top 10 "draws" among world nations—the countries that earn the most from foreign tourists, according to figures released in 1994 by the World Tourism Organization. (The figures are in billions, and reflect the previous year's activity.)

1. U.S.	$56.4
2. France	$23.5
3. Spain	$20.9
4. Italy	$19.5
5. Austria	$15.1
6. United Kingdom	$12.2
7. Germany	$10.6
8. Hong Kong	$7.7
9. Switzerland	$7.7
10. Mexico	$6.1

The top five U.S. destinations for foreign visitors, according to TV's *Weekend Travel Update* show:

1. New York
2. Los Angeles
3. Miami
4. Orlando
5. San Francisco

The top 10 "fantasy island vacations for families," as recently recommended by *Child* magazine:

1. U.S. Virgin Islands
2. Hawaii
3. Barbados
4. Aruba
5. St. Martin/St. Maarten
6. Anguilla
7. Jamaica
8. Nevis
9. Puerto Rico
10. The Bahamas

SOME TIPS FROM THE U.S. STATE DEPARTMENT FOR BEFORE AND DURING A FOREIGN VACATION:

General

• Learn about the places you plan to visit, and the languages you will be dealing with. Try to study and practice at least the basics of the languages as much in advance of your departure as possible. The more time and energy you invest upfront, the more enjoyable and meaningful your trip will be.

• Familiarize yourself with local laws and customs, keeping in mind that U.S. citizenship cannot protect you if you breaks the laws of the country you are visiting. (Consult your library, a travel agent, or tourist bureaus of the countries on your itinerary. Also keep track of what is being reported in the media about any recent developments.

• Don't take anything you would hate to lose. Leave behind all unnecessary credit cards, expensive jewelry or irreplaceable family objects. Even if they're not lost or stolen, the extra mental energy devoted to worrying about them and safeguarding them can only detract from the overall experience.

• Put your name and address *inside* (as well as outside) each piece of luggage and lock it.

• Leave a copy of your itinerary with family or friends at home so they'll be able to contact you in case of an emergency.

• Take photographs of your airline ticket, passport ID page, driver's license and the credit cards you take with you. Leave one set at home and keep another with you in a separate place from these valuables. Leave a copy of the serial numbers of your travelers checks at home, take another with you separate from the checks themselves and, as you cash in the checks, keep a tally of which ones remain unredeemed.

Medical

• Keep medicines in original containers. Ask your druggist for the generic name of any prescribed drug in case you need to refill your prescription. Brand names differ in other countries.

• If you're allergic to certain medications, insect or snakebites, wear a medical-alert bracelet and carry a similar warning in your wallet.

• If you wear eyeglasses or contact lenses, bring an extra pair along with your lens prescription and ample supplies of lens solution and cleaner.

• Carry a summary of your medical records. Be sure to include past illnesses and blood type.

• Make sure your medical insurance coverage provides adequate coverage for you and your family when traveling abroad.

• An increasing number of countries are establishing entry regulations for AIDS, particularly for students and other long-term residents. Check with the embassy or consulate of the individual country to see if this applies to you.

Once you've reached your destination, if you have problems or concerns, visit the American Embassy to register. Let them know where you are staying, the areas you plan to visit, and when you will be returning to the U.S.

If you plan to drive a car while in a foreign country, check with the AAA (Automobile Association of America) to see whether or not you need an international driver's license and to find out where you can purchase supplemental insurance coverage, as needed. You might also want to consider hiring a driver rather than driving yourself, since in many countries the driver is detained in an accident until settlement is made.

Four truly foreign driving rules:

> Bulgaria—must have a fire extinguisher in car
> Ireland—children under 12 may ride in backseat only
> Italy—fines up to $500 must be paid immediately
> Finland—headlights must be on day and night

DON'T **dial 911 to get the police in these foreign cities:**

> Athens—dial 100
> Copenhagen—dial 000
> London—dial 999
> Paris—dial 17
> Stockholm—dial 90000

SIZING UP YOUR FOREIGN SHOPPING TRIP

If you're shopping in foreign lands for clothing or shoes, here's a handy table of approximate equivalents that will help you find the right size. But note: even with the guide, it's still a good idea to try the item on, since metric sizes—like U.S./British sizes—vary slightly from one manufacturer to another. Also, women shopping in Great Britain should keep in mind that shoe sizes run a couple of digits lower than in the U.S., while dress sizes run a couple of digits higher. Remember, too, that clothing may be cut differently abroad due to local styles or national body types. For instance, American women looking for small sizes in Germany reportedly have a hard time of it—one such traveler wound up shopping in children's departments!

Men

Suits	U.S./British	34	36	38	40	42	44	46	48		
	Metric	44	46	48	50	52	54	56	58		
Shirts	U.S./British	14	14 1/2	15	15 1/2	16	16 1/2	17	17 1/2		
	Metric	36	37	38	39	40	41	42	43		
Shoes	U.S./British	7	7 1/2	8	8 1/2	9	9 1/2	10	10 1/2	11	11 1/2
	Metric	39	40	41	42	43	43	44	44	45	45

Women

Suits/Coats, Dresses	U.S./British	8	10	12	14	16	18	20	
	Metric	36	38	40	42	44	46	48	
Blouses, Sweaters	U.S./British	32	34	36	38	49	42	44	
	Metric	40	42	44	46	48	50	52	
Shoes	U.S./British	5	5 1/2	6	6 1/2	7	7 1/2	8	8 1/2	9
	Metric	35	35	36	37	38	38	39	39	40

WORLD'S 15 BUSIEST AIRPORTS

	Airport	Total Passengers*	92/93 %Chg.
1.	Chicago-O'Hare, U.S.	85,077,508	+1.0
2.	Dallas/Ft. Worth Airport, U.S.	49,970,180	-3.6
3.	London-Heathrow, Great Britain	47,898,526	+5.9
4.	Los Angeles-International, U.S.	47,844,794	+1.9
5.	Atlanta, U.S.	47,088,487	+12.0
6.	Tokyo-Haneda, Japan	41,562,084	-2.6
7.	San Francisco, U.S.	32,736,672	+0.4
8.	Denver, U.S.	32,622,587	+5.7
9.	Frankfurt, Germany	32,536,457	+5.8
10.	Miami, U.S.	28,660,396	+8.2
11.	New York-JFK International, U.S.	26,789,801	-3.5
12.	Paris-Charles De Gaulle, France	26,114,620	+3.6
13.	Newark, U.S.	25,612,575	+5.5
14.	Paris-Orly, France	25,368,248	+0.8
15.	Hong Kong	25,155,915	+11.0

*Figures, from the Airport Operators Council International, are for 1993 and represent passenger arrivals, departures and transfers.

THE ARGONNE ANTI-JET-LAG DIET

The Argonne Anti-Jet-Lag Diet is helping travelers quickly adjust their bodies' internal clocks to new time zones. It is also being used to speed the adjustment of shiftworkers, such as power plant operators, to periodically rotating work hours. The diet was developed by Dr. Charles F. Ehret of Argonne's Division of Biological and Medical Research as an application of his fundamental studies of the daily biological rhythms of animals. Argonne National Laboratory is one of the U.S. Department of Energy's major centers of research in energy and the fundamental sciences.

How to avoid jet lag:

1. DETERMINE BREAKFAST TIME at destination on day of arrival.

2. FEAST-FAST-FEAST-FAST on home time. Start three days before departure day. On day one, FEAST; eat heartily with high-protein breakfast and lunch and a high-carbohydrate dinner. No coffee except between 3 and 5 P.M. On day two, FAST on light meals of salads, light soups, fruits and juices. Again, no coffee except between 3 and 5 P.M. On day three, FEAST again. On day four, departure day, FAST; if you drink caffeinated beverages, take them in morning when traveling west, or between 6 and 11 P.M. when traveling east. Going west, you may fast only half day.

3. BREAK FINAL FAST at destination breakfast time. No alcohol on plane. If flight is long enough, sleep until normal breakfast time at destination, *but no later.* Wake up and FEAST on high-protein breakfast. Stay awake, active. Continue day's meals according to meal times at destination.

FEAST on high-protein breakfasts and lunches to stimulate the body's active cycle. Suitable meals include steak, eggs, hamburgers, high-protein cereals, green beans.

FEAST on high-carbohydrate suppers to stimulate sleep. They include spaghetti and other pastas (but no meatballs), crepes (but no meat filling), potatoes, other starchy vegetables, and sweet desserts.

FAST days help deplete the liver's store of carbohydrates and prepare the body's clock for resetting. Suitable foods include fruit, light soups, broths, skimpy salads, unbuttered toast, half pieces of bread. Keep calories and carbohydrates to a minimum.

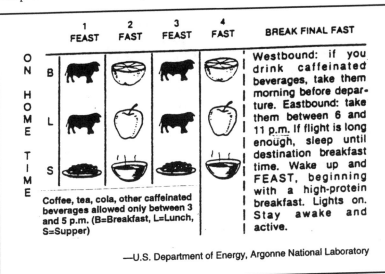

—U.S. Department of Energy, Argonne National Laboratory

AIR-TRAVEL PROBLEMS—AND HOW TO SOLVE THEM

Americans spend billions each year traveling in the United States and abroad. Good planning is a factor in making vacation travel a delight, whether you choose to be your own travel agent or use the services of a professional.

If you use the services of a travel agent, you are buying a service, and the choice of that travel agent should begin with references. It's a good idea to have friends and business associates tell you of the competence or incompetence, good judgment or ineptitude of people who have helped to plan their vacation. Then check their recommendation with the Better Business Bureau.

These are the services travel agencies offer:

• Arrangements, including reservations for air, sea, bus and rail travel, cruises, car rentals and car purchases abroad.

• Preparation of individual itineraries and arrangements for package tours and for personally escorted tours or group tours, within the U.S. and abroad.

• Information on travel and luggage insurance, visas, passports, inoculations, traveler's checks, currency exchange, weather, a practical wardrobe, etc.

To provide efficient assistance, the travel agent will need to have a good idea of your travel budget and your special interests.

Travel agents are compensated from commissions earned from carriers, tour operators, and hotels. Their services are provided at no charge to their customers. However, you may have to pay for any special or unusual services you request.

When you use a travel agent, you have every right to assume:

• That the tour and its accommodations will be exactly as they were represented—the oceanfront hotel will be on the beach instead of a mile away, and a first-class reservation gets you a first-class compartment on the train.

Consider the line that appears (in small print) in many tour brochures: "We reserve the right to change accommodations without prior notice." No one would mind changing accommodations if the facilities are at least equal to those originally contracted for. But what happens if your luxury hotel has no room for you? If you find yourself in a fourth-rate hotel, do you get a pro-rata refund? From whom? And under what circumstances?

• That the charges you pay will match the charges you expected. Unexpected charges can wreck your carefully planned budget.

• That your charter flight will actually get off the ground at the promised time of departure (barring, of course, impossible flying weather, mechanical difficulties or airport strikes).

Surety and Escrow

It is important that you know what these two words mean in relation to air charters.

- **Surety bonds** are required to guarantee that the charter is run and the contractors are paid.

- **Escrow accounts** are deposit accounts in a bank maintained by the charter operator that protect passenger funds until the charter is completed. Before you make your decision to sign up for a charter, find out if there is a surety bond or escrow account established, and to whom payment is made. If you have to sign a contract, make sure it specifies that you pay directly to the escrow account at the bank, and not to the organizer. Also be sure you know the names of both the insurance company that is providing the surety bond and the bank in which the escrow account is maintained.

Air Charters

In the past, travelers who wanted to take advantage of lower prices for air charter tours were faced with an alphabet soup of different charter plans. That has changed. Now among the charters available are:

- Advance booking charters (ABC) offer a fixed price and a fixed date for a round-trip or one-way charter flight. These are not recurring regularly scheduled flights; therefore, signup is usually recommended at least 60 days in advance. There is a discount if you book early.

- Travel group charters (TGC) operate similarly to advance booking charters except that in an ABC the organizer takes a risk in meeting cost; on a travel group charter, the organizer earns a set fee. Vacant seats on the plane may increase the price for each passenger.

- Affinity or pro-rated charters are designed to serve the needs of organized groups whose members have a prior "affinity" or association. If the flight does not sell out, those who do not participate in the flight may absorb the cost of the empty seats.

Your Rights as an Air Traveler

- If an airline overbooks your flight and has to "bump" passengers with confirmed reservations, it is required by the Department of Transportation (DOT) regulations to ask for volunteers to give up their seats. If you volunteer, the airline must offer to pay you for your cooperation. How much they offer is up to them. Each carrier has its own compensation policy.

If there are too few volunteers and you are involuntarily bumped, the airline must give you immediately "denied boarding compensation" of up to $400, depending on the price of your one-way ticket. If the airline can get you alternate transportation that arrives at your destination within two hours of your originally scheduled arrival time (four hours on international flights), they still have to pay you—but half the above rate; this compensation is in addition to the passenger's ticket, which can be used on another flight or refunded. If the airline arranges alternate transportation that arrives at your destination within one hour of your originally scheduled arrival time, no compensation is required. Nor is compensation due if you are bumped as the result of the need to change to a smaller plane, or if you are offered a seat on your original flight but in a different section than specified on your ticket. Also you get no compensation if you have failed to comply with ticketing, check-in or reconfirmation procedures.

• If your flight is canceled, an airline will nearly always put you on its own next available flight, and sometimes on the competition, although—contrary to widespread belief—they are not obligated to do either. (According to DOT representative Timothy J. Kelly, the feeling that an airline is so obligated is a "fallacy . . . constantly recycled by the news media. . . . There are no federal rules on the subject, and there never have been.")

The office that handles airline transportation problems is the Aviation Consumer Protection Division, U.S. Department of Transportation, C-75, Washington, DC 20590, (202) 366-2220.

If your hotel turns out to be 25 miles away from the music festival, the ski slopes or the beach...if the quality of the accommodations doesn't measure up to your expectations, bring it to the attention of the travel agent immediately. If you are not satisfied with the response, get in touch with the nearest Better Business Bureau. If the travel agency is a member of the American Society of Travel Agents (ASTA), you can also register your complaint with them. Their address is: ASTA, 1101 King St., Alexandria, VA 22314.

—Better Business Bureau

424

TRAVEL LOG

Ancient footpaths were the beginnings of the first roads, as primitive people explored their surroundings. As the scope of human activities grew, paths and roads became wider and more numerous. The first modern-type roads were built about 2,000 B.C.—the stone-paved processional boulevards of the cities of Mesopotamia. The first permanent road system was constructed by the Chinese about 1,000 B.C.

Although the Assyrians pioneered large-scale, state-backed road building, their efforts were later dwarfed by those of the Romans during the years of their far-flung empire. Using such materials as dirt, pebbles, mortar, and stone slabs, the Romans built a vast and surprisingly durable network of roads in Europe and the Middle East.

The first road vehicles—in use by the Sumerians by about 3,000 B.C.—were two-wheeled carts, with wheels crudely fashioned from stone. They were the forerunners of the chariot, which was developed by the Egyptians and Greeks, among others.

The origins of water travel and transport remain largely uncharted. Reed boats were developed in Mesopotamia and Egypt, as were dugout canoes in northwestern Europe, about 8,000 to 7,000 B.C. Large cargo boats were being used by Egyptians about 3,000 B.C.

Arabs invented a sailing rig to allow a boat to sail across the wind's direction as well as with it, A.D. 200 to 300. By 1090 the Chinese were using the magnetic compass for navigation, and by 1300 Chinese ships had watertight bulkheads.

The famous—and fearsome—Viking longship was developed about A.D. 800. Viking explorers reached North America (or "Vinland") some 200 years later.

The three-masted ship, which made possible great voyages of discovery, was developed in western Europe about 1400 to 1500.

Although a submarine in the form of a submersible, leather-covered rowboat had been built in Holland in 1620, it was not until 1863 that France developed the first engine-powered sub, the aptly named *Plongeur* ("Diver").

The first railroads were built for use in European mines of the 15th century; the rails were of wood and the trucks they guided were hand-propelled. Wooden rails were iron-plated by the 1690s, and in 1789 the first all-iron rails were laid in Leicestershire, England. The first steam locomotive was built in 1803 by English engineer Richard Trevithick.

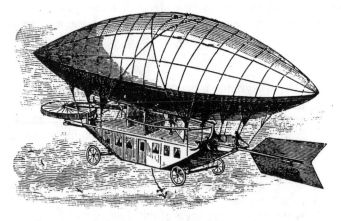

Of all the roads one may travel, none is as akin to the cosmos as the seemingly infinite road of flight. After eons of dreaming of what soaring through air might be like, humans in the late 18th century reached that point in the science of flight where the sophistication of the tools finally began to match the difficulties of the problem. Interest in the development of hot-air ballooning was especially intense in 1783, when several Europeans, including the Montgolfier brothers of France, achieved manned and unmanned ascent. Ballooning would continue to improve, achieving a secure niche for itself in the field of aviation, but the main focus was soon to shift to the development of a heavier-than-air flying machine.

The world's first self-propelled road vehicle was invented in 1789 by French engineer Nicolas Joseph Cugnot. It was a huge, three-wheeled, steam-powered carriage with an average speed of about 3 mph. The world's first motor-vehicle accident reportedly occurred the following year, when an even larger version of Cugnot's machine overturned on a Paris street.

The original one-way street was created in 1791 in New York, near the John Street Theater, to clear up horse-drawn traffic congestion.

English engineer George Stephenson (1781-1848) was a giant among railroad pioneers. He built his first locomotive in 1814, and in 1829 (with the help of his son Robert) he built the classic, state-of-the-art-in-its-day *Rocket*, pictured on next page. The *Rocket*, which saw service on the Liverpool-Manchester Railway, was Stephenson's winning entry in a locomotive-design competition, and therefore had a profound influence on future locomotive developments.

On August 9, 1831, the nation's first steam locomotive made a run between the New York cities of Albany and Schenectady, as rail transport began to boom. By 1840, railroad mileage surpassed that of the canals. By the end of the Civil War, steel had replaced iron as the main construction ingredient, and the first Pullman sleeping car had been introduced.

In 1866 the *New York Times* reported there were about 100,000 Americans living or traveling in Europe, the most popular destination being Paris, followed by German cities.

Credit for building (in 1885) the first vehicle with an internal-combustion, gasoline engine is usually given to German engineer Karl Benz. His countryman Gottlieb Daimler also developed such an engine about the same time.

The bicycle went through various transformations during the 19th century, as improvement followed improvement. In the 1880s and 1890s cycling achieved great popularity in the U.S. and Europe.

Pre-1900 railroad landmarks include the demonstration of the first electric railway, in Berlin (1879); the invention of the diesel engine in Germany by Rudolf Diesel (1892); and the opening of the world's first subway system, between Paddington and London (1863). (The first U.S. subway opened in Boston in 1898.)

On January 25, 1890, *New York World* reporter Nellie Bly completed a trip around the world in 72 days, 6 hours and 11 minutes, thereby beating the fictional 80-day trip of Jules Verne's Phineas Fogg.

On April 25, 1901, New York became the first state to require automobile license plates. The plates for the 954 cars then registered in the state carried their owners' initials.

The American Automobile Association was founded in 1902 primarily to combat the widespread distrust of and antipathy toward motorized vehicles. The group continues to roll along, offering a broad range of information and assistance to the motorist.

On December 17, 1903, at Kitty Hawk, North Carolina, the Wright brothers, Wilbur and Orville, made the world's first successful flights in a man-carrying aircraft powered by a motor. The fourth and final flight, made by Wilbur, lasted 59 seconds and covered 852 feet. (The other three: Orville, 120 feet; Wilbur, 195 feet; Orville, 200 feet.)

Henry Ford introduced the first mass-produced automobile in 1908, the Model T, or "Tin Lizzie." During the years of its availability (1908-27), 15 million Model T's were sold—half of all automobiles sold in the U.S.

Intercity buses, first manufactured in 1921, were called "greyhounds" because they were painted gray. A bus line based in Muskegon, Michigan, adopted the nickname for its vehicles and eventually became the Greyhound Bus Company.

After 1920 the railroad industry entered a long period of decline, the result of increased competition from airplanes and other carriers. By 1951, total U.S. rail mileage was less than that of 1906. Hard times gave rise to a series of belt-tightening mergers; technological improvements kept freight service profitable, but passenger service continued to shrink.

On June 3, 1935, the French oceangoing liner *Normandie* broke the transatlantic speed record on its maiden voyage with a mark of 4 days, 3 hours and 5 minutes.

Aviation research and development, spurred by World War I, made great strides in the first half of the 20th century, as regular airmail and passenger service was introduced, then gradually expanded. Highlights of this adventuresome era include Charles Lindbergh's historic solo flight across the Atlantic (in 1927), the briefly popular transatlantic zeppelin passenger service of the early thirties, and the development of jet propulsion in the late forties. In 1952 the British Overseas Airways Corporation opened the world's first regular jet passenger service (London-Johannesburg).

Post-1960 railroad landmarks include the beginning of bullet-train service at speeds averaging 125 mph in Japan between Tokyo and Osaka (1964) and the setting of the new world speed record by French passenger trains, averaging 132 mph between Lyons and Paris, with a top speed of 170 (1983).

On April 22, 1969, Englishman Robin Knox-Johnston completed the first nonstop voyage around the world, in his ketch (a type of sailboat) in 312 days. On July 19 of the same year another Briton, John Fairfax, arrived at Fort Lauderdale, Florida, after rowing across the Atlantic alone, the first person to do so.

In 1970, the federal government established the National Railroad Passenger Corporation, or Amtrak, a quasi-public agency charged with consolidating and improving intercity passenger service—an increasingly unprofitable area for railroads that had been concentrating instead on freight service as a means of economic survival.

In 1976 the Anglo-French *Concorde* was put into service, carrying up

429

to 100 passengers at speeds of over 1,000 mph and crossing the Atlantic in less than three hours.

ROBERT MERZ

RX FOR LOSTNESS

Should you ever get lost on a sunny day—and should you happen to have a good, old-fashioned, nondigital watch—there is a way to find your way.

What you do is hold the watch level and turn it so that the hour hand is pointing to the sun. South will then be halfway between the hour hand and the 12 on the watch face. And, of course, once you have one direction, you have them all.

NOW IS THE TIME

. . . the microseconds they are a-changin' . . .

Time goes, you say? Ah no!
Alas, Time stays, we go.
　　—AUSTIN DOBSON

Time is the least thing we have of.
　　—ERNEST HEMINGWAY

NOT A MOMENT TOO SOON

Time—that toweringly eternal tick-tock we can ponder and gauge but never quite capture with word-bound definitions—is, always was, and most likely always will be one of the ultimate mysteries of existence. A mystery with which scientists, artists and philosophers have long grappled, their works and findings usually generating more questions than answers.

What is time anyway?

Is it nothing more than an idea, an intangible fiction which helps us order and measure our lives? Or is there something mystical and magical about Time, something that shall ever elude the wheels and dials and electronic pulses we employ to convince us that we are more its masters than its slaves? And what about such bogglesome

431

notions as time warps and relativity?

Unfortunately, neither time nor space permit here the kind of discussion so gigantic a subject deserves. But for those wishing to launch their own pursuit of the truths of time, consider, for starters, the paradox of the present—namely, is it *always* the present, or is it *never* the present?

Is time, in other words, always here waiting, or does it wait for no one?

One school of thought says it is *always* the present because the past is gone forever and the future is not yet here.

Another school of thought holds that it is *never* the present because the future is constantly becoming the past and no part of the present can be pointed to and called "the present," inasmuch as it will always, by that time, have passed.

Something to think about. If you have time . . .

For now, let us concentrate on practicalities, and consider how this vast and enigmatic subject may be measured.

The two natural cycles on which time measurements are based are the day and the year—the time it takes Earth to turn once upon its axis (23 hours, 37 minutes and 4 seconds), and the time required for it to go completely around the sun (365 days and about six hours).

Generally speaking, in the Northern Hemisphere, the seasons from spring to winter begin three weeks into March, June, September and December, respectively, though the exact date may vary from the 20th to the 23rd. The seasons are caused by the tilt of the earth with respect to its yearly journey around the sun, with different parts receiving different amounts of sunlight at different times.

Between late March and late September, earth's Northern Hemisphere is titled toward the sun, giving us spring and summer; the rest of the year, the northern hemisphere is titled away from the sun, giving us autumn and winter. Twice a year days and nights are equal in length—the vernal (spring) and autumnal equinoxes. The summer solstice, marking the beginning of that season, has the longest period of sunlight and the winter solstice, marking that season's beginning, has the shortest.

HOW OUR CALENDAR EVOLVED

The earliest Roman calendar (eighth century B.C.) was divided into ten months, starting in March and ending in December—which explains why September, October, November and December now seem so oddly named, inasmuch as they're derived from the Latin words for seven, eight, nine and ten. (July and August were originally called Quintilis and Sextilis, denoting the fifth and sixth months; their present names derive from Julius and Augustus Caesar.)

The Etruscan king Numa Pompilius (715-673 B.C.) instituted a lunar calendar of 12 months by adding January and February, but the calendar was set aside at Rome after the expulsion of the kings about 510 B.C., then readopted in 153 B.C. At the same time the beginning of the Roman civil year was changed to January 1, which became the day that newly elected consuls took office.

By the time of Julius Caesar the reformed lunar calendar had shifted eight weeks out of phase with the seasons—and so, in 46 B.C., known ever since as the "Year of Confusion," Caesar added 67 days to set it right again. And to keep the calendar accurate he instituted the practice of adding a day to February every four years.—Leap Year Day. That reform, suggested by the Roman astronomer Sosigenes, became part of what is known as the Julian Calendar and remained in use for centuries.

Unfortunately, Sosigenes did a tad too much rounding off, estimating the year at 365.25 days, while it really is 365.2422—which adds up to about 11 minutes too many every year. Although Caesar and his astronomer were long gone before anyone noticed it, some 1,500 years later, the excess time had grown to a sizable—and bothersome—10 days.

That gave rise to our present-day calendar, instituted in 1582 by Pope Gregory, who simply deleted the extra days—a change that took a while to be accepted in non-Catholic countries. Indeed, England and her colonies didn't join in until 1752, by which time the error had grown to 11 days.

Besides dropping the added days, Pope Gregory ruled that not every fourth year would be a leap year. In the Gregorian Calendar, centennial years are leap years only if they can be divided evenly by 400. Therefore, the year 2000 will be one of those rare leap years. (The last was 1600; the next will be 2400.)

Note: Every year has at least one Friday the 13th, but never more than three.

WHY 24, 60?

How come, one might ask, there are 24 hours in a day and 60 minutes in an hour?

According to Dr. J. T. Fraiser, founder of the International Society for the Study of Time, the credit or blame for our current divisions of time goes to the Sumerians of the fourth millennium B.C., who used a mathematical system based on groups of 60, as ours is based on groups of 10. (Sixty has the advantage of being divisible into 2, 3, 4, 5, 6, 12 and 20 equal parts. It also goes 6 times into 360, which was then believed to have been the number of days in a year.)

The Sumerians divided night and day into 12 equal hours each, but the length of the two parts varied with the seasons, as the number of daylight hours and minutes changed. The Chinese divided the astronomical day into 12 equal hours as well. But except for astronomical purposes, equal hours were useless because people lived by the sun. In the West, the eventual division of the day into 24 equal hours did not become useful until the invention of mechanical clocks.

DAYLIGHT SAVING TIME

Daylight saving time, achieved by advancing clocks one hour, is both a private and public boon, increasing one's sunlit hours and trimming utility bills, while helping to conserve natural resources..

In enacting the Uniform Time Act of 1966 (amended 1972), Congress made the observance of daylight ("advanced") time automatic throughout the country for the six-month period from the last Sunday in April to the last Sunday in October. That law, however, allows a state which falls in more than one time zone to exempt itself as a whole, or only that part in the most easterly zone, from the observance of daylight time. In 1977, in addition to the territories, only Arizona, Hawaii and the eastern time zone of Indiana did not observe daylight saving time from April 27 to October 26.

Faced with the energy crisis in 1974, the U.S. government required the use of daylight saving time throughout the year and, as amended later in 1974, it was temporarily observed from January 6 to October 27, 1974, and from February 23 to October 26, 1975.

Time-zone boundaries in the U.S. have been defined—and from time to time relocated—since 1918 by the Interstate Commerce Commission (ICC) and, beginning in 1967, by the Department of Transportation (DOT). Prior to 1966, however, a number of communities in the vicinity of the defined boundaries chose not to recognize them. When the Uniform Time Act became effective in 1967, those communities were confronted with a problem. With its automatic daylight feature, the 1966 act required a far greater degree of nationwide recognition of the boundaries defined by DOT The result has been active urging by state and local governments, as well as hundreds of requests from private citizens, for the relocation of time-zone boundaries.

In 1986, President Reagan signed legislation moving up the start of daylight saving time to the first Sunday in April. DOT has estimated that the earlier starting date helped save more than $28 million in traffic-accident costs, while preventing more than 20 deaths and 1,500 injuries. The new law, opposed by some farm-state lawmakers, took effect in 1987

Note: For the correct way to reset your clock at the two times a year you need to, remember this motto: "Spring ahead, fall behind."

TAKING A FLYING LEAP

On July 1, 1983, clocks around the world were set back one second at midnight Greenwich Mean Time. It was the 11th such "leap second" to be added to the calendar since 1972. The adjustments are made to keep clock time in harmony with astronomical time.

TIME DIFFERENCES OF U.S. CITIES

When it is noon, eastern standard time, here is the time in the following U.S. cities:

City	Time	City	Time
Atlanta, GA	noon	Lincoln, NE	11 a.m.
Baltimore, MD	noon	Los Angeles, CA	9 a.m.
Boston, MA	noon	Miami, FL	noon
Chicago, IL	11 a.m.	Milwaukee, WI	11 a.m.
Cleveland, OH	noon	Minneapolis, MN	11 a.m.
Dallas, TX	11 a.m.	Mobile, AL	11 a.m.
Denver, CO	10 a.m.	New York, NY	noon
Des Moines, IA	11 a.m.	Philadelphia, PA	noon
Detroit, MI	noon	Phoenix, AZ	10 a.m.
Fairbanks, AK	7 a.m.	Pittsburgh, PA	noon
Fort Worth, TX	11 a.m.	Portland, OR	9 a.m.
Hartford, CT	noon	Richmond, VA	noon
Honolulu, HI	7 a.m.	St. Louis, MO	11 a.m.
Houston, TX	11 a.m.	San Francisco, CA	9 a.m.
Indianapolis, IN	noon	Washington, DC	noon
Kansas City, MO	11 a.m.	Wichita, KS	11 a.m.
Las Vegas, NV	11 a.m.	Wilmington, DE	noon

Note: Since a few cities—such as Honolulu, Phoenix and Indianapolis—do not observe daylight time, an adjustment has to be made to determine correct relationships to other cities that *are* on daylight time.

TIME DIFFERENCES OF WORLD CITIES

When it is noon, Eastern Standard Time, here is the time in the following cities:

CITY	TIME	CITY	TIME
Aberdeen, Scotland	5:00 p.m.	Buenos Aires, Argentina	2:00 p.m.
Amsterdam, Netherlands	6:00 p.m.	Cairo, Egypt	7:00 p.m.
Athens, Greece	7:00 p.m.	Calcutta, India	10:30 p.m.#
Bangkok, Thailand	midnight*	Cape Town, South Africa	7:00 p.m.
Barcelona, Spain	6:00 p.m.	Caracas, Venezuela	1:00 p.m.
Belfast, Northern Ireland	5:00 p.m.	Chihuahua, Mexico	11:00 a.m.
Berlin, Germany	6:00 p.m.	Copenhagen, Denmark	6:00 p.m.
Birmingham, England	5:00 p.m.	Dublin, Ireland	5:00 p.m.
Bogotá, Colombia	noon	Edinburgh, Scotland	5:00 p.m.
Bombay, India	10:30 p.m.#	Frankfurt, Germany	6:00 p.m.
Bordeaux, France	6:00 p.m.	Glasgow, Scotland	5:00 p.m.
Brussels, Belgium	6:00 p.m.	Hamburg, Germany	6:00 p.m.
Budapest, Hungary	6:00 p.m.	Havana, Cuba	noon

Helsinki, Finland	7:00 p.m.	Nairobi, Kenya	8:00 p.m.
Istanbul, Turkey	7:00 p.m.	Naples, Italy	6:00 p.m.
Johannesburg, South Africa	7:00 p.m.	Oslo, Norway	6:00 p.m.
Kingston, Jamaica	noon	Panama City, Panama	noon
La Paz, Bolivia	1:00 p.m.	Paris, France	6:00 p.m.
Lima, Peru	noon	Peking (Beijing), China	1:00 a.m.*
Lisbon, Portugal	5:00 p.m.	Prague, Czech Republic	6:00 p.m.
Liverpool, England	5:00 p.m.	Rio de Janeiro, Brazil	2:00 p.m.
London, England	5:00 p.m.	Rome, Italy	6:00 p.m.
Lyons, France	6:00 p.m.	Santiago, Chile	1:00 p.m.
Madrid, Spain	6:00 p.m.	Shanghai, China	1:00 a.m.*
Manchester, England	5:00 p.m.	Stockholm, Sweden	6:00 p.m.
Manila, Philippines	1:00 a.m.*	Sydney, Australia	3:00 a.m.*
Melbourne, Australia	3:00 a.m.*	Tokyo, Japan	2:00 a.m.*
Mexico City, Mexico	11:00 a.m.	Venice, Italy	6:00 p.m.
Milan, Italy	6:00 p.m.	Vienna, Austria	6:00 p.m.
Moscow, CIS (former USSR)	8:00 p.m.	Warsaw, Poland	6:00 p.m.
Munich, Germany	6:00 p.m.	Zürich, Switzerland	6:00 p.m.

*On the following day

India, the time-zone maverick among nations, is 5 1/2 hours ahead of Greenwich Mean Time and 10 1/2 hours ahead of American Eastern Standard Time.

INTERNATIONAL DATE LINE

The International Date Line runs along 180° longitude and is the point at which the date changes. When traveling west over the line, the date must be advanced one day; when traveling east, it must be set back one day. But when and why was it established?

With the expansion of transoceanic shipping and transcontinental rail service in the 1870s, the need for standardized time zones around the world became critical. While accurate measures of latitude and longitude had long existed, they did little to standardize time, since each country designated its own prime meridian (zero degrees longitude) from which longitude (and hence time of day) east and west were measured. During the early 19th century, mapmakers ran prime meridians through Madrid, London, Paris, Rome, Washington, D.C., St. Petersburg and so on.

In 1884, with 14 prime meridians still in use, an international conference held in Washington, D.C., recommended that standard time be based on a single prime meridian running through Greenwich Observatory on the Thames River near London. The Greenwich meridian was chosen because Greenwich time had long been the British standard and so was recognized by Great Britain's many colonies and by other countries using the popular British maps. It was also recommended that the earth's 360-degree circumference be divided into 24 time belts, or zones, of 15 degrees each with zero degrees at Greenwich, putting 180 degrees in the central Pacific Ocean.

The 180th meridian was chosen as the least disruptive place for changing dates, since it passed mainly over water. The International Date Line passes through the Bering Sea between Alaska and Siberia, then deviates westward around the Aleutian Islands before returning to 180 degrees longitude. It deviates once more (this time to the east) to include some of the South Sea Islands with New Zealand and Australia.

In the United States time zones based on Greenwich mean time were adopted in late 1883 by a meeting of railroad managers seeking to bring order to a chaotic system that had many local times. The new time zones (four in the continental United States) remained unchanged until November 1983 when Alaska's four zones were reduced to two. Most of that state now lies in the Alaska (formerly Yukon) time zone, which is one hour earlier than Pacific standard time. A small part of western Alaska and the Aleutian Islands falls in the Bering time zone, two hours earlier than Pacific standard time.

—DAVID LUDLUM

DAYS OF THE WEEK FOR WINNERS, LOSERS
Some key facts to keep in mind about the days of the week:
- Monday is the worst day for a job interview—and the prime time for suicides. But you knew that.
- Tuesday and Wednesday tend to be lackluster on the stock market..
- Thursday doesn't have any obvious strikes against it, so go for it.
- Friday is your best bet for a stock profit, but it's also the day when most firings take place.
- The weekend brings the most heart attacks.

—RIP'N' READ NEWS SERVICE, THE MAYO CLINIC, ROBERT HALF INTERNATIONAL, INC.

TIME RHYMES
A New England proverb to help you remember how many days each month has:

> Thirty days hath September,
> April, June and November;
> All the rest have thirty-one,
> Excepting February alone,
> Which hath but twenty-eight, in fine,
> Till leap year gives it twenty-nine.

• • •

The 12 months, as condensed by George Ellis (1753-1815):

> Snowy, Blowy, Flowy,
> Showery, Flowery, Bowery,
> Hoppy, Croppy, Droppy,
> Breezy, Sneezy, Freezy

437

HERE IS VERSI-FORM DESIGNED
IN A SHAPE WHICH BRINGS
TO MIND, THAT WHEN PUT-
TING THOUGHTS IN
RHYME, YOU'RE
SUPPOSED TO
MEASURE
TIME
BUT THE
MEASURE OF
YOUR OWN, YOU
SHOULD GLADLY LEAVE
UNKNOWN; FOR THERE'S
SCARCELY ANY DOUBT, THAT
YOUR SAND IS RUNNING OUT.

GERALD LYNTON KAUFMAN (GEO-METRIC VERSE)

MOVABLE FEASTS

Although "movable feast" is strictly defined as a religious feast that does not occur on the same date each year, we use the term here more generally, to include any currently observed occasion or event, whether religious or secular, that does not always fall on the same date.

Note: The observance of all Jewish holidays begins at sundown the previous day.

Martin Luther King, Jr., Day. The third Monday in January; commemorates the civil-rights leader's life and accomplishments.

Presidents' Day. The third Monday in February; combines the observance of the birthdays of Abraham Lincoln (12 February) and George Washington (22 February).

Mardi Gras (Fat Tuesday; Shrove Tuesday). The last day before the Lenten season; originally a day of penance, it is now marked by merrymaking and feasting.

Ash Wednesday. The first day of the 40-day Lenten season, traditionally observed by fasting, performing acts of charity and foregoing certain pleasures.

Palm Sunday. The Sunday before Easter; commemorates the entry of

Jesus into Jerusalem.

Good Friday. Two days before Easter; commemorates the Crucifixion, and marked by fasting, mourning and repentance.

Passover. Occurring in March and/or April, the seven-day "Pesach" or Passover commemorates the exodus of the Jews from Egypt in about 1300 B.C.

Easter. The first Sunday following the first full moon on or after the vernal equinox (first day of spring) always between March 22 and April 25.

Arbor Day. The last Friday in April; dedicated to trees and their preservation.

Mother's Day. The second Sunday in May; proposed by Anna Jarvis of Philadelphia in 1907.

Armed Forces Day. The third Saturday in May; honors members of the U.S. Armed Forces.

Memorial Day. The last Monday in May. Originally called Decoration Day, and set aside to honor the memory of those who died in the Civil War, the day is now dedicated to the memory of all war dead; it also marks the unofficial start of summer.

Father's Day. The third Sunday in June; first celebrated June 19, 1910.

Labor Day. The first Monday in September; first celebrated in 1882, as a day to be set aside in honor of labor.

Rosh Hashana (Jewish New Year). Occurring in September or October, the day begins the Ten Days of Repentance, closing with Yom Kippur.

Yom Kippur (Day of Atonement). Described in Leviticus as a "Sabbath of rest," the day is traditionally observed by fasting and praying.

Columbus Day. The second Monday in October; commemorates Christopher Columbus's "discovery" of America.

Great American Smokeout. The third Thursday in November; designated by the American Cancer Society as a day for smokers to break their habit and for nonsmokers to "adopt" a smoker and help him or her through the day.

Thanksgiving. The fourth Thursday in November; informally celebrated until President Lincoln in 1863 proclaimed it a national harvest festival.

Hanukkah (Festival of Lights). Occurring usually in December but sometimes in November, this eight-day feast was instituted by Judas Maccabeus in 165 B.C. to celebrate the purification of the Temple of Jerusalem.

439

PERPETUAL CALENDAR, 1825-2028

Find the desired year (from the period 1825-2028) in the table below. The number following it tells you which calendar to use of the 14 immediately following the table.

1825	7	1859	7	1893	1	1927	7	1961	1	1995	1
1826	1	1860	8	1894	2	1928	8	1962	2	1996	9
1827	2	1861	3	1895	3	1929	3	1963	3	1997	4
1828	10	1862	4	1896	11	1930	4	1964	11	1998	5
1829	5	1863	5	1897	6	1931	5	1965	6	1999	6
1830	6	1864	13	1898	7	1932	13	1966	7	2000	14
1831	7	1865	1	1899	1	1933	1	1967	1	2001	2
1832	8	1866	2	1900	2	1934	2	1968	9	2002	3
1833	3	1867	3	1901	3	1935	3	1969	4	2003	4
1834	4	1868	11	1902	4	1936	11	1970	5	2004	12
1835	5	1869	6	1903	5	1937	6	1971	6	2005	7
1836	13	1870	7	1904	13	1938	7	1972	14	2006	1
1837	1	1871	1	1905	1	1939	1	1973	2	2007	2
1838	2	1872	9	1906	2	1940	9	1974	3	2008	10
1839	3	1873	4	1907	3	1941	4	1975	4	2009	5
1840	11	1874	5	1908	11	1942	5	1976	12	2010	6
1841	6	1875	6	1909	6	1943	6	1977	7	2011	7
1842	7	1876	14	1910	7	1944	14	1978	1	2012	8
1843	1	1877	2	1911	1	1945	2	1979	2	2013	3
1844	9	1878	3	1912	9	1946	3	1980	10	2014	4
1845	4	1879	4	1913	4	1947	4	1981	5	2015	5
1846	5	1880	12	1914	5	1948	12	1982	6	2016	13
1847	6	1881	7	1915	6	1949	7	1983	7	2017	1
1848	14	1882	1	1916	14	1950	1	1984	8	2018	2
1849	2	1883	2	1917	2	1951	2	1985	3	2019	3
1850	3	1884	10	1918	3	1952	10	1986	4	2020	11
1851	4	1885	5	1919	4	1953	5	1987	5	2021	6
1852	12	1886	6	1920	12	1954	6	1988	13	2022	7
1853	7	1887	7	1921	7	1955	7	1989	1	2023	1
1854	1	1888	8	1922	1	1956	8	1990	2	2024	9
1855	2	1889	3	1923	2	1957	3	1991	3	2025	4
1856	10	1890	4	1924	10	1958	4	1992	11	2026	5
1857	5	1891	5	1925	5	1959	5	1993	6	2027	6
1858	6	1892	13	1926	6	1960	13	1994	7	2028	14

JANUARY
```
S  M  T  W  T  F  S
      1  2  3  4  5  6  7
 8  9 10 11 12 13 14
15 16 17 18 19 20 21
22 23 24 25 26 27 28
29 30 31
```

FEBRUARY
```
S  M  T  W  T  F  S
               1  2  3  4
 5  6  7  8  9 10 11
12 13 14 15 16 17 18
19 20 21 22 23 24 25
26 27 28
```

MARCH
```
S  M  T  W  T  F  S
               1  2  3  4
 5  6  7  8  9 10 11
12 13 14 15 16 17 18
19 20 21 22 23 24 25
26 27 28 29 30 31
```

APRIL
```
S  M  T  W  T  F  S
                        1
 2  3  4  5  6  7  8
 9 10 11 12 13 14 15
16 17 18 19 20 21 22
23 24 25 26 27 28 29
30
```

MAY
```
S  M  T  W  T  F  S
      1  2  3  4  5  6
 7  8  9 10 11 12 13
14 15 16 17 18 19 20
21 22 23 24 25 26 27
28 29 30 31
```

JUNE
```
S  M  T  W  T  F  S
                  1  2  3
 4  5  6  7  8  9 10
11 12 13 14 15 16 17
18 19 20 21 22 23 24
25 26 27 28 29 30
```

JULY
```
S  M  T  W  T  F  S
                        1
 2  3  4  5  6  7  8
 9 10 11 12 13 14 15
16 17 18 19 20 21 22
23 24 25 26 27 28 29
30 31
```

AUGUST
```
S  M  T  W  T  F  S
            1  2  3  4  5
 6  7  8  9 10 11 12
13 14 15 16 17 18 19
20 21 22 23 24 25 26
27 28 29 30 31
```

SEPTEMBER
```
S  M  T  W  T  F  S
                     1  2
 3  4  5  6  7  8  9
10 11 12 13 14 15 16
17 18 19 20 21 22 23
24 25 26 27 28 29 30
```

OCTOBER
```
S  M  T  W  T  F  S
 1  2  3  4  5  6  7
 8  9 10 11 12 13 14
15 16 17 18 19 20 21
22 23 24 25 26 27 28
29 30 31
```

NOVEMBER
```
S  M  T  W  T  F  S
               1  2  3  4
 5  6  7  8  9 10 11
12 13 14 15 16 17 18
19 20 21 22 23 24 25
26 27 28 29 30
```

DECEMBER
```
S  M  T  W  T  F  S
                     1  2
 3  4  5  6  7  8  9
10 11 12 13 14 15 16
17 18 19 20 21 22 23
24 25 26 27 28 29 30
31
```

JANUARY
```
S  M  T  W  T  F  S
      1  2  3  4  5  6
 7  8  9 10 11 12 13
14 15 16 17 18 19 20
21 22 23 24 25 26 27
28 29 30 31
```

FEBRUARY
```
S  M  T  W  T  F  S
                  1  2  3
 4  5  6  7  8  9 10
11 12 13 14 15 16 17
18 19 20 21 22 23 24
25 26 27 28
```

MARCH
```
S  M  T  W  T  F  S
                  1  2  3
 4  5  6  7  8  9 10
11 12 13 14 15 16 17
18 19 20 21 22 23 24
25 26 27 28 29 30 31
```

APRIL
```
S  M  T  W  T  F  S
      1  2  3  4  5  6  7
 8  9 10 11 12 13 14
15 16 17 18 19 20 21
22 23 24 25 26 27 28
29 30
```

MAY
```
S  M  T  W  T  F  S
               1  2  3  4  5
 6  7  8  9 10 11 12
13 14 15 16 17 18 19
20 21 22 23 24 25 26
27 28 29 30 31
```

JUNE
```
S  M  T  W  T  F  S
                     1  2
 3  4  5  6  7  8  9
10 11 12 13 14 15 16
17 18 19 20 21 22 23
24 25 26 27 28 29 30
```

JULY
```
S  M  T  W  T  F  S
      1  2  3  4  5  6  7
 8  9 10 11 12 13 14
15 16 17 18 19 20 21
22 23 24 25 26 27 28
29 30 31
```

AUGUST
```
S  M  T  W  T  F  S
               1  2  3  4
 5  6  7  8  9 10 11
12 13 14 15 16 17 18
19 20 21 22 23 24 25
26 27 28 29 30 31
```

SEPTEMBER
```
S  M  T  W  T  F  S
                        1
 2  3  4  5  6  7  8
 9 10 11 12 13 14 15
16 17 18 19 20 21 22
23 24 25 26 27 28 29
30
```

OCTOBER
```
S  M  T  W  T  F  S
      1  2  3  4  5  6
 7  8  9 10 11 12 13
14 15 16 17 18 19 20
21 22 23 24 25 26 27
28 29 30 31
```

NOVEMBER
```
S  M  T  W  T  F  S
                  1  2  3
 4  5  6  7  8  9 10
11 12 13 14 15 16 17
18 19 20 21 22 23 24
25 26 27 28 29 30
```

DECEMBER
```
S  M  T  W  T  F  S
                        1
 2  3  4  5  6  7  8
 9 10 11 12 13 14 15
16 17 18 19 20 21 22
23 24 25 26 27 28 29
30 31
```

JANUARY
S	M	T	W	T	F	S
	1	2	3	4	5
6	7	8	9	10	11	12
13	14	15	16	17	18	19
20	21	22	23	24	25	26
27	28	29	30	31

FEBRUARY
S	M	T	W	T	F	S
					1	2
3	4	5	6	7	8	9
10	11	12	13	14	15	16
17	18	19	20	21	22	23
24	25	26	27	28

MARCH
S	M	T	W	T	F	S
					1	2
3	4	5	6	7	8	9
10	11	12	13	14	15	16
17	18	19	20	21	22	23
24	25	26	27	28	29	30
31

APRIL
S	M	T	W	T	F	S
	1	2	3	4	5	6
7	8	9	10	11	12	13
14	15	16	17	18	19	20
21	22	23	24	25	26	27
28	29	30

MAY
S	M	T	W	T	F	S
			1	2	3	4
5	6	7	8	9	10	11
12	13	14	15	16	17	18
19	20	21	22	23	24	25
26	27	28	29	30	31

JUNE
S	M	T	W	T	F	S
						1
2	3	4	5	6	7	8
9	10	11	12	13	14	15
16	17	18	19	20	21	22
23	24	25	26	27	28	29
30

JULY
S	M	T	W	T	F	S
	1	2	3	4	5	6
7	8	9	10	11	12	13
14	15	16	17	18	19	20
21	22	23	24	25	26	27
28	29	30	31

AUGUST
S	M	T	W	T	F	S
				1	2	3
4	5	6	7	8	9	10
11	12	13	14	15	16	17
18	19	20	21	22	23	24
25	26	27	28	29	30	31

SEPTEMBER
S	M	T	W	T	F	S
1	2	3	4	5	6	7
8	9	10	11	12	13	14
15	16	17	18	19	20	21
22	23	24	25	26	27	28
29	30

OCTOBER
S	M	T	W	T	F	S
		1	2	3	4	5
6	7	8	9	10	11	12
13	14	15	16	17	18	19
20	21	22	23	24	25	26
27	28	29	30	31

NOVEMBER
S	M	T	W	T	F	S
					1	2
3	4	5	6	7	8	9
10	11	12	13	14	15	16
17	18	19	20	21	22	23
24	25	26	27	28	29	30

DECEMBER
S	M	T	W	T	F	S
1	2	3	4	5	6	7
8	9	10	11	12	13	14
15	16	17	18	19	20	21
22	23	24	25	26	27	28
29	30	31

JANUARY
S	M	T	W	T	F	S
		1	2	3	4
5	6	7	8	9	10	11
12	13	14	15	16	17	18
19	20	21	22	23	24	25
26	27	28	29	30	31

FEBRUARY
S	M	T	W	T	F	S
						1
2	3	4	5	6	7	8
9	10	11	12	13	14	15
16	17	18	19	20	21	22
23	24	25	26	27	28

MARCH
S	M	T	W	T	F	S
						1
2	3	4	5	6	7	8
9	10	11	12	13	14	15
16	17	18	19	20	21	22
23	24	25	26	27	28	29
30	31

APRIL
S	M	T	W	T	F	S
		1	2	3	4	5
6	7	8	9	10	11	12
13	14	15	16	17	18	19
20	21	22	23	24	25	26
27	28	29	30

MAY
S	M	T	W	T	F	S
				1	2	3
4	5	6	7	8	9	10
11	12	13	14	15	16	17
18	19	20	21	22	23	24
25	26	27	28	29	30	31

JUNE
S	M	T	W	T	F	S
1	2	3	4	5	6	7
8	9	10	11	12	13	14
15	16	17	18	19	20	21
22	23	24	25	26	27	28
29	30

JULY
S	M	T	W	T	F	S
		1	2	3	4	5
6	7	8	9	10	11	12
13	14	15	16	17	18	19
20	21	22	23	24	25	26
27	28	29	30	31

AUGUST
S	M	T	W	T	F	S
					1	2
3	4	5	6	7	8	9
10	11	12	13	14	15	16
17	18	19	20	21	22	23
24	25	26	27	28	29	30
31

SEPTEMBER
S	M	T	W	T	F	S
	1	2	3	4	5	6
7	8	9	10	11	12	13
14	15	16	17	18	19	20
21	22	23	24	25	26	27
28	29	30

OCTOBER
S	M	T	W	T	F	S
			1	2	3	4
5	6	7	8	9	10	11
12	13	14	15	16	17	18
19	20	21	22	23	24	25
26	27	28	29	30	31

NOVEMBER
S	M	T	W	T	F	S
						1
2	3	4	5	6	7	8
9	10	11	12	13	14	15
16	17	18	19	20	21	22
23	24	25	26	27	28	29
30

DECEMBER
S	M	T	W	T	F	S
1	2	3	4	5	6
7	8	9	10	11	12	13
14	15	16	17	18	19	20
21	22	23	24	25	26	27
28	29	30	31

JANUARY
```
S  M  T  W  T  F  S
            1  2  3
4  5  6  7  8  9 10
11 12 13 14 15 16 17
18 19 20 21 22 23 24
25 26 27 28 29 30 31
```

FEBRUARY
```
S  M  T  W  T  F  S
1  2  3  4  5  6  7
8  9 10 11 12 13 14
15 16 17 18 19 20 21
22 23 24 25 26 27 28
```

MARCH
```
S  M  T  W  T  F  S
1  2  3  4  5  6  7
8  9 10 11 12 13 14
15 16 17 18 19 20 21
22 23 24 25 26 27 28
29 30 31
```

APRIL
```
S  M  T  W  T  F  S
            1  2  3  4
5  6  7  8  9 10 11
12 13 14 15 16 17 18
19 20 21 22 23 24 25
26 27 28 29 30
```

MAY
```
S  M  T  W  T  F  S
                  1  2
3  4  5  6  7  8  9
10 11 12 13 14 15 16
17 18 19 20 21 22 23
24 25 26 27 28 29 30
31
```

JUNE
```
S  M  T  W  T  F  S
      1  2  3  4  5  6
7  8  9 10 11 12 13
14 15 16 17 18 19 20
21 22 23 24 25 26 27
28 29 30
```

JULY
```
S  M  T  W  T  F  S
            1  2  3  4
5  6  7  8  9 10 11
12 13 14 15 16 17 18
19 20 21 22 23 24 25
26 27 28 29 30 31
```

AUGUST
```
S  M  T  W  T  F  S
                     1
2  3  4  5  6  7  8
9 10 11 12 13 14 15
16 17 18 19 20 21 22
23 24 25 26 27 28 29
30 31
```

SEPTEMBER
```
S  M  T  W  T  F  S
      1  2  3  4  5
6  7  8  9 10 11 12
13 14 15 16 17 18 19
20 21 22 23 24 25 26
27 28 29 30
```

OCTOBER
```
S  M  T  W  T  F  S
               1  2  3
4  5  6  7  8  9 10
11 12 13 14 15 16 17
18 19 20 21 22 23 24
25 26 27 28 29 30 31
```

NOVEMBER
```
S  M  T  W  T  F  S
1  2  3  4  5  6  7
8  9 10 11 12 13 14
15 16 17 18 19 20 21
22 23 24 25 26 27 28
29 30
```

DECEMBER
```
S  M  T  W  T  F  S
            1  2  3  4  5
6  7  8  9 10 11 12
13 14 15 16 17 18 19
20 21 22 23 24 25 26
27 28 29 30 31
```

JANUARY
```
S  M  T  W  T  F  S
                  1  2
3  4  5  6  7  8  9
10 11 12 13 14 15 16
17 18 19 20 21 22 23
24 25 26 27 28 29 30
31
```

FEBRUARY
```
S  M  T  W  T  F  S
      1  2  3  4  5  6
7  8  9 10 11 12 13
14 15 16 17 18 19 20
21 22 23 24 25 26 27
28
```

MARCH
```
S  M  T  W  T  F  S
      1  2  3  4  5  6
7  8  9 10 11 12 13
14 15 16 17 18 19 20
21 22 23 24 25 26 27
28 29 30 31
```

APRIL
```
S  M  T  W  T  F  S
                  1  2  3
4  5  6  7  8  9 10
11 12 13 14 15 16 17
18 19 20 21 22 23 24
25 26 27 28 29 30
```

MAY
```
S  M  T  W  T  F  S
                     1
2  3  4  5  6  7  8
9 10 11 12 13 14 15
16 17 18 19 20 21 22
23 24 25 26 27 28 29
30 31
```

JUNE
```
S  M  T  W  T  F  S
      1  2  3  4  5
6  7  8  9 10 11 12
13 14 15 16 17 18 19
20 21 22 23 24 25 26
27 28 29 30
```

JULY
```
S  M  T  W  T  F  S
            1  2  3
4  5  6  7  8  9 10
11 12 13 14 15 16 17
18 19 20 21 22 23 24
25 26 27 28 29 30 31
```

AUGUST
```
S  M  T  W  T  F  S
1  2  3  4  5  6  7
8  9 10 11 12 13 14
15 16 17 18 19 20 21
22 23 24 25 26 27 28
29 30 31
```

SEPTEMBER
```
S  M  T  W  T  F  S
         1  2  3  4
5  6  7  8  9 10 11
12 13 14 15 16 17 18
19 20 21 22 23 24 25
26 27 28 29 30
```

OCTOBER
```
S  M  T  W  T  F  S
                  1  2
3  4  5  6  7  8  9
10 11 12 13 14 15 16
17 18 19 20 21 22 23
24 25 26 27 28 29 30
31
```

NOVEMBER
```
S  M  T  W  T  F  S
   1  2  3  4  5  6
7  8  9 10 11 12 13
14 15 16 17 18 19 20
21 22 23 24 25 26 27
28 29 30
```

DECEMBER
```
S  M  T  W  T  F  S
            1  2  3  4
5  6  7  8  9 10 11
12 13 14 15 16 17 18
19 20 21 22 23 24 25
26 27 28 29 30 31
```

◆ 7 ◆

JANUARY
```
S  M  T  W  T  F  S
                  1
2  3  4  5  6  7  8
9  10 11 12 13 14 15
16 17 18 19 20 21 22
23 24 25 26 27 28 29
30 31
```

FEBRUARY
```
S  M  T  W  T  F  S
         1  2  3  4  5
6  7  8  9  10 11 12
13 14 15 16 17 18 19
20 21 22 23 24 25 26
27 28
```

MARCH
```
S  M  T  W  T  F  S
         1  2  3  4  5
6  7  8  9  10 11 12
13 14 15 16 17 18 19
20 21 22 23 24 25 26
27 28 29 30 31
```

APRIL
```
S  M  T  W  T  F  S
                  1  2
3  4  5  6  7  8  9
10 11 12 13 14 15 16
17 18 19 20 21 22 23
24 25 26 27 28 29 30
```

MAY
```
S  M  T  W  T  F  S
1  2  3  4  5  6  7
8  9  10 11 12 13 14
15 16 17 18 19 20 21
22 23 24 25 26 27 28
29 30 31
```

JUNE
```
S  M  T  W  T  F  S
         1  2  3  4
5  6  7  8  9  10 11
12 13 14 15 16 17 18
19 20 21 22 23 24 25
26 27 28 29 30
```

JULY
```
S  M  T  W  T  F  S
                  1  2
3  4  5  6  7  8  9
10 11 12 13 14 15 16
17 18 19 20 21 22 23
24 25 26 27 28 29 30
31
```

AUGUST
```
S  M  T  W  T  F  S
1  2  3  4  5  6
7  8  9  10 11 12 13
14 15 16 17 18 19 20
21 22 23 24 25 26 27
28 29 30 31
```

SEPTEMBER
```
S  M  T  W  T  F  S
               1  2  3
4  5  6  7  8  9  10
11 12 13 14 15 16 17
18 19 20 21 22 23 24
25 26 27 28 29 30
```

OCTOBER
```
S  M  T  W  T  F  S
                  1
2  3  4  5  6  7  8
9  10 11 12 13 14 15
16 17 18 19 20 21 22
23 24 25 26 27 28 29
30 31
```

NOVEMBER
```
S  M  T  W  T  F  S
      1  2  3  4  5
6  7  8  9  10 11 12
13 14 15 16 17 18 19
20 21 22 23 24 25 26
27 28 29 30
```

DECEMBER
```
S  M  T  W  T  F  S
               1  2  3
4  5  6  7  8  9  10
11 12 13 14 15 16 17
18 19 20 21 22 23 24
25 26 27 28 29 30 31
```

◆ 8 ◆

JANUARY
```
S  M  T  W  T  F  S
1  2  3  4  5  6  7
8  9  10 11 12 13 14
15 16 17 18 19 20 21
22 23 24 25 26 27 28
30 31
```

FEBRUARY
```
S  M  T  W  T  F  S
         1  2  3  4
5  6  7  8  9  10 11
12 13 14 15 16 17 18
19 20 21 22 23 24 25
26 27 28 29
```

MARCH
```
S  M  T  W  T  F  S
               1  2  3
4  5  6  7  8  9  10
11 12 13 14 15 16 17
18 19 20 21 22 23 24
25 26 27 28 29 30 31
```

APRIL
```
S  M  T  W  T  F  S
1  2  3  4  5  6  7
8  9  10 11 12 13 14
15 16 17 18 19 20 21
22 23 24 25 26 27 28
29 30
```

MAY
```
S  M  T  W  T  F  S
         1  2  3  4  5
6  7  8  9  10 11 12
13 14 15 16 17 18 19
20 21 22 23 24 25 26
27 28 29 30 31
```

JUNE
```
S  M  T  W  T  F  S
                  1  2
3  4  5  6  7  8  9
10 11 12 13 14 15 16
17 18 19 20 21 22 23
24 25 26 27 28 29 30
```

JULY
```
S  M  T  W  T  F  S
1  2  3  4  5  6  7
8  9  10 11 12 13 14
15 16 17 18 19 20 21
22 23 24 25 26 27 28
29 30 31
```

AUGUST
```
S  M  T  W  T  F  S
            1  2  3  4
5  6  7  8  9  10 11
12 13 14 15 16 17 18
19 20 21 22 23 24 25
26 27 28 29 30 31
```

SEPTEMBER
```
S  M  T  W  T  F  S
                  1
2  3  4  5  6  7  8
9  10 11 12 13 14 15
16 17 18 19 20 21 22
23 24 25 26 27 28 29
30
```

OCTOBER
```
S  M  T  W  T  F  S
   1  2  3  4  5  6
7  8  9  10 11 12 13
14 15 16 17 18 19 20
21 22 23 24 25 26 27
28 29 30 31
```

NOVEMBER
```
S  M  T  W  T  F  S
               1  2  3
4  5  6  7  8  9  10
11 12 13 14 15 16 17
18 19 20 21 22 23 24
25 26 27 28 29 30
```

DECEMBER
```
S  M  T  W  T  F  S
                  1
2  3  4  5  6  7  8
9  10 11 12 13 14 15
16 17 18 19 20 21 22
23 24 25 26 27 28 29
30 31
```

JANUARY
S	M	T	W	T	F	S
	1	2	3	4	5	6
7	8	9	10	11	12	13
14	15	16	17	18	19	20
21	22	23	24	25	26	27
28	29	30	31			

FEBRUARY
S	M	T	W	T	F	S
				1	2	3
4	5	6	7	8	9	10
11	12	13	14	15	16	17
18	19	20	21	22	23	24
25	26	27	28	29		

MARCH
S	M	T	W	T	F	S
					1	2
3	4	5	6	7	8	9
10	11	12	13	14	15	16
17	18	19	20	21	22	23
24	25	26	27	28	29	30
31						

APRIL
S	M	T	W	T	F	S
	1	2	3	4	5	6
7	8	9	10	11	12	13
14	15	16	17	18	19	20
21	22	23	24	25	26	27
28	29	30				

MAY
S	M	T	W	T	F	S
			1	2	3	4
5	6	7	8	9	10	11
12	13	14	15	16	17	18
19	20	21	22	23	24	25
26	27	28	29	30	31	

JUNE
S	M	T	W	T	F	S
						1
2	3	4	5	6	7	8
9	10	11	12	13	14	15
16	17	18	19	20	21	22
23	24	25	26	27	28	29
30						

JULY
S	M	T	W	T	F	S
	1	2	3	4	5	6
7	8	9	10	11	12	13
14	15	16	17	18	19	20
21	22	23	24	25	26	27
28	29	30	31			

AUGUST
S	M	T	W	T	F	S
				1	2	3
4	5	6	7	8	9	10
11	12	13	14	15	16	17
18	19	20	21	22	23	24
25	26	27	28	29	30	31

SEPTEMBER
S	M	T	W	T	F	S
1	2	3	4	5	6	7
8	9	10	11	12	13	14
15	16	17	18	19	20	21
22	23	24	25	26	27	28
29	30					

OCTOBER
S	M	T	W	T	F	S
		1	2	3	4	5
6	7	8	9	10	11	12
13	14	15	16	17	18	19
20	21	22	23	24	25	26
27	28	29	30	31		

NOVEMBER
S	M	T	W	T	F	S
					1	2
3	4	5	6	7	8	9
10	11	12	13	14	15	16
17	18	19	20	21	22	23
24	25	26	27	28	29	30

DECEMBER
S	M	T	W	T	F	S
1	2	3	4	5	6	7
8	9	10	11	12	13	14
15	16	17	18	19	20	21
22	23	24	25	26	27	28
29	30	31				

JANUARY
S	M	T	W	T	F	S
		1	2	3	4	5
6	7	8	9	10	11	12
13	14	15	16	17	18	19
20	21	22	23	24	25	26
27	28	29	30	31		

FEBRUARY
S	M	T	W	T	F	S
					1	2
3	4	5	6	7	8	9
10	11	12	13	14	15	16
17	18	19	20	21	22	23
24	25	26	27	28	29	

MARCH
S	M	T	W	T	F	S
						1
2	3	4	5	6	7	8
9	10	11	12	13	14	15
16	17	18	19	20	21	22
23	24	25	26	27	28	29
30	31					

APRIL
S	M	T	W	T	F	S
		1	2	3	4	5
6	7	8	9	10	11	12
13	14	15	16	17	18	19
20	21	22	23	24	25	26
27	28	29	30			

MAY
S	M	T	W	T	F	S
				1	2	3
4	5	6	7	8	9	10
11	12	13	14	15	16	17
18	19	20	21	22	23	24
25	26	27	28	29	30	31

JUNE
S	M	T	W	T	F	S
1	2	3	4	5	6	7
8	9	10	11	12	13	14
15	16	17	18	19	20	21
22	23	24	25	26	27	28
29	30					

JULY
S	M	T	W	T	F	S
		1	2	3	4	5
6	7	8	9	10	11	12
13	14	15	16	17	18	19
20	21	22	23	24	25	26
27	28	29	30	31		

AUGUST
S	M	T	W	T	F	S
					1	2
3	4	5	6	7	8	9
10	11	12	13	14	15	16
17	18	19	20	21	22	23
24	25	26	27	28	29	30
31						

SEPTEMBER
S	M	T	W	T	F	S
	1	2	3	4	5	6
7	8	9	10	11	12	13
14	15	16	17	18	19	20
21	22	23	24	25	26	27
28	29	30				

OCTOBER
S	M	T	W	T	F	S
			1	2	3	4
5	6	7	8	9	10	11
12	13	14	15	16	17	18
19	20	21	22	23	24	25
26	27	28	29	30	31	

NOVEMBER
S	M	T	W	T	F	S
						1
2	3	4	5	6	7	8
9	10	11	12	13	14	15
16	17	18	19	20	21	22
23	24	25	26	27	28	29
30						

DECEMBER
S	M	T	W	T	F	S
	1	2	3	4	5	6
7	8	9	10	11	12	13
14	15	16	17	18	19	20
21	22	23	24	25	26	27
28	29	30	31			

JANUARY
S	M	T	W	T	F	S
		1	2	3	4	
5	6	7	8	9	10	11
12	13	14	15	16	17	18
19	20	21	22	23	24	25
26	27	28	29	30	31	

FEBRUARY
S	M	T	W	T	F	S
						1
2	3	4	5	6	7	8
9	10	11	12	13	14	15
16	17	18	19	20	21	22
23	24	25	26	27	28	29

MARCH
S	M	T	W	T	F	S
1	2	3	4	5	6	7
8	9	10	11	12	13	14
15	16	17	18	19	20	21
22	23	24	25	26	27	28
29	30	31				

APRIL
S	M	T	W	T	F	S
			1	2	3	4
5	6	7	8	9	10	11
12	13	14	15	16	17	18
19	20	21	22	23	24	25
26	27	28	29	30		

MAY
S	M	T	W	T	F	S
					1	2
3	4	5	6	7	8	9
10	11	12	13	14	15	16
17	18	19	20	21	22	23
24	25	26	27	28	29	30
31						

JUNE
S	M	T	W	T	F	S
1	2	3	4	5	6	
7	8	9	10	11	12	13
14	15	16	17	18	19	20
21	22	23	24	25	26	27
28	29	30				

JULY
S	M	T	W	T	F	S
			1	2	3	4
5	6	7	8	9	10	11
12	13	14	15	16	17	18
19	20	21	22	23	24	25
26	27	28	29	30	31	

AUGUST
S	M	T	W	T	F	S
						1
2	3	4	5	6	7	8
9	10	11	12	13	14	15
16	17	18	19	20	21	22
23	24	25	26	27	28	29
30	31					

SEPTEMBER
S	M	T	W	T	F	S
		1	2	3	4	5
6	7	8	9	10	11	12
13	14	15	16	17	18	19
20	21	22	23	24	25	26
27	28	29	30			

OCTOBER
S	M	T	W	T	F	S
				1	2	3
4	5	6	7	8	9	10
11	12	13	14	15	16	17
18	19	20	21	22	23	24
25	26	27	28	29	30	31

NOVEMBER
S	M	T	W	T	F	S
1	2	3	4	5	6	7
8	9	10	11	12	13	14
15	16	17	18	19	20	21
22	23	24	25	26	27	28
29	30					

DECEMBER
S	M	T	W	T	F	S
		1	2	3	4	5
6	7	8	9	10	11	12
13	14	15	16	17	18	19
20	21	22	23	24	25	26
27	28	29	30	31		

JANUARY
S	M	T	W	T	F	S
			1	2	3	
4	5	6	7	8	9	10
11	12	13	14	15	16	17
18	19	20	21	22	23	24
25	26	27	28	29	30	31

FEBRUARY
S	M	T	W	T	F	S
1	2	3	4	5	6	7
8	9	10	11	12	13	14
15	16	17	18	19	20	21
22	23	24	25	26	27	28
29						

MARCH
S	M	T	W	T	F	S
1	2	3	4	5	6	
7	8	9	10	11	12	13
14	15	16	17	18	19	20
21	22	23	24	25	26	27
28	29	30	31			

APRIL
S	M	T	W	T	F	S
				1	2	3
4	5	6	7	8	9	10
11	12	13	14	15	16	17
18	19	20	21	22	23	24
25	26	27	28	29	30	

MAY
S	M	T	W	T	F	S
						1
2	3	4	5	6	7	8
9	10	11	12	13	14	15
16	17	18	19	20	21	22
23	24	25	26	27	28	29
30	31					

JUNE
S	M	T	W	T	F	S
		1	2	3	4	5
6	7	8	9	10	11	12
13	14	15	16	17	18	19
20	21	22	23	24	25	26
27	28	29	30			

JULY
S	M	T	W	T	F	S
				1	2	3
4	5	6	7	8	9	10
11	12	13	14	15	16	17
18	19	20	21	22	23	24
25	26	27	28	29	30	31

AUGUST
S	M	T	W	T	F	S
1	2	3	4	5	6	7
8	9	10	11	12	13	14
15	16	17	18	19	20	21
22	23	24	25	26	27	28
29	30	31				

SEPTEMBER
S	M	T	W	T	F	S
		1	2	3	4	
5	6	7	8	9	10	11
12	13	14	15	16	17	18
19	20	21	22	23	24	25
26	27	28	29	30		

OCTOBER
S	M	T	W	T	F	S
					1	2
3	4	5	6	7	8	9
10	11	12	13	14	15	16
17	18	19	20	21	22	23
24	25	26	27	28	29	30
31						

NOVEMBER
S	M	T	W	T	F	S
	1	2	3	4	5	6
7	8	9	10	11	12	13
14	15	16	17	18	19	20
21	22	23	24	25	26	27
28	29	30				

DECEMBER
S	M	T	W	T	F	S
		1	2	3	4	
5	6	7	8	9	10	11
12	13	14	15	16	17	18
19	20	21	22	23	24	25
26	27	28	29	30	31	

JANUARY						
S	M	T	W	T	F	S
					1	2
3	4	5	6	7	8	9
10	11	12	13	14	15	16
17	18	19	20	21	22	23
24	25	26	27	28	29	30
31						

FEBRUARY						
S	M	T	W	T	F	S
	1	2	3	4	5	6
7	8	9	10	11	12	13
14	15	16	17	18	19	20
21	22	23	24	25	26	27
28	29					

MARCH						
S	M	T	W	T	F	S
	1	2	3	4	5	
6	7	8	9	10	11	12
13	14	15	16	17	18	19
20	21	22	23	24	25	26
27	28	29	30	31		

APRIL						
S	M	T	W	T	F	S
					1	2
3	4	5	6	7	8	9
10	11	12	13	14	15	16
17	18	19	20	21	22	23
24	25	26	27	28	29	30

MAY						
S	M	T	W	T	F	S
1	2	3	4	5	6	7
8	9	10	11	12	13	14
15	16	17	18	19	20	21
22	23	24	25	26	27	28
29	30	31				

JUNE						
S	M	T	W	T	F	S
			1	2	3	4
5	6	7	8	9	10	11
12	13	14	15	16	17	18
19	20	21	22	23	24	25
26	27	28	29	30		

JULY						
S	M	T	W	T	F	S
					1	2
3	4	5	6	7	8	9
10	11	12	13	14	15	16
17	18	19	20	21	22	23
24	25	26	27	28	29	30
31						

AUGUST						
S	M	T	W	T	F	S
	1	2	3	4	5	6
7	8	9	10	11	12	13
14	15	16	17	18	19	20
21	22	23	24	25	26	27
28	29	30	31			

SEPTEMBER						
S	M	T	W	T	F	S
				1	2	3
4	5	6	7	8	9	10
11	12	13	14	15	16	17
18	19	20	21	22	23	24
25	26	27	28	29	30	

OCTOBER						
S	M	T	W	T	F	S
						1
2	3	4	5	6	7	8
9	10	11	12	13	14	15
16	17	18	19	20	21	22
23	24	25	26	27	28	29
30	31					

NOVEMBER						
S	M	T	W	T	F	S
		1	2	3	4	5
6	7	8	9	10	11	12
13	14	15	16	17	18	19
20	21	22	23	24	25	26
27	28	29	30			

DECEMBER						
S	M	T	W	T	F	S
				1	2	3
4	5	6	7	8	9	10
11	12	13	14	15	16	17
18	19	20	21	22	23	24
25	26	27	28	29	30	31

JANUARY						
S	M	T	W	T	F	S
						1
2	3	4	5	6	7	8
9	10	11	12	13	14	15
16	17	18	19	20	21	22
23	24	25	26	27	28	29
30	31					

FEBRUARY						
S	M	T	W	T	F	S
	1	2	3	4	5	
6	7	8	9	10	11	12
13	14	15	16	17	18	19
20	21	22	23	24	25	26
27	28	29				

MARCH						
S	M	T	W	T	F	S
		1	2	3	4	
5	6	7	8	9	10	11
12	13	14	15	16	17	18
19	20	21	22	23	24	25
26	27	28	29	30	31	

APRIL						
S	M	T	W	T	F	S
						1
2	3	4	5	6	7	8
9	10	11	12	13	14	15
16	17	18	19	20	21	22
23	24	25	26	27	28	29
30						

MAY						
S	M	T	W	T	F	S
	1	2	3	4	5	6
7	8	9	10	11	12	13
14	15	16	17	18	19	20
21	22	23	24	25	26	27
28	29	30	31			

JUNE						
S	M	T	W	T	F	S
				1	2	3
4	5	6	7	8	9	10
11	12	13	14	15	16	17
18	19	20	21	22	23	24
25	26	27	28	29	30	

JULY						
S	M	T	W	T	F	S
						1
2	3	4	5	6	7	8
9	10	11	12	13	14	15
16	17	18	19	20	21	22
23	24	25	26	27	28	29
30	31					

AUGUST						
S	M	T	W	T	F	S
		1	2	3	4	5
6	7	8	9	10	11	12
13	14	15	16	17	18	19
20	21	22	23	24	25	26
27	28	29	30	31		

SEPTEMBER						
S	M	T	W	T	F	S
					1	2
3	4	5	6	7	8	9
10	11	12	13	14	15	16
17	18	19	20	21	22	23
24	25	26	27	28	29	30

OCTOBER						
S	M	T	W	T	F	S
1	2	3	4	5	6	7
8	9	10	11	12	13	14
15	16	17	18	19	20	21
22	23	24	25	26	27	28
29	30	31				

NOVEMBER						
S	M	T	W	T	F	S
		1	2	3	4	
5	6	7	8	9	10	11
12	13	14	15	16	17	18
19	20	21	22	23	24	25
26	27	28	29	30		

DECEMBER						
S	M	T	W	T	F	S
					1	2
3	4	5	6	7	8	9
10	11	12	13	14	15	16
17	18	19	20	21	22	23
24	25	26	27	28	29	30
31						

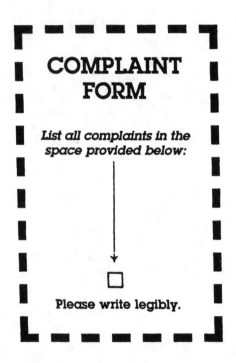

448

COPYRIGHTS AND ACKNOWLEDGMENTS

Pro Football," Sterling Publishing Co., Inc., 387 Park Ave. So., New York, NY 10016, from *Football: Startling Stories Behind the Records* by Jim Benagh © 1987 by Jim Benagh; "On the Ball," copyright, Roger Angell, 1990; "Mysteries of the Curve," from *Science 80-86*, October 1981, copyright © 1981 by the American Association for the Advancement of Science; "The Evolution of Basketball," from *The 1991 Old Farmers Almanac*, copyright © 1991, Yankee Publishing, Inc., Dublin, NH; "Girls and Women in Sport: Test Your IQ," National Association for Girls and Women in Sports. **NOTES FOR THE ROAD**—"First-Aid Kit for Winter Driving" and "How to Jump-Start Your Car Safely," courtesy AAA-Chicago Motor Club; "Beating the Travel-Photo Blahs," courtesy Abigail Foerstner, *Chicago Tribune*; "Air-Travel Problems and How to Solve Them," courtesy Better Business Bureau of Chicago and Northern Illinois *Consumer Resource Book*. **NOW IS THE TIME**—"International Date Line," originally published in *Country Journal* magazine, February 1984, © Cowles Magazines, Inc.

Thanks also to Chicago multimediaist Chuck L'Heureux for his input on various health and food topics, and to California artist Robert Merz for permission to reprint throughout the book 13 of his classic cartoons and drawings from his collection *Merz and More Merz* (Corinth Books, 1964).

And special thanks to two legendary lights of the book business— editors *extraordinaire* Robert B. Wyatt and Iris Bass of St. Martin's Press. Were it not for their initial involvement and encouragement, this book might still be "in progress."

The index was compiled by the Comp Shop of Students Publishing Co. at Northwestern University.

INDEX

B

Bach, Johann Sebastian
   Chinese zodiac sign of, 147
   compared to Beethoven and
      Mozart, 316
Bacon, Francis
   on gardening, 277
   on money, 219
baking soda, uses of, 214-215
Ballanchine, George, 313
bank, tips on selecting, 226-227
Barnum, P. T., on money, 225
Barrymore, John, on sex, 343
baseball, 380-389
   Mets of 1969, 386
   pitches, curveball, 380-382
   selected stats, 383-384
basketball
   evolution of, 389-391
   most valuable players, 391
   original rules for, 390-391
bears, 56
Beatles
   asteroids named for, 36
   rejection of by Decca Records,
      317
   songs by, 320-321
beavers, 53
Beethoven, Ludwig van
   Chinese zodiac signs of, 47
   compared to Bach and Mozart,
      316
Behan, Brendan, 333
Berra, Yogi
   and Berraisms, 387-388
   on observing, 80
Better Business Bureau
   and solar-energy use, 71
   home-improvement hiring
      advice, 275-276
   using to check out merchants,
      232-233, 241
bicycles, 482-484
   safety tips for, 483-484
Bierce, Ambrose, 342, 343
Big Bang theory, 52

first creatures, 52
   "molecular fossils," 52
Bill of Rights, 128-129
blood pressure, classifications, 168-
   169
Bombeck, Erma, 345
bonds, rating of, 231
books, 329
   facts about, 331
   history of, 329
   quotes about, 331-332
Booth, John Wilkes
   in *Julius Caesar*, 327
   in name-finder puzzle, 354-355
Borgia, Cesare, Chinese zodiac sign
   of, 148
boxing, 395-396
Brahe, Tycho, 15
Brecht, Bertolt, 191
Bronson, Charles, Chinese zodiac
   sign of, 149
Buck, Pearl, 148
budget, how to, 228
Burton, Richard, Chinese zodiac sign
   of, 147
business, tips for going into, 249-
   250
Byrnner, Yul, on not smoking, 171
Byron, Lord, on laughter, 153

C

Cage, John, on art and life, 313
calendar, evolution of, 432-433
   perpetual, 440-447
   Roman, 432
camping
   equipment, 400-402
   keeping bears away, 402-403
   lightning, 403
cancer,
   prevention of, 170-171
   warning signs, 170
Capote, Truman, 147
Carson, Johnny, 346
Caruso, Enrico, 149
Castro, Fidel, 147

Q

R

T

U

V

W